THE INTERNATIONAL LABOUR ORGANISATION

By the same author:

An Introduction to Ethics
Selections from the Scottish Philosophy of Common Sense
The Development of Berkeley's Philosophy
International Social Progress
Citizenship in the Industrial World
Berkeley's Commonplace Book

THE
INTERNATIONAL
LABOUR ORGANISATION

ITS WORK FOR SOCIAL AND ECONOMIC PROGRESS

G. A. JOHNSTON

Past Assistant Director-General and Past Treasurer of the ILO

EUROPA PUBLICATIONS
LONDON

EUROPA PUBLICATIONS LIMITED
18 Bedford Square, London, W.C.1

© G. A. Johnston 1970

ISBN: 900362 235
Library of Congress Catalog Card No. 74–112270

Made and Printed in Great Britain by Staples Printers Ltd.,
at their Rochester, Kent, establishment

Contents

PART II: MAJOR PROBLEMS AND PROGRAMMES

PART III: THE FUTURE; CONCLUSION

PART IV: REFERENCE

Acknowledgments

My grateful thanks are due to David A. Morse, who when Director-General of the ILO gave me constant encouragement, to C. Wilfred Jenks, Director-General, who read part of the manuscript and gave much valuable advice, and to Francis Wolf, Legal Adviser, who helped me in many ways. I am greatly indebted to Jane Carroll of Europa Publications for constructive suggestions on remodelling and developing the treatment of the subject, and for her helpful co-operation in implementing them.

G. A. Johnston

Geneva, 1 *June* 1970

Abbreviations

ECA	Economic Commission for Africa
ECAFE	Economic Commission for Asia and the Far East
ECE	Economic Commission for Europe
ECLA	Economic Commission for Latin America
ECOSOC	Economic and Social Council
ECSC	European Coal and Steel Community
EEC	European Economic Community
FAO	Food and Agriculture Organization
GATT	General Agreement on Tariffs and Trade
IAEA	International Atomic Energy Agency
IBRD	International Bank for Reconstruction and Development (World Bank)
ICA	International Co-operative Alliance
ICEM	Intergovernmental Committee for European Migration
ICFTU	International Confederation of Free Trade Unions
IDA	International Development Association
IFC	International Finance Corporation
IFCTU	International Federation of Christian Trade Unions (now WCL)
ILO	International Labour Organisation
IMCO	Inter-Governmental Maritime Consultative Organization
IMF	International Monetary Fund
IOE	International Organisation of Employers
ISSA	International Social Security Association
JMC	Joint Maritime Commission
NGO	Non-Governmental Organisation
OECD	Organisation for Economic Co-operation and Development
OEEC	Organisation for European Economic Co-operation (now OECD)
UAR	United Arab Republic
UK	United Kingdom
UN	United Nations
UNCTAD	United Nations Conference on Trade and Development

UNDP	United Nations Development Programme
UNDP/SF	United Nations Development Programme Special Fund
UNDP/TA	United Nations Development Programme Technical Assistance
UNESCO	United Nations Educational, Scientific and Cultural Organization
UNHCR	United Nations High Commissioner for Refugees
UNICEF	United Nations Children's Fund
UNIDO	United Nations Industrial Development Organization
UNITAR	United Nations Institute for Training and Research
UNRISD	United Nations Research Institute for Social Development
UNRWA	United Nations Relief and Works Agency for Palestine Refugees in the Near East
USA	United States of America
USSR	Union of Soviet Socialist Republics
WCC	World Council of Churches
WFP	World Food Program
WCL	World Confederation of Labour
WFTU	World Federation of Trade Unions
WHO	World Health Organization

INTRODUCTION

THE stages of economic growth and social progress are often not identified until some thought-provoking title is assigned to them. Thus, the "Acquisitive Society" gave place to the "Affluent Society", and the "Paternalistic State" to the "Welfare State". "Backward Territories" have become "Developing Countries" or "Emergent Countries" or "Industrialising States".

The last half-century, the period covered by the history of the International Labour Organisation, has seen economic and social changes in the world so great as to justify the term "transformation". In recent years the chief characteristic of this transformation has been "the revolution of rising expectations". Not only "great expectations" but "rising expectations" have excited the ambitions of the peoples of the world, most of whom are still living in conditions of poverty.

In co-operation with other members of the United Nations family of organisations, the ILO has been sharing in the world-wide enterprise of converting poverty into prosperity.

"Poverty anywhere constitutes a danger to prosperity everywhere." These words in the Declaration of Philadelphia, adopted by the International Labour Conference in 1944, are true whether poverty is due to unemployment of men, machines or natural resources in economically developed countries or to underemployment and low productivity in economically underdeveloped countries.

The Constitution of the ILO has fitted it well for this co-operative endeavour. Composed of representatives of governments, employers and workers, the International Labour Conference and the Governing Body of the International Labour Office constitute a balanced forum for the consideration of social problems in their economic bearings and of economic problems in their social bearings.

Resulting from the deliberations of the Conference at fifty-three sessions, the International Labour Code forms a balanced body of standards for the improvement of conditions of life and labour in a world of full and expanding employment.

Operating on this balanced basis, the ILO has been enabled, through its technical co-operation activities, to give help to developing countries on a wide range of problems on which the attainment of balance between the social and economic aspects of policy is essential.

1

This book is divided into four Parts.

Part I contains a description and discussion of the origins and membership of the ILO, its structure, functions and procedures, its relationships and financial resources.

Part II examines the major problems attacked and the solutions worked for in half a century of endeavour. Throughout the years the efforts of the ILO have been deployed on three broad fronts:

the development of human resources, including manpower planning and employment organisation, and vocational and technical training and rehabilitation;

the improvement of conditions of work and life, including hours of work, wages and incomes, productivity, occupational safety, health and welfare, and social security;

the encouragement of labour and industrial structures and institutions, including labour-management relations, labour administration, management development, workers' education, and co-operative organisation.

For convenience in tracing the historical development of the ILO's contribution in these three wide fields, Part II devotes separate chapters not only to the questions enumerated above but also to certain other sectors, namely, conditions of women, children and young persons, work at sea, agriculture and rural development, and non-metropolitan territories. Human rights receive special consideration.

Within each of its spheres of action, broad or narrow, the ILO has attempted to achieve generally acceptable results, on the one hand by balancing the often conflicting interests of governments, employers and workers, and on the other by balancing the ideally desirable and the practically realisable. In this complicated operation it was not to be expected that success could always be registered; sometimes opportunities have been missed, errors have been made, obstacles have proved insurmountable, courage has flagged, objectives have become blurred. To meet changing world conditions and emerging demands, from developing countries as well as from those with an advanced economy, old methods have had to be revised, time-honoured practices have had to be amended, established techniques have had to be re-tooled, and new procedures have had to be devised. But the underlying aim has remained the attainment of balance in the promotion of social and economic advancement.

Part III is devoted to an attempt to foresee developments in the structure, functions and programmes of the ILO, firstly over the next decade and then over the next half-century.

Part IV provides reference material on the ILO and its activities.

PART I
ORGANISATIONAL
DEVELOPMENT

1. ORIGINS

The Early Precursors

Almost exactly one hundred years before the Paris Peace Conference of 1919, the Congress of Aix-la-Chapelle (1818) was afforded an opportunity of incorporating in its decisions, as the Paris Peace Conference did, international provisions relating to labour and industry. That Congress received a memorial declaring that a prime task for the Governments of Europe was the international fixation of the legal limits of the normal working day for the industrial classes of Europe, and inviting the Congress to appoint a Commission to report on the question. A chance had been given to history to anticipate itself.

History could not anticipate itself, for the memorial came from a voice which at that time was not re-echoed from any country or any community. The memorialist was Robert Owen, a Welshman who had introduced new methods of industrial management in his textile mills at New Lanark in Scotland. Robert Owen was a philanthropist who, reflecting on the evils of child labour, envisaged the possibility of international agreement to regulate labour conditions.

Another early advocate of international action to combat industrial exploitation was Charles Hindley, who managed a cotton-spinning factory in Lancashire. Like Owen, Hindley was representative of the Manchester-school manufacturers who constituted one of the mainsprings of the early nineteenth-century reform movement in England.

The idea next emerged in France. In 1839 Villermé called attention to the abuses which existed in the textile industry and argued that international agreement was necessary because manufacturers in any one country, however good their intentions, could achieve nothing without the agreement of manufacturers in other countries.

At about the same time the French liberal economist Jérôme Blanqui, in his treatise on industrial economics written in 1838–39, impressed by the difficulties encountered by individual employers or even by all the employers in any one country in improving labour conditions owing to the severity of international competition, proposed the conclusion of international treaties to regulate such conditions.

Of all the precursors, however, the most important was Daniel Legrand, a Swiss from Basle, who managed a ribbon-making factory in Alsace. He was no political radical; he supported the monarchy of Louis Philippe and

5

disapproved of the revolution of 1848. From 1838 until his death in 1859 Legrand bombarded not only the French but also the British, Russian and Swiss governments with memoranda in the hope of inducing them to enact "an international law to protect the working class against work excessive in amount and at too early an age, the primary and principal cause of its physical deterioration, its moral degradation and its deprivation of the blessings of family life."

With Daniel Legrand the period of the precursors comes to an end. Their conception of international labour legislation was based on humanitarian and religious principles; it was reformist, inspired by the desire for "social peace"; it was not revolutionary, in no way an expression of the class struggle.

From the outset the concept of international labour legislation was bound up with the idea that competition between manufacturers in different countries is an obstacle in the way of the establishment and development of national legislation. The underlying principle is that certain basic humanitarian requirements should be removed from the sphere of international competition; there should be international agreement to secure certain minimum standards of protection of health, strength and human dignity.

Interesting and indeed valuable as the ideas of the precursors are, their significance in the history of the origins of the International Labour Organisation is not to be overestimated. Differing in nationality and in background, all were alike in this: they were powerless to translate their visions into action.

The conception of international labour legislation could not lead to positive results until the doctrines of economic liberalism that had obstructed its realisation began to lose some of their power. This happened in the second part of the nineteenth century. Under the influence of a developing social consciousness and the ideas propagated in many European countries by the 1848 revolutionary movement, the doctrine of *laissez-faire* began to weaken. The demands for national legislation for the protection of the workers became more clamant, some such legislation was actually enacted, and a vigorous impetus was given to the conception of international labour legislation.

Intergovernmental Action

As the precursors had themselves clearly seen, no practical results could be achieved without intergovernmental action. In the latter half of the nineteenth century persistent efforts were made, at first tentatively and unsuccessfully, to secure such action.

The first step was taken in 1876, when Colonel Frey, afterwards President of the Swiss Confederation, delivered before the Swiss Chamber an address in which he raised the question of the advisability for Switzerland to make treaties uniformly regulating conditions of labour among the several industrial States. In 1880, Colonel Frey took further action and proposed that the Federal Council should enter into negotiations for the purpose of bringing about international factory legislation. In the following year, the Federal Council addressed to the Swiss Legations at Paris, Berlin, Vienna and Rome, and the Swiss Consulates-General in London and Brussels, a note asking them to obtain information which would make it possible to know which States in Europe would co-operate in international regulation of labour. It was not to be expected that the first attempt would succeed. All the governments approached expressed their views with the exception of Belgium, and all were more or less unfavourable.

The next country to show a practical interest was France. A group of French deputies submitted in 1885 a bill indicating willingness on the part of the French government to comply with the overtures of the Swiss government. This bill, which contained the first suggestion that an international labour office should be established, was not adopted.

The initiative now passed to Germany. In 1886, members of the German Social Democratic Party promoted a resolution asking that the Imperial Chancellor should convene a conference of the principal industrial States with a view to formulating a uniform basis for an international agreement for the protection of labour. The resolution was defeated, but the heated discussions gave publicity to the idea of international labour legislation.

In 1889 the Swiss government considered the time ripe for further action. In a circular note to the governments of Europe, it recognised the impossibility of obtaining agreement on a comprehensive programme. It therefore proposed that an international conference should deal solely with questions of the international regulation of Sunday work and the work of women and children. The date of the conference was fixed for May 1890. The persistent efforts of the Swiss seemed to be about to be crowned with success, but at the eleventh hour the government cancelled the conference.

This sudden cancellation was due to one of the interventions of the German Emperor in international affairs. On 4 February 1890, i.e. three months before the conference convened by the Swiss, the German Emperor issued two rescripts. The first rescript was addressed to Bismarck urgently recommending action for improving the condition of the working classes and suggesting the co-operation in particular of England, France, Belgium and Switzerland. When Bismarck found that the Emperor was bent on action, he issued invitations on 8 February to nine European governments; but, as he did not himself approve the Emperor's move, he concentrated on making the proposed conference as innocuous as possible. The conference which assembled in Berlin on 15 March 1890 consisted of representatives of fourteen countries. Several resolutions were adopted, for the most part unanimously.

While on paper these resolutions appeared to have considerable importance, in reality the conference did not lead to any immediate practical results. Of the governments represented, only the Swiss had the foresight, or indeed the desire, to envisage practical action to give effect to the resolutions. A proposal submitted to the conference by the Swiss government is of sufficient interest, in the light of subsequent developments, to warrant quotation:

"Measures should be taken [the Swiss proposal ran] with a view to carrying out the provisions adopted by the Conference. It may be foreseen on this point that the States which have arrived at an agreement on certain measures will conclude an obligatory arrangement; that the carrying out of such arrangement will take place by national legislation, and that if this legislation is not sufficient it will have to receive the necessary additions. It is also safe to predict the creation of a special organ for centralising the information furnished, for the regular publication of statistical returns, and the execution of preparatory measures for the conferences anticipated. The principal task of these conferences will be to develop the arrangements agreed on and to solve the questions giving rise to difficulty or opposition."[1]

While these proposals foreshadowed some of the essential features of the procedure and machinery subsequently embodied in the Constitution of the International Labour Organisation, in 1890 the proposals were premature.

Between the Berlin Conference in 1890 and the establishment of the ILO in 1919, the ideal of international labour legislation was gradually brought nearer to practical realisation by two series of efforts. On the one hand, the International Association for Labour Legislation was created, and through its conferences led to the first really effective steps in international labour legislation. On the other hand, various international workers' conferences, both of a trade union and of a political character, kept before the minds of the workers the importance of the international solution of labour and industrial difficulties. To a certain extent, these developments ran on parallel lines. The International Association for Labour Legislation and

[1] Quoted in *The Origins of the International Labour Organisation* edited by James T. Shotwell, 1934, Vol. I, pp. 24–25.

the workers' internationals consciously or unconsciously influenced one another. If more immediate concrete results were achieved by the former body, the influence of the latter group should not be overlooked, especially in its later phases.

The International Association for Labour Legislation

After a conference in Brussels in 1897, the International Association for Labour Legislation was formally established in Paris in 1900. Leaders in the work of setting up this body were two men distinguished in the public life of their countries, Léon Bourgeois (France) and Ernest Mahaim (Belgium). It was decided that autonomous national sections were to be organised, an International Labour Office was to be set up in Basle, directed by a bureau representing the national sections, and international congresses on labour legislation were to be convened.

Following a series of preparatory meetings an international diplomatic conference in Berne in 1906 adopted two draft Conventions on the prohibition of the use of white phosphorus in the manufacture of matches and on the prohibition of the night work of women. For the first time the principle of international agreement for the regulation of labour conditions had been accepted by a number of industrial states.

Only the briefest mention need be made of the subsequent work of the International Association for Labour Legislation. At a technical conference held in Berne in 1913 two drafts of Conventions were adopted. The first provided for the general prohibition of the night work of young persons under sixteen years of age, and absolute prohibition for all young persons under fourteen. The second concerned the determination of the length of the working day for workers under sixteen and for women. It was intended to submit these two drafts to a diplomatic conference to be held in the following year, but owing to the outbreak of the first world war, that conference was never held.

The International Association for Labour Legislation suffered from fundamental weaknesses as an organism for promoting international agreements on industrial questions. In the first place, it was representative neither of employers' organisations nor of workers' organisations, nor of governments. Although the technical and diplomatic conferences were attended by government representatives, the great majority of those who attended the delegates' meetings were professors, doctors, lawyers and social workers, with a sprinkling of politicians and government officials. In the second place, in its investigations into industrial questions it could not command the necessary information.

Nevertheless, the experience gained in the pioneer work of the Association was of real use in the construction of the framework of the ILO in 1919. Of the dominant conceptions embodied in the Constitution of the ILO no less than three were derived directly from this pre-war experience, namely, (a) periodical conferences for the conclusion of international agreements; (b) a central organ of information and preparation; and (c) supervision over the observance of conventions.

The International Workers' Movement

While the influence exerted by the international workers' movement on the trend of thought which led to the creation of the ILO was very different from the influence of the International Association for Labour Legislation, it was no less important. If the International Association for Labour Legislation adumbrated the technical and diplomatic structure of the new machinery to be established after the war, the international workers' movement helped to supply, directly or indirectly, the power necessary to set it in motion.

As an organised and articulate body of opinion, the international workers' movement did not originate until 1864, when the International Working Men's Association was formed in London. This Association held its first meeting at Geneva in 1866, and adopted a number of resolutions significant for the early formulation of principles which were subsequently incorporated in international conventions.

In 1872 a split took place in the Association which led to its disruption. The Second (Socialist) International was constituted in 1889 in Paris. It adopted a programme including the prohibition of the employment of children under fourteen and in general of night work, an eight-hour day, one day of rest in seven, the establishment of an international minimum wage and the creation of systems of State-supported national and international factory inspection.

In addition to the Second International which concerned itself with the political aspirations of the workers rather than with their trade union demands, another international was set up in 1898, namely the International Federation of Trade Unions. This was a loose federal organisation to which the central trade union organisations of a number of important industrial countries were affiliated. With headquarters in Berlin, it held congresses in various European cities, at which resolutions were adopted relating to concrete aspects of the improvement of conditions of labour in their international bearings.

These two Internationals, the Second (Socialist) International and the International Federation of Trade Unions, were both in their own provinces progressing when the first world war broke out.

Although the United States had not at that time entered the war, the American Federation of Labor in 1914 called for a world labour congress to meet at the same time and place as the Peace Conference.

With a view to following up this proposal Léon Jouhaux, the Secretary of the French General Confederation of Labour, convened a meeting of allied trade union representatives in Paris in May 1916. This paved the way for an Inter-Allied Trade Union Conference in July 1916 in Leeds, whose conclusions exercised a great influence on the subsequent course of the war-time thinking of the workers.

In the following year a conference of workers' representatives from the Central and Neutral Powers met in Berne, and an Inter-Allied Labour and Socialist Conference was held in London.

The last of the pre-Peace Treaty conferences of the international workers' movement, and the only one at which workers of Allied, Neutral and Central Powers were all represented, was held in February 1919 in Berne. From the point of view of international labour legislation, the great achievement of the conference was the detailed Labour Charter which it adopted.

In order to understand the influence exerted on the governments which drafted the terms of the Peace Treaties by these conferences of the workers' movement, it is necessary to appreciate the great change brought about during the 1914–18 war in the relations between the governments and the employers and workers in the belligerent countries.

In several countries, war conditions brought the organisations of employers and workers into much closer relation with the governments. The re-orientation of industry for the production of munitions and for supplying the essential needs of the community gave rise to many problems on which governments found it essential to consult the organisations of employers and workers. As a result governments became much better informed on the thinking of the employers and the workers and much more inclined to give sympathetic consideration to their views.

Government Preparations for the Peace Conference

Long before the Peace Conference met, it had become clear to the governments of the principal belligerent countries that, in order to take account of the thinking of the workers and the employers it would be necessary to promote international action in the Peace Treaties. Gradually, as a result in part of the progressive clarification of the workers' demands and the employers' attitudes, and in part of constructive thinking within government departments, a pattern began to take shape.

Although there was hardly any exchange of information between the

Allied governments in the earlier stages of their respective consideration of the problem, it was found when contact was established between them that their thinking was developing on substantially similar lines.

In January 1919 discussions took place in Paris on British draft proposals between the British delegation, which included Malcolm Delevigne, Harold Butler and Edward Phelan, and members of other delegations, particularly James T. Shotwell of the United States delegation, who made an outstanding contribution to the success of the efforts to secure an agreed draft. Discussions also took place with Arthur Fontaine of the French delegation, Ernest Mahaim of the Belgian delegation, Arnaldo Cabrini of the Italian delegation and Edouard Benes of the Czechoslovak delegation, and also with members of the British Dominion delegations. Finally, an outline of the British proposals was discussed with representatives of the British trade union movement who had been invited to come to Paris for this purpose, and by correspondence with representatives of the British employers. As a result of all these consultations and discussions the British proposals gradually assumed a form on which a substantial measure of agreement had been reached even before the Peace Conference met.

The 1919 Peace Conference

One of the first acts of the Peace Conference was to appoint, on 31 January 1919, a Commission on International Labour Legislation, with the following terms of reference.

"That a Commission, composed of two representatives apiece from the five Great Powers, and five representatives to be elected by the other Powers represented at the Peace Conference, be appointed to enquire into the conditions of employment from the international aspect and to consider the international means necessary to secure common action on matters affecting conditions of employment, and to recommend the form of a permanent agency to continue such enquiry and consideration in co-operation with and under the direction of the League of Nations."

The Commission elected as its President Samuel Gompers (United States) and as its Vice-Presidents G. N. Barnes (British Empire), and M. Colliard (France). Its General Secretary was Arthur Fontaine (France) and its Assistant General Secretary Harold Butler (British Empire).

In the work of the Commission the influence of the United States delegation was very great. It provided the President of the Commission, and in the discussions an important part was played by James T. Shotwell and by A. N. Robinson, a prominent American employer, both of whom were members of the United States delegation. Further, all members of the

Commission were aware that its objectives enjoyed the warm support of President Wilson.

The Commission started work on 1 February 1919, and adopted its report at its thirty-fifth sitting on 24 March 1919. Its task proved difficult and laborious. Although it accepted at the outset as a basis for discussion the British draft which, as has been indicated, had already secured a substantial measure of support from other delegations, difficulties were encountered in the course of discussion, at least three of which proved so serious as to threaten the very existence of its work.

The first difficulty related to the question whether the Commission should propose for inclusion in the Peace Treaty the constitution of a permanent international organisation or the formulation of certain general principles, a sort of Labour Charter. The second main difficulty arose in connection with the representation of groups or interests in the International Labour Conference and Governing Body. The third difficulty concerned the obligations of States in relation to the decisions of the Conference. In the end, all these difficulties were successfully surmounted and complete agreement was reached.

Although in the course of its discussions the Commission dealt with many other important points, one only need be mentioned. The original draft of the Preamble ran as follows: "Whereas the League of Nations has for its object the establishment of universal peace, and such a peace can be established only if it is based upon the prosperity and contentment of all classes in all nations." The Commission decided to amend the second clause, on the proposal of Emile Vandervelde, to read: "and such a peace can be established only if it is based upon social justice." The significance of this amendment lies in the introduction of the two words "social justice" which came to symbolise the main objective of the International Labour Organisation.

The report of the Commission consisted of two Parts, Part I containing the Constitution of the proposed permanent International Labour Organisation, and Part II the Labour Clauses, the enumeration of principles to be incorporated in the Peace Treaty. Part I was adopted by the Peace Conference on 11 April 1919, and Part II (in a redrafted form) on 28 April. These texts were embodied, with minor drafting amendments, in the Treaty of Versailles as Part XIII, and they were later inserted in corresponding positions in the other Peace Treaties concluded in 1919 and 1920.

In spite of all the efforts of the Commission to present a completely harmonious report, a difference of spirit remained between Part I and Part II. The difference could not be eliminated, because Part I was based on a governmental draft designed to provide machinery for securing long-term progress; whereas Part II, while not based on the Labour Charter of the Berne international trade union conference, was inspired by the desire of the workers to incorporate in the Peace Treaty a declaration of principles to which they attached immediate importance. If, in a future age, Parts I and II alone were to survive, without any trace of the discussions which led to them, the scholars of that time would certainly be puzzled by the co-existence in the same document of two texts differing so obviously in character. It is not surprising that when the Constitution was amended in 1946 Part II was omitted.

The resolution adopted by the Peace Conference on 11 April 1919 was of great historical importance, as it not only approved the Constitution of the International Labour Organisation but made provision for the preparation of its first Conference. The resolution was in the following terms:

"That this Conference approves the Draft Convention creating a permanent organisation for the promotion of international regulation of labour conditions which has been submitted by the Labour Commission, with the amendments proposed by the British Delegation, instructs the Secretariat to request the Governments concerned to nominate forthwith their representatives on the Organizing Committee for the October Conference, and authorises that Committee to proceed at once with its work."

Very different are the sober and business-like terms of this resolution from the inflated and repetitive memorials of Robert Owen and Daniel Legrand. But if the early precursors could have looked down on the Peace Conference on that April day, they would surely have recognised in the forty tightly drafted Articles the realisation of their visions.

In a description of the events leading to the establishment of the ILO included in a book published in 1924 the author wrote this somewhat flamboyant passage:

"At the end of a century of endeavour the International Labour Organisation now is. Is it to be regarded, with Thucydides, as the denouement in the unfolding of a mighty drama of the fates, or with Hegel, as the final self-externalisation of the spirit of social progress, or with the materialistic school of history, as a blind event in a sequence of blind events? Whether as dramatic climax, as philosophic culmination, or as materialistic resultant, the real significance of the International Labour Organisation is not to be the end of a sequence but the beginning of a new process."[2]

The years that have passed have confirmed that "the real significance

[2] *International Social Progress*, 1924, p. 36.

of the International Labour Organisation is not to be the end of a sequence but the beginning of a new process".

It will be for the chapters that follow to describe and assess "the new process".

2. MEMBERSHIP

Universality

From the outset the ILO has been inspired by the will to become all-embracing. Whenever a new member has been admitted, its accession has been hailed with joy as a further stage towards the goal of complete universality, and whenever a member has withdrawn sorrow at its decision has always been tempered by the conviction that sooner or later it would return.

Three times in the Preamble to the Constitution the world-wide mission and character of the Organisation are stressed.

An international labour organisation which did not aim at universality would indeed be a contradiction in terms. The peace and prosperity of the world as a whole may be endangered by the eruption of social agitation in any country where large masses of the workers are subject to poverty and privation.

One of the most penetrating commentators on the Constitution, Georges Scelle, emphasised that the universality of the Organisation is the essential consequence of the mission assigned to it. "The psychological and moral basis of the Organisation is the eternal and universal need of justice in the soul of man. Little would have been done for the cause of peace if this need of justice were not satisfied. In the case of the technical international agencies whose aim is to develop material, economic and social solidarity universality appears to be necessitated by the very nature of the solidarity aimed at. This is particularly true of the ILO, whose social vocation cannot be otherwise than ecumenical."[1]

But universality does not mean uniformity. This was emphasised by the Credentials Committee in a report to the 1954 Conference. "Paramount in that concept (i.e. universality) is the idea that the aims and purposes of the ILO and the action that it takes must correspond with the needs of all the peoples throughout the world, whatever social or economic regime exists in their countries. The principle of universality means also that the functioning of the ILO should not be designed solely to fit any given social system or to impose a pattern of social structure to be uniformly applied."[2]

It is because of such considerations as these that the formal resolution

[1] Georges Scelle: *L'Organisation Internationale du Travail et le B.I.T.*, 1930, pp. 38–39.
[2] *Record of Proceedings*, International Labour Conference, 1954, p. 436.

adopted by the Conference in admitting a new member includes the following clause:

> "Recalling that it has always been the firm conviction of the International Labour Organisation that its ends can be more effectively advanced if the membership of the organisation could be made universal."

Original Members

At first the ILO was far from even approaching the goal of numerical universality. The forty-two original members of the ILO were, in accordance with the Treaty of Versailles, the original members of the League of Nations. But these did not include the United States, nor Germany, nor Soviet Russia, nor a number of other States, such as Austria, Bulgaria, Finland, Hungary, Mexico and Turkey. The absence of these States constituted a very serious gap in the membership of the Organisation, and the question was even asked whether it could carry out its work without the participation of three of the chief industrial powers in the world, powers moreover in which labour legislation and industrial relations were developing on such very different lines.

Growth of Membership

One of the first acts of the ILO was to take the first step towards a more balanced membership. In 1919 the first session of the Conference decided to admit Germany and Austria.[3]

In 1920 Finland and Luxembourg, together with Albania, Bulgaria and Costa Rica, automatically became members of the ILO in virtue of the decision of the First Assembly of the League of Nations to admit them to the League. Also in virtue of decisions of the Assembly of the League, in 1921 Estonia, Latvia and Lithuania became members, in 1922 Hungary, in 1923 Ethiopia and the Irish Free State and in 1924 the Dominican Republic.

In 1927 the first withdrawal from the League became effective. In that year Costa Rica ceased to be a member of the League and as it had not indicated any desire to remain a member of the ILO it ceased also to be a member of that Organisation.

[3] For this decision the way had been prepared by the Supreme Council of the Peace Conference. When, in the course of the peace negotiations with Germany and Austria, the question was raised of the participation of these countries in the ILO, the Supreme Council authorised the ILO to settle the question as it wished.

Abandonment of the Doctrine of the Identity of Membership of the ILO and the League of Nations

For a short time after 1926 the membership of the ILO and the League was identical, as Austria and Germany were admitted to the League in 1920 and 1926 respectively.

As early as 1920 the doctrine of the compulsory participation of members of the League in the ILO had been contested. In that year El Salvador maintained that while it had become a member of the League by adhering to the Covenant, it had not signed any of the Treaties of Peace containing the Constitution of the ILO, and that it therefore had no obligations to the ILO. It therefore did not consider itself a member of the ILO and refused to pay a contribution in respect of the budget of the ILO. In the end, although El Salvador maintained its legal contention, it recognised its membership of the ILO, paid its arrears of contribution and sent delegations to the Conference.

In 1926 a different problem arose, namely the question whether a State which withdrew from the League could continue to belong to the ILO. In 1926 Brazil and Spain declared their intention of withdrawing from the League but stated at the same time that they wished to remain members of the ILO. Although Spain returned to membership of the League before the expiry of the period of notice of two years required by the Covenant, Brazil did not change its mind and actually left the League in 1928. In 1929 the Assembly found a solution inspired by common sense and the practical interests both of the League and the ILO. After statements had been made by the Secretary General of the League and the Director of the ILO, the constitutional and legal issues involved were left entirely open, but it was accepted that Brazil remained a member of the ILO.

The Brazilian case is important because, though the constitutional issue whether identity of membership of the two organisations was necessary had been left open, the practical precedent created, added to the German and Austrian case, facilitated the decision taken by the Conference in 1934 to invite the United States to become a member of the ILO. That decision amounted to the *de facto* abandonment of the doctrine of identity of membership of the two organisations.

Admission of the United States

From the outset, Albert Thomas and the leading members of the Governing Body and the Conference had realised how important it was for the Organisation to have the United States as a member, and contacts were established, as and where possible, with workers' and employers' organisations and individuals in the United States interested in international relations. The election of Roosevelt as President and the change of the political climate which accompanied it opened the way for action. Roosevelt himself, as long before as 1919 when he was Assistant Secretary of the Navy, had met Harold Butler in Washington and shown an interest in the ILO. Frances Perkins, his Secretary of Labor, had visited Geneva and had a full understanding of, and respect for, the work of the Organisation. It was necessary, however, to move very cautiously with the formulation of the procedure for securing admission. On the side of the United States care had to be taken not to alarm those members of Congress who might see in membership of the ILO the first step in a move to join the League. On the side of the ILO care had to be taken to ensure that the League would raise no objection on constitutional grounds to admission by the Conference to membership of the Organisation.

On 19 June 1934 President Roosevelt signed a joint resolution of Congress authorising the President to accept membership in the Organisation. This was communicated to the Conference on 21 June, and on the following day the Conference unanimously adopted a resolution inviting the Government of the United States to accept membership in the Organisation. The President, exercising the authority conferred on him by the joint resolution of Congress, accepted the invitation, effective 20 August 1934.

This special procedure was ingeniously devised with a view to avoiding objections being raised either on the side of Congress or on the side of the League. The normal procedure under which a State becomes a member of an international organisation is for the State to submit a formal application for membership and for the Organisation formally to admit the State. But if this procedure had been followed in the case of the United States, the risk of objection both from Congress and from the League would have been greatly increased. From the side of Congress there was an important difference between authorising the President to apply for membership in the ILO (when there was considerable doubt whether the Conference was competent to admit to membership) and authorising the President to accept an invitation from the Conference to become a member. From the side of the League there was an equally important difference between the assumption by the Conference of the Assembly's power to admit to membership and the giving by the Conference of an invitation to become a member. In the result the special procedure was successful. Congress adopted the joint resolution, unanimously in the case of the Senate, with a two-thirds majority in the case of the House. On the side of the League, while the League's legal advisers were convinced that the action of the Conference was *ultra vires*, the League very wisely refrained from raising any objection.

Relations with the United Nations in respect of Membership

The difficulties that had arisen out of the doctrine of identity of membership between the ILO and the League were borne in mind when the Charter of the United Nations was being drawn up, and accordingly the Charter contains no provision requiring identity of membership between the United Nations and the specialised agencies. When the Constitution of the ILO was amended in 1945–46 and the ILO entered into relationship with the United Nations, the arrangements were such that difficulties between the two bodies in respect to membership were effectively precluded. The new rules were largely a codification of the practice that had developed over the previous few years.

In the first place, while membership of the United Nations does not carry with it membership of the ILO, any original member of the United Nations and any State subsequently admitted to membership of the United Nations may become a member of the ILO by communicating to the Director-General its formal acceptance of the obligations of the Constitution of the ILO.

In the second place, if a State which is not a member of the United Nations applies for membership of the ILO, the amended Constitution of the ILO formally confers on the Conference the right to admit to membership which it had assumed *de facto* during the period of the relationship of the ILO to the League.

The provisions of the amended Constitution with regard to membership have worked smoothly. In the case of members of the United Nations, membership of the ILO can be acquired, as has been indicated, simply by the communication of formal acceptance of the obligations of the Constitution. But the acceptance of the obligations must be complete. The Constitution does not permit acceptance with reservations. When in 1953 the Soviet Union communicated to the Director-General its acceptance, subject to specified reservations, of the obligations of the Constitution, the Director-General pointed out in reply that the Constitution does not make any provision for reservations, and in the following year the Soviet Union communicated its acceptance of the obligations of the Constitution without any reservations.

After this brief discussion of the constitutional relationship of the ILO to the League of Nations and the United Nations respectively in respect of membership, it is time to return to the chronology of the changes in the membership of the ILO from 1930 until the time of writing.

Fluctuations in Membership, followed by Renewed Growth

The years from 1930 until 1970 fall into three clearly delimited periods, first a period of growth, then a period of decline and finally a period of renewed and sustained growth.

In 1931 Mexico was admitted, in 1932 Iraq and Turkey, in 1934 the United States, Afghanistan, Ecuador and the USSR, and in 1936 Egypt. All these States, with the exception of the United States and Egypt, became members of the ILO in virtue of their membership of the League.

In 1935 the period of decline of membership began and lasted until 1942. Germany withdrew in 1935, followed in 1937 by Paraguay, in 1938 by Austria, Guatemala, Honduras and Nicaragua, in 1939 by Italy and El Salvador and in 1940 by Japan. In 1940 the USSR ceased to be a member of the ILO on its expulsion from the League, and in 1941 and 1942 Spain and Romania withdrew. 1942 marked the "all-time low" in the membership of the ILO.

From 1944 onwards, as soon as the victory of the allied democracies appeared assured, a double movement of growth of membership developed. On the one hand, States whose membership had ceased in the pre-war and war-time period rejoined the Organisation. Thus, in 1944 Costa Rica was readmitted, in 1945 Guatemala and Italy, in 1947 Austria, in 1948 El Salvador, in 1951 the Federal Republic of Germany and Japan, and also Yugoslavia which had withdrawn two years previously, in 1954 the Soviet Union, in 1955 Honduras, in 1956 Paraguay, Romania and Spain, and in 1957 Nicaragua.

Simultaneously with the readmission of former members, the membership of the ILO was added to by the admission of States whose accession to full sovereignty was of recent date. Thus, in 1945 Iceland became a member, in 1947 Syria and Pakistan, in 1948 Burma, Ceylon, Lebanon and the Philippines, in 1949 Israel, in 1950 Indonesia and Viet-Nam, in 1952 Libya, in 1956 Jordan, Morocco, Sudan and Tunisia and in 1957 Ghana and Malaya. From 1958 onwards membership increased even more rapidly as nearly all the countries which attained independence were admitted.

From the geographical standpoint, the most striking transformation in the membership of the ILO is in Africa. In 1919, Africa was represented in the ILO by only two States – South Africa, a very active member for many years, and Liberia, which took hardly any interest in the ILO. In 1969, although South Africa had withdrawn, thirty-seven African countries were ILO members.

Since the war the membership has more than doubled. At the end of 1969 it numbered 121. The vast majority of the new members are from Asia and Africa. As a result, decisive changes are being effected in the policies, programmes and power-structure of the ILO. Though these changes create fresh problems for the ILO, they are to be welcomed; otherwise the ILO would cease to be able to serve a changing world. A list of members will be found in the Reference section.

The Position of Non-Metropolitan Territories

Although few non-metropolitan territories now remain, when the ILO was established there were many. From the outset the ILO was fully conscious of the importance of its relationship to such territories. Under whatever name they have borne – colonies, possessions, protectorates, mandated territories, trust territories – these areas have shared a common quality: they are not self-governing or not completely self-governing. So long as their status is of this order, such territories cannot become members of the Organisation.

Nevertheless, under special provisions, some non-metropolitan territories, which afterwards became self-governing and were admitted to membership, had for some years previously been associated with the work of the ILO.

The revised Constitution provides that each member which is responsible for the international relations of non-metropolitan territories may appoint as additional advisers to each of its delegates: (a) persons nominated by it as representatives of any such territory in regard to matters within the self-governing powers of that territory; and (b) persons nominated by it to advise its delegates in regard to matters concerning non-self-governing territories.

In 1954 the Governing Body decided that tripartite delegations from non-metropolitan territories might be invited to attend the Conference as observers. In accordance with this decision the Gold Coast (now Ghana) was represented at the Conference in 1954. In subsequent years several other non-metropolitan territories were also represented. Thus in 1969 observer delegations from Bermuda and Grenada were present.

In regard to one category of dependent territory the Organisation has always been in a special relationship. After the first world war certain non-metropolitan territories ("mandated territories") were placed under the special protection of the League; after the second world war the mandates system was replaced by the trusteeship system under the United Nations, and the "trust territories" enjoyed the special protection of the United Nations.

When under the League a Permanent Mandates Commission was set up to supervise the operation of the mandates, it was agreed that the ILO should have the right to appoint an expert who might attend all meetings of the Commission at which questions relating to labour were discussed. Through collaboration in the Permanent Mandates Commission the ILO was able to stimulate labour legislation in the mandated territories and the authorities in these territories became acquainted with the aims and procedure of the ILO. It was therefore not surprising that as soon as mandated territories such as Iraq, Syria, Lebanon and Israel attained independence, one of their first acts was to seek membership of the ILO. In view of the fruitfulness of the collaboration of the ILO with the Permanent Mandates Commission, it was natural that when under the United Nations a Trusteeship Council was set up arrangements were made for the participation of the ILO in its work.

Through contacts with representatives of such territories at meetings of the Mandates Commission and the Trusteeship Council preparation has been made for their admission to membership of the Organisation when they attain independence.

Although some of the other specialised agencies in relation with the United Nations have introduced into their Constitutions provisions enabling them to admit as "Associate Members" States not fully self-governing, the ILO, in spite of its constant urge towards universality, has, like the United Nations itself, refrained from creating a second category of membership.

Cessation of Membership

In every organisation cases arise in which for one reason or another members wish to withdraw, and detailed provision for this is made in the Constitution of the ILO.

Under the Constitution no member may withdraw without giving two years' notice, during which it remains bound to discharge its obligations. Since the second world war five members have given notice of withdrawal, but in three cases the member has returned to the ILO.

In June 1947 Yugoslavia gave notice of withdrawal, on the grounds that "the Constitutional provisions and the structure of the ILO have become incompatible with the economic and social conditions in the Federal People's Republic of Yugoslavia and do not reflect the general trends of developments in those fields in the post-war world." In May 1951 Yugoslavia was readmitted to the ILO.

In May 1955 Venezuela gave notice of withdrawal, alleging that, arising out of certain incidents occurring on the occasion of a meeting of the ILO Petroleum Committee held in that country on the invitation of the government, the Officers of the Governing Body had attempted to impose a sanction on the government involving intervention in its internal affairs.

The ILO in reply made it clear that no action of ILO representatives at the time was to be regarded as a sanction and they had no intention of intervening in the internal affairs of Venezuela. The withdrawal did not take effect, Venezuela resuming normal relations with the ILO.

Indonesia and Albania gave notice of withdrawal in March and August 1965. These notifications were based on political grounds; while Indonesia returned to the ILO before the withdrawal became effective, Albania has remained outside.

In March 1964 South Africa informed the ILO of its decision to withdraw. For some years relations between the ILO and that country had been increasingly difficult. The South African policy of *apartheid* was completely at variance not only with the ILO Convention on Discrimination in Employment and Occupation but also with the whole philosophy of human rights on which the ILO is based. Things came to a head at the 1963 session of the Conference when all the other African delegates withdrew from that session in noisy protest. As a widespread desire was expressed that South Africa should be expelled from the Organisation, and as the Constitution of the ILO makes no provision for expulsion, the Governing Body, meeting in February 1964, agreed on proposals for submission to the Conference, which adopted amendments to the Constitution to provide for the suspension or expulsion of a member in specified circumstances. This action was accompanied by a vigorous condemnation of the policy of *apartheid*. The reaction of South Africa was to withdraw from the ILO, as it had already done from the Food and Agriculture Organization.

Before and during the second world war, the massive withdrawals which took place (Germany, Italy, Japan and countries under their influence) were all motivated by political considerations. After the war all those States sought and obtained readmission to the ILO.

Thus, the only cases of withdrawal which have remained effective are those of South Africa and Albania.

The withdrawal of a member has always been regarded by the Organisation as a serious matter, much more serious than the simple subtraction of one numerical unit. For the Organisation is not merely the mathematical total of its members. As the human body is not merely the arithmetical sum of all its limbs and organs, but is rather the unity of these various parts, so the ILO is more than a mere list of States. It is a living association of these States, organised for a common purpose – the attainment of balanced economic and social progress in an expanding world economy.

3. THE INTERNATIONAL LABOUR CONFERENCE

IN structure the ILO is extremely simple. It consists of an International Labour Conference, a Governing Body and an International Labour Office. The Conference is the supreme policy-making and legislative organ; the Governing Body the executive council; and the Office the secretariat, operational headquarters and information centre.

Of all the innovations made by the Constitution of the Organisation the most original is its tripartite character. In the Conference and the Governing Body, side by side with government representatives, sit employers' and workers' representatives, equal in status. Unique in this respect among international organisations, the ILO has owed its vitality and a large measure of its success to the balanced collaboration in its activities of governments, management and labour.

Except for an interruption due to the war, the International Labour Conference has continued, since the first session in 1919, to meet at least once a year. The annual session of the Conference has become a tradition in the field of industrial relations; whenever the need for maintaining this tradition has been examined the consensus of the governments, the employers and the workers of the world has been that an annual session is necessary.

Composition of the Conference

The Conference is composed of four representatives of each member, of whom two are government delegates and two are delegates representing respectively the employers and the workers of the member concerned. All delegates may be accompanied by advisers, not exceeding two for each item on the agenda.

The 2+1+1 basis of representation at the Conference has been a subject for acute difference of opinion. In particular, it was fully discussed in 1919 in the Commission on International Labour Legislation of the Peace Conference and in 1946 in the Committee on Constitutional Questions of the International Labour Conference. In 1946 as in 1919 the underlying argument in favour of the 2+1+1 system was that it was essential that the governments should have a voice at least equal to that of the employers and workers combined, since otherwise it would often happen that Conventions

25

adopted by a two-thirds majority of the Conference would be rejected by the legislatures of the various States, and the influence and prestige of the Conference would be quickly destroyed.

Employers' and Workers' Delegates of States with a Socialised Economy

The most difficult constitutional question the Conference has had to consider is the position of employers' and workers' delegates of States with a socialised economy. In 1936, two years after the USSR became a member of the Organisation, the Conference, on the request of the employers' group, asked the Governing Body to examine the question of the representation of States with a socialised economy. The question remained under consideration for the next two years. By 1938 the USSR had ceased to participate actively in the ILO, and the Conference, with a sigh of relief, simply took note of a non-committal report from the Governing Body.

The question was not again considered until 1946. In that year the Conference Delegation on Constitutional Questions in their report to the Conference said: "They desire to emphasise that appropriate provision for the representation of socialised management and of different sections of the labour movement of member States can be made within the framework of the present system of representation."[1] In its turn, the Conference Committee on Constitutional Questions, in stating that proposals for the revision of the composition of the Conference had been withdrawn, added: "The agreement reached by the Committee on this basis was facilitated by the unanimous wish of the Committee to make it clear that the International Labour Organisation desires and will welcome the active participation in the Organisation of all the members of the United Nations and of all important sections in the labour movement of all member States."[2]

In 1946 it was still fresh in men's minds that the USSR had been aligned with the Western World in the struggle for freedom, and there was a unanimous desire to facilitate its return to the Organisation. In 1954, when the USSR had again become a member, the political situation was very different; there was no unanimous desire to facilitate her participation in the work of the ILO.

At the 1954 session of the Conference, the Chairman of the employers' group lodged objection to the credentials of the employers' delegations of the USSR, Bulgaria, the Byelorussian SSR, Czechoslovakia, Hungary, Poland and the Ukrainian SSR. The ground for the objection was that they did not

[1] *Report II* (1), Int. Lab. Conf., 1946, p. 94.
[2] *Rec. Proc.*, Int. Lab. Conf., 1946, p. 358.

represent employers in the context of the tripartite structure of the ILO. This objection triggered off a prolonged series of reports and discussions in the Governing Body and Conference. The Conference continued every year to accept, by a majority, the credentials of the employers' and workers' delegates of Communist States, but the employers' group of the Conference (consisting of the non-Communist majority) refused to propose the inclusion, in the "voting section" of any committees, of the employers of Communist States.

In 1959 the Conference adopted by a majority a *modus vivendi* under which every delegate has the right to be appointed to all the working committees of his choice, but the Conference groups select the members of each committee who have the right to vote. A delegate not included by his group in the "voting section" may appeal to a three-man Appeals Board appointed by the Conference consisting of "persons of internationally recognised independence and impartiality". The Board may add a maximum of two delegates to the "voting section" of any one group in a committee. The decision of the Board is final and no debate upon it may take place in the Conference. Obviously this *modus vivendi* has no logical basis. It is a pragmatic device, accepted reluctantly, by a majority, as an ingenious way of overcoming a difficulty which had proved otherwise insurmountable.

At the sessions of the Conference from 1959 to 1967 the employers' group appointed no delegate from Communist States to the "voting sections". These delegates duly appealed to the Board, and the Board seated the maximum of two of these delegates in the "voting section" of each committee. At the 1959 session all the employers' delegates of the non-Communist countries walked out of the committees in protest against the seating of the Communist delegates; they maintained that this violated the tripartite character of the committees and that the Conference had shirked its responsibilities in setting up an Appeals Board. At the following sessions the employers' group, respecting the individual freedom of its members, agreed to leave it to each member to decide whether to sit in the committees along with the Communist delegates. In fact very few employers' delegates refused to sit in the committees.

At the 1968 session the employers' group made an important change in its procedure. It decided, on an experimental basis, to abstain from making a recommendation to the Selection Committee on the composition of the voting sections of the employers' group in the Conference committees. Accordingly, the employers' group merely transmitted lists of the employers' members of those committees, with an indication of those members who had requested to be entitled to vote.

The meaning of this new procedure was explained to the Conference by the Chairman of the employers' group, Pierre Waline. After referring to the debates on the matter since 1954, he said: "The situation in 1968 is no longer what it was in 1954 or even in 1959. The increase in the number of members of the Organisation, the extreme diversity of national situations, the evolution which has been taking shape or trying to take shape in certain Eastern European countries in recent years, and the objection of employers from these countries, and from all other countries, to the system which I have just mentioned[3] are the four major reasons which have led the employers' group to reconsider carefully whether the methods it has followed in recent years for the composition of Conference committees are still appropriate. . . . The group hopes, in adopting this new attitude, that it will allow the different national situations to be better taken into account in the work of the Conference. It hopes, also, that in this way it will contribute to improving the atmosphere of the Conference, which it wants to proceed smoothly to the exclusion of political controversy."[4]

At the 1969 session of the Conference, and also at the 1969 Preparatory Technical Maritime Conference, the new procedure continued to be followed by the employers' group.

This change in the attitude of the employers' group is a major contribution to improvement in the relations in the ILO of the "free enterprise" and the "socialised" economies of the world.

At the same time it must be noted that at the 1969 session the Committee on the Programme and Structure of the ILO, set up to undertake a general review of the Governing Body working party's reports on the same subject, found that it was not yet ready to make any firm recommendations on certain problems of structure, one of which was "the composition of the Governing Body, including the relationship between elective and non-elective seats, and the relationship between the employers' group and socialised management not represented as such therein".

From all these developments two encouraging conclusions may be drawn. Thanks to patience and accommodation on both sides the crisis which threatened to disrupt the ILO in 1954 seems unlikely to recur. Hope may also be found in the fact that "talks are continuing"; even if they take another fifteen years to result in complete agreement, the time will not have been wasted in the endeavour to find a solution of this crucial problem.

These and other adjustments in the procedures and methods of work of the Conference have enabled tripartite delegations from countries with a socialised economy to participate effectively in its work. In spite of the

[3] The system mentioned by the speaker was the reference of appeals to the Appeals Board set up in 1959.
[4] *Rec. Proc.*, Int. Lab. Conf., 52nd session, Geneva, 1968, p. 13.

controversies arising from differences in political outlook, the tripartite principle has continued to be respected. Indeed, the contribution of the ILO to the balanced economic and social progress of the world would not have been possible without the vigorous presence in its councils of workers and management representatives of countries in a wide range of political, economic and social development.

Representative Character of the Conference

Because of its representative character, the Conference is, according to Georges Scelle, "already at an advanced stage of international evolution".[5] It is more closely akin to a representative law-making parliament than the Assemblies either of the League of Nations or the United Nations.

But Troclet goes too far when he writes: "Thus, the four delegates of each State, thanks to the freedom of attitude, speech and vote guaranteed by the Constitution of the ILO, come to the Conference as the members of a Parliament and not as the representatives of a State at a diplomatic Conference under instructions which are imperative or which may at any time become so. This freedom is evidenced even more in the votes which they cast, as they do not commit the State which they represent," and he adds in a footnote, "except, however, to a certain extent, in the case of the government delegates at least, in respect to the budget and the allocation of contributions."[6]

While it is true that the employers' and workers' delegates vote in complete freedom from their governments, the Conference has itself more than once expressed the view that when government delegates vote for a Convention or for the adoption of the budget, this vote should be regarded as a commitment on the part of the Government concerned to take steps to promote the necessary legislative or other action in their own countries to give effect to these decisions.

Although the Constitution contains no stipulation as to the manner of appointment of government delegates, most States appoint as their delegates ministers, diplomats or officials subject to government instructions. In practice, well-organised government delegations come to the Conference with general instructions covering the main questions on the agenda; the delegation meets every morning, and in the light of the general instructions decides on the attitude to be taken by the various members of the delegation in the committees on which they sit on the detailed issues expected to emerge that day. Whenever in the course of the discussions in the Conference a question arises on which the head of the delegation

[5] Georges Scelle: *L'Organisation Internationale du Travail et le BIT*, 1930, p. 141.
[6] Léon-Eli Troclet: *Législation sociale internationale*, 1952, pp. 344–345.

considers that he needs further instructions from his government he seeks these by telegram or telephone.

Under the Constitution employers' and workers' delegates are to be nominated by the governments of their countries "in agreement with the industrial organisations, if such organisations exist, which are most representative of employers or workpeople, as the case may be, in their respective countries".

In many countries the task of determining which is the most representative organisation is not an easy one. It is not an easy one because almost every case differs from every other one. Suppose there exists side by side with the central organisation a special industrial organisation not affiliated to the central body and having a larger membership? Or suppose a special organisation appears to be more representative of the particular category of employers or workers affected by the agenda of a particular session of the Conference? Or suppose there is no central organisation, but instead a number of trade unions or employers' associations with no regular relationship between them? Although governments have benefited from the decisions, year by year, of the Credentials Committee, and from an advisory opinion of the Permanent Court of International Justice, fresh puzzles continue to be presented at almost every session of the Conference to the experienced wisdom of the Credentials Committee.

Disputed Credentials

The most frequent objection to the credentials of workers' delegates is that they are not the true representatives of the workers of their particular countries.

On the employers' side, the most important case of disputed credentials – employers' delegates from countries with a socialised economy – has already been mentioned.

It is rare for the credentials of government delegates to be disputed. Nevertheless, over the years some dozen protests have been lodged against government delegates, usually on political or constitutional grounds.

Although each year ten or more credentials are disputed, the Credentials Committee usually finds that the appointment has been made in accordance with the Constitution. Under the Standing Orders, to avoid time-consuming debate in plenary sitting, if the Credentials Committee's report is unanimous, the Conference takes note of it, without discussion.

Freedom of Speech

The discussions in the Conference, whether in group meetings, in committees or in plenary sittings, have always been marked by freedom of speech. This freedom of speech is, indeed, one of the characteristics which has been most highly valued by employers and workers alike. It always appealed particularly to Sir John Forbes Watson, who for many years led the employers' group, but it has no less attraction for the workers' delegates.

In recent years, while all three groups are anxious to maintain the tradition of freedom of speech, there have sometimes been cases in which individual speakers have overstepped the limits of normal parliamentary language. It has therefore become customary for the President at some appropriate stage in the proceedings to draw the attention of delegates to the need for observing a reasonable degree of moderation in their inter-ventions in debate. At the 1969 session, for example, the President said, "Freedom of speech is the life-blood of the International Labour Organisa-tion. There is no immunity in the ILO from criticism for anyone – a government, an employer or a worker – but if we are to practise freedom of speech with mutual respect we must all accept a common discipline to ensure the proper progress of our work".[7]

The limits of debate in Conference have been set out in principles unanimously approved by the tripartite Working Party on the Programme and Structure of the ILO in its fourth report, para. 58, which runs as follows: "In periods of acute political tension the ILO has a two-fold responsibility – to uphold the values of human freedom and dignity enshrined in its Constitution, and to circumscribe rather than extend the area of inter-national tension by ensuring the fullest possible degree of continued co-operation in pursuit of the objectives of the ILO."

It was found desirable to draw up that statement in order to prevent the work of the Conference and particularly the discussion of the Director-General's report becoming an arena for charges and counter-charges of a political nature. The ILO lives and works in a political world, but there has always been general agreement that the place for political discussion is elsewhere, and that the ILO should confine itself to its own field.

Systems of Voting

The general principle is one man, one vote. At plenary sittings of the Conference that means that governments have twice as many votes as either employers or workers, as each delegation is composed, in accordance with the Constitution, of two government delegates, one employers' delegate and one workers' delegate. If a government sends only one government delegate, he has only one vote; if a government sends an

[7] *Prov. Rec.*, Int. Lab. Conf., 53rd session, Geneva, 1969, p. 13.

employers' delegate and no workers' delegate, or a workers' delegate and no employers' delegate, that delegate has no vote. A member in arrears with its contribution may lose the right to vote.

On most matters a simple majority of votes is sufficient, but on others a two-thirds majority is required, e.g. record votes on the adoption of the budget, of a Convention or Recommendation, or an amendment to the Constitution.

In the committees of the Conference, except in the Selection Committee where the 2+1+1 system is observed, the three groups have equality of voting strength. As, however, the number of members of each group on a committee is rarely the same, being determined at each session in accordance with the requests of the groups for membership of particular committees, a system of weighting is employed in order to maintain equality of voting strength. At the 1969 session, for example, the Committee on Holidays with Pay comprised 48 government members, 27 employers' members, and 35 workers' members. The Finance Committee of Government Representatives, the only non-tripartite committee, consists of one government representative of each member State represented at the Conference.

Continuity of the Conference

The International Labour Conference is essentially a living organism, continuing from year to year. True, when a session of the Conference has disposed of its agenda, it adjourns *sine die*; it is only that session which is closed, not the Conference as such. The Conference is a permanent body, meeting in separate sessions, but continuing its essential activities from session to session.

Each session has certain continuing duties – the discussion of the Report of the Director-General, the review of the annual reports on the application of Conventions and Recommendations, together with financial and administrative functions. In addition, certain duties are performed at specified intervals, such as the election of the Governing Body. Finally, the Conference at each session considers the specific technical questions on its agenda, with a view to the adoption of Conventions or Recommendations.

Although the advisers change from session to session in accordance with the particular questions on the agenda, at every session of the Conference a large proportion of the delegates have been present at one or more previous sessions. In this way continuity in the general policy of the Conference has been facilitated; this has proved of inestimable value to the Organisation as a whole.

Procedure of the Conference

As in the case of all representative assemblies, the procedure of the Conference has gradually crystallised as a result of experience. In its formative period the Conference owed much to the practical wisdom of the President of its third and fourth sessions, Lord Burnham. Detailed rules of procedure have been formulated in the Standing Orders which the Conference itself has always been free to adopt and amend as necessary. The combination of orderliness and flexibility which characterises the procedure of the Conference has been of great value in the furtherance of its work. "All progress is secreted in the interstices of procedure," wrote Sir Henry Maine, and this has been amply exemplified in the case of the International Labour Conference.

It was in the International Labour Conference that simultaneous telephonic interpretation was first used. This was in 1926. Prior to its introduction, all speeches made at international meetings were translated, after the speaker's words, into one or more languages successively. This not only wasted a great deal of time but also interrupted the continuity of debate. Edward Filene of Boston first suggested to the ILO that arrangements might be made to provide simultaneous telephonic interpretation and, to back up his suggestion, he put a sum of money at the disposal of the Office to devise the necessary equipment. A temporary official of the Office, Gordon Finlay, invented apparatus which, after some experiments, was manufactured by the International Business Machines Corporation.

With such equipment, which has since been produced also by other companies, each delegate in a meeting, provided with a telephonic receiver, can dial to receive interpretation into the language he selects out of two, three or more languages into which interpretation is provided simultaneously with the delivery of the original speech. This system of simultaneous telephonic interpretation has gradually come into general use both in international meetings of all kinds and in national parliaments in countries in which more than one national language is recognised.

An illustration of the day-to-day procedure of the Conference may be drawn from the 50th anniversary session, 1969. Although that session had special features, it followed otherwise the standard pattern. The number of delegates and advisers amounted to over 1,200; in addition there were officially designated observers from countries not members of the ILO, representatives of the United Nations, specialised agencies and other official international organisations, of non-governmental international organisations with which consultative relationships have been established, and of non-governmental international organisations invited by the Governing Body to be represented at the Conference.

On 4 June, at 10.15 a.m., the chairman of the Governing Body (George Weaver, Special Assistant for International Affairs to the United States Secretary of Labor) declared the session open. After a rapid review of events since the previous session and a survey of the items on the agenda, he called for nominations for the office of President of the Conference. Yoshihiro Nakayama, Ambassador and Permanent Delegate of Japan in Geneva, proposed, on behalf of all the government representatives of Asia, the election of Jean Möri, workers' delegate of Switzerland. That proposal was supported by Rudolph Faupl, workers' delegate, United States; Pierre Waline, employers' delegate, France; Pyotr Pimenov, workers' delegate, USSR; Naval Tata, employers' delegate, India; and others. In the absence of other nominations, Jean Möri was declared unanimously elected President.

The election of a workers' delegate to the chair was an innovation; at each of the preceding sessions of the Conference, the President was a government delegate. In the months before the Conference a feeling had been growing that a departure from that tradition on the 50th anniversary of the ILO would be an appropriate gesture to show the attachment of all three groups to the tripartite principle on which the ILO is based; there was agreement on Jean Möri, who for many years had been the influential and respected chairman of the workers' group of the Governing Body.

After the President's address, the Conference adjourned, and the three groups met separately to make their proposals for vice-presidents of the Conference and for membership of the Selection Committee (the steering or business committee).

At 3 p.m. the Conference resumed, approved the proposals, and appointed as vice-presidents, A. Tzankov, government delegate, Bulgaria; Edwin P. Neilan, employers' delegate, United States; and Albert Monk, workers' delegate, Australia. The Conference also took note of the appointments made by each of the groups of their chairmen, vice-chairmen and secretaries.

Immediately on the adjournment of the Conference, the Selection Committee, composed of twenty-four government members, twelve employers' members and twelve workers' members, met and elected its chairman, Calderon Puiz, government member, Mexico, and its vice-chairmen, Gullmar Bergenström, employers' member, Sweden, and Abid Ali, workers' member, India. The committee then agreed on a number of items relating to the setting up of Conference committees and the order of business of the Conference, embodied in its first and second reports to the Conference.

At 4 p.m. the Conference met again and approved the reports. In accordance with the proposals contained in these reports, the Conference decided to set up the following committees: Finance Committee of Government Representatives, Committee on the Application of Conventions and Recommendations, Committees on the Technical Items on the agenda, viz. Labour Inspection (Agriculture), Social Security, Holidays with Pay, Minimum Wage, Youth Schemes, Programme and Structure of the ILO.

The Conference approved the membership of each of these committees, and also lists of international organisations invited to be represented at each of the technical committees. Finally, the Conference approved the composition of the Credentials Committee which consists of only three members, one from each group, and also the Drafting Committee comprising the President and Secretary-General of the Conference (David A. Morse, the Director-General), together with C. Wilfred Jenks, Principal Deputy Director-General of the Conference, Francis Wolf, Legal Adviser of the Conference, and Nicholas Valticos, Chief of the International Labour Standards Department of the ILO.

Thus, by the evening of the first day, all committees had been set up, and could settle down to work in accordance with the detailed timetable arranged daily by the Selection Committee. In addition, the general programme and order of business for the Conference as a whole had been approved and made known to all participants in the Conference.

In general, plenary sittings of the Conference are held at the same time as committees are meeting in committee rooms. On the second day, the Conference was therefore able to begin the discussion of the Director-General's Report, copies of which had been distributed some months previously. At the outset of the discussion the President drew attention to principles relating to the orderly procedure and conduct of debate, and then called on the first speaker, John Agudela-Rios, Minister of Labour and Social Security, Colombia. Other speakers included Ministers of Labour of Morocco, Peru, Uganda, and also employers' and workers' delegates from other countries. As usual, the discussion of the Director-General's report covered a very wide area, as delegates commented on, with praise or criticism, the activities and programmes of the ILO, particularly the World Employment Programme on which the Director-General had asked specially for their views. Delegates also referred, from the government, employers' or workers' standpoints, to problems and solutions in their own countries. The debate did not conclude until 21 June, and the Director-General replied on 24 June.

At a special sitting on 10 June the Conference was addressed by Pope Paul VI, who had come to Geneva expressly for that purpose. At other special sittings addresses were delivered by Haile Selassie, Emperor of Ethiopia, Kenneth Kaunda, President of Zambia, and El Hadj Ahmadou Ahidjo, President of the Federal Republic of Cameroon.

The outstanding feature of the 1969 Conference, which differentiated it from all previous sessions, was the solemn sitting on 18 June to celebrate the 50th anniversary of the ILO. A brief note on that historic occasion is contained on page 42.

In the course of its regular sittings the Conference discussed, prior to the detailed examination undertaken by the Finance Committee of Government Representatives, the Programme and Budget Proposals for 1970–71; set up the Resolutions Committee, took note of several unanimous reports of the Credentials Committee, did not approve a proposal to grant the right of vote to Bolivia in arrears with payment of its contribution (see Chapter 9 on Finance); took note of the results of the voting in the electoral colleges for the election of members and deputy members of the Governing Body for the period 1969–72 (see Chapter 4 on the Governing Body); took note of ratifications of Conventions by several States, and adopted on a record vote the budget and the allocation of expenses among States members for 1970–71.

During all this time the various technical committees set up on the first day had been steadily advancing with their work, and their reports containing summaries of their proceedings, resolutions and conclusions began to appear in the daily printed *Provisional Record*, ready for consideration by the Conference in plenary session.

On 23, 24 and 25 June the Conference adopted conclusions and Resolutions relating to the placing of items on the agenda of the 1970 session, with a view to the adoption of (a) a Convention, revising the Holidays with Pay Convention, 1936, (b) a Convention concerning Minimum Wage Fixing Machinery and Related Problems with Particular Reference to Developing Countries, and (c) a Recommendation concerning Special Youth Employment and Training Schemes for Development Purposes.

The Conference also adopted the reports of the Committees on the Application of Conventions and Recommendations and on the Programme and Structure of the ILO, and took note of the election of members for 1969–72 of the three regional advisory committees – Asian, African and Inter-American.

Finally, the Conference adopted on record votes two Conventions concerning Labour Inspection in Agriculture, and Medical Care and Sickness Benefits, and two Recommendations on the same subjects. The voting was:

Labour Inspection in Agriculture (Convention) – for, 312; against, 0; abstentions, 30.

Labour Inspection in Agriculture (Recommendation) – for, 321; against, 0; abstentions, 19.

Medical Care and Sickness Benefits (Convention) – for, 260; against, 5; abstentions, 67.

Medical Care and Sickness Benefits (Recommendation) – for, 231; against, 47; abstentions, 48.

Further reference to these Conventions and Recommendations and also to the items for the agenda in 1970 is contained in later chapters relating to the questions concerned.

After short speeches from the three Vice-Presidents, the Secretary-General, and the President, the Conference adjourned *sine die*.

Special Features of Various Sessions

Each session of the Conference has had some special quality or has met in some special circumstance which has differentiated it from other sessions. To chronicle separately each of the sessions would result in a catalogue as uninspiring as Homer's Catalogue of the Ships. Nevertheless, it may be of some value to distil in a few words the essence of some sessions which either singly or in groups were outstanding in the history of the Organisation.

At its first session in Washington, the Conference produced twelve detailed constructive international agreements which were adopted not only as the basis, but as the text, of future international action. It thus laid the foundation of a system of international labour legislation immeasurably in advance of anything that had previously been considered possible.

The decisions of the second session, held in Genoa, although they constituted the foundation of the International Seafarers' Code, do not entitle it to a high place in the apostolic succession of the Conference. Carved on the lid of an old chest in the Palazzo San Giorgio, in which the Conference met, was the following motto: *Ubi ordo deficit nulla virtus sufficit*. There was the secret of the comparative failure of the Conference. It possessed "every virtue, every grace" – except method.

In 1921 when the third session met in Geneva, the spirit of optimism which pervaded the minds of men immediately after the first world war had given place to doubt, and in some cases to worse than doubt. Had peace made the world safe for democracy? Were employers and workers finding in co-operation the solution of their conflicts? The delegate who asked himself these questions looked out upon a world suffering from an unemployment crisis of unexampled intensity.

The sessions held between 1922 and 1929 were marked by certain similarities. These years constituted a gradual return to one of the rare periods of relative economic and political stability in the recent history of the world. The violent alternation of boom and slump had given place in most countries to ample employment, expanding production and stable prices. In the political sphere it was confidently hoped that the 1914–18 "war to end war" would prove to have accomplished its aim. The work of the Conference followed a rhythm that became almost standardised.

While the delegates included each year some new names, familiar faces were seen in increasing numbers. The leading personalities, who came year after year, had acquired a certain prestige and authority; among the government delegates, rotund and choleric De Michelis of Italy, academic Mahaim of Belgium, judicial Paal Berg of Norway, Sir Atul Chatterjee of India, Monsignor Nolens of the Netherlands; among the employers Lambert Ribot, immensely powerful French metallurgist, inventive Olivetti of Italy, fiery but kindly Clydeside shipbuilder Sir James Lithgow; among the workers Jouhaux of France. The Secretary-General of the Conference, Albert Thomas, alternately beaming and flashing through his spectacles, and the Deputy Secretary-General, Harold Butler, imperturbable, were always in their accustomed places. Urbane Arthur Fontaine, too, was always there, the Chairman of the Governing Body.

It was in this period that the phrase "the atmosphere of Geneva" was coined, applying equally to ILO Conferences and meetings of the League of Nations. This "atmosphere of Geneva" has been well described by F. P. Walters in his *History of the League of Nations*. "From the early days there had been observed an unexpected, yet constantly recurring pheno- menon – the successful issue of conferences . . . which had been preceded by many signs of discord and seemed destined to lead to complete deadlock. . . . Such experiences were often ascribed to a sentimental or even a mystical state of mind induced by what was known as 'the atmosphere of Geneva'. There was, in truth, an atmosphere of Geneva, but it was in no way mystical, nor was it, in the usual sense of the word, sentimental."[8]

The sessions held in the 1930's were marked by a gradually growing sense of frustration and a gradually increasing dread of impending catastrophe. Economically as well as politically the early years of the decade presented a conjuncture of deepening crisis.

In 1933–34 the morale of the Conference sank to its lowest point. The intensity of the economic crisis, the menacing political situation, combined with the loss of the dynamic and inspiring personality of Albert Thomas, seemed to some to jeopardise the very existence of the Organisation.

At this dark hour aid came from the West. In 1935 a strong American delegation brought as its special contribution the results of recent develop- ments in that country in industrial relations and did much to enlarge the outlook of the Conference. The whole delegation voted for the contro-

[8] F. P. Walters: *A History of the League of Nations*, p. 296.

versial Forty Hour Week Convention, including the employers' delegate in spite of the opposition of the great majority of the employers' group. In addition, the government delegate made a constructive suggestion for the future programme of the ILO, urging an enquiry into the world position of the textile industry. As a result, in 1937 the ILO organised in Washington the World Textile Conference, which discussed not only labour conditions in the textile industry but also its economic aspects. That conference therefore contributed to the widespread recognition of the need for the ILO to consider economic aspects as well as social aspects of labour and industrial problems – a policy which Harold Butler had strongly advocated.

In the closing years of the decade any hope that the world would be spared the devastation of another war gradually faded. Doubts and uncertainties about the future gradually gave way to an uneasy conviction that the impending catastrophe could not much longer be delayed. When the twenty-fifth session of the Conference met in June 1939, no delegate knew that within three months the world would be at war, but almost every delegate felt that there would be no 1940 session.

Although the war caused the postponement of the 1940 session the Governing Body convened a special Conference of the Organisation for October 1941 in New York. That Conference provided a unique opportunity for the expression of the social aspirations of the free world. Its importance was underlined by statesmen who bore the ultimate responsibility for high policy in their respective countries – by President Roosevelt, who addressed the closing sittings at the White House, by Winston Churchill, who delegated Clement Attlee to represent the British Government, by Field Marshal Smuts of South Africa, by Prime Minister Mackenzie King of Canada, by Foreign Ministers Paul-Henri Spaak of Belgium and Jan Masaryk of Czechoslovakia. At that critical moment in the history of the world, the Conference was the only medium through which the free peoples could give collective expression of their views. They did so, in the words of Edward Phelan, who was Secretary-General of the Conference, "with a volume, with an authority, and with a determination which I believe mark a significant change in the moral aspect of the conflict with which the world is faced at this moment".[9]

The 1944 Session marked the beginning of a new era in the history of the Organisation. Meeting at Philadelphia, delegations representing forty-one States came together for the first time during the war in a regular session of the Conference. An atmosphere of tension pervaded the Conference; after four and a half years of war the freedom-loving peoples of the world were stirring with the confidence of approaching victory and liberation. Against this background the Conference courageously seized

[9] *Rec. Proc.*, Conference of the International Labour Organisation, 1941, p. 155.

the vast possibilities of social advance which it was confident would open up after victory had been won. Its objective and its programme were based on the conception of an expanding and balanced economy directed towards raising the standards of life and work of the peoples of all lands. "The Declaration of Philadelphia" has as its chief characteristic the re-statement of the principle that the promotion of material and spiritual well-being "in conditions of freedom and dignity, of economic security and equal opportunity" must constitute the central aim of national and international policy.[10]

The five sessions held from 1945 to 1948 each met in a different city, three on one side of the Atlantic (Seattle, Montreal and San Francisco) and two on the other (Paris and Geneva).

It was a particular pleasure to the delegates that the first session after the cessation of hostilities was held in Paris (1945) in which the Organisation had been born in 1919. The delegates were welcomed with special warmth by General de Gaulle.

The session in San Francisco (1948) owed much to the dynamic influence of J. D. Zellerbach, then employers' Vice-Chairman of the Governing Body, and the delegates were entertained by President Truman.

The period was one of economic and political reconstruction. Although many countries suffered from financial difficulties and some from internal political unsettlement, the general picture was one of full employment, rising standards of living, and political stabilisation. Such conditions provided a climate in which the Organisation could effectively get on with its work.

During these years the Conference, by amending the Constitution, re-modelled the Organisation; by approving a formal Agreement with the United Nations, established an organic relationship with the new international system; and by adopting successive budgets provided the necessary means for re-equipping the Organisation. Thus the Organisation laid

[10] The origins of the Declaration of Philadelphia are to be found in two earlier instruments. One was the Atlantic Charter of 1940, the other the Declaration of Havana of 1939. Of the eight common principles announced in the Atlantic Charter and afterwards subscribed to by all the United Nations, three defined a common approach to international social and economic problems. These principles had all been endorsed by the ILO Conference held in New York and Washington in 1941, which pledged the full co-operation of the Organisation in their implementation. The Declaration of Havana, adopted by the Second Session of the American Regional Conference which met soon after the outbreak of the war, in Havana (November 1939) proclaimed unshaken faith in the promotion of international co-operation and unwavering support for the International Labour Organisation. When the Philadelphia Conference was being planned, the idea that a solemn declaration should be adopted by that Conference had its germ partly in the substance of the Atlantic Charter and partly in the form of the Declaration of Havana.

the foundation for implementing the new social charter embodied in the Declaration of Philadelphia.

After the *Wanderjahre* of the war-time and immediate post-war period the Conference once again settled down to meet regularly in Geneva, and all the sessions from 1949 onwards have been held there. But this geographical tranquillity did not reflect a world at peace.

In the earlier years of the period the political differences which had already begun to cast a shadow on the work of the Organisation grew rapidly more acute. When war broke out in Korea, it had political and economic repercussions in practically all the States of the Organisation, and the work of the ILO was necessarily profoundly affected by it.

In 1953, when the Conference assembled in Geneva, there were mounting hopes that the negotiations for an armistice in Korea would lead in the early future to the end of the war. It was therefore in a spirit of optimism that the delegates set themselves to secure that that session would mark a further advance towards the goal of peace and social justice. Senator Irving Ives of the United States, in a presidential address of vigorous optimism, insisted that the Conference "stood at the gateway of opportunity". Speaking with an urgency which reflected that of the Director-General's report, the Australian Minister of Labour and National Service called upon the delegates to give "some organised attention" to the problem of making "a really buoyant and prosperous economy a natural outcome of a more peaceful era". Sir Walter (later Viscount) Monckton, Minister of Labour of the United Kingdom, urged that the Organisation must be quick to identify new problems as they arose and must be looking within the framework of the Constitution for techniques supplementary to its legislative procedures.

In 1954 and the following sessions the Conference faced problems arising from the re-admission of the USSR, the admission of the Byelorussian and the Ukrainian Soviet Socialist Republics, and the resumption of active participation in the Organisation of several Eastern European members. Most of the employers' and workers' delegates and some of the government delegates expressed doubts as to the sincerity of the desire of the USSR and the other Eastern European countries to co-operate with the ILO, and suggested that their aim was to disrupt it or use it for their own propaganda ends. Other government delegates urged that differences of political ideology or economic structure should not be a barrier to effective co-operation in the work of the ILO which was in a technical field. The delegates of the USSR and the Eastern European countries emphasised that they sincerely desired to co-operate with all other countries in reducing international tension which stood in the way of social progress.

In the following years the question of relations between the free enterprise countries and those of socialised economy continued to be debated in one form or other. The tension mounted again in 1959 in connection with the decision taken by a majority of the Conference to set up an Appeals Board. Thereafter a better atmosphere was gradually created, the practical results of which were shown in the procedural developments already described. Further, the diminishing intensity of the "cold war" in world relations undoubtedly contributed to relaxing tension in the councils of the ILO. Thus, as the years passed, West and East, working together on ILO programmes for balanced social and economic development, succeeded in substituting for hostile co-existence a measure of active co-operation.

Concurrently, during the 'fifties and 'sixties, the Director-General decided to include in his annual Report to the Conference, in addition to the traditional review of developments and trends in world social and economic policy, together with a survey of the activities of the ILO during the previous year, a discussion of some particular problem to which the attention of the Conference was specially invited. These subjects included automation (1957); the ILO in a changing world (1958); unemployment and underemployment, social problems of economic development; institutions and social policy (1959); youth and work (1960); labour relations (1961); older people, work and retirement (1962); and programme and structure of the ILO (1963, 1964 and 1965). In 1966 the Report dealt with industrialisation, in 1967 with non-manual workers, in 1968 with human rights, and in 1969 with the World Employment Programme. As a result, the discussion in the Conference each year of the Director-General's Report became more purposeful, as delegates tended more and more to direct their speeches upon that central question.

At the 53rd session (1969) the ILO celebrated its 50th anniversary. As has been mentioned earlier in this chapter, the opportunity was taken by several heads of State and Prime Ministers to attend the Conference and express on behalf of their countries their continuing support for the Organisation.

At a special Celebration sitting the Secretary-General of the United Nations, the President of the International Court of Justice, and the Presidents of international employers' and trade union organisations paid tributes to the ILO and emphasised their confidence in its future. Speaking of what the ILO had done over the past fifty years to give substance to the ideal of an international community, the Director-General of the ILO enumerated five ways in which the ILO had been able to give expression to the concern of all nations for the improvement of the general welfare of the working men and women of the world. First, the ILO had given the international community a sense of social purpose, a commitment to translate that purpose into affirmative action, and a legal and institutional framework through which effective and practical programmes could be implemented.

Secondly, the ILO had put forward a plan of action for the realisation of these broad and ambitious programmes. Thirdly, the ILO had given expression to the fundamental principle that the whole of mankind has a collective responsibility for eliminating poverty and injustice wherever it exists. Fourthly, the ILO through its tripartite structure had given the working man a voice in shaping the national and international policies which affected him. Finally, the ILO had made a substantial contribution, through its efforts to improve the lot of the working man, towards achieving social justice, thereby providing, as U Thant had said, an essential ingredient of universal and lasting peace.

Wit and Humour in the Conference

Before closing this section I cannot refrain from adding a few lines on wit and humour in the Conference. Surprise is often expressed by those who attend international gatherings for the first time that the proceedings are so rarely relieved by a witty remark or a humorous touch. If the International Labour Conference be compared with a national legislative assembly, there is a great difference in the extent to which members permit themselves in their speeches to try to "raise a laugh".

Why is this? The delegates who attend the Conference are not lacking in wit and humour. There have been many outstanding instances to the contrary. The main reason is to be found in the nature of wit and humour. Wit and humour normally depend for their effect either on allusion or on word-play. But much, perhaps most, allusion is national; it is allusion to national literature or music or painting, or to national proverbial wisdom, or to national politics, or to national sport or some other national feature. Sometimes such national allusions will be internationally understood, for example a reference to Ulysses or Falstaff or Figaro or Gargantua, or to the Mona Lisa or the Night Watch or even on a different plane to Grock or Brigitte Bardot. But such cases are rare; most national allusions are not understood beyond the borders of a particular country.

Still less international is the wit and humour that is expressed in a play upon words. Very few puns are translateable. In a national committee a spontaneous remark involving an apposite play upon words will be received with joy; in an international committee three-quarters of the members will look blank and wonder why the others laugh.

Nothing is so disconcerting to the speaker who makes a joke as to find that it has proved a damp squib. The result is that those who on their home ground are noted for their wit and humour refrain completely in the international arena from indulging in any verbal fireworks.

There is also another and more serious reason for their abstinence from international joking. In an international gathering it is painfully easy for jokes to be completely misunderstood, and for what the speaker intends as a harmless piece of comic relief to be resented by a delegate as a personal attack. Time and again this has occurred, particularly when the person who imagines himself insulted has had to depend on the interpreter's version of the speaker's witticism.

Although there is, for these reasons, little wit and humour in the proceedings of the Conference, laughter will be heard in the lobbies, round the dinner tables and at the cocktail parties. For example, one President of a Conference was noted for the slowness and uncertainty with which he gave his rulings; a member of the Conference parodied the standard opening phrase of the daily communiqué, "the Conference met under the presidency of Mr X", by murmuring "Today the Conference met under the hesitancy of Mr X". At the 1921 session of the Conference, when cocktails with exotic names were in favour, the barman, capitalising on the items on the agenda, concocted a cocktail "White Lead and Anthrax". At another session, Humbert Wolfe (now best remembered as a poet), who represented the British Government, was advocating a certain measure which had encountered opposition from Monsignor Nolens, a Church dignitary who for many years represented the Netherlands Government. In his final speech urging adoption of the measure, Humbert Wolfe began, "Nolens volens, we will get this measure through." At the Genoa session, when an Italian workers' delegate who at the particular sitting had, in accordance with the Standing Orders, authorised one of his advisers to take his place at that sitting and thereby divested himself of his right to speak, changed his mind in the course of an exciting debate and loudly tried to intervene, Albert Thomas, seated at the side of a powerless President, boomed, "You may shout as loud as you like, *but you are not here!*" An anecdotic history of the ILO could record many such humorous comments or witty rejoinders.

Is the Conference worth while?

This chapter should close on a more serious note. The question may well be asked: "What is the end-product of this heavy machine that swings into action once a year in the month of June in Geneva?" The cynical observer might point out that for delegates from any part of the world June in Geneva is very pleasant, and that some of them at least appear to take very lightly their official duties.[11] "No wonder," he would say, "that they are all

---

[11] Once when George Bernard Shaw was in Geneva, he was taken to see a committee at work. As he left the room he remarked: "Deplorable; the only time any delegate showed the slightest interest was when a pretty typist came into the room."

in favour of continuing to have the annual Conference at Geneva." Whatever grain of truth there may be in that sneer, the truth is, of course, that it is not the delegates who decide whether the trip to Geneva is necessary; it is the governments, the employers' organisations and trade unions who have to detach from their regular work at home some of their best men for several weeks; it is the governments who pay. Governments, employers' organisations and trade unions base their decisions to send delegates on their realistic assessments of the value to them of what is done at Geneva.

A more pertinent criticism of the Conference is that it is used as a platform for political argument and propaganda. Undoubtedly the Conference has been used as a propaganda sounding-board by governments anxious to proclaim to the world the excellence of their labour legislation or their system of socialised economy. In doing so, they have sometimes attacked other governments and even their leaders and thus provoked the danger of political debate. There has also sometimes been "infighting", when workers' delegates of a certain country attack the policies of the employers or governments of their own country. However, the action taken recently to draw the attention of delegates to the inadmissibility of such practices has had a large measure of success.

In the last few years the ILO has been undertaking self-examination. Like any business firm it is anxious to improve its organisation and to step up its performance. It has been asking itself many questions. Is the Conference not too heavy and cumbrous a machine? Is the expense of sending delegates every year not too great, particularly for small States? Are Conventions and Recommendations still useful; is there any need under present conditions for new ones? Does the discussion on the Report of the Director-General serve any useful purpose? Since 1963, the Conference, the Governing Body and the Office have been seeking answers to such questions. As a result, steps have been taken to streamline the procedure of the Conference and facilitate the effectiveness of its debate. No doubt the discussion on the Director-General's report takes up too much time, but it has to be remembered that the Conference has a parliamentary character, and as Churchill once said, "talking is better than shooting". There has been general agreement in all three groups that an annual session of approximately three weeks continues to be necessary.

An important by-product of the Conference is the opportunity it affords for conversations, discussions and negotiations between delegates on matters of mutual concern outside the agenda. Ministers of Labour often take advantage of their presence at the Conference to have talks with Ministers of Labour of other countries in the informal atmosphere and neutral ground of the Conference. Experts attending as advisers in all three groups at sessions dealing with technical subjects such as social insurance and occupational health and safety consult experts from other countries on points unconnected with the Conference agenda. Such bilateral talks are not confined to intergovernmental exchanges. Employers' and workers' delegates also find it useful to discuss points of common interest with their opposite numbers in other countries. Finally, it is not unknown for employers and workers from the same country to find the climate of Geneva conducive to more friendly contacts than their relationships at home permit.

4. THE GOVERNING BODY

WITHIN the family of international organisations there is no organ constitutionally comparable to the Governing Body. Meeting three or four times a year, it has a general responsibility for co-ordinating the activities of the ILO into an over-all programme which can be fulfilled within the limits of the financial resources available and modified rapidly when necessary to take account of changing needs or priorities.

Composition of the Governing Body

The Constitution has thrice been amended in order to make the Governing Body more fully representative. These amendments have not affected the proportions in which governments, employers and workers are represented. The 2+1+1 system in the Conference has also always been applied in the Governing Body.

At first the Governing Body consisted of 24 members, no fewer than 20 of whom came from European countries. The membership is now 48, of whom 24 represent governments, 12 employers and 12 workers. It is interesting to note, as an illustration of the shift in the geographical balance of power in the ILO, that in each of the three groups European members are now in a minority.

The government members of the Governing Body are governments and not persons; it follows that the person representing a government may change from session to session. In practice, however, most governments appreciate the importance of maintaining continuity by refraining from changing too frequently the persons who represent them. On the other hand the employers' and workers' members of the Governing Body are elected by the electoral colleges of the Conference as persons, and all such members retain their mandates for the three years of their appointment, even if owing to changes in the employers' or workers' movements in their countries they cease to hold any representative position in those countries. The Conference often re-elects the same persons again and again.

The government group comprises ten governments representing the States of chief industrial importance, plus fourteen governments elected by an electoral college of the Conference including all governments except those of chief industrial importance. The 24 governments having seats on the Governing Body now include four West Europeans, three East

47

Europeans, two North Americans, four Latin Americans, five Asians, four Africans and two from the Middle East. The workers' group comprises four West Europeans, one East European, one North American, two Latin Americans, one Asian, three Africans and none from the Middle East; and the employers' group four West Europeans, no East European, one North American, two Latin Americans, two Asians, two Africans, and one from the Middle East.

The government and workers' panels therefore form a reasonably balanced representation of the main regions of the world, and any apparent anomalies are to some extent corrected by the regional distribution of the panels of the deputy members. The employers' group, however, cannot claim to represent equitably world management, as it includes no employers' delegate from Eastern European countries.

In addition to the titular members, each group is entitled to a further twelve deputy members, also elected by the electoral colleges. These deputy members have the right to attend and, with the permission of the chairman, to speak, but not to vote.

A relatively new feature of Governing Body meetings is the attendance of representatives from organisations with which the ILO maintains relations (*see* Chapter 8).

States of Chief Industrial Importance

From the point of view of constitutional history, the provision that certain States, those of "chief industrial importance", should have the right to nominate government representatives on the Governing Body is of deep significance. In the International Labour Conference all member States, from the largest or most important to the smallest or least important, have exactly the same rights; the principle of equality is completely respected. But it was recognised, when the Constitution was being drafted, that it would be unrealistic not to ensure that the government membership of the Governing Body should include some of the more important industrial States. In the ILO therefore, as in the League of Nations and subsequently in the United Nations, an exception was made to the principle of equality. Just as in the Council of the League and in the Security Council of the United Nations certain States of outstanding political importance were assured of permanent seats, so in the ILO States of "chief industrial importance" were from the first entitled to representation on the Governing Body.

Inevitably, the determination of the list of members of chief industrial importance has often given rise to great difficulty. A certain prestige attaches to a State declared to be of "chief industrial importance", and

States have therefore always been eager to qualify for admission to the charmed circle and even more reluctant to be removed from it.

The first list of States of chief industrial importance (eight in number in accordance with the original Constitution) consisted of, in alphabetical order, Belgium, British Empire, France, Germany, Italy, Japan, Switzerland and the United States (Denmark to occupy the place assigned to the United States until that country became a member). In 1935 a revised list comprised France, Germany (replaced by Canada when Germany's notice of withdrawal became effective in 1935), India, Italy, Japan, United Kingdom, USSR and United States. In subsequent years some amendments of this list occurred owing to withdrawals of members. In 1954 a new list was drawn up, with the assistance of a Committee of Statistical Experts, to take account both of an amendment of the Constitution increasing the number of States of chief industrial importance from eight to ten, and the readmission of Germany (Federal Republic), Japan and USSR. This list comprised Canada, China, France, Federal Republic of Germany, India, Italy, Japan, USSR, United Kingdom, United States. No change has since been made.

Functions of the Governing Body

In the attempt to synthesise the functions of the Governing Body in a single term, it has been called the Executive Committee of the ILO, or the Board of Directors, or the Control Tower, or the Power House. None of these names is really satisfactory, as a brief enumeration of its duties will show.

The Governing Body draws up the agenda of each session of the Conference and decides what specific action should be taken on the resolutions passed. It follows up the application by member States of the Conventions and Recommendations adopted by the Conference.

It appoints the Director-General. It scrutinises the programme and budget submitted by him and the financial estimates and accounts presented to the Conference for adoption.

It settles the date, duration and agenda of all regional and technical conferences and committees, receives their reports, and decides on the action to be taken.

An example will illustrate how the Governing Body carries out its duty of determining the agenda of the Conference. Looking forward at its March 1969 session to the agenda "technical questions", i.e. items for possible Conventions or Recommendations, for the 1971 session of the Conference, the Governing Body requested the Director-General to submit to its November 1969 session reports on national law and practice in various countries together with further proposals on the following subjects: The World Employment Programme (general discussion); child labour; paid educational leave; dock labour; inland navigation (minimum age for admission to employment, medical examination, vocational training and certificates of competence). On the suggestion of the Governing Body, the 1969 session of the Conference undertook some general discussion on the appropriateness of these questions for the 1971 agenda, and that discussion was taken into consideration by the Governing Body in November 1969 when it finally determined the agenda for the 1971 session of the Conference.

Committees of the Governing Body

With the increase in the work of the Governing Body, it soon became impossible for all questions on its agenda to be debated in full session. A certain number of these questions were therefore referred for consideration, in the first place, by committees set up by the Governing Body.

In spite of the drawbacks of the committee system, without it the Governing Body could not dispose of its large volume of business with any reasonable degree of method and celerity. If the committee system could possibly have been dispensed with when the Governing Body consisted of 24 members, it has become indispensable in a Governing Body composed of 48 members, the very great majority of whom take a keen and active interest in the proceedings.

The committee system would become intolerable if the Governing Body were to show a disposition to re-open in plenary sitting the questions which had been discussed in committee. Fortunately, although each member of the Governing Body, whether or not he has been a member of a particular committee, has a perfect right to initiate in a plenary sitting a discussion on any question reported on by a committee, the general consensus in the Governing Body is that when, as is usually the case, a committee makes a unanimous recommendation to the Governing Body, the Governing Body should be satisfied to accept that recommendation without discussion. On the other hand when, as sometimes happens, a committee fails to reach agreement, and its recommendation is made by a majority vote, it is normal that discussion on the merits of the question should be re-opened in the Governing Body itself.

The Governing Body committees include the following: Financial and Administrative; Allocations; Standing Orders and Application of Conventions and Recommendations; Industrial Committees; International Organisations; Operational Programmes; Freedom of Association; Discrimination. There are also three Regional Advisory Committees – Asian, African and Inter-American.

Continuity of the Governing Body

In spite of the changes in the Governing Body the dominant impression that remains when its work is passed in review is one of continuity – continuity in membership and continuity in policy and outlook.

Throughout the years there has in fact, in spite of political and industrial vicissitudes, been a surprising degree of stability in the membership of the Governing Body. This has ensured constructive continuity of policy and the establishment of certain valuable traditions. International life, like parliamentary life, requires for its full fruition a period of apprenticeship. In the early years it was once said that the Governing Body was not a body and it did not govern. Time was needed for a corporate sense of power and authority to develop.

Whether the continuity of the Governing Body has been in any respect affected by the frequency with which it has met in the same place is a question on which students of history might well differ. But the psychologist might argue that when any deliberative body meets regularly in the same hall in the same city, sitting in the same seats, looking at the same pictures on the same walls, with the same trees shading the same windows, these material surroundings may exercise some undefined influence in the direction of continuity of outlook and policy.

The great majority of the sessions have been held in Geneva in the dignified Governing Body room decorated with works of art presented by many of the members. Though more than once enlarged, the Governing Body room retains its essential original features, and in it the members always feel at home.

Some interest, other than merely geographical, attaches to the list of cities in which the Governing Body has met: Berlin, Brussels, Geneva, Genoa, Interlaken, London, Madrid, Montreal, Mysore, New York, Paris, Philadelphia, Prague, Quebec, Rome, San Francisco, Stockholm, Warsaw, and Washington. Such meetings away from headquarters have often had considerable political and industrial importance.

Outstanding Personalities of the Governing Body

Throughout the years the Governing Body has been fortunate in having among its members some very remarkable men. From among those whose service to the Governing Body and the Organisation as a whole was particularly noteworthy, seven names may be singled out, three government representatives, two employers' representatives and two workers' representatives.

Arthur Fontaine, outstanding French administrator (and shrewd connoisseur of French impressionist art), was Chairman of the Governing Body for the first twelve years of its existence. Respected for his transparent integrity and unwavering courtesy, his friendly and tactful authority did much to ensure the collaboration of the three groups in the first formative years of the Organisation.

Hans Christian Oersted, distinguished Danish jurist, was the spokesman of the employers for many years. His mind was naturally constructive, and even when he felt obliged on some question of principle to oppose the other two groups (as he could do with both brilliance and forcefulness) he never lost his sense of loyalty to the Organisation.

Corneille Mertens, Belgian trade union leader and Senator, impetuous, choleric, enthusiastic and something of an opportunist, was quick to seize a tactical advantage. But an engaging frankness and a ready sense of humour endeared him even to those whom he might attack most fiercely in his championship of social justice.

Sir John Forbes Watson was noted in the Governing Body for the Scots forthrightness with which he expressed his views as leader of the employers' group. If he was often severely critical of the other groups and also the administration of the Office, that was because he believed fervently in the mission of the ILO. During and after the war he saw in the Organisation one of the great bastions of freedom, and he laboured hard to help to ensure its proper place in the post-war world.

Léon Jouhaux will always have a place in the trade union and political history of France, but perhaps his most enduring monument will be the ILO. In the councils of the ILO he had little use for reports and papers, but a singularly retentive memory and an uncanny knack of isolating essentials, together with a ringing gift of persuasive oratory, made him formidable whether as opponent or as advocate. His two consuming passions were the promotion of world peace (recognised by the award of the Nobel Prize) and the furtherance of the ILO.

Sir Atul Chatterjee, who had been responsible for initiating in India far-reaching reforms in factory and mining legislation, largely influenced by international labour conventions, brought to the chairmanship of the Governing Body a mathematician's sense of clarity and precision. As an "elder statesman" his wise counsel was of the greatest value.

Sir Guildhaume Myrddin-Evans, twice Chairman of the Governing Body and also President of the International Labour Conference, combined with Celtic fire a character of steel and great kindliness of heart. He rendered particularly memorable service to the ILO in the difficult negotiations connected with the separation of the ILO from the League of Nations and its association with the United Nations.

Among others whose work on the Governing Body in more recent years will be specially remembered are – in the government group Roberto Ago (Italy), Luis Alvarado (Peru), Amasasp Arutiunian (USSR), Barboza Carneiro (Brazil), Alexandre Parodi and Paul Ramadier (France), G. C. H. Slater (United Kingdom); in the employers' group Gullmar Bergenström (Sweden), Lord McCorquodale, Sir George Pollock and Sir Richard Snedden (United Kingdom), Yllanes Ramos (Mexico), Naval Tata (India), Pierre Waline (France), J. D. Zellerbach (United States); in the workers' group Paul Finet (Belgium), Lord Collison, Sir Joseph Hallsworth and Sir Alfred Roberts (United Kingdom), Albert Monk (Australia), Jean Möri (Switzerland).

5. THE INTERNATIONAL LABOUR OFFICE

The Director-General of the ILO

Under the Constitution, the Director of the ILO (since 1946 Director-General) is appointed by the Governing Body and, subject to the instructions of the Governing Body, is responsible for the efficient conduct of the International Labour Office and for such other duties as may be assigned to him.

The International Labour Office has had, as Directors or Directors-General, men differing in nationality, in background and in approach, but similar in their devotion to the ideals of the Organisation.

Albert Thomas (1920–32), Harold Butler (1932–38), John G. Winant (1939–41), Edward Phelan (1941–48), David A. Morse (1948–70), C. Wilfred Jenks (1970–) – these six men have been entrusted with the task of directing the International Labour Office. The services rendered by these public servants epitomise the history of the ILO.

Albert Thomas has now become an almost legendary figure. Although very few of those who now attend the International Labour Conference ever met Thomas, his name is held in such respect that any reference to him is sure to evoke a sympathetic response. Employing to the full all his natural endowments, he made a creative contribution to every aspect of the work of the Organisation. It was thanks to his gifts as a negotiator that the Governing Body and the Conference developed an *esprit de corps* that was stronger than any of the disintegrating elements within them. It was thanks to his political and parliamentary experience that the Conference became not only an efficient piece of legislative machinery but a world forum for the frank international discussion of problems of labour and industry. It was thanks to his conception of "the policy of presence" that the members of the Organisation were brought into closer relation with Geneva. It was thanks to his qualities as an administrator, a keen disciplinarian but a kindly chief, that the Office developed into a balanced, harmonious and efficient organism.

When Butler was appointed Director in 1932 after the death of Thomas, it was clear that troubled times were ahead. In the economic sphere the world was under the shadow of the Great Depression. In the political field the clouds were no less lowering. Butler considered it to be elementary prudence to do everything possible to strengthen the Organisation with a view to equipping it to weather the storm if the storm should burst. It was

54

clear to Butler that the greatest single reinforcement that could be looked for was the entrance of the United States into the Organisation, and he worked unremittingly for that. He also did all he could to make more effective the participation of other extra-European countries. He realised, sooner than others, that the centre of gravity of the world was shifting, and that it was necessary, if the effectiveness of the Organisation were to be maintained and developed, that the centre of gravity of the Organisation should also shift. With rare perspicacity he addressed himself to the task of readjusting the Organisation to these changing conditions. In three new directions he initiated or encouraged development. One was the regional consideration of industrial problems at regional conferences, another was the international discussion of the problems of particular industries in technical tripartite meetings (the precursors of the post-war Industrial Committees) and the third was the provision to governments of technical advice and assistance. The enduring importance of these initiatives was to be clearly demonstrated in the post-war history of the Organisation.

John G. Winant, appointed Director in 1939 after Butler's resignation, rendered invaluable service at the most critical moment of its whole existence. In 1940 Winant, with foresight and courage, assumed the responsibility of moving a nucleus staff across the Atlantic, and with the generous co-operation of the Prime Minister of Canada, who was a personal friend, established the working centre at Montreal. Both the Governing Body and the Conference subsequently paid tribute to Winant's services, which had preserved the life, spirit and freedom of action of the Organisation. In 1941 he resigned to accept appointment as United States Ambassador in London.

Edward Phelan worked with Butler in the Organising Committee for the Washington Conference and was his right-hand man in Washington. In 1920 Thomas appointed him Chief of the Diplomatic Division. In 1933 he became an Assistant Director, in 1939 Deputy Director and in 1941, on Winant's resignation, Acting Director. In 1946 he was appointed Director-General, the appointment being made retroactive to 1941. At the 1948 Conference on the eve of Phelan's retirement the Chairman of the Governing Body paid a tribute to his contribution to the Organisation: "It was he who brought the Organisation so triumphantly through the supremely difficult years of the war; it was his foresight and sagacity which enabled the Organisation to survive and to grow in strength when other international organisations disintegrated. It was the proposals which he laid before the 1944 session of the Conference which enabled the Organisation to re-formulate its aims and purposes in the Declaration of Philadelphia in language the historic quality of which was emphasised by President Roosevelt."[1]

[1] *Rec. Proc.*, Int. Lab. Conf., 1948, p. 4.

When David A. Morse was elected Director-General in 1948, he came to his duties with a brilliant record in his own country as a lawyer, a soldier and an administrator. As United States Government member of the Governing Body since 1946 and government delegate of his country at three sessions of the Conference, he had a record of experience in the directing and controlling organs of the Organisation that none of his predecessors had approached.

In his first report to the Conference as Director-General, he indicated clearly his view of the direction in which the Organisation should move. "It is my view", he wrote, "that the new emphasis in ILO policy is essential if the Organisation is to maintain its leadership in the field of international labour and social policy and if it is to render to its member Governments the services which they need and expect in the solution of their problems."[2] Morse drew attention in particular to the demands of the new States for industrialisation, for increasing production, for a quickening in the pace of improving standards of living. There was a world demand for an intensification and expansion of the advisory work of the ILO as the complement of its legislative function.

The frequent references throughout this book to the action initiated by David Morse bear testimony to the pervading influence exercised by him in every field of the activities of the Organisation. While his name will be specially associated with the development of its operational and promotional activities, he always insisted that there is no conflict between the traditional standard-setting and information work and the new technical assistance and educational programme. "They are each part of one whole."

When David Morse resigned in 1970 the Governing Body elected as his successor C. Wilfred Jenks, the Principal Deputy Director-General. In a lifetime of outstanding and devoted service to the ILO, Wilfred Jenks has established a position of personal authority in the broad fields of international law and social policy that has gained world-wide recognition.

Functions of the Office

When Albert Thomas was appointed the first Director of the Office it became clear that he intended to make the fullest use of the constitutional powers of the Office. The Office, it was true, was controlled by the Governing Body, but Thomas insisted that he and his staff were not there merely to record passively the decisions of the Governing Body. He emphasised that the Office as such should always have and express a point of view, an attitude, on every question that arose.

Thus, from the outset papers submitted by the Office to the Governing

[2] *Report of the Director-General*, Int. Lab. Conf., 1949, p. 1.

Body on the items on its agenda were not confined to the provision of information for the Governing Body's decision; they nearly always included the detailed proposals of the Office as to the decision that might be taken. Further, the reports prepared by the Office on the items on the agenda of the Conference were not limited to setting forth the law and practice in the different countries; they contained the detailed proposals of the Office on the terms of the Conventions or Recommendations that might be adopted.

This wide conception of the rights and powers of the Office necessarily brought Thomas into conflict with some members of the Governing Body, who considered that the Office should be merely an organ of preparation, of recording and of execution, that it should not express any opinion of its own on the questions which came before it, and that it should not on its own responsibility undertake any action for which explicit authority had not been given by the Governing Body.

In recent years no difficulty has been experienced in avoiding conflict between the Governing Body and the Office in respect of duties and responsibilities.

The main duties of the Office may be briefly summarised: to organise, compile reports and provide secretarial services for the International Labour Conference, the Governing Body and other conferences, meetings and committees, and to prepare the first drafts of international labour standards and promote their effective application; to assemble and disseminate information, and to undertake research and enquiries and publish the results; to implement operational programmes and carry out technical co-operation projects.

Internal Organisation

As circumstances have required, changes have been made in the internal organisation of the Office when the needs of States members have altered or new problems have had to be tackled. The most recent reorganisation was effected in 1965–66, following upon the discussions in the Governing Body and Conference on the programme and structure of the ILO.

Under the Director-General, the work of the Office is apportioned among ten departments. Each of these, except the Research and Planning Department, which reports direct to the Director-General, reports to a Deputy Director-General or Assistant Director-General. The Legal Adviser of the Office reports direct to the Director-General.

The names of the departments are shown in a list of senior officials, effective 1 June 1970, in the Reference section of this book. Mention of their work will be found in the chapters relating to the problems with which each is concerned.

The Staff of the Office

Among the constitutional provisions relating to the staff, one of the most important is the requirement that, so far as is possible with due regard to the efficiency of the ILO, the Director-General shall, in appointing the staff, select persons of different nationalities.

The question has sometimes been asked whether recruitment of staff on this wide geographical basis involves some sacrifice of quality. To that question the answer cannot be a simple yes or no. On the one hand, everyone who has spent a period of years in a responsible position in an international organisation would agree that, in every nationality alike, outstanding, average and indifferent officials may be found. No nationality has a monopoly of good officials – or of poor ones. On the other hand, many of the newly independent countries experience acute shortages of well-qualified officials for their own administrations and they are not unnaturally often reluctant to release one of their best men for service with an international organisation; in these circumstances it has happened that the international organisation has had to recruit a "second-best". Nevertheless, from such countries some of the best among the present ILO officials have come.

Perhaps a supplementary question may be put: does not the obligation to recruit officials of different nationalities result in some loss of efficiency? In international organisations a considerable proportion of the work of headquarters consists in drafting official correspondence and writing reports or other documents in English or French, or much less frequently in Spanish. If an official whose maternal language is not one of those is employed on such work, what he produces may require extensive revision. On the other hand, many posts exist where professional or technical qualifications are more important than an impeccable knowledge of one of the official languages – accountants, statisticians, doctors, actuaries, librarians, and the wide range of specialist skills possessed by experts participating in technical co-operation projects; in all of these, language deficiencies due to nationality are usually no handicap.

The difficulties that arise in the day-to-day routine of international administration are not due solely to differences of language. They result also from differences in national modes of thought and action, national systems of administration, national customs, traditions and institutions. All these differences render extraordinarily difficult the speedy understanding and adjustment required in every efficient administration. They make it easy for misunderstandings to occur between officials, for personal friction to develop. That these obstacles are so often successfully overcome is a tribute to the emergence of a genuine international civil service.

Taking "efficiency" in a broad sense, the presence of officials of many nationalities is of positive advantage to an international organisation. In the ILO, conferences and other meetings succeed one another throughout the year, and officials of various nationalities, whatever their regular job, are called upon to keep in touch with the delegates from their countries. Such liaison activities, appreciated by the delegates, are necessary for the Office. Further, all international organisations are necessarily sensitive to trends, tendencies, and currents of opinion in all their States members; in addition to all the services rendered in that respect by regional, area and national branch offices, the presence of officials of many nationalities is an indispensable condition of their overall efficiency.

The staff consists of two categories, Professional and General Service, each classified in several grades. Salary scales, determined by the Assembly of the United Nations, are applied with minor adaptations to ILO staff by decision of the Governing Body.

Recruitment to the normal starting grades is effected on the basis of competitive written examination, together with interview of a short-list of the best candidates, or by selection on the basis of qualifications combined with interview. In order to ensure appropriate balance on the one hand of nationalities, and on the other of the special requirements of the various departments, recruitment for particular posts is usually restricted to specified languages, or professional or technical qualifications, e.g. statisticians, lawyers, economists, accountants, stenographers.

In an organisation concerned with the promotion of industrial relations throughout the world, the ILO's staff regulations naturally provide for the participation of staff representatives, appointed by the Staff Union Committee, on the Administrative Committee, a joint body authorised to submit to the Director-General proposals regarding recruitment, promotion and status. The staff regulations specify procedures relating to contentious cases, involving in the last resort appeal to the ILO Arbitration Tribunal, composed of three judges – Letourneur (French Conseil d'Etat), Grisel (Swiss Federal Tribunal), and Rt. Hon. Lord Devlin (United Kingdom).

In numbers the staff has increased with the years to meet the demands resulting from the expansion of the functions and programmes of the ILO. At the end of 1921 the staff consisted of over 250 officials, belonging to 19 nationalities, in 1930 it consisted of 400, belonging to 35 nationalities, in 1948 over 600, in 1969 approximately 1,800, belonging to over 100 nationalities. The figure of 1,800 in service in 1969 does not include over 1,000 experts in the field engaged in ILO technical co-operation projects.

In recent years efficiency has benefited as a result of staff training and increased use of office machines and other modern equipment; the Office includes an Electronic Data Processing Unit.

In view of the criticism sometimes heard that the staff live a sheltered existence, it may be recalled that if to all the members of the staff the war spelt adventure, to some it meant disaster. When hostilities broke out and the *blitzkrieg* swept across Poland and Norway, the majority of the staff had their contracts terminated or suspended under conditions fixed by the Assembly of the League of Nations and approved by the Governing Body. Although these conditions were not financially ungenerous, the officials concerned found their careers broken at a time when it was difficult if not impossible for most of them to start a new career.

In the spring of 1940 – perhaps the loveliest spring that Geneva had ever known – when the Panzer divisions began to break into France, Belgium and Holland, and invasion of Switzerland was awaited from one day to the next, the Director advised the remaining members of the staff to be ready at a moment's notice to take to the mountains with their families, rucksacks on their backs. Happily, Switzerland was spared invasion, and the departure of the officials and their families was effected by more conventional means. As a result of a second series of terminations and suspensions of contract, most of the remaining officials were scattered. Many of them, together with their families, were able to reach, by rail or road, Bordeaux or Marseilles, whence on colliers or other craft they gained British or North African ports. Others succeeded, sometimes after weeks of cross-country journeying, in reaching Lisbon or Cadiz, and thence sailed to Latin American countries. Some were less fortunate; in traversing France they were captured by the Germans and interned as civilian prisoners until the end of the war.

Most of the small nucleus staff who were retained for wartime service with the Organisation were transported by coach across unoccupied France, Spain and Portugal to Lisbon, whence they went by sea to New York en route for Montreal.

The position of the former members of the staff, even if they succeeded in reaching their own countries, was often far from enviable. Families were often widely dispersed and they knew at first hand the evils of unemployment. Ultimately most succeeded in obtaining employment either in the armed forces or in the public administrations of their countries. In a particularly awkward situation were the French ex-members of the staff. The great majority refused to collaborate with the Pétain administration and either threw in their lot with de Gaulle's Free French overseas or became active in the Resistance movement in France.

On the conclusion of the war, when it became possible for the ILO to rebuild its staff, a large number of its former officials were gradually brought together again from all over the world to rejoin the Office in Montreal or Geneva.

The Seat of the Office

The Office was first established in London early in 1920 in a house made available by the British Government, at 7 Seamore Place, off Park Lane, not far from Sunderland House, the headquarters of the Secretariat of the League of Nations. The description of the League's quarters given by Mr F. P. Walters in his history of the League of Nations could well be applied also to the ILO building, "a pretentious, ugly, uncomfortable and inconvenient mansion". But for the few months during which the house was occupied by the ILO it served well enough.

In June 1920, although the Council of the League had at that time taken no decision to move its Secretariat to Geneva, the Governing Body approved the immediate transfer of the International Labour Office to that city.

From 1920 until 1940 the Office continued to operate in Geneva, at first in temporary premises but from 1926 onwards in a building on the shore of Lake Geneva. Although this office was once stigmatised as "Labour's Home of Luxury" its cost was in fact modest, as it was built during a period of economic depression on a splendid site provided free by the Swiss Confederation. In 1932–33, 1950–51 and 1956–57 wings were constructed, which provided additional committee rooms and offices. A new building is expected to be ready for occupation in 1972/73.

During the war, when the working centre was transferred to Montreal, a small skeleton staff continued to work in the Geneva building, and care was always taken to avoid any statement that the seat or headquarters of the Office had moved to Montreal. Officially, the war-time working centre of the Organisation was established in Montreal, but the seat remained Geneva.

Towards the end of the war and immediately thereafter much consideration was given to the question whether the seat of the Organisation should remain in Geneva. In the minds of some, Geneva was still too closely associated with the failure of the League of Nations and it would be preferable for the Organisation in the new order of things to sever completely its old ties with Geneva. Furthermore, a strong current of opinion was running in favour of bringing together all the specialised agencies at the seat of the United Nations. On the other hand, some pointed out that in Geneva the ILO had an excellently equipped office building with its specialised library and archives, and that in any case it might be preferable for it to operate at some geographical distance from the United Nations; the ILO had had sad experience of too close relationship with a political organisation, and it would be desirable to avoid any risk of a repetition of that experience.

In 1946 the problem constituted a serious dilemma for the Organisation. The Constitution was being revised and an Agreement was being negotiated with the United Nations. In neither document could the inclusion of something about the seat or permanent headquarters of the Organisation be avoided. On the other hand, if the question of the location of the seat or permanent headquarters of the Organisation were to be submitted for formal decision to either the Governing Body or the Conference, it was clear that the voting would be so equally divided as to seriously prejudice the future of the Organisation.

The question was handled with a high degree of tact and discretion. By tacit consent, the matter was not raised as an issue either in the Governing Body or the Conference. In the revision of the Constitution and in the drafting of the Agreement with the United Nations formulae were found which, though somewhat equivocal, avoided prejudicing the future.

After these documents were approved, two years were to elapse before the question of the seat or permanent headquarters could be regarded as settled. In those two years four things contributed to bring the question to a point at which it was no longer a live issue. In the first place the League of Nations, formally dissolved in 1946, had passed into the limbo of history, and the memories of association with it in Geneva were no longer a menace. In the second place, the Conference met in Geneva in 1947 and sessions of the Governing Body were also held there; delegates appreciated the well-remembered amenities and conveniences offered by Geneva. In the third place, partly in order to service the Conference and Governing Body, most of the staff were moved from Montreal to Geneva and re-established in the Office building. In the fourth place, it was noted that all the other specialised agencies were avoiding, for one reason or another, establishing their permanent headquarters under the shadow of the United Nations in New York. In these circumstances, when the decision was taken by the Director-General towards the end of 1948 to transfer to Geneva all the international staff still at Montreal, no voice was raised in opposition. Beyond any dubiety, Geneva was the seat of the ILO.

This happy solution of a problem which, if treated unwisely, might have given rise to much bitterness, was undoubtedly contributed to by the establishment in New York, in 1946, of the ILO Liaison Office with the United Nations. Of all the specialised agencies, the ILO was the first to set up a Liaison Office with the United Nations. The establishment of this Liaison Office constituted the best possible proof that if the seat of the ILO was not to be in New York, nonetheless the ILO would remain in day-to-day relation in New York with the United Nations.

Regional and other Offices

In addition to the headquarters staff in Geneva and the Liaison Office in New York, the ILO has a far-flung network of external services. From 1920 onwards Branch Offices and National Correspondents were set up in some of the more important industrial countries, and since the war a chain of field and regional offices has been organised. This decentralisation is intended both to facilitate operational activities and to provide for on-the-spot contact with United Nations regional Commissions and other regional bodies. It also assists in maintaining close and continuous relations with governments, employers and workers in the regions and countries served.

Regional offices have been set up in the three continents where the ILO carries on most of its operational activities: Addis Ababa for Africa, Lima for Latin America, Bangkok for Asia. The Middle East is served by the ILO Area Offices in Istanbul and Beirut. Each office is headed by a regional co-ordinator who supervises the area offices responsible for a particular country or group of countries as the case may be. A special liaison office has been opened in Santiago, which is also the headquarters of the Economic Commission for Latin America. The regional offices are in constant touch with headquarters and its technical branches, which in some cases second specialists to the regional offices. Arrangements have been made for local liaison with such regional bodies as the Organization of American States, the Organization of African Unity, the League of Arab States and a number of European organisations.

6. REGIONAL AND TECHNICAL CONFERENCES AND COMMITTEES

WITHIN the Organisation an important role has been played by regional and technical committees and conferences.

The committees and conferences differ greatly both in their composition and in the functions assigned to them. In some cases the members of committees are representatives of governments and employers' and workers' organisations; in other cases they are appointed as experts in a personal capacity. In some cases they have a continuing existence, meeting periodically; in other cases they have a single *ad hoc* meeting. In some cases the conferences are called to discuss some technical problem on an international basis covering the Organisation as a whole; in other cases only the problems of a particular region are under discussion and the conference is open only to members in the region or with special interests in the region.

As these committees and conferences are so numerous, it would be impossible within any reasonable compass to discuss all of them; in these circumstances reference will be limited mainly to the Regional Conferences and the Industrial Committees.

Regional Conferences

The ILO initiated regional activity before any other international organisation; its first regional conference was held as long ago as 1936. Historically, the concept of regional activity within the ILO was derived from the increasingly active participation of non-European countries in the work of the ILO and from a growing recognition of the special problems of those countries and of the special contribution which governments, employers and workers in those countries can make to the efforts of the Organisation to solve the problems.

In the early 1930's the region of the world in which labour and industrial problems appeared to be particularly ripe for consideration on a regional basis was the American continent. Accordingly, the Governing Body convened the first Regional Conference to meet in Santiago, Chile, in 1936. When the Conference assembled for its opening sitting in the imposing Parliament Building in Santiago, there was a general feeling among the delegates that history was being made. History was indeed being made, for

64

the pattern which the Santiago Conference wove served as a model, with only minor modifications, for all subsequent Regional Conferences, whether held on the American continent or in other regions.

The first Asian Regional Conference was held in 1947 at New Delhi, the first European Regional Conference in 1955 at Geneva, and the first African Regional Conference in 1960 at Lagos.

Further regional conferences have been held in America, Asia and Africa at approximately three-year intervals. By the end of 1969, eight conferences had been held in America, in seven different countries; six in Asia, in four different countries; and three in Africa, all in different countries. All regional conferences are tripartite in composition.

The agenda of regional conferences is determined by the Governing Body in consultation with the countries invited to participate, and their resolutions are addressed to the Governing Body, which is responsible for taking decisions and following them up.

The resolutions have naturally related to questions of special interest to the particular region at the time. For example, the first American conference adopted a resolution on fundamental principles of social security, which later played a major role in the elaboration of the social security legislation of the Latin American countries. The fifth (1952) gave special attention to ILO standards on freedom of association and protection of the right to organise, and made practical suggestions for the smooth working in the region of the international procedure laid down for the prevention of infringements of trade union rights. It was the eighth (1966) which adopted the plan known as the Ottawa Plan for Human Resources Development.

The Asian conferences have considered a wide range of social problems of first importance to millions of Asian workers, such as the creation and improvement of systems of social security, the setting up of co-operative societies, the development of employment services and vocational guidance schemes, and above all the bettering of the working conditions of women and young people. The principal resolution adopted at the fifth conference (1962) recognised that "the questions of employment promotion, vocational training and the improvement of labour–management relations . . . are essential features of a development policy based on full utilisation of human resources", and thus set human resources development firmly within the wider framework of national development as a whole.

The African conferences have adopted resolutions on certain problems of key importance for that continent: relations between employers and workers, particularly those concerned with freedom of association, joint consultation and collective agreements; vocational training schemes for agriculture, industry and commerce; methods and principles of wage regulation and the employment and conditions of work of women; labour administration; technical co-operation and employment policy.

These conferences have been remarkably successful in avoiding political issues and in concentrating on practical measures for social justice and economic development. They have always been particularly conscious of the interrelations of economic and social factors. For example, the first Asian conference had on its agenda "The economic background of social policy, including problems of industrialisation", and the report of the Director-General submitted to an American conference (1960) bore the sub-title "Economic Growth and Social Policy". These conferences have in fact made a special contribution to "balanced economic and social progress" in their regions. Increasingly, the practical implementation of the resolutions of the conferences has been helped by the availability of funds under the technical co-operation programmes of the United Nations and by the advice given by ILO experts assigned to their countries.

Industrial Committees

Among the war-time and post-war innovations in the structure and work of the ILO one of the most important was the inauguration in 1945 of Industrial Committees to deal with some of the principal international industries. The decision to set up the Committees was taken by the Governing Body in war-time London to the accompaniment of exploding enemy bombs.

It was due to the far-sighted statesmanship and deep understanding of the potentialities of the ILO shown by Ernest Bevin, then British Minister of Labour and National Service, and later Secretary of State for Foreign Affairs, that the Industrial Committees came into being. Bevin realised that after the war new methods and procedures would be needed to supplement and in some cases to supersede the old, that post-war problems would have to be treated internationally with the same directness, realism and immediacy as they had been tackled nationally, and that the ILO would be able to respond to the new demands only if its methods and machinery were overhauled and renovated. Bevin's conception was elaborated in detail by Sir Frederick Leggett, British Government member of the Governing Body.

The industries for which the Governing Body decided to set up Industrial Committees were: coal mining; inland transport; iron and steel; metal trades; textiles; building, civil engineering and public works; petroleum; and chemicals. All these industries have an international importance and are faced with international problems. Each of the countries represented on a Committee is entitled to appoint six representatives –

two for the Government, two for the employers and two for the workers, together with advisers.

On the whole the tripartite composition of the Industrial Committees has worked well. Bevin's own idea was that, like the Joint Maritime Commission, they should be bipartite; he was a great believer in leaving employers and workers to grapple with their own problems without the intervention of governments. But the decision of the Governing Body to include government representatives in the Committees has been vindicated by experience.

In connection with the work of the Committees, problems have of course arisen, in particular the problem of the implementation of the conclusions reached by them. Suggestions have been made that a measure of obligation should be assigned to at least some of these conclusions. Such suggestions have not been approved. There is room within the framework of the Organisation for the experiment conducted by the Industrial Committees under which reliance is placed on voluntary action rather than on legislative enactment. The results already achieved afford evidence that this new machinery is a valuable addition to the Organisation's means of stimulating national action and establishing the conditions of social and economic balance in some of the key international industries of the world.

Some evidence of the usefulness of the Industrial Committees is to be found in the number of requests that have come from other industries to have Industrial Committees constituted for them also. Although the Governing Body has examined all such requests, it has avoided complicating unduly the machinery of the ILO and overburdening its limited budget. No additional Industrial Committees have therefore been set up, but meetings similar to Industrial Committees have been held of the Committee on Work on Plantations and the Advisory Committee on Salaried Employees and Professional Workers (which superseded two pre-war committees). *Ad hoc* technical tripartite meetings have also been held during the 1950's and 1960's for civil aviation, mines other than coal mines, timber, printing and allied trades, the food industries, clothing, hotels, restaurants and similar establishments, woodworking, and leather and footwear.

The Governing Body exercises close control over the Committees, allocating budgetary credits for the meetings, fixing the agenda, receiving their reports and resolutions, and taking action on them.

From time to time the Governing Body has also undertaken a general assessment of the value of the work of the Committees. In 1966 it agreed that the objectives of these meetings were still substantially the same as in 1945, namely: (i) to break down the barriers between peoples by bringing them together in the matters which touch them most closely, the conditions of their daily lives in their chosen occupations; (ii) to develop mutual understanding between management and labour in order to achieve the largest possible measure of agreement on effective ways of improving working and living conditions and thereby enhancing the welfare of the whole community; and (iii) to promote the prosperity, on a world-wide basis, of the great world industries. In 1969 it decided that the ILO's industrial activities should be not only continued but strengthened, and from 1971 onwards should form part of an "ILO Programme for Industrial Activities".

It is not easy to identify in precise terms the concrete results of the work of the Industrial Committees. Certainly their discussions and resolutions have made some contribution, in a few cases a major contribution, on the one hand to the preparation of items to be placed on the agenda of the Conference, with a view to the adoption of Conventions and Recommendations, and on the other to the formulation of programmes of technical co-operation in developing countries. In addition, instances can be recalled where suggestions made by Industrial Committees have led to concrete action which, but for those suggestions, might never have been taken. For example, the Inland Transport Committee in 1947 requested the Governing Body to take action aiming at the international regulation of social security and conditions of work in navigation on the Rhine. As a result, a conference adopted two agreements on conditions of employment and social security, and the final texts were approved at a meeting of the six governments concerned in 1950. These agreements have been fully applied, and have been of real value to navigation on the Rhine. Another proposal made by the Inland Transport Committee led to the adoption of regulations on the individual control book for drivers in road transport, which have been incorporated in some national legislation and also in a regional agreement worked out by the United Nations.

Since 1945 some 80 meetings of Industrial Committees have been held. In connection with labour-management relations and productivity they have examined the impact on the various industries of automation and the application of computers and electronic devices. They have also facilitated in developing countries the processes of industrialisation. In many countries, developed as well as developing, the guidelines worked out by Industrial Committees for consultation with a view to collective agreements or other forms of joint negotiation have stimulated action by management and trade unions to secure an effective balance between economic growth and social advance.

Details of some of this work are given in the chapters relating to major problems attacked by the ILO.

Perhaps, however, the main value of the Industrial Committees lies not in what they have done but in what they are. Their chief contribution has been made not in the technical field but in relations. Their meetings have provided clinical examples of how industrial relations should be conducted, and for many of the workers' and employers' members the experience of participating in these discussions has been of permanent educational value.

The Joint Maritime Commission

Although the Joint Maritime Commission is similar to the Industrial Committees in that it is concerned with a particular occupational group, it has some special characteristics that are noteworthy. In the first place, it was set up in 1920, long before the Industrial Committees were even thought of. When the Versailles Peace Treaty was being drafted, the seamen, who had rendered outstanding service in the war, claimed the creation of a special office of maritime labour. The Governing Body decided, as soon as it was appointed, that a Joint Commission would facilitate the work of the ILO in the consideration of problems relating to maritime labour and would, at least to some extent, not only meet the wishes of the seamen, but be acceptable to the shipowners.

In the second place, unlike the Industrial Committees, the Joint Maritime Commission includes no government members. It consists only of shipowners' and seafarers' representatives. From time to time suggestions have been made that government members should be added, but this was opposed by the shipowners, and the only concession made has been to provide that sub-committees might be tripartite if governments were specially concerned with the subjects with which the sub-committees were to deal.

Throughout the history of the ILO, the JMC has played an extremely important role in preparing the way for the adoption of Maritime Conventions and Recommendations and in securing the continuing loyalty to the ILO of the shipowners and seafarers of the world.

Other Commissions and Committees

Reference to other ILO commissions and committees will be found in the chapters relating to the fields in which their contributions have been made; they include the Committee of Experts on the Application of Conventions and Recommendations; the Fact-Finding and Conciliation Commission on Freedom of Association; the Permanent Agricultural Committee; and the Committee of Social Security Experts. Panels of consultants have also been appointed on several questions, and two joint ILO–WHO committees, on occupational health and health of seafarers respectively.

7. TRAINING AND RESEARCH INSTITUTES

In the course of his journeys throughout the world on the business of the ILO, the Director-General became increasingly impressed by the urgency of the need for leaders, particularly in the developing countries – leaders in government service, in employers' organisations and industrial and commercial undertakings, in trade unions and in rural communities. To meet that need action was taken by the ILO. The Governing Body, after considering the Director-General's proposals, set up the International Institute for Labour Studies in Geneva, which became operational in 1962, and the International Centre for Advanced Technical and Vocational Training in Turin in 1965.

The Geneva Institute

The Geneva Institute is designed to meet the needs of three main groups – emerging leaders in the new countries who may be expected to shape future social policy and industrial relations; men charged with managerial and similar responsibilities in industrialised countries who welcome the opportunity for round-table discussion of their problems; and research workers of various academic disciplines devoting themselves to studies on labour and industry.

The Institute's educational work is directed towards public policy rather than technical studies. It is intended to respond to an accelerating demand for responsible leadership in government and in a variety of organisations concerned with making and carrying out social policy.

In its first few years, it concentrated exclusively on educational work. Some 40 participants at a time from all over the world attended intensive three-month courses on various aspects of economic and social policy.

Each year since 1962 international study courses on labour problems in economic and social development have been held. A special course on industrial relations for Latin American engineers was held in 1966. In 1967 an East African seminar on labour problems in economic development was held in Nairobi for participants from seven countries of the region. Symposia on current policy issues have also been organised yearly since 1965. The one held in Denmark in 1967 dealt with wage policy issues in economic development. In 1969 advanced courses, mainly for participants from Latin American countries, were organised in Mexico and Argentina. The results already achieved have led to an expansion of the work of the Institute in bringing together responsible policymakers to discuss current socio-economic issues.

It has become clear, however, that an international institute cannot by itself hope to meet this need for training leaders in rational methods of policy making. In addition, therefore, the Institute now conceives its role as encouraging and assisting university centres in developing areas to provide this type of educational service locally. The Institute in Geneva has become, as it were, an educational laboratory developing new methods and programmes of leadership education so that these improved programmes can be put to work in national education centres where they reach larger numbers of people.

The Institute's research complements that of the ILO and fills somewhat different needs. It is concerned with long-term trends in society whereas the ILO research is more orientated towards applications through current action programmes. In the freedom of initiative which the Institute has in research, and in the fact that individual authors rather than institutions are responsible for the views expressed, the Institute is more like a university. It also serves as a link between the academic community and the ILO, and is the world intellectual centre concerned with development of social policy. The Institute took the lead in establishing in 1966 the International Industrial Relations Association, which links national associations of industrial relations specialists in most of the highly industrialised countries of the world and encourages the formation of such associations for other countries.

Various international research projects are now being carried out or planned, usually with the participation of research institutes and scholars in different countries. All of them fit within three broad areas of interest: firstly, the changing institutional relationships in industrial societies (for example, a major study is under way on workers' participation in management); secondly, the integration of social groups which still remain outside or not fully participant in industrial or modernising societies – such as the rural communities in less developed countries – and thirdly, the prospection of new opportunities for international action in the social field.

The Board of the Institute consists of the Director-General of the ILO as chairman, together with twelve members, six of whom are members of the Governing Body of the ILO. The functions of the Board are to prepare the programme for the Institute, to present an annual report on its work to the Governing Body and to prepare its annual budget for approval by the Governing Body.

The Turin Centre

The International Centre for Advanced Technical and Vocational Training was established essentially as an extension of, and complement to, the field projects carried out under the vocational training and management development programmes of the ILO.

The need for such a Centre had been indicated in resolutions adopted by the International Labour Conference in 1960 and 1961, and also by Regional Conferences in Africa (1960) and the Americas (1961). In 1961 the Italian government offered to put at the disposal of the ILO some of the buildings erected for the Exhibition in Turin in order to create an international training centre under ILO auspices. As a site for such a centre Turin had several specific advantages. The offer was accepted by the Governing Body and the Centre was opened in 1965.

The initial programme of the Centre was defined as follows: to provide advanced technical and vocational training at various levels, primarily for the benefit of developing countries, for persons considered suitable for more advanced training than any they could obtain in their own countries or regions; to provide advanced training for persons connected with the development of small-scale industry and production co-operatives; to provide instruction in teaching methods for technical co-operation experts.

During the first four-year period (1965–68) the work of the Centre consisted mainly in providing courses of vocational training for chiefs of national services and vocational training institutes; instructors and technicians; instructors of industrial drawing; automobile mechanics; general mechanics, etc. In 1966 the first management courses were organised. Participants in these courses, an average of 500 each year, came from 102 countries.

In 1968 the Board of the Centre approved the management and technical training programmes proposed by the Director for the second four-year period, 1969–72. With respect to technical training, the Board reaffirmed that advanced technical training of instructors and foremen should remain a basic element in programmes, priority being given to the training of trainers. While it was understood that the Centre should continue to cater primarily for the needs of the developing countries, the Board agreed that the Centre should be used as a meeting place for economists and managerial staff from industrialised countries with different economic and social systems to study management problems and their solution. The ILO Governing Body endorsed these conclusions and the programmes of the Centre have been gradually reorientated in consequence.

A particularly significant feature of this development has been the extension of management training. The management training programmes of the Turin Centre provide a complement at the international level to the training activities of the ILO at the national level. The Centre now offers a range of twelve-week courses for senior and middle-level managers in general management, marketing management, production management, personnel administration and management accounting.

In addition to this standard range, the Centre also conducts special programmes for, or in conjunction with, such international organisations or agencies as UNESCO, UNCTAD/GATT, EEC and ICEM.

The Chairman of the Board is the Director-General of the ILO.

An evaluation of the Centre carried out in 1969 by Sir Eric Wyndham-White, former Secretary-General of GATT, contained the following conclusions:

> "The technical programmes of the Turin Centre constitute a net addition to ILO training activities at the national level, meet needs which exist and will continue to exist in the relevant future, and justify the operating costs;
> "the management training programmes of the Turin Centre provide a service which is not obtainable elsewhere and do so at a reasonable cost. The long-term future of the Centre would appear to be secure in this field in view of the high premium put on management skills in all parts of the world. There are definite advantages in undertaking management training for developing countries in an international environment, which provides an indispensable link between management theories and practices appropriate on the one hand to a sophisticated environment and on the other to conditions of imperfection."

While the continuing need for the Centre is clearly established, its future will depend on a long-term solution of the problem of financing its operations, a matter which at the time of writing is under active consideration.

8. RELATIONSHIPS

THE ILO was never intended to live and work in isolation. It never has lived and worked in isolation. The reason for this was well stated in a report submitted to the Philadelphia Conference: "The International Labour Organisation cannot, consistently with the proper discharge of the broad responsibilities which have been entrusted to it, be in the world but not of it. Daily and intimate contact with all parts of the intricate machinery through which international policies with social repercussions are formulated and applied is a *sine qua non* of the vitality and effectiveness of the Organisation."[1]

As an association of States it has been necessary for the Organisation to establish close relations with the governments of those States. These relations have been maintained on the one hand by visits of the Director-General or senior members of the staff to heads of governments and Ministers of Labour, supplemented by the day-to-day contacts through Branch offices and National Correspondents; on the other by attendance at the Conference, Governing Body and other ILO meetings of Ministers of Labour, other political personalities, and high departmental officials of the various governments.

As a tripartite organisation, it has been necessary for the ILO to establish equally close relations with the other two sides of the triangle – the employers and workers. These relations also have been two-way relations, relations with the employers' and workers' associations in the countries concerned, and relations within the various organs of the Organisation. From the outset the ILO has realised that, if the equality in status within the Organisation of employers and workers with governments were not fully implemented in practice, the whole system would collapse.

As an intergovernmental organisation, it has been necessary for the ILO to establish relations with other intergovernmental organisations. As the number of these bodies has grown, the system of relationships established between them and the ILO has assumed a complexity and an importance undreamt of when it came into being.

Finally, as an organisation for social and economic progress, it has been necessary for the ILO to establish relations with a multiplicity of international associations, voluntary or semi-official, whose action tended in the

[1] *Future Policy, Programme and Status of the International Labour Organisation,* 1944, p. 22.

same general direction as its own. Some of these associations are important, some are not. In some cases the relations of the Organisation with these bodies might be compared to the friendship, in the fable, of the lion and the mouse. However unimportant an association might appear to be, it could sometimes have the opportunity to render a service to the ILO; and through its contacts with these specialised associations the ILO has often had occasion to influence sectors of opinion that otherwise would have been closed to it.

Relations with Trade Unions

At the outset in many countries the trade unions were disappointed with the structure and powers of the ILO. Thomas saw very clearly that it was necessary, if the new Organisation was to develop or even to survive, to overcome the lukewarmness and hesitancy of the trade unions and to enlist their active and vigorous support. He therefore made a point of attending and addressing the annual congress of the International Federation of Trade Unions and also congresses of trade union federations in the principal industrial countries. The value of this active "policy of presence", which continued to be implemented after his death, was two-fold. In the first place, it helped in securing the whole-hearted allegiance to the ILO of the majority of the organised workers of the world. In the second place, the philosophy of the trade union movement was gradually and in part unconsciously influenced away from the class-struggle towards co-operation in industrial relations.

Although the war radically curtailed the activities of the ILO great importance was attached to maintaining, in spite of all difficulties, relations with the workers' organisations. For this there were two reasons. In the first place it was recalled that in the first world war the membership and influence of the trade unions had greatly increased, and it was a safe assumption that in this respect history would repeat itself. In the second place, and here again it seemed probable that history would prove a reliable guide, it was to be expected that after the war the organised workers could exercise an influence, perhaps a decisive influence, on the form which would be assumed by the intergovernmental organisation for dealing with questions of labour and industry. In a nutshell, if after the war the workers were determined to scrap the ILO and put something else in its place, the chances were that this would be done. On the other hand, if the workers were satisfied that the ILO with all its defects was the organisation in the field of labour and industry best fitted to contribute to the tasks of social and economic reconstruction after the war, the ILO would not only survive but would grow in strength.

With considerations such as these in mind, during the war the ILO took care to maintain the Workers' Relations Service with its lists of addresses, and it continued to correspond with the principal international and national workers' organisations and to supply them with the publications of the Office and such information as the Office could provide from its restricted resources. When the New York Conference of the Organisation was held in 1941 and the Philadelphia Session of the International Labour Conference in 1944, the workers' representatives made it clear that they were solidly in support of the ILO with its tripartite structure, its social philosophy, its background of experience, and its programme for the future.

After the war the pattern of relations with workers' organisations was affected by a change in the Constitution providing for consultation with international organisations of workers, and also by the establishment of Industrial Committees. The international workers' organisations having consultative status now comprise the International Confederation of Free Trade Unions, the World Confederation of Labour, and the World Federation of Trade Unions. In virtue of this consultative relationship these organisations are entitled to send representatives to all sessions of the International Labour Conference and the Governing Body, as well as to such meetings as those of Industrial Committees.

The setting up of Industrial Committees affected relations with the trade unions in two ways. In the first place, as each of the eight Committees provided for the attendance of two workers' delegates from each country represented on the Committee, a large number of trade union representatives in a wide variety of industries who would not otherwise have had an opportunity of coming into contact with the ILO were enabled to participate in its work. Further, by an application by analogy of the new constitutional provision for consultative relationship, the Governing Body granted permission to the international organisations of workers in the particular industries to send observers to attend the meetings of the Committees.

Relations with Employers' Organisations

When the ILO came into being, while the employers' organisations agreed to participate in the work of the Conference and the Governing Body, their general attitude to the ILO was at first one of reserve or even of open hostility. The hostility of the employers was accentuated by their suspicion that the ILO, instead of functioning as a neutral civil service, was being used as a propaganda agency on behalf of the workers. Gradually, however, a degree of positive co-operation was established, due in part to the personal influence of Thomas. Even when the employers were most strongly opposed to him they never doubted his sincerity and they could not resist his charm, his *bonhomie* and his humour. On one occasion when some threat had been made that the employers might leave the ILO altogether, Thomas remarked: "The employers have often said that their function is to put on the brake, but in order to put on the brake the brakesman must himself be on the train!"

When the war broke out the ILO fully realised the importance of maintaining relations with the employers' organisations, and from its working centre in Montreal its publications continued to be distributed to them. More particularly, the Office remained closely in touch with the employers' leaders who, as members of the Governing Body or its Emergency Committee, had a special responsibility for planning for its survival during the war and its reconstruction after the war.

At the two Conferences held during the war the employers' delegates affirmed their whole-hearted support of the Organisation. At the New York Conference in 1941 the keynote of the discussions, stressed by the employers, was that the experience of organised management and organised labour should be brought to bear directly upon the planning and execution of international economic policies, and that the ILO was a unique instrument for that purpose. When the 1944 session of the Conference met at Philadelphia the employers' delegates took an active part in the discussions relating to the future policy, programme and status of the Organisation and unanimously voted for the Declaration of Philadelphia in which the essential aims and purposes of the Organisation were re-stated. Sir John Forbes Watson pointed out that the Declaration was a creed, and its essence was the preservation of freedom; the Organisation itself was "the international trustee of democracy" and that was "a very sacred trust". In the Philadelphia discussions it was made clear that the employers were determined to participate fully in that sacred trust.

After the war relations with the employers' organisations developed in a totally different climate to that which had chilled relationships when the ILO came into being after the first world war. The reason is not far to seek. Whereas the employers had almost nothing to do with creating the ILO they had a very great deal to do with re-creating it. In the process of re-modelling and re-equipping the ILO undertaken by the Conference and its Delagation on Constitutional Questions in 1945–46, the employers' representatives played an active and in some respects a determining role. For the employers after the war the ILO was *their* organisation in a sense in which they had never felt it to be their organisation before the war; it was now their organisation as completely as it was the workers' organisation.

The setting up of Industrial Committees had an effect on relations with

the employers' movement by broadening the area of contact between the
ILO and the employers of the countries represented on the Committees. As
in the case of the workers, large numbers of employers in the eight important industries covered by the Committees were enabled to come into
contact with employers in other countries and to gain some experience at
first hand of the working of the ILO. Although the employers severely
criticised some aspects of the work of the Industrial Committees, they
never declined to participate in their meetings.

Under the 1946 Constitution the International Organisation of Employers was brought into consultative relationship with the ILO and thus
became entitled to send representatives to all sessions of the International
Labour Conference and of the Governing Body as well as to such meetings
as those of Industrial Committees.

Relations with Intergovernmental Organisations

When the League of Nations was formally dissolved in 1946 the ILO
entered into formal relationship with the United Nations. The agreement
with the United Nations, approved by the International Labour Conference
in September 1946 and by the General Assembly of the United Nations in
December of the same year, was the first of the relationship agreements to
be concluded between the United Nations and the specialised agencies,
and it served to a large extent as a model for subsequent agreements.

The negotiations in 1945/46 which culminated in this Agreement were
difficult and at times critical. In January 1945 the Governing Body,
meeting in wartime London, unanimously adopted a statement affirming
the desire of the ILO for association with the new international political
organisation that was then contemplated to supersede the League of
Nations. It also appointed representatives to present this statement to the
Conference convened at San Francisco to decide on the form of the new
organisation.

At the San Francisco Conference the representatives of the ILO were
received coldly if not discourteously. The main reason for this was that at
that Conference powerful influences urged a clean sweep not only of the
League of Nations but also of all the organisations linked to the League.
The San Francisco Conference was organised and attended by the vic-
torious powers who had scant regard for the neutrals. Some of them
pointed out that most of the neutrals were members of the League and the
ILO, that the League sheltered in a neutral country during the war, and
that the executive heads of the three League organisations, the Secretariat,
the International Labour Office, and the Permanent Court, were all
nationals of neutral countries. So far as the ILO in particular was concerned,

while they admitted that it had wisely transferred its working centre to Montreal during the war, they doubted whether it would be able to untangle the constitutional ties which bound it to the League. In the result, the Charter of the United Nations, adopted at San Francisco, contained no reference to the ILO.

In these circumstances it was very difficult for the International Labour Conference, meeting in October–November 1945, to decide what action to take. In this situation of uncertainty, the Conference wisely decided to limit mention of the United Nations, in amending the Constitution, to two Articles. In regard to membership, it provided that "Any original Member of the United Nations and any State admitted to membership of the United Nations by a decision of the General Assembly in accordance with the provisions of the Charter may become a Member of the International Labour Organisation by communicating to the Director-General of the International Labour Office its formal acceptance of the obligations of the Constitution of the International Labour Organisation." This provision was a gesture of approach to the United Nations, as it facilitated access of their members to membership in the ILO. On the other hand it did not prejudice in any way the independence of the ILO.

In regard to finance, it provided that "The International Labour Organisation may make such financial and budgetary arrangements with the United Nations as may appear appropriate. Pending the conclusion of such arrangements or if at any time no such arrangements are in force . . ." (here follow detailed financial and budgetary provisions). This formula was an inspiration of genius. On the one hand, it was known that in United Nations circles the view was strongly advocated that the United Nations should have a central budget, to be adopted by the General Assembly, from which all the specialised agencies would be financed. On the other hand, the ILO, with its experience of financial dependence upon the League of Nations, was most anxious to secure complete budgetary and financial autonomy. The formula took account of this situation, without prejudicing the future in one direction or in the other, and also made practical provision for the immediate need of financing the work of the Organisation.

In addition to making these Constitutional amendments, the Conference adopted a carefully worded resolution, in which it confirmed the desire of the ILO to enter into relationship with the United Nations on terms to be determined by agreement, and authorised the Governing Body to enter, subject to the approval of the Conference, into such agreements with the appropriate authorities of the United Nations as might be necessary or desirable.

When, in the early months of the following year, negotiations began with a view to the conclusion of the Agreement that was contemplated, at first between officials of the ILO and the United Nations and then between representatives of the ILO Negotiating Delegation and representatives of the Economic and Social Council, the climate was very different from that of San Francisco. On the side of the United Nations there was manifest willingness to welcome as the first specialised agency to be brought into relationship with the United Nations an organisation with the experience and record of the ILO. On the side of the ILO there was relief and satisfaction that it would not be subjected to vexatious restrictions and that it would retain the authority essential for the discharge of its responsibilities under its Constitution and the Declaration of Philadelphia.

The change of climate did not mean that the negotiations were easy. They were not easy, but they were pursued in a spirit of mutual confidence and goodwill and their successful conclusion owed much to the two chairmen, Mr Myrddin-Evans (later Sir Guildhaume Myrddin-Evans), Chairman of the ILO Negotiating Delegation, and Sir Ramaswami Mudaliar, Chairman of the Committee on Negotiations with Specialised Agencies of the Economic and Social Council.

As soon as the ILO was brought into formal relationship with the United Nations, it took the initiative in entering into formal agreements with other specialised agencies, as they were set up, such as the Food and Agriculture Organization, UNESCO, the World Health Organization, and the International Civil Aviation Organization.

The Agreement between the ILO and FAO which entered into force in 1947 was the first of such inter-agency agreements to be concluded. In eleven articles, the Agreement provides for reciprocal representation at meetings, ILO–FAO joint committees, exchange of information and documents, personnel arrangements, statistical services, financing of special services, and revision and termination. The Agreement is supplemented by two detailed Memoranda of Understanding agreed by the Directors-General of the two organisations. One relates to responsibilities for migration for land settlement (1951), the other to responsibilities in the fields of migration for land settlement, vocational training in agriculture, co-operatives and rural industries (1955).

Perhaps reflection on the vast complex of inter-organisational relationships that has gradually been built up may sometimes lead to the cynical suspicion that among these organisations the word "co-operation" has acquired a religious or mystical significance. Be that as it may, the ILO at least has shown itself aware that the mere enunciation of the sacred word "co-operation" was not enough to solve any question; arrangements for effective inter-organisational relationship can only be worked out the hard way.

These Agreements may be regarded as "treaties of amity and goodwill".

In implementing them surprisingly few difficulties have been experienced. No major jurisdictional disputes have occurred. On the other hand, as is inevitable in the life of vigorous and growing organisms, some questions of frontier adjustment have arisen from time to time.

Implementation of the Agreement with the United Nations has been greatly facilitated by two bodies, established by the United Nations, the Administrative Committee on Co-ordination (ACC), consisting of the Secretary-General of the United Nations and the executive heads of all the specialised agencies, and the Advisory Committee on Administrative and Budgetary Questions (ACABQ), composed of persons of recognised administrative and financial competence appointed by the General Assembly.

While, on the whole, the various intergovernmental organisations have loyally tried to avoid overlapping and have refrained from initiating action in a field in which one or more other organisations might have an interest without first consulting them, the importance of the regulative and co-ordinating functions exercised by the Economic and Social Council and ACC should not be underestimated. Without their vigilant and at times vigorous action wasteful "proliferation" and anarchic dissipation of energy would have been almost inevitable.

The ILO's network of relationships has been supplemented by agreements with regional organisations with which its interests are closely linked, such as the Organization of American States, the Council of Europe, the Organization of African Unity and the League of Arab States. In establishing these relationships the ILO has recognised that since the war regional sentiments and regional loyalties have strongly developed, and that it is necessary in pursuing its own international aims to take account of such trends and tendencies.

Relations with Non-Governmental Organisations

The term "non-governmental organisations" includes a great variety of bodies, international or regional, differing in function and purpose. The first two groups of organisations differ from the others in having special relationships with the ILO.

By a unanimous decision of the Governing Body in 1920 a special Service was set up in the ILO to collect information on the co-operative movement and to keep in touch with co-operative organisations. Throughout the whole of the pre-war period the ILO continued to maintain close relations with the co-operative movement, which were facilitated by the inclusion of particulars about co-operative societies in the annual editions of the *International Labour Directory*, and by the issue by the ILO of a multigraphed periodical containing information of interest to the co-operative movement. After the war the Governing Body approved the revival of relations with the co-operative movement. The Correspondence Committee on Co-operation was reorganised and enlarged. Under the 1946 revision of the Constitution the International Co-operative Alliance has been brought into consultative relationship with the ILO, and has been regularly represented at sessions of the Conference and of the Governing Body.

In the pre-war period when the Conventions and Recommendations in the field of social insurance adopted at various sessions of the Conference were gradually building up an international code of social insurance legislation, the ILO endeavoured to ensure that the administration of social insurance should keep pace with the rapid increase in national legislation under the stimulus of the developing international code. In particular the ILO encouraged the creation of an international association of national institutions responsible for the administration of social insurance funds. Immediately after the war the Association was reconstituted and, in addition to institutions concerned with the administration of social insurance, governments were admitted to membership. The relationship of the ILO to the International Social Security Association has involved not only the rendering of services but also direct budgetary expenditure. The Governing Body has agreed that it is important for the ILO in its work on social security to have the assistance of voluntary organisations throughout the world which could bring independent minds to bear on this very important sphere of activity.

Since 1940 the ILO has also maintained close relationships with another social security body, the Inter-American Committee on Social Security. The creation of this body, like ISSA, was directly influenced by the social security activities of the ILO.

The other non-governmental organisations with which the ILO maintains relations are very numerous, including the International Red Cross, Inter-Parliamentary Union, World Assembly of Youth, International Association for Social Progress, International Social Service and many others. These organisations do not enjoy "consultative status" with the ILO, but each year the Governing Body invites a list of them to be represented at the Conference.

Relations with Religious Bodies

In the early years of the ILO Albert Thomas on several visits to Rome examined with the Vatican methods of establishing relations on a permanent basis. It was agreed that a priest should be appointed as a member of the personnel of the ILO, and since 1926 a priest has always been on the

ILO staff to advise the Director-General on relations with the Catholic world.

In 1931 in his annual Director's Report, Albert Thomas referred to the similarity of the objectives pursued by the ILO and the Catholic Church in respect of social policy. In the same year Pope Pius XI emphasised in the Encyclical *Quadragesimo Anno* the remarkable concordance between the principles laid down in the Constitution of the ILO and the Encyclical *Rerum Novarum*.

In the years after the second world war Pope Pius XII received on various occasions the participants in ILO meetings held in Rome. In particular he granted a special audience to the Governing Body at its session in Rome in 1954.

Pope John XXIII stated in 1961 in the Encyclical *Mater et Magister*:

"We are happy to express our cordial esteem for the International Labour Organisation. For several decades it has been making its effective and valuable contribution to the establishment in the world of an economic and social order infused with justice and humanity, where the legitimate claims of the workers find their expression."

In 1969 when the ILO was making preparations to celebrate its 50th anniversary the Director-General sent an invitation to Pope Paul VI to come to Geneva to address a special sitting of the International Labour Conference. The invitation was accepted; on 10 June the Pope addressed the Conference and afterwards spoke informally to each of the three groups of delegates, representing respectively governments, employers and workers. In his speech to the Conference he said: "We are an attentive observer of the work you accomplish here, and more than that, a fervent admirer of the activity you carry on, and also a collaborator who is happy to have been invited to celebrate with you the existence, functions, achievements and merits of this world institution, and to do so as a friend."[2]

Albert Thomas also established contacts with the international movements within the non-catholic Churches which paved the way for the formation of the World Council of Churches. He sent a representative to the Jerusalem Conference of the International Missionary Council, which aimed at co-ordinating missionary policy and action mainly in the underdeveloped countries of Africa and Asia. The ILO was also represented at the Stockholm Conference on Christian Life and Work in 1925 which did much to define and clarify the social attitude and policy of the Churches in the modern world. That ecumenical gathering readily supported the idea of a world organisation concentrating on the problems of social justice in modern society.

[2] *Prov. Rec.*, Int. Lab. Conf., 53rd session, Geneva, 1969, p. 76.

In the following years the contacts thus established were intensified, and when the World Council of Churches was set up in Geneva, close relations were maintained with the various activities which it organised, leading up to the World Conference on the Churches and Society in 1966. At that assembly the attention of the Churches was focussed on the new and dynamic forces that had arisen to challenge their predominantly Western view of world social and economic order. In 1969, on the occasion of the 50th anniversary of the ILO, Dr Carson Blake, Secretary-General of the World Council of Churches, addressed the Conference. "We in the Churches", he said, "surely need the illumination and the example of organisations such as the ILO. . . . Social justice will advance most surely if it is in constant encounter with the theologians and the philosophers – indeed with all those who believe that true justice is more than a set of abstract rational principles or the accumulation of technical 'know-how'."[3]

Although the contacts of the ILO with the Christian world have been closer than with those of other religious communities, it has always recognised the value of the social programmes of other far-flung religious disciplines, and it has been more than ready to get into touch with them.

Sometimes the ILO has been criticised for "wasting time" on relations with voluntary associations and particularly with religious bodies. Such an attitude is near-sighted and unhistorical. Whatever one's personal position may be in respect of religious belief and observance, there can be no doubt that the great religious systems have, throughout all the period of the existence of the Organisation and, indeed, for long centuries before, been powerful influences in giving a moral and social content to the law of nations which the ILO has been contributing to build.

Friendships, it has been said, must be kept in repair; in order to keep in repair all this multiplicity of friendly relationships the Relations and Conference Department of the ILO includes five branches respectively for Official Relations, Employers' Relations, Workers' Relations, International Organisations, and Non-Governmental Organisations.

[3] *Prov. Rec.*, Int. Lab. Conf., 53rd session, Geneva, 1969, pp. 269–270.

9. FINANCIAL RESOURCES

INEVITABLY, the work of the ILO is conditioned by the financial resources available. Lord Balfour once said that the greatest danger to the development of international organisations lies in the problem of financing them. The financing of its work has always presented problems for the ILO and sometimes these problems have given rise to acute anxiety.

For the first thirty years of its life the ILO depended for its funds almost exclusively on the contributions of its member States. During the existence of the League of Nations its budget, though prepared by the Governing Body, was adopted by the Assembly of the League, and contributions were not paid to the ILO directly, but (except in the case of States not members of the League) were paid to it by the Treasurer of the League, who collected them. This system necessarily gave rise to some friction and the ILO was happy to secure financial autonomy when the League of Nations was dissolved in 1946. In that year the International Labour Conference, for the first time, adopted the annual budget and a scale of contributions for which member States would be assessed.

Throughout the pre-war period, the annual budget of the ILO was stabilised at around the equivalent of 1·5 million dollars. Since the war, in order to provide for the expansion of the activities of the ILO, the growth of its staff, the provision of additional accommodation and other charges, the annual budget has increased year by year from 3·75 million dollars in 1947 to nearly 27 million in 1969. As, however, during this period the number of members grew from 51 to 121, the contribution from each member has not increased in the same proportion.

On budgetary and financial matters close relations have always been maintained with the United Nations.

In 1969 a major budgetary change was made when the Conference adopted, instead of the usual annual budget, a budget on a two-year basis, to cover the period 1970–71. This first biennial programme and budget was considered to have certain advantages, both for the States members whose financial commitments to the ILO would be known for two years in advance, and for the ILO which could plan its programmes further into the future. A summary table of the budget for 1970–71, amounting to $59,671,000, will be found in the Reference section. This contains, under each programme and other item, 1970–71 estimates, together with 1969 budget and 1968 expenditure.

85

The expenses of the ILO are allocated among the States members on a percentage basis. Each State's contribution is assessed as a percentage of the total budget. While certain problems relating to allocation still await solution the principle of assessment continues to be "capacity to pay". There is a fixed minimum contribution rate applicable to States with the lowest capacity to pay. For 1971 that has been fixed at 0·08 per cent, amounting to $23,868. The percentages allocated to certain States are: USA 25 per cent, USSR 10·45 per cent, United Kingdom 9·12 per cent, France 6·07 per cent. A table showing the assessment of each State will be found in the Reference section.

In respect of collection of contributions the Governing Body and the Conference have more than once laid it down as a principle that nothing less than 100 per cent collection could be regarded as satisfactory. In practice the rate of collection has fallen slightly short of that target. Particulars of arrears due by States are always submitted to the Governing Body and the Conference. Although delay in payment of contributions sometimes causes serious anxiety to the Treasurer, the cases in which arrears have had to be written off are remarkably few.

The audited accounts are passed by the Conference on the recommendation of the Governing Body.

Extra-Budgetary Funds

The work of the ILO could not have developed as it has in recent years if its regular budget had not been substantially supplemented by money from other sources. The policy of receiving large extra-budgetary funds was initiated in 1950, when the Governing Body accepted an offer made by a number of members of the ILO who were also members of the Organisation for European Economic Co-operation to provide approximately one million dollars. In the following year large resources began to be placed at its disposal annually under the Expanded Programme of Technical Assistance. In addition, during 1960 operations began under the United Nations Special Fund for Economic Development. In 1969, mainly from these two Funds (UNDP/TA and UNDP/SF) merged in the United Nations Development Programme, over 24 million dollars was estimated to be available to the ILO, for financing technical co-operation programmes. A table showing annual expenditure on technical co-operation each year since 1950 will be found in the Reference section.

Finally, two bodies set up by the ILO and operating under its auspices draw their income largely from funds external to the regular ILO budget. The International Institute for Labour Studies is financed substantially from an endowment fund contributed by governments, employers' and workers' organisations and other donors. The International Centre for Advanced Technical and Vocational Training depends for its resources mainly on specially-contributed funds.

10. STANDARD-SETTING

STANDARD-SETTING is the first of the three functions of the ILO, all of which are closely interrelated.

When, after the first ten years of the ILO, a chronicle of the first decade was published it contained the following sentence: "The functions of the International Labour Organisation can be summed up in two words: legislation and information."[1]

At that time, it was a correct and complete enumeration of the functions of the Organisation. In the original Constitution only two main functions were explicitly assigned to the Organisation, although they were not specified to be exclusive of other possible functions.

In the first place, the International Labour Conference was to adopt International Labour Conventions and Recommendations, which, in a sense to be defined later, would constitute a body of international labour legislation. This is the legislative or standard-setting function.

In the second place, the International Labour Office was charged with the duty of collecting and distributing information on all subjects relating to the international adjustment of conditions of industrial life and labour. This is the research and information function.

When the Constitution was revised in 1946, a third main function was added. It was provided that, subject to such directions as the Governing Body may give, the Office will accord to governments at their request all appropriate assistance within its power in connection with the framing of laws and regulations on the basis of the decisions of the Conference and the improvement of administrative practices and systems of inspection. This is the technical assistance or operational function.

While there is an essential continuity in the work of the Organisation throughout the whole of its existence, a significant change of emphasis occurred after the war. When David A. Morse was appointed Director-General in 1948 he took the view that, in the spirit of the new orientation given to the Organisation by the revised Constitution and particularly by the Declaration of Philadelphia it would be desirable for the Organisation to respond to the demands of member States for direct assistance in the solution of their social and industrial problems; the Organisation had to develop a practical operational approach.

[1] *The International Labour Organisation: the First Decade*, 1931, p. 68.

These three functions are closely interrelated, both in the rendering of service to individual States and in the international work of the ILO.

When individual governments need guidance in developing social policy and legislation designed to promote the welfare of the working populations in their countries they are able to obtain help from the standards set in Conventions and Recommendations and from the publications of the ILO. When they need further individualised help in setting up administrative machinery and in putting into effect policies for improving the skills, earning capacity and living standards of their workers, they are able to call upon the ILO for practical technical assistance. In providing such individualised technical assistance the ILO experts benefit from the background afforded by the International Labour Code and the ILO publications.

In the international work of the ILO, the three functions are also closely inter-related. Many of the technical and regional meetings convened by the ILO have devoted attention to operational questions, and have advised how the ILO can best provide technical assistance in particular fields or in particular regions. Many ILO regional technical assistance projects have originated as a result of discussions at such regional conferences. Conversely, the operational programme has been influencing the publications programme and also the work of the Conference. More publications of the "manual" type have been issued, designed to be of practical usefulness to government officials and employers and workers. In the Conference, not only has much attention been devoted to technical assistance policy and programmes, but a more practical approach to the discussion of other problems has sometimes been manifested.

In recent years increasing emphasis has been laid on the adoption of educational or promotional methods by the ILO. When in 1958 the Director-General submitted to the Conference a review of the response of the ILO to world developments in the previous decade, together with a forward look at the future, he drew special attention to the importance of the educational approach.

To some extent, indeed, all the activities of the ILO are educational. The standard-setting work involves the education of wide sectors of opinion in the understanding, acceptance and implementation of these standards. The operational activities offer education, training and advice in the acquisition of know-how and technical skills. The research activities provide, through the wide distribution of ILO publications, the basic documentation for educational programmes, aiming at balanced social and economic development.

But the recent emphasis on the educational or promotional aspect of the ILO's responsibilities goes further. It has led to new approaches in promoting labour–management relations, workers' education and management development, and in contributing to the strengthening of labour administration and institutions of social organisation. Still further progress in this direction is being made as a result of the setting up by the ILO of the International Institute of Labour Studies, and of the International Centre for Advanced Technical and Vocational Training.

International Labour Legislation

In the early days of the ILO much emphasis was laid on its function in building up a body of international labour legislation.

But the term "international labour legislation" is open to misinterpretation, and when reference is made to the legislative function of the Conference, it is particularly necessary to be clear as to what is meant. The Conference is not legislative in the sense that a national parliament is legislative. Its decisions do not have immediate force of law in any country. The powers of the Conference may more properly be called quasi-legislative or pre-legislative.

When the original Constitution was being drafted at the Paris Peace Conference in 1919 proposals were made that the International Labour Conference should be given full legislative powers. The French and Italian delegations in particular supported the workers' claims that the Conference should be a legislative assembly in the fullest sense of the term, adopting laws which would be obligatory upon all the members of the Organisation. Very wisely, as experience has proved, most of the delegations took the view that the attribution of such supra-national powers to the Conference would not be accepted by the majority of States as consistent with the exercise of their sovereignty. The Constitution therefore limited the basic obligation of members to the submission by them of Conventions and Recommendations to the national competent authority (in most cases the legislature) for the enactment of legislation or other action.

Under the Constitution, therefore, none of the decisions of the Conference have compulsory effect, and no member is under any obligation to ratify them. Nevertheless, the special provisions relating to the procedure of the Conference in the adoption of its decisions constitute an important step forward as compared with the procedure of former diplomatic conferences. The significance of this advance is often overlooked.

In the procedure of the Conference the concept of unanimity which had previously appeared to be the necessary corollary of the sovereign rights of States was definitely set aside. No member has a right of veto at any stage in the procedure leading to the adoption of a Convention or a Recommendation.

When the Governing Body draws up the agenda of a session of the

Conference, its decisions are taken by a simple majority. If a member objects to the inclusion of any item on the agenda it has a right of appeal to the Conference, but the Conference can decide by a two-thirds majority to keep the question on the agenda. Similarly, when a final vote is being taken on a Convention or Recommendation a hostile vote by one member cannot force a negative decision, because in this case also the rule of the two-thirds majority has been substituted for the rule of unanimity.

Further, the obligations imposed upon States under the Constitution are identical whether its government has voted for or against the decisions. No matter how its delegates have voted, all governments are bound to submit the Conventions or Recommendations adopted by a two-thirds majority of the delegates to their national competent authorities. The government has the right to propose to its competent authority that no action be taken on a Convention of Recommendation against which it has voted, but it cannot simply ignore it.

If care is taken to avoid claiming for the corpus of ratified Conventions a value and importance greater than is warranted by their legal status, the use of the term "international labour legislation" is justified by the facts. The position was well put by the Conference Delegation on Constitutional Questions, on the basis of whose report the Constitution was revised in 1946, in the following passage: "The 902 ratifications of the 67 Conventions so far adopted which, despite the immense difficulties created during the last fifteen years by the depression, the rise of totalitarian aggression, and the second world war, have been registered by 50 countries since 1920, represent a more far-reaching network of international obligations than have been created in any other field of social or economic policy."[2]

Sometimes, instead of the term "international labour legislation", the expression "International Labour Code" is employed. Although "International Labour Code" began to be used in the early days of the Organisation, it did not come into general currency until 1941, when the Office published, under the title "The International Labour Code, 1939" a codification of the Conventions and Recommendations. This was followed by a second edition, amplified and brought up to date, entitled "The International Labour Code, 1951". The latter work presents in an orderly and convenient form the provisions of the 100 Conventions and 92 Recommendations which had at that time been adopted by the Conference. With the annual addition of new Conventions and Recommendations the Code gradually became a more comprehensive and interdependent whole.[3]

The International Labour Code is a code of standards. In terms which

[2] *Report II* (1), *Constitutional Questions*, Int. Lab. Conf., 1946, p. 37.
[3] *See* Francis Wolf: *L'interdépendance des conventions internationales du travail*, 1968.

are bold, but not unjustifiably so, the Director-General claims, in a foreword to the volume: "These standards have now been one of the main formative influences on the development of social legislation in many countries for three decades. When the fullest allowance has been made for all the limitations of what has been achieved there has been nothing comparable to this achievement in the whole course of human history."[4]

How have these Results been Attained?

A large part of the success of the standard-setting work of the Conference is due on the one hand to the wise selection by the Governing Body of items for the agenda, and on the other hand to the careful documentary preparations undertaken by the Office.

The Governing Body has always taken very seriously its duty of selecting the items for the agenda of the Conference. Experience has shown that if a question is placed on the agenda before it is sufficiently mature for international consideration, the Conference is unlikely to succeed in adopting a Convention or Recommendation. On the other hand, if the Governing Body waited to place an item on the agenda until there was one hundred per cent certainty that a Convention or Recommendation could be adopted the Organisation would tend to become a sort of recording machine of progress rather than an initiator of progress.

A wise choice of the right items for the agenda of a Conference to be held eighteen months ahead always involves a careful balancing and evaluation of many factors. This balancing and evaluation has to be effected by a tripartite body, representative of governments, employers and workers from countries of different regions of the world and of different stages of economic and social development.

Although it rarely happens that the Governing Body's decisions on the items to be placed on the agenda of the Conference are unanimous, the decisions are loyally accepted by the minority, whether that minority is composed of employers' members or workers' members or government members or of members from two or more groups. It is only on the rarest occasions that a government has availed itself of its right under the Constitution to appeal to the Conference against the inclusion of an item on its agenda. The most important instance of this was in 1921, when the French Government moved (unsuccessfully) the deletion from the agenda of all the items concerning agriculture.

In addition to the normal procedure under which the agenda of the Conference is determined by the Governing Body, the Constitution empowers the Conference itself, by a two-thirds majority, to place a

[4] *The International Labour Code, 1951*, ILO, 1952, p. VI.

question on the agenda of its following session. Except, however, to provide for the second discussion of an item under the double-discussion procedure, this power has very rarely been used. From the outset the Conference has recognised that it is in many ways ill fitted to select a new question for inclusion on its agenda; it has been satisfied to leave the determination of its agenda to the Governing Body.

As soon as the agenda of the Conference has been fixed, the Office starts the documentary preparation. The procedure is not defined in the Constitution, and it has gradually been modified and adjusted in the light of experience. The history of the procedural developments does not indicate any instability in the Organisation or any desire to make a change for change's sake. The evolution may have been a discontinuous evolution, but it has always been evolution and not either revolution or regression. As the historian looks back over the experience of fifty years, he can identify three clear principles, firstly, to ensure the most thorough preparatory technical objective study of the questions under consideration; secondly, to provide for the fullest preliminary consultation of governments; and thirdly, to safeguard the authority and continuity of the work of the Conference.

The Conference now normally proceeds to a discussion at two succeeding sessions of questions placed on its agenda with a view to the adoption of international regulations. While the detailed rules governing the procedure of discussion in the Conference have frequently been amended, the basic principle has remained unchanged since the first session. That principle is that the Conference normally refers each item on its agenda to a tripartite committee consisting of government, employers' and workers' members for consideration and report back to it; the final decision being taken by the Conference itself in plenary sitting after consideration of the Committee's report.

The standard-setting decisions of the Conference take the form either of Conventions or of Recommendations. From the constitutional and legal standpoint there is a fundamental difference between the two types of decision. Conventions are designed as obligation-creating instruments. On the other hand Recommendations are designed as guidance-providing instruments. In other words, after Conventions have been ratified by governments, they become binding international obligations, whereas Recommendations are essentially guides to national action without the creation of international obligations. The number of ratifications required to bring a Convention into force is fixed in every case by the terms of the Convention; in the great majority of cases any two ratifications are sufficient.

In the course of the history of the Organisation frequent discussions have taken place on the relative appropriateness of Conventions and Recommendations for dealing internationally with various types of question. Perhaps the best concise survey of the matter is contained in the report of the Conference Delegation on Constitutional Questions, on the basis of which the Constitution of the Organisation was revised in 1946.

"The obligations resulting from ratified Conventions have a number of functions the relative importance of which varies from one case to another. In addition to giving a certain stability to the main outlines of social legislation, thereby strengthening the forces of social progress, and giving a social content to the law of nations which promises a great accession of needed strength to the growing world community, they also fulfil a variety of more immediately tangible and measurable purposes. When ratified and applied, they constitute codes of fair international competition; they afford protection for workers employed in countries other than their own; they furnish the necessary legal basis for the international co-ordination of placing arrangements and social services; they resolve conflicts of laws and conflicts of jurisdiction in regard to the application of social legislation; they create rights of an international character, such as the pension rights of migrant workers, which could not be effectively established by action of any one country; they make possible reforms, like the marking of the weight on heavy packages transported by vessels, which it is impossible to make effective without concerted action by a number of countries.

"Recommendations, like Conventions, are designed to fulfil a variety of purposes. In some cases the principal objective of a Recommendation is the creation of a measure of international uniformity as regards matters in respect of which such uniformity is desirable; the promotion of such uniformity by a Recommendation may facilitate the acceptance at a later date of international obligations where such are desirable, and in other cases may make the acceptance of such obligations for the purpose of ensuring uniformity unnecessary, and thus secure some of the advantages of the existence of a network of obligations, while preserving greater freedom of national action. In some cases a Recommendation is primarily a contribution to the creation of a common social consciousness extending beyond frontiers; the imperfect development of such a consciousness hitherto would seem to have been the characteristic weakness of the international community as a community. Frequently the main function of a Recommendation is to contribute to the wise handling of social and labour problems as national problems by the formulation in an authoritative manner of standards or principles which embody conclusions drawn from the experience of a large number of countries, supplemented by research into new problems and a careful evaluation of new aspirations and the practicability of giving effect to them."[5]

Although at various times it has been proposed that either the Convention technique or the Recommendation technique should be abandoned, there has always been a strong consensus of opinion in favour of maintaining them both.

Flexibility

At the first session of the Conference special provisions relating to India, Japan, China, Persia and Siam were included in four of the Conventions. In the Hours of Work (Industry) Convention, for example, designed to secure an 8-hour working day and a 48-hour working week, provision was made for specified modifications for Japan, and a 60-hour week for India; the Convention did not apply to China, Persia and Siam, but provisions limiting hours of work in those countries were to be considered at a future Conference.

Although special clauses for Asian countries are contained in twelve ILO Conventions, the practice was soon abandoned. For that there were two main reasons. Changes in political and economic conditions rendered it increasingly difficult to secure the general approval of the Conference for differing standards for different parts of the world. Further, the national pride of the developing countries has made them increasingly reluctant to seek the inclusion of derogatory provisions in the Conventions.

In these circumstances the flexibility required by the continued existence in the world of wide differences in the conditions determining economic and social policy has had to be secured in other ways. In recent years new expedients have therefore been devised. Some Conventions contain optional or alternative parts and provide that members, when ratifying, shall make declarations indicating the extent of the obligations which they undertake by ratification. Certain Conventions permit the substitution by specified countries of a prescribed standard lower than the normal standard laid down in the Convention, provided the member makes an appropriate declaration when ratifying the Convention. Other Conventions give the parties a limited discretionary power to except sparsely populated or otherwise underdeveloped areas from all or certain of their provisions. In some cases a degree of latitude is given to governments in the methods of application, which can be appropriate to national conditions (legislation, collective agreements, and so on). Sometimes the flexibility is achieved through including only statements of principle in a Convention, supplemented by more precise and detailed standards in a Recommendation.

[5] *Report II (I), Constitutional Questions*, Int. Lab. Conf., 1946, pp. 36–38.

With the exception of certain instruments on fundamental human rights, almost all the Conventions adopted since 1946 contain flexible formulae of one kind or another.

An example of flexibility is provided in the Wages, Hours of Work and Manning Convention (Revised), 1958. That Convention, which contains six Parts, permits exclusion of Part II (wages), but any member making a declaration of exclusion must supply information showing the basic monthly wages of an able seaman in a vessel to which the Convention applies. Two further elements of flexibility are supplied by a provision that (a) a member making a declaration of exclusion may subsequently notify the Director-General that it accepts Part II, and (b) while the declaration of exclusion remains in force the member may declare its willingness to accept Part II as having the force of a Recommendation.

By providing in these and other ways for options, alternatives and adjustments, the ILO is increasingly attempting to take account in realistic fashion of the differences between its members in respect of economic, industrial and social development.

A further element of flexibility in its standard-setting work is provided by the power of the Organisation to revise Conventions and Recommendations. This power was not explicitly conferred by the Constitution, but clearly follows from the power to adopt Conventions or Recommendations. There are two main reasons why Conventions have been revised.

In some cases experience has shown that ratification of Conventions has been prevented by provisions in a Convention of minor importance or provisions the terms of which were drafted with unnecessary rigidity. In such cases revision has been undertaken in order to remove these obstacles to ratification while maintaining the essential prescriptions of the Convention. An example of such revision is the Protection against Accidents (Dockers) Convention, adopted in 1929 and revised in 1932.

In other cases progress over the years in a particular field of labour legislation has made it possible to raise the standards embodied in Conventions. An example of such revision is the Minimum Age (Sea) Convention adopted in 1920 and revised in 1936.

The ILO has used with discretion its power to revise Conventions. It does not show any repugnance to revising Conventions where revision is clearly desirable to remove obstacles to implementation or to enable Conventions to keep pace with the world they serve.

By 1969 the total number of standard-setting instruments adopted by the Conference in the course of its 53 sessions amounted to 130 Conventions and 134 Recommendations. Of the 130 Conventions, 25 adapt earlier ones to take account of the passage of time or the lessons of experience.

Lists of Conventions and Recommendations will be found in the Reference section.

Obligations of Member States

When delegates leave the Conference do they conveniently forget about it and fail to implement in their own countries the provisions of the Conventions and Recommendations adopted? In reply to this question, it is worth examining in some detail the obligations which members assume.

The obligations of members in respect of Conventions and Recommendations are precisely defined in the Constitution. Each member undertakes that it will, within the period of one year at most from the closing of the Session of the Conference, or if it is impossible owing to exceptional circumstances to do so within the period of one year, then at the earliest practicable moment and in no case later than eighteen months from the closing of the Session of the Conference, bring the Convention or Recommendation before the authority or authorities within whose competence the matter lies for the enactment of legislation or other action. This basic obligation, laid down in the original Constitution, was not altered when the Constitution was revised in 1946.

The other obligations were substantially clarified and amplified in the revised Constitution.

These obligations are as follows:

(a) Members shall inform the Director-General of the measures taken to bring Conventions and Recommendations before the competent authority or authorities, with particulars of the authority or authorities regarded as competent and of the action taken by them.

(b) If a Convention fails to obtain the consent of the competent authority no further obligation shall rest upon the member except that it shall report to the Director-General, at appropriate intervals as requested by the Governing Body, the position of its law and practice in regard to the matters dealt with in the Convention and showing the extent to which effect has been given or is proposed to be given to any of the provisions of the Convention by legislation, administrative action, collective agreement or otherwise and stating the difficulties which prevent or delay the ratification of such Convention.

(c) If no legislative or other action is taken to make a Recommendation effective no further obligation shall rest upon the member except that it shall report to the Director-General, at appropriate intervals as requested by the Governing Body, the position of the law and practice in the country in regard to the matters dealt with in the Recommendation and showing the extent to which effect has been given or is proposed to be given to the provisions of the Recommendation and such modifications of these provisions as it has been found or may be found necessary to make in adopting or applying them.

Obligations of Federal States

The Constitutional revision effected in 1946 includes also an important amendment designed to clarify and in some respects to extend the obligations of federal States. When the Constitution was being drafted in 1919 the question of the obligations of federal States proved so difficult as almost to wreck the negotiations for setting up the Organisation. The solution then adopted was to provide that in the case of a federal State whose power to enter into Conventions on labour matters is subject to limitations the government may treat a Convention to which such limitations apply as a Recommendation. The Peace Conference recognised that this solution was not really satisfactory, as it placed federal States under a less degree of obligation than other States, but it recognised also that "the solution is the best possible under the circumstances".

The 1946 solution, also reached after most difficult negotiations, which was embodied in the revised Constitution, specified that in respect of Conventions and Recommendations which the federal government regards as appropriate under its constitutional system for federal action the obligations of the federal State shall be the same as those of other members; and in respect of Conventions and Recommendations which the federal government regards as appropriate in whole or in part for action by the constituent States, provinces or cantons rather than for federal action, the federal government is required (a) to make effective arrangements for the reference of such Conventions and Recommendations to the appropriate federal State, provincial or cantonal authorities for the enactment of legislation or other action; (b) to arrange, subject to the concurrence of the State, provincial or cantonal governments concerned, for periodical consultations between the federal and the State, provincial or cantonal authorities with a view to promoting within the federal State co-ordinated action to give effect to the provisions of such Conventions and Recommendations; and (c) to communicate information to, or send reports to, the Director-General similar to the information and reports sent by other members in respect to the action taken by them and the position of their law and practice.

While the non-federal members of the Organisation appreciated the readiness of the federal States to accept some extension of their obligations, they could not regard this solution as entirely satisfactory, in as much as the obligations of federal States were still not identical with those of the other members. They were obliged to recognise, however, as a basic fact of constitutional law and history, that between the federal form of government on the one hand and the non-federal on the other there are ultimate differences which will always involve lack of identity in respect of the international obligations of these two categories of states. But they drew some consolation from the reflection that the internal constitutional arrangements of federal States are not static and that in many of them the growing complexity of economic and social problems has necessitated a far-reaching extension of federal action, the further development of which might be expected to lessen, in practice, the difference between them and non-federal States relating to their obligations in respect of Conventions.

The adoption by the Conference of all these amendments, both those relating to the obligations of federal States and those relating to the obligations of other members, provided one of the most striking evidences of the growing confidence of governments in the Organisation, after twenty-seven years of its operation, and of their increasing willingness to shoulder fresh burdens. The acceptance of these new obligations is all the more remarkable as some of them were clearly designed to strengthen the system of mutual supervision through the machinery of the ILO.

The System of Mutual Supervision

Of all the innovations made by the Constitution one of the most far-reaching was the system of mutual supervision of the application of ratified Conventions. The early history of national labour legislation had shown that such legislation proved ineffective unless measures were taken to provide machinery for the supervision of its application. But the setting up of international supervisory machinery involved the problem of respect for national sovereignty; when at the Berne Conference of 1906 the first two international labour conventions prepared by the International Association for Labour Legislation were adopted, it was found impossible to agree on the appointment of an international supervisory commission, even with merely consultative functions.

In 1919 the Peace Conference took the bold step of including in the Constitution of the ILO machinery for the supervision of the application of ratified Conventions. In the first place, each of the members agreed to make an annual report to the International Labour Office on the measures which it had taken to give effect to the provisions of Conventions to which it is a party. In addition, there was procedure for complaints, enquiries and sanctions.

When the Constitution was revised in 1946, the system was not altered, except in three respects, all of which are of real historical interest.

In the first place, organisations of employers and workers are enabled to participate more fully in the system, in consequence of a new provision that each member shall communicate to the representative organisations of employers and workers copies of the reports and information communicated to the Director-General.

In the second place, the provisions concerning the imposition of economic sanctions contained in the original Constitution are deleted, as the experience of the League of Nations showed that such economic sanctions were ineffective, and a general provision is substituted to the effect that in the event of any member failing to carry out the recommendations of a Committee of Enquiry or the International Court of Justice the Governing Body may recommend to the Conference such action as it may deem wise and expedient to secure compliance.

Finally, the importance of reliance upon due process of law is emphasised by a new provision enabling the Conference to appoint a tribunal for the expeditious settlement of any dispute or question relating to the interpretation of a Convention.

Such is the constitutional framework of the system of mutual supervision.

Implementation of the System

In marked contrast to the boldness of the constitutional provisions was the caution of the early approach of the Organisation to their implementation. There was, indeed, one lacuna in the Constitution; it provided that a summary of the reports on the application of Conventions should be communicated to the Conference, but it did not say what the Conference should do with them. In fact the Conference, at its first few sessions, did practically nothing with them. For this inactivity there were two reasons. On the one hand, it was difficult for the Conference, in a session of three or four weeks, to undertake, in addition to its special agenda, a detailed and careful scrutiny of these reports, the number of which was rapidly increasing. On the other hand, and perhaps more important, was the realisation by the Conference that the whole question of mutual supervision was full of dynamite, and their consequent disinclination to touch it.

Be that as it may, it was not until 1926 that the Conference took steps to deal with the situation. When, however, it had at last made up its mind to seize the nettle, it seized it firmly. It recommended that in future each session of the Conference should appoint a special Committee to examine the reports presented under the Constitution; it also invited the Governing Body to consider appointing a Committee of Experts to carry out a preliminary study of the reports. This procedure was put into practice in the following year, and has been maintained ever since.

There are two successive phases: first, an examination of the reports by a Committee of Experts of an advisory character, which submits its observations to the Governing Body; in the next place, an examination by a Committee of the Conference, which has before it the summary of the reports of the governments prepared by the Office as well as the report of the Committee of Experts. The report of the Conference Committee, which has been called the "conscience of the ILO", is submitted to the Conference.

Since the war, fortified by the new provisions of the revised Constitution, the system of mutual supervision has become more and more firmly established and more and more effective. To say that it has become more and more effective does not mean that it has ever approached even the neighbourhood of one hundred per cent effectiveness.[6]

Every year the two Committees record in their reports the progress made in the operation of the machinery of mutual supervision. The picture is always in chiaroscuro, a blend of light and shade. Nevertheless, the Committees have been able to point to many cases in which, as a result of their observations, governments have taken action to bring their national legislation into line with the international standards.

The question may be asked, to what extent can the ILO put pressure on governments to ratify Conventions, or when ratified to observe them? The word "pressure" is never used in the ILO. Nevertheless, influence can be, and is, exercised. For example, the observance by States of the constitutional obligation to submit Conventions and Recommendations within a year or in exceptional cases eighteen months to the competent authority for enactment of legislation or other action was at first extremely unsatisfactory. As a result of continued action since 1948 by ILO supervisory bodies, the position, while not yet satisfactory, has definitely improved, and now about half the States members usually comply with the prescribed limits.

In regard to the influence exerted by the supervisory bodies to bring national legislation into conformity with Conventions ratified by them, it has been noted that over the past six years more than 450 discrepancies have been eliminated as a result of intervention by these two bodies. A general assessment of the effectiveness of the procedure was made in a recent survey[7] of the cases – totalling several thousand – dealt with by the

---

[6] *See* N. Valticos: *Un système de contrôle international: la mise en oeuvre des conventions internationales du travail*, 1969.

[7] E. A. Landy: *The Effectiveness of International Supervision. Thirty Years of ILO Experience*, 1966.

supervisory bodies over thirty years. It showed that in three-quarters of the cases no discrepancy was found to exist. In the other cases where discrepancies were detected, the proportion in which governments took action to eliminate them, completely or partially, exceeded sixty per cent.

A case in which comments of the Committee of Experts were followed by national action is provided by the report of the United Kingdom Court of Inquiry into certain matters concerning the Shipping Industry (Cmnd. 3211, 1967). Following comments by the Committee of Experts concerning provisions of the Merchant Shipping Act, 1894, laying down penal sanctions for various breaches of discipline among seamen, the provisions of the Merchant Shipping Act were reviewed by a Court of Inquiry under Lord Pearson. The Court's final report made detailed and far-reaching recommendations for amendment of the Merchant Shipping Act, including the provisions that were the subject of the comments by the Committee of Experts.

Further, under the provision of the Constitution relating to the reporting by governments of the position in law and practice in their countries in respect of unratified Conventions and of Recommendations, the observations made by the Committee of Experts have led in a number of cases to action by the government to ratify or at least to give effect to some of their provisions.

In addition to action by the supervisory bodies, special machinery was set up in 1950 to protect freedom of association, and action has been taken under Article 26 of the Constitution to appoint Commissions of Enquiry. A further development occurred in 1968 with the appointment of a study group of independent persons to examine the labour and trade union situation in Spain. As all the action taken under these procedures has related either to freedom of association or forced labour, details will be found in the chapter on Human Rights.

The development of supervisory procedures bears witness on the one hand to the continuing need for supervision, and on the other to the determination of the ILO to encourage and stimulate governments to implement the international standards. Despite their special features, the supervisory procedures are alike in having recourse to semi-judicial methods, associated with independent persons whose impartiality ensures the confidence essential if any form of international supervision is to be effective.

The difficulty of ascertaining and assessing results in terms of practical application has prompted the suggestion, made more than once in the Conference and elsewhere, that only through an international system of labour inspection could the effect given by states to their international obligations in the field of labour law be adequately supervised. Reflection on the political and administrative implications of the suggestion has always led to the conclusion that the world is not yet ready for such a development. The ILO has, however, been active in emphasising the importance of adequate national systems of labour inspection and in providing guidance to governments on practical methods of organisation and administration.

Results Achieved

From the outset it has been recognised that the first, though not the only, yardstick for measuring the results of the standard-setting work of the Organisation is the number of ratifications registered. After a slow start progress became more rapid, and continued steadily until the outbreak of the war. By 1926 over 200 ratifications had been registered, by 1932 over 500, and by 1938 over 800. During the war, as was to be expected, ratifications were brought almost to a standstill. Immediately after the war ratifications began to flow in, and succeeding years witnessed a sustained increase. The 900 mark was passed in 1946, the 1,000 mark in 1949, the 1,100 mark in 1950, the 1,300 mark in 1952, the 1,500 mark in 1955, the 2,000 mark in 1960, and the 3,000 mark in 1965. By 1 December 1969 over 3,500 ratifications had been registered coming from 120 States. While that is an imposing total, it works out as an average of only 29 per State. Details of ratifications will be found in the Reference section.

The number of ratifications varies widely according to the country and the Convention. For example, 25 countries have each ratified at least 40 Conventions, 16 countries at least 50 and 8 countries over 60 (France, with 80, is the country with the most ratifications), while 15 countries have ratified fewer than 10 Conventions. The average number of ratifications is 45 for the West European countries, 39 for the East European countries, 31 for the American countries, 23 for the African countries, 19 for the Middle Eastern countries, 16 for the other countries of Asia and 36 for Oceania (Australia and New Zealand).

Similarly, the number of ratifications varies according to the Convention. Thirty-two Conventions have received at least 40 ratifications, 23 at least 50 and 13 at least 60. The six Conventions which are regarded as being more directly concerned with fundamental human rights have received on average 85 ratifications and one of them has even passed the hundred mark.

In addition to these ratifications, Conventions have, under Article 35 of the Constitution, been the subject of a large number of declarations regarding their application to non-metropolitan territories. As these have become independent and joined the ILO, they have as a rule confirmed that they remained bound by the obligations previously accepted on their behalf by the State responsible for their international relations. The same has been true of States which have been formed by breaking away from other States; 655 ratifications on behalf of 45 States have been registered in this way.

Since the war, the influence of standards has been particularly noteworthy in newly independent countries. As the Minister of Labour and Social Welfare of Malaya told the Conference in 1958: "Whenever labour legislation is contemplated or any changes are considered, our first thought is always: 'What do ILO Conventions say on the matter?'." Or, as the Secretary of Labour of the Philippines said in 1955, his government was implementing a set of labour laws, "most of them patterned after ILO Conventions".

In any survey of ratifications one black point stands out prominently; perhaps it would be better to call it a red point – for danger. That is the number of countries which have neglected their obligations almost completely. The Conference is becoming more and more alive to the importance of stimulating the social conscience of the more reluctant countries, and at recent sessions pressing appeals have been made to members to translate into positive action the obligations imposed by membership of the ILO.

While ratification affords the most tangible indication of the impact of the international labour code on national law and practice, this is by no means the only evidence. Even when a Convention is not ratified by a particular country, it may still exercise an influence in that country; some of its provisions may be applied in new legislation or in fresh collective agreements. Further, although Recommendations are not subject to ratification, their influence on national law and practice may be widespread and substantial. Two examples may be given, one a Convention, the other a Recommendation. Although the Washington Hours Convention was poorly ratified, it exerted a powerful influence in the 1920's and 1930's in securing the generalisation and maintenance in industrial undertakings of the eight-hour day and forty-eight-hour week. The Seamen's Welfare in Ports Recommendation, 1936, has determined the whole pattern of seamen's welfare organisation in many countries.

Since the 1946 revision of the Constitution imposed on governments the obligation to report on unratified Conventions and Recommendations fuller information has become available on the effectiveness of the standard-setting work of the Organisation.

While collective agreements are more frequently used to give effect to Recommendations than to Conventions, cases are found where collective agreements or regulations made by bodies on which employers and workers are represented are used, sometimes in conjunction with legislation, in the application of Conventions. For example, in the United Kingdom under the Merchant Shipping Act, 1948, which enabled five maritime Conventions to be ratified, collective agreements are associated to a limited extent with their application, and the Holidays with Pay (Agriculture) Convention, 1952, is implemented by Wages Orders of the Agricultural Wages Board, a statutory body composed of employers' and workers' representatives and independent members.

Ratification of a Convention does not necessarily mean that any real influence has been exerted in the country concerned. National legislation may have been in conformity with, or even in advance of, the provisions of the Convention when it was adopted. Even when amendments have been introduced in national legislation or new legislation has been adopted subsequent to the adoption of a Convention which bring national legislation into conformity with the Convention, it may not follow that the Convention has in fact exercised influence. The argument *post hoc, ergo propter hoc* must always be distrusted.

Since 1955 the ILO has been publishing in the *International Labour Review* a series of articles analysing the influence exerted by ILO standards on legislation in countries representing a wide range of political and economic development.[8] The study on the United Kingdom, published in 1968, assembles substantial evidence of solid and enduring influence exerted by ILO standards in that country.

Although, throughout the world, ratifications have attained a considerable total, much still requires to be done to render the ratification situation completely satisfactory. The Committee of Experts on the Application of Conventions and Recommendations has devoted continuous attention to

---

[8] *See* N. Valticos: "The influence of international labour Conventions on Greek legislation", Vol. LXXI, No. 6, June 1955, p. 593; V. K. R. Menon: "The influence of international labour Conventions on Indian labour legislation", Vol. LXXIII, No. 6, June 1956, p. 551; A. Berenstein: "The influence of international labour Conventions on Swiss legislation", Vol. LXXVII, No. 6, June 1958, p. 495; "The influence of international labour Conventions on Nigerian legislation", Vol. LXXXII, No. 1, July 1960, p. 26; Luisa Riva-Sanseverino: "The influence of international labour Conventions on Italian labour legislation", Vol. LXXXIII, No. 6, June 1961, p. 576; Karl Nandrup Dahl: "The influence of ILO standards on Norwegian legislation", Vol. XC, No. 3, Sept. 1964, p. 226; Amor Abdeljaouad: "The influence of international labour Conventions on Tunisian legislation", Vol. 91, No. 3, Mar. 1965, p. 191; Jan Rosner: "The influence of international labour Conventions on Polish legislation", Vol. 92, No. 5, Nov. 1965, p. 353; Ratko Pešić: "International labour standards and Yugoslav legislation", Vol. 96, No. 5, Nov. 1967, p. 443; G. A. Johnston: "The influence of international labour standards on legislation and practice in the United Kingdom", Vol. 97, No. 5, May 1968, p. 465; and L.-E. Troclet and E. Vogel-Polsky: "The influence of international labour Conventions on Belgian labour legislation", Vol. 98, No. 5, Nov. 1968, p. 389.

the reasons which have prevented ratification of certain Conventions by particular countries; in 1969 its examination of the problem was published under the title, "The Ratification Outlook after Fifty Years: Seventeen Selected Conventions". These seventeen Conventions are representative of the major areas of ILO concern; they also illustrate the impact of standard-setting throughout the five decades of the ILO existence.

After reviewing the results of this examination, the Committee states, as one of its conclusions, "As the ILO enters its second half-century of existence, this survey confirms two definite trends: at the international level the range and content of the International Labour Code have further expanded and efforts have been made to develop techniques facilitating the gradual implementation of ratified Conventions; at the national level, measures tending towards fuller compliance with Conventions and, where possible, their ratification testify to the continued vitality of the Organisation's standard-setting activities."[9]

[9] *Op. cit.*, Geneva, 1969, para. 325.

11. RESEARCH AND INFORMATION

THE research and information function of the ILO, like its standard-setting function, had its roots in the past. In 1901, when the International Association for Labour Legislation set up the first International Labour Office at Basle, it did so in the belief that this Office could do valuable work by collecting and publishing information on labour legislation.

The activities of the Basle Office, and especially its translations of labour laws, were well known to many members of the Commission on International Labour Legislation of the Paris Peace Conference and they had no hesitation in including an information function among the duties of the new International Labour Office to be set up by the Peace Conference.

Collection of Information

From the outset the collection of information involved the co-ordination of the work of a group of departments in the ILO for some of which information collection was their sole or most important function, for others a subsidiary or ancillary function.

The first of these departments was naturally the library. The nucleus of the library of the ILO was formed by the library set up at Basle, consisting principally of publications contributed by public administrative bodies. Subsequently the ILO also acquired the library of the International Association against Unemployment at Ghent.

The most important function of the library has always been to act as a circulating agency within the Office. It is not merely a receptacle into which books and periodicals are deposited. It is definitely a workshop library.

The Central Library and Documentation Branch, as it is now called, receives over 6,000 periodicals and 10,000 books every year; it issues daily within the Office a list of bibliographical references, keeps the card-index catalogues up to date, and supplies publications on loan to officials as required.

In addition to fulfilling its primary function, the library has become a centre to which research students interested in labour and industrial questions resort for study. Long ago Bergson emphasised that in the case of all scientific work it is indispensable to constitute a number of centres where there is a certainty of finding all the publications on any particular subject. In its own sphere the ILO has attempted to become the international centre with the completest collection of books, pamphlets and periodicals in its particular field.

The ILO also gives favourable consideration to applications to undertake research in its archives from professors, graduate students and other responsible persons. Archives have sometimes been called "by-products of administration". In the ILO, files originally created to keep correspondence properly arranged and readily available for reference are, after this "first age" of immediate usefulness, appraised in accordance with a records retirement programme, and either destroyed or passed for preservation into the archives. There they remain available either for ILO consultation as precedents or for other reference purposes, or for research in virtue of their historical interest or value.

Research

Within the ILO, while research is undertaken by nearly all the departments in the fields for which they are responsible, the Central Research and Planning Department is responsible for keeping a close watch, through its economic and statistical branches, on world developments and trends and, in collaboration with other departments, preparing policy and programme proposals for submission to the Director-General. Although "research" is nowhere mentioned in the Constitution it early assumed an important place in the information work of the ILO. From the outset the ILO did not confine itself to collecting information; it worked on that information; it became an important research agency.

As the questions with which the Organisation deals are nearly all controversial, it was inevitable that in the early years the research work of the Office sometimes became a target for bitter criticism.

It was unfortunate that the first major research project undertaken by the Office was in a particularly controversial field. This was the Enquiry into Production, authorised by the Governing Body in June 1920. As the preparation of the report proceeded, at session after session of the Governing Body opposition was voiced to the continuation of the enquiry. When the report was published it was seen that the suspicions and fears that had been expressed were groundless; the report was an objective and impartial international study, the value of which was widely recognised when in 1927 the World Economic Conference was convened by the League of Nations.

But the ILO learnt an important lesson from this affair. It learnt that it was not sufficient for its research work to be objective and impartial; on specially controversial questions it should surround itself with outside guarantees. Experience showed that these guarantees could most readily be provided through consultations of committees of experts, with or without tripartite representation of the Governing Body. Whenever a report was to be prepared on some question on which opinion was sharply divided, the Office has since consistently followed the practice of consulting outside experts. Thus, when in the 1950's the question of productivity assumed great importance in the work of the Organisation, the Office was careful to secure the collaboration and advice of committees of experts before publishing reports on the subject.

As the years passed, the objectivity of the research work of the Office was more and more widely recognised. Though the criticism is still sometimes heard that this or that report is subjective, biased or tendentious, such criticism was much more rarely voiced in the 1950's or 1960's than in the 1920's and 1930's.

At a recent ILO Conference one of the government delegates, who had the previous year entered the service of the government of his country after spending some years as an official of the ILO, was asked by a former colleague how he liked government service. "Well," was the reply, "it's terribly difficult to maintain ILO standards of objectivity."

Distribution of Information

The information function of the Organisation was defined in the Constitution as including not only the collection of information but also its distribution. Such distribution can be performed in two ways; on the one hand, by replying to particular requests for information from governments and associations; on the other hand, by issuing publications and giving them a wide circulation.

From the earliest days requests for information reached the Office in large numbers from governments, employers' and workers' organisations, public and private administrations, universities, libraries, philanthropic and other institutions, belonging to most of the members of the Organisation. When governments requested information, they frequently stated that the particulars were required with a view to the preparation of new national laws or administrative measures. In such cases, the Office enabled governments to avoid the expense necessitated by the undertaking of special research. Many requests for information have always come from States which had recently attained to complete sovereignty. In endeavouring to set up a system of labour and industrial legislation, they have found the documentation which the Office was able to supply of the greatest value.

Throughout the first two decades of its existence the work of replying to requests for information constituted a very substantial part of the activity of the Office.

After the war requests for information again began to come to the ILO from governments, employers' and workers' organisations and individuals, and the flow has not ceased. If such requests relate specifically to a matter dealt with by a particular unit in the ILO that request is routed to the unit concerned. In some cases, where this informational activity has become particularly intense, a special unit has been organised.

Of these the most important is the International Occupational Safety and Health Information Centre, commonly known as the CIS. Established in 1959 with the help of the International Social Security Association and West European accident prevention institutions – known as National Centres – the CIS gained the support of WHO. The task of the thirty-three National Centres includes collecting and scrutinising for the CIS the information available in their countries and sending an abstract of each document to Geneva together with a copy of the original publication. The basic activity of CIS is the issue of abstract colour-coded cards relating annually to over 2,000 documents on occupational hazards and their prevention. Since 1963 the abstracts are also reproduced in the monthly "Occupational Safety and Health Abstracts" bulletin which is easier for small and medium-sized undertakings to consult. CIS publications distributed to subscribers have since 1962 been supplemented by information sheets and bibliographies issued at irregular intervals. Organisation of collection and dissemination of information in this particular field has not only forged closer links between the ILO and institutions concerned with prevention of health hazards and accidents but has made the information readily available to industry precisely where the most effective action can be taken to eliminate or reduce such occupational hazards.

The Publications of the ILO

The Editorial and Translation Branch, responsible for editorial, translation, printing and sales, performs the functions of a large publishing house. Its budget for the biennium 1970–71 amounts to over 2·25 million dollars. Full lists of the periodical and other publications issued, together with information on subjects covered, will be found in the Reference section of this book.

While the quality and accuracy of ILO publications are very generally recognised, some are open to the criticism that they are voluminous and diffuse. It is of course essential for the ILO to issue reports that are both factually complete and balanced from the standpoint of policy. In view of these requirements, how to reduce quantity in compilation of facts and limit pros and cons in weighing policy considerations is not an easy problem. Perhaps something might be done in the case of technical reports, in distinction from publications for a wider public, by aiming at a high degree of concise and even terse presentation.

Historically, one of the most interesting features of the publications programme is that, while in the course of the years changes have been made in the character and presentation of individual publications to adapt them to the varying needs of the time, and minor publications have been inaugurated, suspended, merged with others or discontinued, the programme as a whole is virtually the same now as it was in 1921. This continuity has not been due to any reluctance to make changes or to any unwillingness to review the programme. The Governing Body in particular has from time to time undertaken a thorough-going survey of the programme, with a searching analysis of the usefulness of each of the publications. The continuity in the programme has been due above all to the essential soundness of the original conception. When the publications programme was being planned in 1920 a systematic survey was made of the needs to be met by the Organisation in carrying out its essential functions and of the kinds of publications best adapted to meet those needs.

The difficulties involved in carrying out the publications work of the ILO have inevitably been greatly aggravated by the number of languages in which they have had to be produced. The language difficulty suggested to the first Chief of the Scientific Division the following law: "The difficulty of gathering, compiling and publishing information increases with the number of languages involved, not in simple direct ratio, but in the cube of the number of languages involved."

Translation of technical documents is an art, the difficulties of which are not always recognised, and one of the greatest staff difficulties of the Office has been the recruiting and building up of a team of qualified expert translators. An experienced translator has written: "The ordinary translator is a kind of Charon, whose duty it is to transport ideas, which to him are dead, across the waters of Styx. He receives on the one bank gibbering ideas, and when he has ferried them across, it is to a land which to the translator is, after all, merely a land of shades. Only when the translator is an expert interested in his subject does translation cease to be material transportation and become spiritual transfiguration."

In producing its many publications the Office has been animated with the desire to carry out the spirit of its Constitution. The peoples of the world need to be told of each others' success in grappling with the problems of labour and industry. If it is true, as Plato has said, that the man who most benefits the world is he who makes men acquainted with one another, then it may truly be added that the Organisation which most benefits the world is that which lets all countries know of the endeavours, the difficulties, the failures and the successes of others.

It has been increasingly recognised that the ILO also has a duty to inform and educate the public with regard to its aims, its difficulties and its achievements. It has a responsibility to promote its objectives. These objectives cannot be secured solely as a result of the action of governments and employers' and workers' organisations; the effort to attain them must, if it is to succeed, draw its strength from the everyday life of the people. Taking account of this responsibility, the Conference has in recent years included in the budget an appropriation for public information.

The Public Information Branch is responsible for the Press and visual and radio media communiqués, releases, photographs, films, etc., on ILO meetings and other activities; for issuing, in addition to an illustrated periodical, *ILO Panorama*, leaflets, booklets, posters, and other informational material in a great many different languages; and for replying to requests for information on the ILO.

12. OPERATIONAL ACTIVITIES

OPERATIONAL activities include two main types of work, one of which is more direct and immediate than the other. In a national Ministry of Labour, for example, the work of finding employment for workers through employment service offices is one form of operational activity. An operational activity of another kind is the sending of officials to some other country to give advice and assistance in establishing employment service organisation.

In the annals of the ILO, operational activities of the former type have only once been undertaken. Although that adventure brought in its train frustration rather than satisfaction, it has a bearing on at least one chapter of the subsequent history of the Organisation.

Placing Refugees in Employment

After the first world war a High Commissariat for Russian and Armenian refugees was set up under the auspices of the League of Nations with Dr Nansen as High Commissioner. By 1924 it appeared that the political questions involved had been largely settled, and that the principal remaining task was to place the refugees in employment. Dr Nansen suggested that, as the ILO seemed better equipped than any other organisation to carry out that work, the High Commissariat should be transferred to it. In spite of the reluctance of the Governing Body, the Assembly of the League decided to effect the transfer.

Although the ILO did everything in its power to find employment for the refugees, after three years only 50,000 had been placed in employment, mainly in France, Canada, Egypt, Argentina and Paraguay.

In 1929 it was decided to re-transfer responsibility for Russian and Armenian refugees to the High Commission under the auspices of the League. The main reason for this decision was stated as follows in the Report of the Director to the 1929 session of the Conference. "For the refugees who are not yet settled it has become necessary to set up institutions for vocational re-education and above all colonisation. This double work, political and financial in character, could no longer be carried out by the Office."[1]

These words illustrate, in striking fashion, the distance travelled by the

[1] Int. Lab. Conf., Vol. II, Geneva, 1929, p. 32.

Organisation since 1929. If the ILO had been requested by governments in recent years to undertake operational activities involving vocational training and land settlement, it would have had no hesitation in accepting the assignment.

Although the 1929 refusal may appear pusillanimous, it was undoubtedly right in the circumstances of the period. The ILO was still in process of building up its basic legislative and research structure; it had often been accused of exceeding the limits of its competence. At that time the diversion of its energies to direct operational work might have seriously detracted from its ability to establish its position securely in the fields of standard-setting and research.

It was out of its standard-setting and information activities, as a natural growth, that its operational activities in the second sense of the term – technical assistance – were destined to develop.

Origins of Technical Assistance

Although constitutional sanction for the providing of technical assistance was not formally granted until 1946, technical assistance had in fact been given by the ILO from a much earlier date.

As the Conference began to build up an International Labour Code, and the staff of the Office gradually acquired a measure of authority as international experts on various aspects of labour legislation, governments began to turn to the Office for help. If they had difficulty in understanding the precise significance of a provision in a Convention which they proposed to ratify, they requested the Office for an explanation or an interpretation. Some governments went further and communicated to the Office for its comments and advice drafts of national labour legislation which they proposed to introduce, or plans for administrative organisation, for example the setting up or reorganisation of departments of labour, labour inspection services or schemes of social insurance. At first the "technical assistance" afforded by the Office in response to these requests was purely documentary; the Office communicated its observations and advice by letter. Later on governments began to request the Office to send officials to their countries to assist them in assessing the needs for social legislation and in devising appropriate legislative and administrative measures for meeting those needs.

Similarly, in respect of information, as the research programme of the Office developed, governments began to turn to it for information which they needed to guide them in the formulation of new national legislation or the framing of new systems of labour administration. At first all that governments requested was documentary information on the action taken by other governments to regulate this or that problem. Gradually, however, some governments began to go further. They not only asked the Office to provide documentation on what other governments had done; they asked it to bring its international experience to bear on their problems and to suggest solutions which would be appropriate to meet the special circumstances in their countries. It was clear, however, that the suggestions which the Office could give would be more practical if an official of the Office had an opportunity of seeing for himself exactly how the problem presented itself in the particular country. Hence the invitations to the Office to send advisory missions to survey conditions and make suggestions for action by the governments concerned.

Early Development of Technical Assistance

Although the technical assistance function of the ILO thus developed naturally from its legislative and information functions, a decade was required for this development. If the development was natural, why was it so slow? Undoubtedly the essential reason is to be found in the reluctance of governments to do anything that might appear in any way to prejudice their national sovereignty. No government wished to see the ILO interfering or intervening in its affairs, and all were anxious to avoid any situation in which officials of an international organisation coming in as advisers might by their presence or by their actions aggravate social tensions or provoke labour demands. A subsidiary reason lay in distrust of the technical competence of the ILO officials. The ILO had to build up its technical reputation from zero. At first very few of its officials were known outside their own countries. As officials of the Office their work was largely anonymous. It took time for the collective technical competence of the staff to be recognised.

It was not until 1930 that the first technical assistance missions (or "advisory missions", as they were more generally called at that time) were sent out by the ILO. These were missions to advise on schemes of social insurance in Greece and Romania.

From then until the outbreak of the war, a number of advisory missions were carried out, of which the following may be mentioned. 1931, China (organisation of factory inspection); 1932, Egypt (survey of labour conditions and organisation of labour department); 1934, Cuba (organisation of labour department); 1936, United States (social security) and Venezuela (labour code and organisation of labour department); 1937, Morocco (co-operative organisation); 1938, Canada (unemployment insurance) and Venezuela (labour legislation, social insurance and immigration and land settlement); and 1939, Ecuador (social insurance), Egypt (industrial health), Turkey (social insurance) and United Kingdom (workmen's compensation). It will be noted that most of these missions were concerned with social insurance, and that in the case of two countries (Egypt and Venezuela) more than one mission was organised.

When the war broke out and the standard-setting work of the Organisation was stopped and its information work seriously curtailed, the ILO succeeded from its working centre in Montreal in continuing and in some ways intensifying its technical assistance work. Most of this activity was undertaken in the field of social security in North, Central and South America (Bolivia, Canada, Chile, Costa Rica, Haiti, Mexico and Venezuela). Technical assistance on labour statistics was given to Argentina, Brazil, Canada, Chile and Uruguay. Outside the American continent special mention should be made of the missions by ILO officials to the United Kingdom for consultation in connection with the preparation of the Beveridge Report, and to Algiers to co-operate with the French Provisional Government in drafting social legislation.

In the immediate post-war period the Office sent officials on technical assistance missions to Czechoslovakia (social insurance), Egypt (social insurance), Greece (revision of labour legislation), India (social insurance) and Iran (labour legislation and co-operative organisation).

In these early post-war years, as in the pre-war period, the technical assistance work of the ILO was of relatively slight importance, in comparison with its standard-setting and information activities.

Emphasis on Operational Activities

In 1948, when David A. Morse was appointed Director-General, one of his first acts, as has been mentioned elsewhere, was to give a powerful impetus to the technical assistance or operational activities of the Organisation. The Director-General's initiative was warmly welcomed by the Governing Body and the Conference, and the technical assistance or operational function of the ILO rapidly assumed great importance.

The time was indeed ripe for this development. Post-war political and economic changes had brought in their train a series of urgent industrial and labour problems, particularly in countries which had recently achieved independence or were in process of industrialisation. The ILO through its legislative and information work had established a solid foundation of technical equipment to enable it to give practical assistance. The need was there, the means of satisfying the need was there; all that was required was the machinery for bringing into contact those who needed technical assistance and those who could give it.

The necessary machinery could not be provided without money. The regular budget of the Organisation was both limited in amount and inelastic in structure but, thanks to the spirit of comprehension shown by the governments both on the Governing Body and in the Conference, sufficient funds were made available under the regular budget to enable a special operational manpower programme to be launched in 1948.

The Manpower Programme

The operational manpower programme was at first directed toward European problems, but soon extended to other regions as well. The programme covered employment service organisation, vocational guidance and training, and migration. Manpower Field Offices were established in Asia in 1949, in Latin America in 1950, and in the Middle East in 1952, the headquarters Office itself covering Europe. The field offices proved to be a valuable instrument in the execution of the manpower programme and in 1952 their scope was broadened so as to make them general operational field offices.

This operational manpower work had one common characteristic, which distinguished it from operational work carried out subsequently; it consisted of only one form of technical assistance, namely the provision of manpower experts almost all of whom were permanent officials of the ILO. The greatly intensified operational work carried out since 1950 was marked by the engagement of a large number of outside experts for a variety of technical assistance missions.

The Special Migration Programme

In 1950 it proved possible to expand greatly the operational programme in one special field of manpower, namely migration for employment. Impressed by the urgent need to take action to facilitate overseas emigration from European countries with a view to overcoming population surpluses in Europe and population shortages overseas, certain States members of the ILO, also members of the Organisation for European Economic Co-operation, made available to the ILO, outside its regular budget, special funds amounting to approximately one million dollars.

Financed from this source, the Special Migration Programme was largely based on recommendations made by the ILO Preliminary Migration Conference, held in 1950. This programme was co-ordinated with other related activities of the United Nations and specialised agencies, and machinery was set up in the emigration and immigration countries.

The practical experience gained in the field missions and field offices during implementation of the Special Migration Programme (1950–52) was of great value when operational activities increased on a large scale under the Expanded Programme of Technical Assistance.

The Regular Operational Programme

Although the Special Migration Programme and the Expanded Programme were superimposed on the regular operational programme of the ilo and were much wider in scope, the regular programme continued to develop as an essential activity. Since 1950 the ilo has had a modest fellowship programme under its regular budget, and in the 1957 budget provision was made for the first time for a trainee programme.

Most important of all, expert assistance to governments continues to be provided under the regular budget. ilo experts have thus been sent in recent years on fact-finding and advisory missions to Bolivia, Ceylon, Egypt, Greece, India, Iran, Iraq, the Philippines, Turkey and Venezuela and other countries; regional activities have included seminars on social security and other problems.

Beginning in 1956 the budget also makes provision for a programme of workers' education, and from 1960 onwards a management development programme. A rural development programme is also in operation.

Under special arrangements the ilo has afforded technical assistance to the Council of Europe, the European Coal and Steel Community and the Organisation for European Economic Co-operation (replaced in 1961 by the Organisation for Economic Co-operation and Development).

The United Nations Programmes

The Expanded Programme of Technical Assistance for Economic Development of Under-developed Countries, launched in 1950, provided the framework and the financial resources for the bulk of the technical assistance activities not only of the ilo but of the other international organisations associated with the United Nations. The Expanded Programme was based on a resolution of the Economic and Social Council, passed at its ninth session (1950) and subsequently amended. The principles laid down by the Council for the guidance of the participating organisations provide, *inter alia*, that these organisations should regard it as a primary objective to help countries strengthen their national economies through the development of their industries and agriculture with a view to ensuring the attainment of higher levels of economic and social welfare.

In 1959 the Expanded Programme was joined by a partner in the field of technical assistance, the United Nations Special Fund for Economic Development.

Finally, in 1966 the Expanded Programme and the Special Fund were merged to form the United Nations Development Programme. References to projects under these schemes use the abbreviations UNDP/TA and UNDP/SF.

In course of time, as these programmes of technical assistance were implemented, it became clear that the activities concerned should more properly be called "technical co-operation", a term which more truly represents the spirit and character of the operation.

Planning the ILO Programme of Technical Co-operation

In planning the ILO programme the main problems have been to determine what its scope and composition should be; what relative importance should be assigned to projects in the different fields of competence of the ILO; what criteria should be used for determining priorities; and whether the priorities and criteria should be the same for all the regions of the world. Another problem has been to decide to what extent, in view of the resources of the programme, effort should be concentrated or dispersed geographically. It has also been necessary to consider what relative importance should be assigned to the different kinds of assistance – experts, fellowships, group training courses, equipment, etc.

But planning by the ILO has been subject to limiting factors which sometimes militate against a satisfactory balance either by country or by subject. No technical co-operation activity can be undertaken except at the request of a government, and at any given time some countries may ask for much assistance from the ILO and others for very little. Again, a large proportion of the requests from all the countries may be for assistance in one particular field at the same time. Hence, the priorities of governments inevitably – and rightly – condition the ILO's own planning. Further, the ILO is only one of the organisations providing technical co-operation. Finally, there is the restriction imposed by the funds available, which prevents any one organisation from doing all that is requested of it.

Subject to these limitations, the over-riding consideration in the selection of projects for implementation has been their technical soundness and the prospect they offer of making an appreciable and lasting contribution to the balanced economic and social development of the countries concerned.

In the planning of the programme, and particularly in the determination of the policies on which the programme rests, an active part has been played by the Conference and the Governing Body. The Conference gave special consideration to this matter in 1952 in the light of a chapter on "Operational Work and Problems Encountered" in the Director-General's Report, and in 1954 and 1961 on the basis of special reports on Technical

Assistance. In addition, each year the Conference has had before it, in the Director-General's report and the Budget documents, information on the general and financial development of the programme. The Governing Body, for its part, has exercised, through its Technical Assistance Committee, and more recently its Operational Programmes Committee, close supervision over planning and programming.

Implementing the ILO Programme

The first phase of operations under the Programme was characterised by a number of survey missions undertaken at the request of governments to help them in making an assessment of needs and priorities. Thereafter, as a result of this exploratory work, missions have been concerned with advisory activities at the national level or in connection with a pilot scheme or training centre. ILO experts spend a great deal of their time giving practical advice on specific technical and organisational problems in national departments concerned with labour questions, in individual training centres and industrial establishments, and among groups of villagers and handicraftsmen. Their function is not primarily to do the job themselves – though this is often necessary for demonstration purposes – but to train nationals of the countries, especially those in key positions, so that they can themselves operate the new services and in turn train many others in the newly acquired techniques. An ILO expert who had spent two years on a productivity mission in Nicaragua found that the techniques of productivity improvement were known in many undertakings, and books on the subject had been read, but "what they did not know was how to apply these techniques in practice".

The ILO's work under the programme covers nearly all the technical fields falling within its competence. In some of these technical fields far more assistance has been called for and given than in others. Calculated on a basis of expenditure, in 1969 the programme of human resources development, including in particular vocational training, accounted for 82 per cent, social institutions development 12 per cent, improvement of conditions of work and life 5 per cent, and other programmes 1 per cent.

Classified by regions in 1969, also on a basis of expenditure, 40·6 per cent was in Africa, 17·5 per cent in the Americas, 19·4 per cent in Asia, 13·5 per cent in Europe, 5·4 per cent in the Middle East, and 3·6 per cent was on inter-regional projects.

For work on the projects (in 90 countries) the ILO assigned 1,157 experts in 1969.

Statistical and other tables relating to technical co-operation will be found in the Reference section.

Operational Problems

In the administration of the technical co-operation programme many problems have, of course, been encountered.

In the first place, the recruitment of suitable experts has proved to be one of the most difficult problems, as it is certainly one of the most important.

The Economic and Social Council has emphasised the importance of selecting experts who are not only technically qualified but possess the requisite personal and human qualities essential in an international expert. These include: adaptability to strange conditions; readiness to accept hardships; tact in his dealings with government officials and others with whom he has to work; infinite patience in the face of delays and frustrations; an international outlook which will save him from trying to impose his own national experience as the only solution; and a spirit of service towards the people whom he is sent to assist. In addition to these qualities, the expert must have high technical qualifications and usually specific linguistic abilities.

Clearly, to have all these attributes, a man would need to be more than human. The surprising thing is that it has been possible to find men who, with all their defects, have been able to render really effective service. In the fields of competence of the ILO a great many of the experts have been found in the administrative and technical services of governments, although universities and technical and professional institutions have also been a valuable source of recruitment. It is now often possible to obtain the services of experts who have already gained valuable experience in working on projects which have been brought to a successful conclusion.

To an increasing extent, as a result of the successful implementation of the programme, some developing countries have been able to provide, from among their own nationals, experts to be sent to other developing countries. Such experts are not likely to fall into the error sometimes made by experts from industrialised countries of thinking that methods appropriate in a highly developed economy can be applied without modification in a developing economy.

Since the inauguration of the programme, the ILO has recruited experts from over 80 different countries. The largest number have come from the United Kingdom (nearly 500), closely followed by France; other countries providing more than 100 are Belgium, the Federal Republic of Germany and the United States, while from India (a "developing" country) 75 have come.

Experts engaged for short-term projects under the regular budget or UNDP/TA are usually given initial contracts for one year, sometimes for two years. For projects under UNDP/SF which may be planned to continue for up to five years, the initial contract is for one year which may be extended for a further period of up to four years, depending on the planned duration of the project.

In some countries the term "expert" is thought to have a pretentious sound and is therefore disliked. "Specialist" would perhaps be an improvement; technical co-operation "experts" are simply men or women with the special qualifications, skills and abilities required to advise, demonstrate or instruct on a particular matter, whether it be the actuarial basis of a pension scheme or the maintenance of diesel engines.

The criticism is sometimes heard that experts employed on technical co-operation "live in luxury". Luxury is an ambiguous term. If the expert's duties keep him usually in a town with good hotels and houses, he will live on a standard comparable to that to which he has been accustomed in his own country. On the other hand, if his assignment lies mainly in outlying areas he will live and work in somewhat primitive conditions or even in considerable discomfort.

However carefully experts are chosen, experience has shown that they must be adequately briefed if they are to make a success of their assignment. Since the background and experience of most of the experts is primarily national, one of the purposes of briefing is to help them to acquire an international outlook. The process of briefing relates therefore not only to the particular job for which the expert is engaged, but also includes background information on social, economic and political conditions in the country, together with practical hints on pitfalls to be avoided in "getting on" with the people with whom he will be in contact. It is emphasised that he is there on an international mission, and not in any sense as a representative or envoy of the country of which he is a national.

Briefing is a continuous process and does not end with the first visit of the expert to Headquarters or the Regional Office. The ILO keeps in touch with the experts during the course of their assignment, giving them help and guidance as necessary, and officials from the Area Offices visit them for consultations.

A number of difficult operational problems have arisen in awarding fellowships to nationals of developing countries for training abroad. The first type of problem concerns the selection of fellows. Care has to be taken to select them at a level which will enable them to obtain the maximum benefit, both for themselves and for their countries, from the training planned for them. Governments of developing countries, however, are generally short of qualified staff and sometimes find it hard to release the most promising candidates for any long period of study abroad. In some cases also there are language difficulties: candidates otherwise suitable lack the necessary linguistic qualifications to profit from training in the countries whose experience is likely to be most useful to them.

The placement of fellows is arranged by the ILO in close co-operation with the "host" countries. In deciding what "host" country to select for a particular fellow, account has to be taken of the qualifications of the fellow (including knowledge of foreign languages) and of the degree of development in the technical field both in the home country and in the "host" country. It is increasingly difficult to find "host" countries.

There has been considerable criticism of the fellowship side of technical co-operation. Mistakes in selection and placement have been made, and occasionally the fellowship has tended to become a pleasure trip rather than a study tour. In other cases the fellow has found it impossible to adapt himself to conditions in the "host" country.

In 1968, 1,053 fellowships and study grants were awarded.

The worker-trainee programme may be considered as a specialised aspect of the fellowship programme. It makes provision for placing foremen and skilled workers in industrial establishments abroad for training. Experience has shown that certain conditions must be fulfilled if a scheme is to give results of real value, in particular the trainees must have the basic skill and knowledge to enable them to absorb supplementary training rapidly, and there must be a reasonable assurance that on return to their countries the trainees will have an opportunity to make use of their new skills, and that they will be able to pass them on to others.

When technically possible, the workers are sent in batches rather than individually, so that they will not feel unduly isolated in a strange country. In some cases a carefully selected team was sent out; for example, the engineers and technicians who were trained to run the Sariyar hydro-electric plant in Turkey. Under a Yugoslav scheme over 1,000 foremen, technicians and skilled workers have been placed for training in over 400 factories in 12 different European countries

As a concrete example of the results attained by the Yugoslav project, the case of one of the worker-trainees may be cited. Joze Planinc, worker in an electrical factory in Ljubljana, was sent to Germany to train on the manufacture of fluorescent lighting. Back in his old factory, he was put in charge of a group of eighty workers. He introduced new techniques resulting in a fourfold increase of production with reduced costs.

But the results of these worker-trainee schemes are not to be assessed merely in terms of increased productivity. Another trainee, J. Ivancic, wrote of his experience in a Belgian factory: "We formed friendships with workers of ten different countries working at our side under a similar training programme. I will remain eternally grateful for the ILO's efforts in bringing people of different nations closer together."

Where necessary the ILO has provided intensive language training courses to give the trainees a basic vocabulary for their daily life and their trade. The language difficulty has not proved to be so formidable an obstacle as had been feared. Very frequently the language training continues in the host country, and the trainees often live with workers' families, where they have opportunities for conversation.

Seminars are a specialised form of fellowship training and are intended to give the participants from a given group of countries with similar problems an opportunity to discuss these problems with the help of international experts. Collective lectures and field visits are combined with group discussion. The ILO has organised regional group training courses in the fields of social security, labour statistics, labour inspection, vocational training, employment service and co-operation.

Experience with some of the earlier seminars organised by the ILO, which lasted an average of three to four weeks, suggested that their value would be enhanced if their duration were increased and more time allotted to field work. Special difficulties have been encountered when the training, background and experience of the participants have been so widely different as to make it impossible to choose an optimum level at which to conduct the training.

These are only a few of the operational problems that have been encountered. Others have arisen in connection with the procurement and supply of technical equipment and the co-operation of the governments requesting assistance. Some difficulties have been due to the limitations imposed by the currencies available for financing operations.

Assessment of Results

Assessment of the results of technical co-operation is important not only as a measure of the benefits that have accrued but also as an aid to future programme planning. It is a valuable aid in verifying existing priorities and in testing methods after they have been put to trial in the field.

Assessment is a matter of some complexity. The tests to be applied and the procedure to be followed may have to vary from project to project and from country to country. An obvious test is to find out the immediate and direct result of the project – a comparison of the situation "before" and "after". Another important test is the prospect of follow-up action by the country on the termination of the project. A third is to discover the impact of the project on economic and social conditions. The findings must be compared with the objectives of the project planned, in order to measure the degree of success achieved. Such an evaluation should also serve to test the efficacy of existing methods and techniques of implementation in relation to their cost and the results obtained.

While the creation of additional skills through vocational training is essential to long-term economic development, more direct results may sometimes be achieved by improving the efficiency of the existing production process. For example, the rational organisation of cottage industries and the improvement of techniques and processes may show immediate concrete results. The organisation of producers' co-operatives has proved valuable for the introduction of better tools and methods. On-the-job training of factory foremen and skilled workers in industrial establishments abroad may start a drive for more efficient methods of work when they return to their own countries. The organisation of employment in such a way as to increase the mobility of labour is another means of achieving increased productive efficiency. Other projects, like those designed to assist in improving industrial relations and in preventing accidents, also affect the national output.

No less important than these projects, which improve the technical efficiency of production, are those primarily concerned with improving working and living conditions. Other projects are concerned with social security, which the governments of many developing countries consider an essential part of their social policy. Labour legislation cannot play its full part in social and economic progress unless it is effectively administered, and ILO projects in this field therefore have consequences far beyond their immediate impact. The training of specialised personnel – inspectors, conciliation officers, welfare officers, employment exchange managers, and the staff of social security institutions – is closely linked with the industrial development of a country.

Responsibility for assessing the practical results of the project rests by no means exclusively with the ILO; indeed, that of the developing countries themselves is in several ways even more important. Here not only the governments, which naturally shoulder the major burden, but employers' and workers' organisations and other non-governmental bodies as well can play a significant part. On the termination of the project, it is for the governments, firstly to give consideration as soon as possible to the recommendations formulated by the expert and, secondly, to take the necessary financial, administrative or other steps to continue the work begun.

Unfortunately it has occurred more often than it should that after a project has been completed and the expert's recommendations have been transmitted to a government, nothing has happened. There may be many reasons for this. Perhaps since the project was requested, political changes have taken place in the country and the new government has no interest in the project. Perhaps the government is not prepared to find the money necessary to implement the recommendations. Perhaps the departmental inertia which is to be found in all countries, economically developed as well as economically underdeveloped, results in the recommendations being pigeon-holed.

In other cases, while the government has been anxious to carry out the recommendations made by the expert, local resources in qualified staff are lacking. Or again, in the case of a vocational training project, the local instructors who have been trained prove unable to carry on the work alone; in such cases it has sometimes been possible to convert failure into success by reactivating the project for a further year.

The failure or near-failure of a project may also lie on the side of the ILO. However carefully an expert has been selected, medically examined, and briefed it is impossible to foresee every contingency. Cases have arisen where an expert has fallen seriously ill and has had to resign, or where he has continued in post in spite of ill-health. In the former case delays have occurred in finding at short notice a suitable successor, in the latter the expert's work has proved unsatisfactory. In other cases the expert has failed because although he has the "know-how" he has not succeeded in the "show-how" necessary to convey his knowledge and skill to the trainees; in other cases again he has been unable to adjust himself to strange conditions and to "get on" with those he has come to assist and thus to gain their confidence.

Finally, cases have occurred where the failure of the project is due in the main to misunderstandings in its planning and preparation. Before any agreement is signed by the ILO and a government to undertake a project, discussion has taken place between representatives of the ILO and the government on the nature of the need to be met, on the kind of assistance to be provided by the ILO, and on the arrangements to be made by the government in assigning "counterpart" personnel to be associated with the expert and in providing local facilities for the mission. Misunderstanding on any of these points results in the preparation by the two parties being out of alignment; the project gets off to a bad start from which it does not fully recover.

The ILO has rightly laid great stress on the importance of follow-up. It has emphasised that technical assistance is in itself not a goal, but is a means of supplying the countries that need it with temporary help in promoting balanced social and economic development. Missions of international experts and studies abroad of technicians can produce lasting results only to the extent that these projects are integrated with national development plans drawn up with the intention of mobilising the technical and financial resources of the countries concerned.

When the Conference adopted a resolution on the implementation of the programme in 1954 it included the following paragraph: "Urges the Governments of countries in receipt of technical assistance to develop their arrangements for the central co-ordination and follow-up of such assistance, in order to ensure that full benefit may be derived from it, and to arrange, where appropriate, for active co-operation of employers' and workers' organisations and other appropriate bodies in the preparation of programmes for the utilisation of such assistance, in the development and execution of projects and in the evaluation of results."[2]

In 1955 the Governing Body had before it a first report submitted by the Director-General on the evaluation and assessment of the results of the technical assistance work of the ILO. In that report were embodied the findings of a special enquiry undertaken to study the results of the ILO programme in four countries – Ceylon, Haiti, Israel and Yugoslavia – selected from different parts of the world where the ILO programme had been in operation for some years. The Governing Body noted that cases in which national action had ceased after the departure of ILO experts had been relatively few. Similar reports assessing results in other countries have continued to be submitted in more recent years.

There can be no doubt that an overall assessment of the ILO's operational work based on more than twenty years' experience would show that the most worth-while results have been secured from long-term projects closely integrated with comprehensive national development planning.

An example of such a long-term programme may be taken from Venezuela. Between 1959 and 1965 an ILO expert in supervisory training and management development worked in Venezuela, financed to a large extent by trust fund arrangements. During that period the Venezuelan Productivity Institute (an official body) was created in 1961, and in 1965 a UNDP/SF five-year project in management development and productivity was signed, with the ILO as executing agency. That project aims at strengthening and enlarging the Productivity Institute and extending management development and productivity to field centres throughout Venezuela.

Another example can be provided from India. That scheme, centred in the Central Labour Institute in Bombay, started on a modest scale. The Indian government decided in 1950 to set up the Central Labour Institute, its first branch being the Industrial Safety, Health and Welfare Centre, organised with the assistance of ILO experts. That Branch was later added to with an Industrial Hygiene Laboratory, and a Training within Industry Centre to promote the training of supervisors and instructors. In 1955 the work was further extended by the establishment of a Productivity Centre

[2] *Rec. Proc.*, Int. Lab. Conf., 1954, p. 582.

to promote the development of industrial productivity by training management and workers. Sixteen international experts co-operated with the Centre.

The success of the Institute led to the decision of the government to set up three regional Institutes. The ILO was designated as the executing agent for the project under an UNDP/SF programme. The experts gave assistance in organising and operating the three regional Institutes and also took part in seminars and training courses and were called in to advise managements of industrial firms. In view of the success of the Institutes in contributing to increasing the productivity of Indian industry through the active co-operation of management and labour, the government is considering setting up similar institutes or centres in other industrial areas.

In order to overcome weaknesses and shortcomings revealed by experience in the operation of technical co-operation, joint action has been taken, particularly since 1968, by the United Nations, the ILO and other specialised agencies to cut out waste and improve the overall effectiveness of the system. That action has included joint pilot evaluation missions, on-the-spot inspection investigations, and supervisory administrative and financial measures, together with the work of the Pearson Commission and the "Capacity Study" of Sir Robert Jackson. As a consequence of this process of constructive self-examination, the future may see important decisions affecting the development of technical co-operation.

The Social Objective

From the outset the ILO has always assigned fundamental importance to the social objective. That is the significance of the emphasis on social justice in the Preamble to the Constitution. That is the essence of the Declaration of Philadelphia. And in 1949 when the Conference was discussing the participation of the ILO in the Expanded Programme of Technical Assistance which was then being planned, it urged that technical assistance should have a social objective. The resolution of the Economic and Social Council establishing the Expanded Programme, although it does not disregard the social aspect, places primary emphasis on economic development. It has been the task of the ILO, particularly in the comprehensive projects which it has undertaken jointly with other agencies, to ensure that the social objective is not overlooked or sacrificed. In participating in programmes designed to contribute primarily to economic growth, the ILO has emphasised that such action should help to secure a proper balance between economic and social progress.

Nevertheless, the ILO considers it important to abstain from trying to impose any doctrine on the countries it assists. Each country must plan its own course; each must work out its own destiny. What the ILO can do, and does do, is to give information and advice on the solutions which international experience has shown to be useful in dealing with problems similar to their own.

PART II
MAJOR PROBLEMS AND
PROGRAMMES

13. HUMAN RESOURCES AND EMPLOYMENT

AMONG the problems that have confronted the ILO throughout the course of its history, the complex issues involved in manpower and employment are perhaps the most important.

This was one of the first questions to be attacked by the ILO in 1919, and in 1969 when its 50th anniversary was celebrated a decision was taken to launch the World Employment Programme, destined to concentrate its main endeavours in the coming years.

As the implementation of that Programme will thus be a task for the next decade, its purpose, projects and procedures will be described and discussed in the Part of this book entitled "The Future".

Although manpower problems occupied a prominent place in the work of the Organisation before the war, the word "manpower" is rarely found in the reports issued by the ILO in that period. At that time the various manpower questions were looked at separately and dealt with in isolation from one another. In the years after the war, influenced by the wartime experience of the principal belligerent countries, the ILO has recognised the interdependence of the various manpower problems, and has treated them as interrelated aspects of one big problem.

A further difference between the pre-war and the post-war treatment of the problem is that the negative pre-war attitude has been replaced by the positive post-war approach. Instead of "the prevention of unemployment" which was an essential part of the 1919 programme, the ILO after the war committed itself, in co-operation with the United Nations, to positive action, including operational activities, to help to secure the implementation of the policy of full employment. "Full employment", and later, "expanding employment", became the keystone of all the work of the Organisation in this field, unifying its activities on the particular aspects of the prevention of unemployment, employment service organisation, planning of public works, vocational guidance and technical training, and migration for employment.

Prevention of Unemployment

Students of social economics today sometimes find it difficult to understand why unemployment formed such a cardinal preoccupation of the governments and of the workers of the 1920's and the 1930's. The explanation is a simple matter of figures. Between 1920 and 1929 the number of unemployed in the world never fell below ten million. In certain industrial countries the proportion of unemployed never represented less than a tenth of the total number of workers and, when winter came to aggravate an economic crisis, this proportion even rose to one-third. In the early 1930's, in the Great Depression, the total number of unemployed in the world attained astronomic figures. Small wonder, therefore, that throughout the pre-war period the struggle against unemployment was a major task for the ILO.

In 1919 unemployment was already serious and the Washington Conference adopted a Convention and Recommendation on the subject. The Convention requires States (a) to communicate to the ILO all available statistics and information on unemployment, and (b) to establish a system of free public employment agencies under the control of a central authority.

The Recommendation urges that each member should (a) establish an effective system of unemployment insurance, and (b) co-ordinate the execution of all work undertaken under public authority, with a view to reserving such work as far as practicable for periods of unemployment and for districts most affected by it.

While these provisions undoubtedly stimulated government action at the time in a certain number of countries, they were only general outlines. Several years elapsed before the Conference adopted detailed instruments, in 1934 the Convention ensuring benefit or allowances to the involuntarily unemployed, supplemented by the Recommendation concerning unemployment insurance and various forms of relief for the unemployed, in 1937 the two Recommendations concerning respectively international co-operation in respect of public works and the national planning of public works.

In the meantime it had begun to be realised that all these "remedies for unemployment", placing in employment, unemployment insurance or assistance and even planning of public works, valuable as they undoubtedly were, were merely palliatives. They did not attack the causes of unemployment, which, it was beginning to be generally suspected, were essentially of economic and financial origin.

The treatment of unemployment at that time may be compared with the contemporary treatment of malaria. Keep the patient warm, dose him with "medicines", and hope for the best. After much suffering, the patient usually recovered, thanks to the strength of his constitution. So with unemployment, the body politic, after being plied with "remedies", and after much suffering, usually recovered, again thanks to the strength of its constitution. But just as medical science was aware that its "medicines" were mere palliatives and continued to seek the radical causes of the malady, so social and economic science endeavoured to discover the root causes of unemployment.

Causes of Unemployment

In 1921 the Conference asked the Office to undertake an enquiry into the national and international aspects of the unemployment crisis of that period, and requested the assistance of the League of Nations in solving the economic and financial questions which might be brought to light during the enquiry. In accordance with this resolution the first World Economic Conference was held in Genoa in 1922, but it gave merely formal satisfaction on the subject of unemployment, only adopting a recommendation which repeated the terms of the Convention of the Washington Conference.

In 1923 the ILO and the Economic Organisation of the League set up a Mixed Commission on Economic Crises, the first task of which was to consider the indices of economic forecasting, frequently referred to as "economic barometers". In 1924 the ILO presented a report on the subject to the Economic Committee of the League of Nations, and this led to a series of studies which were partly responsible for the progress made in research work by special institutes in various countries.

At the same time the ILO began a general study of the unemployment crisis of 1920–23 which showed that, in addition to several other causes, the monetary policy of certain States had been an important factor in the crisis. Several later studies confirmed these conclusions and showed that the application of the resolutions on currency adopted by the Economic Conference at Genoa could help to increase stability of employment. In the light of the reports submitted by the ILO the Mixed Commission recognised in 1929 that the cyclical fluctuations in economic activity which led to unemployment could to a great extent be restricted if account were taken, in the distribution of credits, of the various economic factors involved, and more particularly of the trends of the labour market and the movement of prices. Moreover, in order to ensure monetary stability, essential to successful economic organisation and a condition for stability of employment, it recommended that all the national currencies should be stabilised on the basis of a gold standard and that collaboration should be instituted between the central banks of issue. These ideas were accepted; the Bank for International Settlements was in one aspect an application of the latter recommendation.

Interrelation of Social, Economic and Financial Factors

Throughout these years there had been a gradually growing recognition that the solution of the problem of unemployment required co-ordinated international action in the interrelated social, economic and financial fields.

The economic history of the inter-war years can be divided into three main periods, 1919–24, 1925–29 and 1930–39. From 1919 to 1924, under-production rapidly gave way to overproduction and a slump in markets. This situation was further aggravated by an unprecedented financial upheaval and it culminated in acute unemployment. Up to the end of 1924, all national and international efforts were directed towards the mitigation of the effects of these crises.

From 1925 to 1929, although the same problems still persisted and unemployment was on the up-grade, the world was able to set about reorganising its economic activities on new principles which it was hoped would prevent the return of a similar situation.

From 1930 onwards the world was under the shadow of the Great Depression. Unemployment soared. Every department of trade, industry and commerce was affected. International commercial transactions became more hazardous as currency fluctuations were added to price fluctuations and customs barriers were raised. Restrictions on trade and foreign exchanges were multiplied by governments in their efforts to safeguard their balance of payments. Economic warfare and the political antagonisms engendered by it were intensified. Financial, economic and social security were progressively undermined. It was only, the cynics pointed out, when armaments production gave a stimulus to industry that the economic situation began to improve.

Throughout the whole period there was, indeed, collaboration between the ILO and the League of Nations. The outstanding instance was the World Economic Conference of 1927, convened by the League, at which the ILO was represented and to which it submitted several reports. But there was widespread dissatisfaction and disappointment, particularly among the workers, with the results of all this study and collaboration. In spite of all the research, all the discussion, things seemed to get steadily worse.

It was one of Harold Butler's major contributions to the ILO to empha-sise, throughout his term as Director, that the Organisation should not abandon hope of finding a solution. Each of his annual reports to the Conference was presented against the background of an analysis of the international economic situation. The titles which he gave to these economic chapters in his successive reports from 1933 to 1938 constitute a revealing synopsis of the fluctuation of the economic barometer during the period of his directorship: "The March of the Depression", "The Effort towards Recovery", "Recovery and Employment", "Recovery or Relapse", "The Extent of Recovery", "Prosperity Regained – or Lost?" In his view the Great Depression had made it plain that the cure for social evils – and particularly unemployment, the worst of all social evils – could not be found without advancing into the wider spheres of financial and economic policy. Economic and financial policy, in his view, was inseparably bound up with social policy. As financial, economic and social questions could not be disentangled and treated in isolation, it was as imperative to study the social implications of financial and economic policy as it was to consider the financial and economic implications of social policy.

The question may well be asked whether, if Harold Butler's views on the causes of unemployment and the measures to be taken to overcome it had been generally accepted by governments, the gravity of the crisis in the 1930's could have been lessened. As early as 1933 Butler wrote in his Report to the Conference: "It is now becoming more and more generally accepted that the root of the crisis lies in the failure of purchasing power. Unemployment breeds unemployment, because the fewer the number of wage earners, the fewer the number of effective consumers. . . . There appears to be a growing volume of opinion in favour of making every effort to expend money destined for the relief of the unemployed in a manner which will provide them with work rather than merely in the distribution of cash."[1]

Though Butler's views were in line with the ideas which John Maynard Keynes afterwards developed in *The General Theory of Employment, Interest and Money* (1936), they did not make any appreciable impact at the time either on the Conference or on economic thinking in member States; it was not until the Philadelphia Conference (1944) that his views on employment and on the interdependence of social and economic policy gained general acceptance.

Employment Organisation during the Transition from War to Peace

On the basis of those views, when the second world war was drawing to a close, the ILO emphasised the great importance of doing everything possible to prevent a recurrence of the difficulties which, after the first world war, had completely disorganised the employment market. At its 1944 (Philadelphia) Session the Conference therefore adopted a Recommendation on employment organisation during the transition from war

[1] Int. Lab. Conf., 17th session, Geneva, 1933, pp. 21, 23.

to peace, and a Recommendation on the national planning of public works. These Recommendations were supplemented by a resolution on economic policies for the attainment of social objectives.

These Recommendations, addressed to governments exactly at the time they were needed, and containing not only the formulation of principles but detailed guidance on the implementation of the principles, were welcomed and widely applied. They undoubtedly contributed substantially to ensuring that in the principal belligerent countries the processes of military and industrial demobilisation and of re-conversion of the national economies from a war to a peace footing were carried out with a minimum of dislocation and waste of national effort. Not less important, perhaps, was the influence of these Recommendations in paving the way for the long-term implementation of the policy of "full employment" launched both by the ILO and the United Nations as the pole-star policy for the post-war world.

Full Employment

When in 1944 the Conference adopted the Declaration of Philadelphia it included the following paragraph:

"The Conference recognises the solemn obligation of the International Labour Organisation to further among the nations of the world pro-grammes which will achieve:

(a) full employment and the raising of standards of living."

In the following year the San Francisco Conference included in the Charter of the United Nations a mandate to promote full employment.

In the post-war period, therefore, both the United Nations and the ILO were entrusted with the mission of promoting full employment. The progress made since the Covenant of the League of Nations and the Constitution of the ILO were adopted in 1919 was due on the one hand to the research and the recommendations of the League of Nations and the ILO which at the time often appeared theoretical and sterile, and on the other to the expansion of the area of economic and financial relations on which governments were finding it desirable to consult one another.

In implementing its mandate the United Nations has enjoyed advantages in respect both of organisation and resources which no other international body ever before possessed. The Economic and Social Council in virtue of its co-ordinating functions has been able from its inception not only to survey the whole field of economic affairs but also to benefit from the co-operation of all the specialised agencies. Certain important matters bearing upon conditions of full employment fall within the sphere of the

ILO, the World Bank and the International Monetary Fund; and their information, advice and recommendations on these matters have always been available to the Council.

That the post-war world has been largely spared the alternation of booms and slumps which the inter-war period suffered is due in substantial measure to the regular surveys and recommendations of the ILO and the Economic and Social Council and the increasing attention paid to them by governments in the formulation of their economic and financial policies.

Almost every year in the discussion of the Director-General's Report, the Conference has debated the employment situation in the various countries and the implementation of the recommendations to maintain full employment.

At the 1961 session of the Conference special attention was devoted to employment problems and policies. The Conference considered two main topics. The first was the problem of creating employment opportunities, including measures to overcome underemployment, in economically less developed countries. The second related to employment problems in the more advanced countries with reference to technological change and shifts in patterns of world trade and the co-ordination of employment policies and anti-inflationary measures. The resolution adopted by the Conference calls upon all countries to adopt, as a major goal of social and economic policy, the objective of full, productive and freely chosen employment.

Following up that resolution, the Conference adopted in 1964 the Employment Policy Convention. Particular importance attaches to Article 1, as it defined the policy which the 1969 "World Employment Programme" is designed to implement:

"With a view to stimulating economic growth and development, raising levels of living, meeting manpower requirements and overcoming unemployment and underemployment, each Member shall declare and pursue, as a major goal, an active policy designed to promote full, productive and freely chosen employment.

"The said policy shall aim at ensuring that – (a) there is work for all who are available for and seeking work; (b) such work is as productive as possible; (c) there is freedom of choice of employment and the fullest possible opportunity for each worker to qualify for and to use his skills and endowments in a job for which he is well suited, irrespective of race, colour, sex, religion, political opinion, national extraction or social origin.

"The said policy shall take due account of the stage and level of economic development and the mutual relationships between employment objectives and other economic and social objectives, and shall be pursued by methods that are appropriate to national conditions and practices."

The objective of the ILO and the United Nations is not merely "full employment". The United Nations aims at "full employment without inflation". The ILO aims at "full employment and the raising of standards of living". These amplifications of the ideal of full employment amount essentially to the same thing. In each case the ultimate goal is social.

As co-ordinated detailed contributions towards the promotion of full employment and the raising of standards of living, the ILO has taken action along two main lines: firstly, the improvement of employment service organisation; secondly, the encouragement of vocational and technical training.

Employment Promotion

In 1948 the Conference adopted the Employment Service Convention which marked a great advance on the Unemployment Convention of 1919. In the first place, the 1948 Convention links employment service organisation directly with full employment by specifying that the essential duty of the employment service shall be to ensure, in co-operation where necessary with other public and private bodies concerned, the best possible organisation of the employment market as an integral part of the national programme for the achievement and maintenance of full employment and the development and use of productive resources. In the second place, the Convention lays down in considerable detail the principles of organisation and operation of an employment service working in this wider framework. These principles in turn are more fully developed in the Recommendation adopted by the Conference in the same year, which contains specific advice with regard to the organisation of the system, the employment market information to be collected, the drawing up of an annual manpower budget and the facilitation of mobility of labour.

These two instruments, supplemented by the technical advice given by the ILO, rapidly exercised a great influence on national practice. The philosophy which lies behind the texts has inspired almost every employment service set up or reorganised since the war and the very words of the Convention have been embodied in the laws of many countries.

In 1949 the Conference revised the Fee-charging Employment Agencies Convention, adopted in 1933. The revision was in line with the post-war emphasis on positive rather than on negative action. The emphasis of the 1933 Convention is on the abolition of fee-charging employment agencies; the revised 1949 Convention recognises that in some countries and in some sectors fee-charging agencies can usefully supplement public employment services, and it lays emphasis on supervision and regulation of such fee-charging agencies rather than on their immediate abolition.

A particularly useful, if unspectacular, piece of work was completed in 1958, when the ILO published the "International Standard Classification of Occupations". This volume provides detailed definitions of 1,600 occupational categories in terms of the work functions involved. It is being used by a number of countries in Europe, Asia, Latin America, the Near and Middle East and Africa for developing and improving their national classification systems for use in employment services and for similar purposes.

Vocational and Technical Training and Apprenticeship

Before the war the ILO had already made a substantial contribution to the solution of the closely connected problems of vocational guidance, vocational and technical training and apprenticeship. Although in 1935 the Conference by adopting the Unemployment (Young Persons) Recommendation went on record as favouring the generalisation of measures for vocational training, and although in 1937 it adopted the Vocational Education (Building) Recommendation, it was not until 1939 that the Conference dealt with the question as a whole and adopted two Recommendations, one on Vocational Training, the other on Apprenticeship.

These pre-war standards related only to young people, and in 1950 they were supplemented by a Recommendation on vocational training of adults including disabled persons. That Recommendation contains guiding principles on the organisation of the training of adults, a post-war problem of special interest to the less developed countries endeavouring to build up new industries and to increase productivity. In order to complete the provisions relating to disabled persons in the 1950 Recommendation, the Conference adopted in 1955 a Recommendation on vocational rehabilitation of the disabled, including those disabled in war and industry and those born with handicaps. This Recommendation is inspired partly by the desire to provide maximum opportunities for the physically handicapped to live full lives, and partly by the desire to enable a world in which full employment is an economic and social goal to make the most complete use of the capabilities of the disabled members of the community.

On vocational guidance the Conference adopted a Recommendation in 1949 which lays down in reasonable detail guiding principles and methods of vocational guidance for (a) young persons including those in school, and (b) adults (employment counselling).

In line with the post-war emphasis on the operational responsibilities of the ILO the formulation of these international standards was followed by practical assistance and advice to governments in overcoming their national difficulties in applying these standards.

At the 1961 session of the Conference, a resolution adopted on "economic and technical assistance for the promotion of economic expansion and social progress in developing countries" recommends priority for the training of national personnel urgently needed for the promotion of economic and social development.

The field experience acquired by the ILO in the course of technical co-operation activities revealed the need for reconsidering some of the provisions of the Recommendations. Accordingly vocational training was examined by the 1961 and 1962 sessions of the Conference for the purpose of revising existing standards. In this connection the Conference was able to take stock of the lessons learned by the ILO in its technical co-operation work and of the principal current requirements for ILO action on training.

As a result the Conference was able to adopt in the latter year a Recommendation which not only brought up to date previous Recommendations but set guide-lines and standards for future ILO action in this field. The basic principle of the Recommendation is that "training is not an end in itself but a means of developing a person's occupational capacities . . . and of enabling him to use his abilities to the greatest advantage of himself and the community".

In this field the work of the ILO has made an important contribution towards helping countries in the formation of balanced economic and social policy. In order to achieve economic growth under modern conditions, countries have to organise courses of training to teach the necessary skills to workpeople and technicians of varying grades of education and experience. These people do not only have to acquire new skills, they have to learn in many cases to adjust themselves to new ways of living and to unaccustomed conditions of routine and discipline. In developing countries in particular the solution of such problems contributes to balanced economic and social progress.

Migration for Employment

In its approach to the problem of migration the ILO has experienced many disappointments and even setbacks.

When the first Session of the Conference met in 1919, migration appeared so obviously a matter requiring international regulation that the Conference had no hesitation in requesting the Governing Body to set up an international Commission which, without infringing national sovereign rights, might propose suitable measures for regulating the migration of workers and protecting wage-earners residing in foreign countries. The Commission, under the chairmanship of Viscount Ullswater, a former Speaker of the House of Commons, adopted several resolutions on the international co-ordination of protective measures for migrants, the placing of migrants in employment, equality of treatment for national and foreign workers, State supervision over emigration agencies and other matters. This body of resolutions constituted a comprehensive programme which largely determined the work of the ILO in the inter-war period.

In attempting to implement this migration programme the Conference made a good start. In 1922 it adopted the Migration Statistics Recommendation, under which members should communicate to the Office, if possible every three months, all information available concerning emigration, immigration, repatriation and transit of emigrants. This Recommendation made the ILO a recognised international depository of information on migration, a position which it has succeeded in retaining, sometimes with great difficulty.

In virtue of its informational responsibilities the ILO produced in the inter-war period a great mass of publications on migration.

Although the ILO thus carried out assiduously its task of collecting and publishing information on migration, the Conference, until 1939, was able to touch only a fringe of the question.[2]

This was due to the growing tendency of governments to declare that immigration or emigration was a domestic question. Any attempt to regulate it internationally was resented as an interference with their sovereignty.

In the development of this attitude, the United States had set the example in 1917 by prohibiting the immigration of "undesirables". In 1921 and 1924 much more restrictive measures were adopted under the Quota Acts. The British Dominions soon followed suit, and later certain States of Latin America. In the 1930's there was not a single immigration country which had not protected its labour market by unilateral restrictive legislation. This was chiefly due to the economic difficulties of the time, but nationalism, which was so strong in many countries, also played an important part.

Certain emigration countries followed the same movement. Here again it was claimed that emigration was a domestic question, and a vital one. Examples of this policy were provided by Italy and Spain; other countries in Southern Europe and also in Central and Eastern Europe adopted stricter supervision over emigration, directing it only towards countries where conditions appeared to them to be acceptable.

All these measures, whether their origin was political or economic and social (and the first was undoubtedly the most important at the time), limited the area in which the ILO could work.

[2] In 1926 the Conference adopted a Convention and Recommendation on the simplification of the inspection of emigrants on board ship.

It was not until the eve of the war that opposition to the international treatment of this question could be overcome to the extent of securing agreement to its inclusion on the agenda of the Conference. In 1939 the Conference adopted a detailed Convention on the recruitment, placing and conditions of labour of migrants for employment, supplemented by two Recommendations.

Although, as a result of twenty years of effort in the field of migration, the ILO could now point to the existence, in its international labour code, of substantial instruments, a further disappointment was in store. As the years passed, it became clear that no government would ratify the Convention. This was partly because it included too many details and partly because the war had affected the conditions of migration for employment.

In 1949 the Conference therefore adopted a revised Convention on migration for employment supplemented by a revised Recommendation. Although governments were slow to ratify the Convention, even in its revised form, it did secure some ratification both by emigration and immigration countries, and the principles and standards embodied in the two instruments constituted a practical and workmanlike basis for the post-war operational activities of the ILO.

In 1950 a Preliminary Migration Conference, bringing together emigration and immigration countries to consider their respective problems, recommended a series of practical steps to be taken by both types of countries and by international organisations in order to clarify the aims and improve the machinery and procedures for migration and related services. This set of recommendations became the working basis of a Special Migration Programme, initiated by the ILO in the same year, under which technical advisory services were furnished to governments of emigration and immigration countries. More than twenty projects were put into operation in Latin American countries of immigration and European countries of emigration, each directed towards carrying out one part or another of the conclusions of the Preliminary Migration Conference.

At the same time, the ILO was aware that the mere provision of technical assistance would not solve the operational problems involved in moving people from a country which could not use them to a country which wanted them. The Office therefore worked out detailed proposals for helping the countries primarily concerned to overcome the practical obstacles to migration (including the problem of transport and its financing, but emphasising the fact, borne out by long experience, that transport is only one of the many important things which enter into the whole migration process). The plan incorporating these proposals was submitted to a Special Migration Conference in Naples in 1951.

That Conference proved a severe disappointment. The plan submitted to the Conference included the establishment of a fund to provide for transportation of migrants and related costs and the setting up within the framework of the ILO of a special migration administration. At the outset of the Conference, however, the majority of the delegates made it clear that they were not in a position to discuss a migration aid fund, transport operations or the proposed migration administration. This came as a complete surprise to the Office. As a result of preliminary consultations with certain governments specially concerned in the problem, it had understood that its plan would receive support at the Conference. If the negative attitude of the majority of the governments had been foreseen, the Conference would probably never have been held. As it was, the Conference added another chapter to the ILO's history of unsuccess in approaching the problem of migration.

Nevertheless, the failure of the Conference on the main issue did not mean a denial of the usefulness of the technical work of the ILO in the migration field. On the contrary the Conference agreed that the ILO should continue to render technical assistance on migration particularly on vocational training aspects, and should expand its efforts to facilitate, at the request of the countries concerned, the conclusion of bilateral agreements for migration.

The ILO co-operated from the outset with the Intergovernmental Committee for European Migration, the body set up after the Naples Conference to be responsible for the transportation of migrants from European countries. In 1960 it co-operated with the European Economic Community in establishing a comparative table showing the occupational skills required for trades entering into international migration.

Work done by the ILO for the protection of migrant workers in respect of social security is described in Chapter 17.

In a somewhat limited field further action on behalf of migrant workers was taken by the Conference in 1955. In that year a comprehensive Recommendation was adopted on the protection of migrant workers in underdeveloped countries and territories.

In all its post-war work on migration the ILO has co-operated with the other international organisations concerned. Within the United Nations family, it has been recognised to have primary responsibility in the migration process. Close working relationships have been established with WHO on medical selection of migrants, with FAO on land settlement, with UNESCO on cultural assimilation, and with the United Nations on economic development and its repercussions on migration and on the protection of migrants. By these various means the ILO has advanced not only its own programme in the migration field but those of other organisations, thus underlining its own concept of the problem as one requiring effective co-ordination of responsibility at the international level.

Operational Activities

The operational responsibilities of the Organisation received practical implementation when the manpower programme, initiated in 1948, took shape in response to specific needs in one region after another. It was the first effort to develop the ILO's direct operational activities on a regional basis, and the experience gained laid the foundation for similar work in other fields.

While each country in each region had its own special problems, each of them had the same concern to get the right number of workers in the right jobs in the right places at the right time, to see that they possessed or were being trained for the right skills, and to ensure that human resources were not simply being conserved but were used to good effect in the whole process of economic and social development. The problem was to know how to do all these things and to build up the plans and technical and administrative services which could assist in getting them done.

From 1949 onwards, first in Europe, then in Asia, next in Latin America and in the Near and Middle East, the ILO developed a series of technical advisory activities on manpower.

From the start of the ILO's participation in the Expanded Technical Assistance Programme, more than half the projects have been in the manpower field. Within this field the great bulk of the projects are concerned with vocational education and training, because of ever-increasing recognition of the importance of technical "know-how" as an essential component of economic and social development. Experience in this field has emphasised the need for careful definition of the types of training needed in each particular situation and equally careful assessment of the numbers of people to be trained.

Vocational and Technical training

Skill is the world's greatest single need. It is not only the developing countries, with more than half the world's population, that need skills. Rapid technological developments make it necessary for industrialised countries to maintain up-to-date training programmes.

The ILO's work in training has included four main types:

(a) Training of youth under various forms of apprenticeship or in vocational training centres or by a combination of both methods.

(b) Training of adults in basic skills or in the improvement of existing skills at special training centres or through on-the-job training or by a combination of both.

(c) Training of technicians, foremen and supervisors in both technical and non-technical aspects of their work.

(d) Training of instructors of various kinds.

A special field in which the ILO has done much work is rehabilitation – enabling physically disabled men and women to earn their livelihood. Among the countries to which the ILO has sent experts to give assistance are Austria, Brazil, Burma, Ceylon, Egypt, Guatemala, Indonesia, Morocco and Yugoslavia. In Egypt, for example, blind men have been trained to weave twenty different varieties of rugs in brilliant colours they will never see; Braille signs in tinplate tell them the shades of the wool. In Brazil the ILO expert, himself blind, has assisted in setting up a pilot rehabilitation centre and operating workshops for training the blind in different trades. At a demonstration arranged by the ILO in Geneva the chairman, a Russian, called on an American doctor to show the successful treatment of two former paralytics, a Greek pilot and a French jockey, who after many years in bed had been trained to walk again and obtain employment.

In some cases, the manpower projects are devised to have cumulative results for many countries in the same area. The Brazilian SENAI (National Apprenticeship Service) training project is an example of such regional co-operation. The ILO provided vocational instructors in the skills needed to expand the range of Brazilian vocational training; and Brazil offered trade scholarships to enable workers from other Latin American countries to be trained in skills needed for the development of these countries.

Some of these projects, particularly those connected with training, have continued over several years. Thus, a project in Haiti, involving the complete reorganisation of technical schools, was completed after five years' work. The ILO's participation in the regional courses in marine diesel mechanics, held in Burma, in five years provided training for nationals of nine Asian countries. Burma was a key centre because its inland water transport board operates the largest inland water fleet in the world. In co-operating with the ILO in running this training centre Burma not only helped herself but provided a friendly service to her neighbours, who were also replacing sail and steam by diesel-powered craft.

The regional Training Institute in Istanbul was attended by young government officials from several Near and Middle East countries before being transferred to the Turkish Government five years later.

In 1954, at the request of the Pakistan Government, then engaged in a vast project for reclaiming the Sind desert, the ILO began to provide technical assistance in setting up a training centre for operators and mechanics of heavy earth-moving equipment – bulldozers, tractors, excavators, etc.; after a short time the school was turning out operators and mechanics at the rate of fifty every six months.

In Karadj, near Teheran, the Iranian Government set up a pilot accelerated training centre under a team of five ILO experts and instructors. This proved so successful that the government organised a series of similar centres, also with ILO assistance. The ILO also organised a seminar on accelerated training attended by specialists from seven Middle Eastern countries.

Other more recent examples reflect equal variety. Tunisia and the United Arab Republic having decided to modernise their railways, the ILO has helped them in organising rolling-stock repair shops. In Gabon and in Kenya it has helped in setting up centres for the training of office personnel. It is training rural craftsmen on the Andean plateau, and hotel staff in Cyprus and Nigeria.

In addition to such special schemes, the ILO co-operates in the creation of national vocational training services, and in training administrative staff and instructors for them. These are long-term projects the implementation of which usually extends over some years; they have been undertaken in many countries including Chile, Colombia, India, Israel, Kenya, Mauritius, Nigeria, Pakistan and the United Arab Republic.

This work is expanding; ILO projects for vocational training approved by the Special Fund Governing Council in 1969 include national schemes in Algeria, Ecuador, Iraq, Jamaica, Malaysia, Philippines; and also specialised projects in other countries, e.g. an institute for training personnel for the hotel and tourist industries in Tunisia, establishment of an in-plant training scheme in Chile, and training of mechanics for marine diesel engines in New Caledonia.

The principle of co-ordinated action has guided the ILO's work in the whole manpower field, at the national as well as at the international level. Each manpower project has had to fit into the whole picture of national and international effort. Each result had to be judged in relation to the overall process of economic and social development. The employment services set up or improved with ILO assistance operate in that framework. Training schools or centres help workers to gain the skills they need in a given situation. Migration can only be of help where it meets a reciprocal need in sending and receiving countries. In each field the types of advisory assistance that the ILO and other agencies can provide will only promote balanced socio-economic development in so far as that assistance is properly timed and co-ordinated in relation to national needs and possibilities of achievement.

Balanced Economic and Social Policy

Experience has shown that in many developing countries the overall manpower situation has similar characteristics. A substantial proportion of the population are chronically under-employed: if they have a regular occupation, it is not full-time work; if at certain seasons they work full-time, at other seasons they have nothing at all to do. Further, owing to rapid population growth, the numbers of those needing employment is increasing fast. Such situations call for decisions of public policy, in which a balance of social and economic considerations is particularly important. From the economic standpoint the more people who are engaged in regular productive full-time employment, the higher will be the rate of national production. From the social standpoint a wide measure of regular full-time employment is desirable because it provides people with incomes. So far the economic and social objectives coincide.

But cases may and do arise in which social and economic conditions conflict. Some regular full-time employment is not directed to useful production, or if it is the rate of productivity may be low. From a narrow social standpoint it may be advocated that, as the people concerned do have some income, it is better to let things be, rather than take economic measures which would throw them out of employment completely. From a narrow economic standpoint it may be claimed that a policy of re-organisation and redeployment should be adopted which would result in a higher level of national production, even if many of the workers concerned would become completely unemployed.

When the ILO is invited to provide technical advice on manpower in a particular country, it inevitably meets with situations such as these. While it is clear that the aim should be to arrive at a properly balanced economic and social policy, the application of that policy in the special conditions of the particular country is not easy. In order to give practical assistance in this field, a group of ILO experts examined in 1960 the nature and place of employment objectives in economic development and the conditions of conflict between more employment and more economic growth. Their report helps to provide answers to certain questions on what level of employment should be aimed at in given circumstances, and in what places and industries new jobs should be provided. Answers to such questions are necessary if the ILO is to give practical advice in helping countries to develop a balanced economic and social policy.

14. HUMAN RIGHTS IN THE ECONOMIC WORLD

ON the tenth anniversary of the Universal Declaration of Human Rights, the International Labour Conference unanimously pledged the ILO's continued co-operation with the United Nations for the promotion of human rights. The promotion of human rights is indeed of basic importance for the fulfilment of the objectives of the ILO; unless its activities are pursued with respect for human personality they will not provide a sound foundation for social and economic progress.

In this sphere the ILO's work covers principally the safeguarding of freedom of association, the abolition of forced labour, the elimination of discrimination in employment and the promotion of the principle of equal pay for work of equal value. But it should not be overlooked that other aspects of the work of the ILO, such as the free choice of employment, fair remuneration and working conditions, protection of the right to social security and protection against unemployment also fall within the broad framework of human rights.

Freedom of Association

"Freedom of association", said Sir Abubakar Tafawa Balewa, then Prime Minister of Nigeria, in opening the first ILO African Regional Conference in Lagos in 1960, "is one of the foundations on which we build our free nations."

On one respect or another freedom of association has been important in the work of the ILO throughout the whole course of its existence.

Pre-war preparation

The Preamble to the Constitution expressly recognised the principle of freedom of association as one of the means of improving the conditions of the workers and establishing universal peace. In the early days the workers did not press that this principle should be guaranteed by a Convention, obviously considering that its full recognition was the very basis of their collaboration in the work of the ILO. This belief subsequently turned out to be insufficiently founded. When complaints concerning the restriction of trade union rights reached the Office, it proved impossible to require

States to apply a principle laid down in the Treaty but not yet embodied in a Convention ratified by them.

Efforts at the 1927 session of the Conference to complete the first stage of the procedure for the adoption of a Convention were unsuccessful, and the pre-war action of the ILO was limited essentially to the collection and distribution of information. In 1923 the Office had been authorised by the Governing Body to begin a study of freedom of association. The enquiries undertaken, which covered both trade union law in the separate States and a comparative study of the various judicial systems, appeared in the form of five substantial volumes in 1927–30,

In 1924 the Conference requested the Office to include in its programme the study of collective agreements and conciliation and arbitration. This work included the preparation of separate studies on conciliation and arbitration procedure in fifteen countries and a general comparative study, together with a comparative study of collective agreements. At that time collective agreements, although already a recognised feature of industrial regulation in Great Britain, in the Scandinavian States and in one or two other countries, were still somewhat of a novelty elsewhere.

From 1926 onwards the Office published an annual survey of legal decisions on labour law, containing a selection of such decisions in France, Germany, Great Britain, Italy and the United States – countries which exemplified the principal types of legal procedure.

In addition to entrusting to ordinary courts of law responsibility for hearing disputes arising in connection with the application of labour law, a movement was developing at the time to set up special labour courts providing a simpler, cheaper and more rapid procedure. The Office made a special study of the functions and operations of these labour courts in several countries and published a comparative survey.[1]

Thus, throughout the whole of the pre-war period, the work of the Organisation in the broad field of freedom of association was limited to information. After the 1927 setback the trade unions, the party most immediately concerned, refrained from urging that the question should again be placed before the Conference. The reason for the attitude of the trade union movement was not that the workers ever ceased for one moment to attach importance to freedom of association. But they feared that any Convention that might be adopted by the Conference during a period which was characterised on the whole by reactionary tendencies would not provide the guarantees they required. "The times were out of joint", and it was necessary to wait for better days.

---

[1] Since the war the movement to set up labour courts has shown little extension and, apart from publishing a report on labour courts in Latin America in 1949, the ILO has devoted no special attention to it.

The post-war opportunity

Although the post-war world was full of industrial dynamite, the situation created for the ILO a challenge which it could not refuse to accept. Some elements in the situation were, indeed, favourable.

The war had stimulated the growth of national trade union movements, increased their responsibilities and enlarged their activities. In many countries labour had become a recognised partner in the economic and social effort which had won the war, and there was a measure of agreement that the workers could play an equally important role in peacetime as a vital part of a healthy democracy.

Still, over the world as a whole, the trade union position was far from secure. In many countries there was evidence that basic trade union rights – a workers' right to join a union of his choice or to take part in its activities – were not being respected either in law or in practice. At the international level, emphasis on the definition of human rights in economic and social terms made any violation of trade union or employer rights a matter of international concern. All these factors combined to produce a situation in which the ILO had both a special responsibility and a clear field for action.

As was to be expected, the immediate impetus came from the trade union movement itself. In 1947 the World Federation of Trade Unions and the American Federation of Labor brought the whole problem of trade union rights before the United Nations Economic and Social Council. The latter immediately referred the matter to the ILO with the request that freedom of association be placed on the agenda of the next session of the Conference. This was done and the Conference, in 1947, took the first important step.

With the adoption in 1947 of a resolution concerning freedom of association and protection of the right to organise and to bargain collectively the Conference initiated a broad programme aimed at the international regulation of industrial relations.

Adoption of Conventions and Recommendations

In 1948 the first of the connected series of Conventions and Recommendations was adopted. This was the Freedom of Association Convention, which lays down the fundamental guarantees which workers' and employers' organisations should have from the time they are set up until the time they are disbanded. Briefly, these are that all workers and employers, without discrimination of any kind, shall possess the right to establish and join organisations of their own choice without prior government authorisation; that these organisations shall have the right to draw up their own rules, elect their own representatives and function freely, without interference from the public authorities; that workers' and employers' organisations cannot be dissolved or suspended by administrative authority, but only by normal judicial procedure; and that these organisations shall have the right to join federations and to affiliate with international organisations of employers and workers. A further article reconciles these basic guarantees with the law of the land, stipulating that the organisations shall respect the law in exercising their rights but that the law shall not impair the guarantees provided in the Convention. Finally, the Convention states that each ratifying government shall undertake to take all necessary and appropriate measures to ensure that workers and employers can, in fact, freely exercise the right to organise.

In the Right to Organise and Collective Bargaining Convention, adopted in 1949, the Conference specified what these measures should be. The principal stipulations are that workers shall enjoy adequate protection against acts of anti-union discrimination in respect of their employment; and that workers' and employers' organisations shall enjoy equal protection against any acts of interference by each other or each other's agents or members in their establishment, functioning or administration. Particulars of the acts concerned are detailed in the Convention. The Convention also specifies that measures appropriate to national conditions shall be taken to encourage and promote the full development and utilisation of machinery for voluntary negotiation between employers or employers' organisations and workers' organisations with a view to the regulation of terms and conditions of employment by means of collective agreements.

These two basic Conventions have been extensively ratified. By 1 January 1970 the 1948 Convention had received 77 ratifications and the 1949 Convention 90; these ratifications had come from countries in all parts of the world, with different economic and social systems and in all stages of development.

In addition to the regular annual procedure for the supervision of ratified Conventions, the Conference has undertaken on several occasions special reviews of the effect given to the freedom of association Conventions, and evidence has been forthcoming that even where they have not yet been ratified, the standards have exerted a real influence on national practice. This has been reported not only in countries in which workers' and employers' organisations are still struggling to establish themselves, but also in countries with long experience of industrial relations.

International machinery for safeguarding trade union rights

Step by step with the standard-setting work, action was taken to supplement the normal ILO machinery with a view to dealing objectively and expeditiously with alleged violations to trade union rights, in particular the right of freedom of association. The arrangements finally devised were based on a series of consultations and agreements between the United Nations and the ILO. At the beginning of 1950, the Governing Body established a Fact-Finding and Conciliation Commission, composed of outstanding authorities on labour law and industrial relations.

It was further decided that a preliminary examination of cases should be made by a Governing Body committee, including experienced workers' and employers' representatives as well as government members. The Committee on Freedom of Association looks at the evidence, taking account of any observations the government concerned may have to offer, and reports back to the Governing Body.

The Committee on Freedom of Association

One of the principles which has guided the Committee in its work is the necessity to avoid two opposite dangers; on the one hand it must not be distracted from its task by attempting to deal with a wide range of cases which it is neither appropriate nor necessary to examine internationally, and on the other hand it must not hesitate to discuss in an international forum cases which are of such a character as to affect substantially the attainment of the aims and purposes of the ILO.

By the end of 1969 the Governing Body Committee had carefully analysed, examined and reported on some 600 cases. All these cases related to complaints of infringement of trade union rights addressed directly to the ILO or referred to it by the Economic and Social Council. Some of these complaints, as was to be expected, have been of a purely or mainly political character, and one of the most difficult tasks of the Committee has been to decide what to do about them. In dealing with such cases the Committee has been guided by the general principle that it is inappropriate for the ILO to discuss political questions directly relating to international security, but that situations which are political in origin may have social aspects which the ILO may be called upon to examine by appropriate procedures.

The recommendations made by the Committee on the complaints submitted to it fall into three categories.

(a) Some complaints the Committee recommends should be dismissed without being communicated to the government concerned for its observations. These are complaints which the Committee considers to be obviously unfounded because they are not substantiated by any evidence.

(b) Other complaints the Committee, after considering the information furnished by governments, recommends should be dismissed. In some of these cases the Committee does not regard the position relating to freedom of association in the country concerned as satisfactory but it finds that the particular allegation of infringement of trade union rights submitted to it is not substantiated.

(c) The third type of recommendation made by the Committee is that the case merits further examination by the Governing Body. These are cases in which the information supplied by the government is too vague and imprecise to enable the Committee to reach a positive conclusion on the merits of the allegation or in which the government concerned has refused to furnish information.

In its work the Committee has shown impartiality and wisdom worthy of the International Court of Justice itself. Most governments have recognised this; they have furnished information to the Committee and where necessary have taken steps to eliminate the cause of the grievance either on their own initiative or in response to recommendations made by the Governing Body on the advice of the Committee. By these means, and through consultation with the governments, the ILO has been exercising a considerable influence in bringing national practice closer to international standards and in achieving the general aim of respect for trade union rights. In particular cases, men imprisoned have been released, and men under sentence of death have been reprieved.

As publicity is specially important in the protection of trade union freedom, the ILO publishes all the reports of the Committee on Freedom of Association.

The Fact-Finding and Conciliation Commission

The first case to come before the Fact-Finding and Conciliation Commission concerned Japan. From 1958 onwards various international and Japanese trade union organisations submitted a series of complaints of alleged infringements of trade union rights for government employees. These were examined by the Governing Body Committee on Freedom of Association between 1958 and 1963, and in 1964 the government of Japan agreed to the reference of the case to the Fact-Finding and Conciliation Commission.

The Commission consisted of three members and worked in 1964 and 1965, during which period it visited Japan. Recommendations, accepted by the government of Japan, were that Japan should ratify the Freedom of Association and the Right to Organise Convention, 1948, and that the habit of mutual consultation between the government and labour organisations should be developed. Before the conclusion of the procedure the government ratified that Convention and high-level talks and regular exchanges of views between the government and the labour organisations were initiated. The Commission's report was accepted by both parties as a basis for the progressive solution of outstanding questions. The report is regarded as a landmark in the history of industrial relations in Japan.

In 1965 the Governing Body referred to the Commission, with the consent of the Greek government, a complaint alleging violations of trade union rights in Greece, sent to the ILO by the Greek General Confederation of Labour. The complainant later withdrew the complaint, and the Commission, after hearing the two parties, agreed that it would not be appropriate to continue the case.

A further development in procedure occurred in 1968 when the Governing Body, at the request of the Spanish government, appointed a study group, whose chairman was Paul Ruegger (Swiss), a member of the Permanent Court of Arbitration, which, after a detailed factual analysis of the labour and trade union situations in Spain, formulated its findings in conclusions entitled, "Towards Reform of the Trade Union Law". The two main points developed in these conclusions are: "Firstly, the future of the labour and trade union situation in Spain can be determined by Spaniards alone"; and, "Secondly, the world, Spain herself, and Spain's place in the world are all changing at an unprecedented rate." The study group terminated its report with the following words: "These being the two decisive factors in the situation, we make only one formal recommendation, but regard it as of fundamental importance. It is that the fullest opportunities should be afforded for the widespread diffusion and completely free discussion of the whole of our report throughout Spain and throughout the international trade union movement, and that special steps, similar to those taken in connection with our third report, should be taken to give the fullest publicity to our conclusions."

The emphasis laid by this first study group on the importance of publicity and discussion in the solution of complex labour problems, apart from its immediate objective of solving Spain's own problems, seems likely to lead to requests from other governments, faced by intractable difficulties connected with freedom of association, for help from the ILO in catalysing their problems.

Still another procedure appropriate for examining questions relating to freedom of association (provided for in Article 26 of the Constitution) was used in 1969 when the Governing Body appointed a Commission of Enquiry to examine a complaint submitted by delegates to the Conference concerning observance by Greece of the two Conventions on freedom of association. The three-man Commission, whose chairman is the Rt. Hon. Lord Devlin (United Kingdom), submitted its first report to the Governing Body in October 1969 and is continuing its work.

Factual surveys

The continuing concern of the ILO over a period of years with the problem of ensuring respect for freedom of association showed the need for fuller factual information about the conditions in each country which affect the extent to which freedom of association is respected. The Governing Body, therefore, decided in 1958 that on-the-spot surveys should be undertaken and published. The surveys are designed to elicit the facts and to present them objectively; they are not to relate those facts to specific allegations of failure to respect trade union rights.[2]

The first two invitations from governments to undertake surveys came from the United States and the Soviet Union. Carried out in 1959, the surveys were published the following year.

When the report on the Soviet Union appeared, it was severely and in some cases violently criticised in the United States. It was stigmatised as an attempt to "whitewash" the Soviet trade unions; the ILO was attacked for "leaning over backwards" to present Soviet practice in a favourable light. But on the whole the two reports were widely welcomed as fair and impartial assessments of the facts relating to the position of the trade unions in the two countries. In particular it was noted that the report on the USSR was the first to be made by an independent enquiry for over forty years.

These reports have been followed by others relating to a variety of other countries, including the United Kingdom and Sweden.

Forced Labour

As will be shown in the chapter on Social Policy in non-Metropolitan Territories, the ILO did useful work before the war in the elimination or restriction of forced labour. But although the instruments adopted in 1930 applied to the metropolitan areas of members as well as the non-metropolitan territories, they were aimed mainly at the prevention of the exploitation of the labour of subject peoples.

The post-war approach of the ILO has been much wider. It was linked to the general promotion of human freedoms. The first step was an impartial enquiry into the nature and extent of forced labour. This enquiry was undertaken by an *Ad Hoc* Committee on Forced Labour under the chairmanship of Sir Ramaswami Mudaliar, appointed jointly by the Secretary-General of the United Nations and the Director-General of the ILO. Issued in 1953, the Committee's report revealed the existence of two

---

[2] A comprehensive enquiry had been carried out in 1955–56 into the extent of the freedom of employers' and workers' organisations from government domination and control in the seventy States which were members of the ILO at that time. The enquiry was conducted on behalf of the Governing Body by an independent committee of a quasi-judicial character under the chairmanship of Lord McNair, former President of the International Court of Justice.

main systems of forced labour affecting the populations of fully self-governing countries, one used primarily as a means of political coercion or punishment, the other primarily for economic purposes. These systems, the Committee concluded, should be abolished in all their forms, so as to ensure respect for, and observance of, human rights and fundamental freedoms.

Following upon the findings of the Committee, action taken by the ILO included the adoption in 1957 of the Abolition of Forced Labour Convention.

That Convention outlaws any form of forced or compulsory labour – (a) as a means of political coercion or education or as a punishment for holding or expressing political views ideologically opposed to the established political, social or economic system; (b) as a method of mobilising and using labour for purposes of economic development; (c) as a means of labour discipline; (d) as a punishment for having participated in strikes; and (e) as a means of racial, social, national or religious discrimination. Each member ratifying the Convention agrees to take effective measures to secure the immediate and complete abolition of these forms of forced or compulsory labour.

The Convention has been rapidly and widely ratified. By 1 January 1970 the number of ratifications had reached 88. Further, with a view to assessing the effect given to this Convention and also to the 1930 Forced Labour Convention by States which have not ratified them, the Governing Body decided in 1961 that these States should be requested to forward reports on the action taken by them on the provisions of the Conventions and the two 1930 Recommendations.

In addition, the work of examining current information on forced labour practices, begun by the joint *Ad Hoc* Committee, is being carried forward by the ILO Committee on Forced Labour.

Throughout its work on this front, the ILO has been inspired by a sentence in the report of the *Ad Hoc* Committee: "Apart from the physical suffering and hardship involved, what makes the system most dangerous to human freedom and dignity is that it trespasses on the inner convictions and ideas of persons to the extent of forcing them to change their opinions, convictions and even mental attitudes to the satisfaction of the State."

Non-observance of the provisions of the two Forced Labour Conventions is examined in the usual way by the ILO committee of experts on the application of Conventions and Recommendations. But in 1961, arising out of complaints made by Ghana against Portugal and by Portugal against Liberia, two Commissions of Enquiry were set up under Article 26 of the Constitution. Each Commission, consisting of three independent persons of high standing, heard the parties as well as witnesses, and in one case the

Commission made on-the-spot investigations (in the Portuguese colonies of Angola and Mozambique) to gain first-hand knowledge of the situation. The recommendations contained in the reports of these two Commissions were accepted by all parties and were followed by various measures taken by the governments concerned. The Committee of experts on the application of Conventions and Recommendations was then entrusted with the task of following up the action taken to implement the recommendations of the Commissions of Enquiry.

Discrimination in Employment and Occupation

Problems of discrimination in employment and occupation clearly fall into the broad field of the protection of human rights. In recent years the ILO has intensified its activities aimed at safeguarding and promoting equality of opportunity and treatment in respect of employment and occupation. While a number of Conventions and Recommendations dealt with specific aspects of non-discrimination policy, many other aspects remained untouched. Although discrimination in employment and occupation is obviously contrary to the social policy on which the ILO is based, it was not till 1958 that a comprehensive Convention and Recommendation were adopted.

Under the terms of the Convention each member agrees to declare and pursue a national policy designed to promote equality of opportunity and treatment in respect of employment and occupation. The Recommendation defines the areas in which a non-discrimination policy should be applied and the principles which should be followed.

The term discrimination includes any distinction, exclusion or preference which deprives a person of equality of opportunity or treatment in employment and occupation and which is made on the basis of race, colour, sex, religion, political opinion, national extraction or social origin.

In adopting these instruments the Conference recognised that while a statement of principle was fundamental, a strictly legislative approach to the complex and multifarious problems of discrimination was both inadequate and inappropriate. The underlying issues could not be determined by formal legal prohibitions. An educational approach, directed towards encouraging the attitudes and opinions necessary for preventing discrimination, was clearly more suitable for the long-term task of promoting equality of opportunity in this area of human rights. In 1961 the Governing Body approved a detailed educational and promotional programme of action.

That promotional programme, comprising publications, meetings, studies and other educational measures to encourage the acceptance in word and in deed of the principles of equality of opportunity and treatment has continued to be implemented by the ILO. Publications include *ILO's action against discrimination in Employment*, and *Fighting discrimination in Employment and Occupation* (a workers' education manual).

In 1968, following consideration by the Conference, the Governing Body committee on discrimination adopted detailed proposals for intensified action. These include a greater effort to mobilise public opinion against discrimination through the preparation of posters, leaflets, model lectures, etc.; preparing studies to determine areas where new international agreements on discrimination could be useful; organising educational seminars; and emphasising the ILO's function as a clearing-house of information on discrimination in employment and occupation. Some evidence is available that this promotional approach has had some impact, particularly in countries which have adopted similar methods in the struggle against discrimination.

Equal Remuneration for Work of Equal Value

One of the forms of discrimination based on sex which the ILO has done something to remove is inequality in respect of payment for work of equal value.

The principle that men and women should receive equal remuneration for work of equal value was one of the general principles embodied in the 1919 Peace Treaty[3] and when the Constitution of the Organisation was revised in 1946 this principle was included in the Preamble.

In the inter-war period, although the principle of equal remuneration was reaffirmed in the Minimum Wage-Fixing Machinery Recommendation adopted by the 1928 Session and in resolutions adopted by the 1937 and 1939 Sessions of the Conference, the differences in actual practice in most countries between men's and women's wages were at that time so great that it was impossible to do anything to give concrete international application to the principle.

During the war, particularly in the belligerent countries, differentials between men's and women's wages decreased sharply and it was generally accepted that sooner or later there would have to be widespread and effective application of the principle. Within the ILO the first reflection of this development occurred in the 1944 Recommendation on employment in the transition from war to peace, which includes the following: "In order to place women on a basis of equality with men in the employment

---

[3] Prior to 1919 the claim had been made for "equal pay for equal work"; the more precise drafting in the 1919 Peace Treaty was due to Lord Balfour.

market . . . steps should be taken to encourage the establishment of wage rates based on job content, without regard to sex."

The further action of the ILO in the direction of giving concrete international form to the principle of equal remuneration for work of equal value was stimulated in part by the World Federation of Trade Unions and in part by the United Nations Commission on the Status of Women. In 1948 the Economic and Social Council, which had placed on its agenda, at the request of the World Federation of Trade Unions, the application of the principle of equal pay for equal work, and had considered a recommendation on equal pay adopted by the Commission on the Status of Women, reaffirmed the principle and invited the ILO to proceed as rapidly as possible with the further consideration of the subject.

A Convention, adopted by the Conference in 1951, contains three main provisions; each member shall, by means appropriate to the methods in operation for determining rates of remuneration, promote and, insofar as is consistent with such methods, ensure the application to all workers of the principle of equal remuneration for men and women workers for work of equal value; where such action will assist in giving effect to the provisions of the Convention measures shall be taken to promote objective appraisal of jobs on the basis of the work to be performed; and differential rates between workers which correspond, without regard to sex, to differences, as determined by such objective appraisal, in the work to be performed shall not be considered as being contrary to the principle.

Although the extremely careful balance in the phrasing of this Convention (some might say its unstable equilibrium) did not give complete satisfaction to the women's organisations, the fact that it was possible to adopt it at all is a striking illustration of the distance the world has travelled since the inter-war period. At no time before the war could the Conference have adopted such a Convention owing to the opposition that would have been manifested by a majority of the governments, employers and workers.

The adoption of this Convention and its implementation by a large number of countries constitute a noteworthy contribution to the attainment of balanced social and economic progress.

Human Rights and Social and Economic Progress

In all these areas of social policy the ILO has been endeavouring to promote greater equality of opportunity and greater respect for human rights. Some may find that its approach has been opportunist and its solutions haphazard and piecemeal. It would be truer to say that it has had to take the world as it is, to identify and isolate particular problems requiring urgent solution, and then adopt such measures as were practicable in the circumstances of the time. The problems it has attacked and the solutions it has worked out are deeply rooted in the whole complex of political, economic, social and cultural trends which make up the changing world in which we live.

At the 1968 Conference the Director-General, taking a fresh look at methods of action for promoting the application of the rights and freedoms which more directly concern the ILO, concentrated on rights related to the four major objectives in the Declaration of Philadelphia – freedom, dignity, economic security and equal opportunity. He emphasised that the application of these rights does not call for a separate ILO programme; rather, the promotion of respect for human rights should pervade the implementation of all its programmes.

Writing on *Human Rights and International Labour Standards*, C. Wilfred Jenks has said: "We live in an age and in a world in which the search for a 'new birth of freedom' dominates the public consciousness as it has never done before. . . . It is perhaps the only force which gives a moral dignity to the economic problems and conflicts of our time" (p. 3).

15. CONDITIONS OF WORK, INCOMES, AND PRODUCTIVITY

In this chapter an account will be given of the activities of the ilo on hours of work, night work, weekly rest, holidays with pay, wages and incomes policy, and productivity. Within this group of problems, wide differences can be discerned in the attention devoted by the Organisation before and after the war respectively. In no other major field of activity has the action of the ilo been so discontinuous.

Throughout the whole of the pre-war period "hours of work" dominated the Conference, the Governing Body and the Office; indeed in the last few years before the war that question unduly absorbed the energy of the Organisation. After the war, on the other hand, many years elapsed before the question again figured on the agenda of the Conference.

Conversely, the question of productivity, which before the war the Organisation had been able to approach only very tentatively and in the face of determined opposition, has since the war proved one of its major concerns. Not only has productivity been discussed by the Conference and by expert committees, but the ilo has been called upon to provide technical co-operation on it.

These differences in the attention devoted to the two questions before and after the war constitute striking evidence that the ilo is no theoretical institute, but is a practical medium for catalysing the needs of the particular time and for taking balanced measures to meet those needs.

This does not mean that the action taken by the ilo has always been judicious or timely. As a tripartite body, the ilo has sometimes been unduly influenced by one of the three elements that compose it. In the pre-war treatment of hours of work and productivity, the historian can have little hesitation in finding that the course of the ilo was deflected owing on the one hand to the excessive insistence of the workers on the reduction of hours of work and on the other hand to the excessive resistance of the employers to the consideration of certain aspects of productivity.

Conditions of Work

The eight-hour day in industry

Long before the first world war the eight-hour day was the principal demand of the workers' organisations. The war evoked a general desire to

163

build a better industrial order; the minds of men were prepared to give a favourable reception to the old demands of the workers. In the Constitution reference to the eight-hour day was made in the Preamble; and Article 427 stated that one of the first objects of the new Organisation must be "the adoption of an eight-hour day or a forty-eight-hour week as the standard to be aimed at where it has not already been attained".

When the Conference held its first Session in 1919, the first item in its agenda was "the adoption of the principle of the eight-hour day and the forty-eight-hour week". At the outset the Conference faced the difficulty of defining in the same Convention the various adaptations of the eight-hour day which would be compatible with occupations so widely different as industrial work, work on board ship, agricultural work and office work, to mention only the main branches. In these circumstances, two decisions were taken; firstly to restrict the task of the 1919 Conference to drafting a Convention on the eight-hour day in industrial undertakings, including mines and railways, and secondly to convene a special session of the Conference to consider the regulation of hours of work in maritime occupations. The question of extending the principle of the eight-hour day to other categories of workers was reserved for the future.

With only one dissentient vote, the Conference succeeded in adopting a detailed Convention which provides that the working hours of persons employed in any public or private industrial undertaking, or in any branch thereof other than an undertaking in which only members of the same family are employed, shall not exceed eight in a day and forty-eight in a week.

When the Convention was enthusiastically adopted it was confidently expected that it would be rapidly and widely ratified. This expectation appeared all the more justified because the principle on which the Convention was based – the eight-hour day and the forty-eight-hour week – was already applied in some national systems of legislation.

The reluctance of governments to ratify the Convention was due in part to the rigidity of some of its provisions, and in part to the attacks on the principle of the eight-hour day which were made in many industrial countries either on the ground of the danger of foreign competition or because of the reduction in output alleged to be the result of the operation of the eight-hour day. In any case members did not wish to bind themselves by ratifying unless their economic competitors did the same. For this reason some members ratified the Convention conditionally on its being ratified by certain other States.

In spite of the slowness of ratification, the Governing Body three times, in 1921, in 1929 and in 1932, rejected formal proposals that the revision of the Convention should be placed on the agenda of the Conference. The workers' group remained unalterably opposed to revision, partly because they feared that revision would weaken the Convention and partly because although the Convention had been so poorly ratified, they realised that it had exercised an influence on national legislation and practice out of proportion to the extent of its ratification. If from this distance of time one looks back to the industrial history of the 1920's there can be no shadow of doubt that in many countries, if "the Washington Convention" of 1919 had not existed, the rule of the eight-hour day and forty-eight-hour week would have been abandoned.

With the 1930's and the Great Depression came the fight for the forty-hour week, which played the same sort of role in that decade as the battle for the implementation of the Washington Convention had played in the 1920's. Before that epic struggle, two other Conventions were adopted on hours of work, the Hours of Work (Commerce and Offices) Convention, 1930, and the Hours of Work (Coal Mines) Convention, 1931 (revised in 1935). Although these two Conventions were adopted in the 1930's they both belong to the social philosophy and economic policy of the 1920's.

Reduction of hours of work

Throughout the whole period from 1932 to 1939 the reduction of hours of work was a continuing preoccupation of the ILO. The problem was attacked from every angle and by every conceivable method. New procedures were devised and dangerous expedients were invented. Sometimes a little ground was gained here, only to be lost there. Experiment after experiment was tried, adventure after adventure was risked.

The history of the treatment of this problem by the ILO may be regarded either as a melancholy chronicle of repeated failure or as an inspiring saga of sustained refusal to accept defeat. If one looks at the record, not as a mere succession of proposals for Conventions most of which were defeated, but, as the historian must, against the background of the social, economic and political currents of the time, there can be no doubt that the latter conception is nearer the truth. For the ILO the 1930's were indeed years of trial and years of endurance. If it later succeeded in surviving the war, that was due in no small degree to the qualities of resistance and resilience which the critical pre-war years helped it to acquire.

It may appear surprising that, in spite of the bitter disappointment of the trade unions with the results of the efforts of the ILO to regulate hours of work, they should have continued to press so hard, throughout almost the whole of the 1930's, for the continuation, and indeed for the intensification, of its activities in this field. During the 1930's reduction of hours of work was advocated by the workers on two main grounds. These grounds were not always clearly formulated and often they were not even clearly understood. Reduction of hours of work was urged in the first place as a remedy for unemployment, and in the second place as a means through which the workers might share in the benefits of technical progress. Although both preoccupations were present in the minds of the workers throughout the whole period, the former was more prominent in the earlier years of the decade when unemployment had reached levels never previously known. As unemployment decreased in the later years of the decade the pressure behind the movement for reduction came mainly from the desire of the workers to obtain some advantage from the great increases in the technical productivity of the industries in which they were employed. As time went on, without any substantial successes being gained by the workers, the reduction of hours of work began to acquire for them something of the power of a religious dogma, and they continued to fight for it almost blindly with a mystical sense of crusade.

It was in 1933 that the issue was first squarely joined. In that year a Tripartite Preparatory Conference was held to consider the question of Hours of Work and Unemployment. Following upon that, efforts were made at the International Labour Conference in 1933 and 1934 to secure the adoption of general Conventions for the reduction of hours of work. Not only were these efforts unsuccessful, but they gave rise to unprecedented constitutional crises.

In 1935 the Conference succeeded in adopting, by 79 votes to 30, a Convention on the principle of a forty-hour week, in which members declare their approval of the principle of a forty-hour week applied in such a manner that the standard of living is not reduced in consequence, and the taking or facilitating of such measures as may be judged appropriate to this end, and undertake to apply this principle to classes of employment in accordance with the detailed provisions to be prescribed by such separate Conventions as are ratified by the member.

The Convention was stigmatised by its opponents as "empty propaganda", as "meaning nothing at all"; even its warmest partisans had no illusions that it would be widely ratified. Nevertheless, its momentary importance was great, because at one of the most critical periods in the history of the Organisation it gave a measure of satisfaction to the aspirations of the workers. And it also had a more lasting significance; as the Director well said in his closing speech at the Conference, the effect of the Convention was to substitute a new objective for the standard of the eight-hour day and forty-eight-hour week laid down in the Constitution.

At every succeeding session of the Conference until the outbreak of the war, the reduction of hours of work figured on the agenda in some shape or form. As a result of an immense amount of effort, only three

Conventions of minor importance were adopted, on public works undertaken or subsidised by governments, the textile industry, and glass-bottle works.[1]

Although the workers' delegates were bitterly disappointed that the efforts made continuously at each session of the Conference over a period of many years had ended in unsuccess, they showed a sense of realism and indeed of statesmanship in their appreciation of the position. On the one hand they saw that the international political tension which appeared to be rapidly reaching a climax was due to forces beyond the control of the governments represented in the Organisation. On the other hand they recognised that in all the organs of the ILO the utmost consideration had been given to trying to meet their demands, and that even by their most determined opponents they had always been treated with respect on a basis of equality. It was reflections such as these that contributed, when war came, to secure the continued loyalty of the workers to the ILO.

The war-time and post-war scene

During the war the intensification of production in all the belligerent and most of the neutral countries left no room for any question of reduction of hours of work. After the war the successful implementation of the policy of full employment together with the insatiable demand for all kinds of goods and services continued to keep the question of the reduction of hours far in the background.

In seeking to secure for the worker a fair share in the benefits of technological progress and increased productivity, whereas in the 1930's the aim of the workers' movement was to obtain reduction of hours of work with the maintenance of existing standards of living, after the war the aim in most countries was to secure improved standards of living without reduction in hours of work.

The question, however, was not dead. At successive sessions of the Conference, in the discussion of the Director-General's report, speakers indicated that the reduction of hours of work remained on the programme of action of the workers' movement. Resolutions adopted by the Conference showed that the workers wished to keep the matter alive.

Agreement appeared to be general that when the reduction of hours of work again came before the Conference for a formal decision, the programme should be launched at a timely juncture. In the case of the industrial relations programme, which converted pre-war failure into post-war success, a great part of the result was due to the happy timing of

---

[1] During the 1930's two other Conventions on hours of work were adopted, relating respectively to automatic sheet-glass works and road transport, but these were not regarded as "reduction of hours".

the action of the Conference. For the success of an hours-of-work programme, timing would be equally important.

In due course an appropriate moment arrived; a Recommendation was adopted in 1962 which differs in two important respects from the 1919 Convention. Whereas the Convention related essentially to conditions in industrialised countries, with specific exceptions or adjustments for named underdeveloped countries, the Recommendation took account fully of the position and prospects in developing countries in general. It therefore recognised the need for gradual progress, and urged, apart from the immediate reduction of hours to forty-eight a week, a progressive reduction towards the target already set in 1935, namely the forty-hour week. Further, that progressive reduction would take account in each country of various factors, such as the level of economic development, the danger of creating inflationary pressures, the advances resulting from the application of modern technology, automation and management techniques, and the need for improving the standard of living. The Recommendation therefore embodies the policy of balance in social progress and economic development.

Night work

The regulation of working hours is not only a matter of the limitation of the total number of hours worked per day and per week; the period of the twenty-four hours in which these hours fall is also important, particularly in the case of women and young persons, for whom regular night work is often harmful to health. The work of the Conference relating to night work for women and young workers is described in the chapter on Women, Children and Young Persons.

In the case of men the Conference has never taken any general action. This is because it is recognised that under modern conditions of industrial operation night work is often indispensable either on technical or on financial grounds. Technically, it is indispensable in all cases in which operations by nature of the technical processes involved, are necessarily carried on without a break at any time of the day, night or week. Financially, it is indispensable in all cases in which the cost of the machinery is so great that the capital invested in installing it would not be amortised unless the machinery could be made to work continuously day and night. For these reasons, while the Hours Conventions have included some provisions for the regulation of shift work, it has never been considered practicable or desirable to attempt to undertake prohibition of night work for men.

There is, however, one particular industry in which night work is not due to necessarily continuous processes or the use of expensive machinery, but has become the rule through long custom; this is the baking industry. An opportune moment for an international Convention prohibiting night work in bakeries appeared to arrive in 1925. In that year a Convention was adopted prohibiting any person engaged in the manufacture of bread in bakeries from working during specified night hours.

Perhaps the main value of the Convention was to lead to an advisory opinion of the Permanent Court of International Justice which, although it was given in a particular case and at a particular time, was of general import and of permanent application in safeguarding the competence of the Organisation.[2]

Weekly rest

The weekly rest is obviously closely connected with hours of work, and is in fact the necessary corollary of the limitation of weekly hours of work.

In 1921 the Conference adopted a Convention for workers in industry and transport, while a Recommendation dealt with the application of the weekly rest to commercial establishments.

In 1956–57 the Conference returned to the question of the weekly rest in Commerce and Offices and in the latter year adopted a Convention and Recommendation.

Holidays with pay

Although holidays with pay had been under discussion in the ILO for many years previously, it was not until 1936 that the Conference adopted a Convention.

The Convention provides that every person to whom the Convention applies shall be entitled after one year of continuous service to an annual holiday with pay of at least six working days, and if under sixteen years of age at least twelve working days. When the Convention was adopted it was widely felt that the minimum duration for the holiday with pay fixed by the Convention was low. At the time, however, it was not possible to secure general agreement on the fixing of a higher minimum, as even the modest standards of the Convention were strongly opposed by most of the employers. At a plenary sitting one of the delegates said: "I say that to ask my

[2] The employers' members of the Governing Body, objecting to a provision of the Convention, requested the Governing Body to obtain an advisory opinion from the Court as to the competence of the ILO to regulate the personal work of employers. In its opinion the Court confirmed the competence of the Organisation "to draw up and to propose labour legislation which, in order to protect certain classes of workers, also regulates incidentally the same work when performed by the employer himself". This advisory opinion of the Court, added to the two advisory opinions of 1922 on the competence of the Organisation in respect to agriculture, confirmed a wide interpretation of its competence.

country to embrace this Convention is to ask my country to commit industrial suicide."[3]

After the war a longer holiday with pay than that provided in the Convention had become so general that it proved possible for the 1954 session to adopt a Recommendation providing that the duration of the annual holiday with pay should be proportionate to the length of service performed with one or more employers during the year concerned and should be not less than two working weeks for twelve months of service.

In 1969 the time appeared ripe to bring up to date the 1936 Convention, and the Conference undertook a first discussion with a view to its revision in 1970. A revising Convention was adopted in 1970 (*see* p. 313).

Improvement in working conditions

Over the whole field of working conditions the improvement in the last half-century has been spectacular. At the beginning of the period in the more developed countries the industrial worker generally worked ten hours day, sixty hours a week, while in the non-industrialised countries the twelve-hour day was the rule. He enjoyed no holiday, except the few public or religious holidays or national days; the factory was dark and grimy; welfare facilities were limited to sanitary conveniences required by law, and even these were not always available.

Today, in industrialised countries, the typical industrial worker usually has a working week of from forty to forty-eight hours. Factories are better lit and ventilated and cleaner. Annual holidays with pay of two, three or even four weeks are general. Welfare facilities often include, in addition to sanitary, drinking-water and washing provision, first-aid and medical services and other amenities such as eating places and recreation grounds. In developing countries conditions are generally less good, but they are rapidly improving.

Wage Regulation

Although there was never any doubt that the regulation of wages came within the purview of the Organisation, it approached the problem with some caution. The mandate, indeed, was clear. The Preamble to the Constitution mentions the conditions of labour which involve injustice, hardship and privation to large numbers of people, and specified among the improvements which are urgently required "the provision of an adequate living wage". When the Declaration of Philadelphia was adopted, it included among the obligations of the Organisation "the raising of standards of living and the furtherance of policies in regard to wages and

[3] *Rec. Proc.*, Int. Lab. Conf., 1936, pp. 459–460.

earnings . . . calculated to ensure a just share of the fruits of progress to all, and a minimum wage to all employed and in need of such protection".

The ILO therefore has a right and a duty to tackle the question of wages internationally. Its hesitancy in beginning the job was due to its realisation that the international regulation of wages was an even more difficult matter than the international regulation of hours of work. Hours of work could be regulated internationally because there was a common yardstick; hours, minutes and seconds were the same measure of time in every country in the world. Wages were in an entirely different position; they were paid in a wide variety of currencies, and, when the ILO began to function, the relationship of these currencies to one another fluctuated from day to day in the most disconcerting manner. Further, there is no objective way of determining what is an "adequate living wage". Very different views may very reasonably be held on the matter, and what is an adequate living wage in one country may not be adequate in another. Again, the "raising of standards of living" may be accomplished either by increasing the aggregate national income or by redistributing the national income, or by a combination of both. Wages questions inevitably involve extremely controversial issues, not only of social justice but also of economic, financial and political policy.

Wage statistics

In these circumstances the ILO very wisely began its work on wages by attempting to secure an improvement in national wage statistics and by endeavouring to work out a method of establishing international comparable index numbers of real wages.

In 1924 as currencies became stabilised, the Office began to compile statistics of real wages in a certain number of occupations in the capitals of the chief industrial countries. The statistics were regularly published both in the *International Labour Review* and in the *Year Book of Labour Statistics*.

In pursuance of recommendations from the International Conference of Labour Statistics, the Conference adopted in 1938 a Convention concerning Statistics of Wages and Hours of Work. Under the Convention members undertake to compile statistics of wages and hours of work, to publish them as promptly as possible, and to communicate them to the Office. The ILO has supplemented its purely statistical studies on wages by issuing either in the *International Labour Review* or as special reports international studies on wages in particular industries. Reference may be made to one pre-war and one post-war study.

The special concern of the Organisation in the 1920's with conditions in coal mines led to the issue in 1925 and 1927 of reports which determined for each of the principal European coal-producing countries hourly wages, wages per shift and annual earnings. But the most important figures were those given at the conclusion of the study for each country. The figures for real wages, that is, for purchasing power, provided an indication of the social standards of miners, and the figures for wages per ton of saleable coal showed the wages costs for the industry and their importance in the economic life of mining countries.

This was the first occasion on which an enquiry into wages had enabled these two figures to be determined with such accuracy. These studies on wages in mines were the first of a series. Although they did not lead to the adoption of international regulations they were of undoubted value in providing a measure of the standard of living, often very unequal, of workers in one and the same occupation in different countries; and in throwing light on a question which after the war attracted even more attention, namely, wages as a factor in the cost of production.

In 1952 a report on textile wages was issued, following discussion by the Industrial Committee on Textiles. In spite of over thirty years of effort by the ILO and by governments to improve labour statistics, the Office had to draw attention to the limitations of the study: "The comparisons and analysis attempted in the report have been severely limited, first by the inadequacy of the available data, and secondly by the methodological difficulties involved in any international comparison of purchasing power or 'real wages'."

The reservations in this conclusion contain the best possible explanation why the ILO has displayed great caution in dealing with wages at the Conference.

Minimum wage regulation

It was in 1926 that the Governing Body first placed on the agenda of the Conference the question of wages, with a view to the adoption of international rules for the creation of minimum wage-fixing machinery. The Conference adopted a Convention in 1928.

Each State which ratifies undertakes to create or maintain machinery whereby minimum rates of wages can be fixed for workers employed in certain of the trades or parts of trades (and in particular in home-working trades) in which no arrangements exist for the effective regulation of wages by collective agreement or otherwise, and in which wages are exceptionally low.

When the Convention was adopted it was recognised to be of particular importance for countries which were industrially less highly developed and where workers in industry were not yet organised in trade unions which could discuss working conditions with the employers and prepare collective agreements. Its greatest service, however, was in its application to home-workers, who are generally inadequately protected and the majority of whom are women.

Protection of wages

After the war the Conference adopted Conventions on two somewhat disparate aspects of wage regulation and protection. The first of these, and in some ways the more important, was the Protection of Wages Convention.

Under the Convention, adopted in 1949, wages payable in money shall be payable only in legal tender, provided that the competent authority may permit or prescribe the payment of wages by bank or postal cheque or money order in certain circumstances. Nevertheless, national laws or regulations, collective agreements or arbitration awards may authorise the partial payment of wages in the form of allowances in kind.

This Convention, like the Minimum Wage Fixing Machinery Convention, was on the whole of greater interest to developing countries than to advanced industrial countries.

Labour clauses in public contracts

On the other hand, the Convention on Labour Clauses in Public Contracts, also adopted in 1949, was perhaps of greater interest to advanced industrial countries. The Convention provides that public contracts as defined in the Convention shall include clauses ensuring to the workers concerned wages (including allowances), hours of work and other conditions of labour not less favourable than those established for work of the same character in the trade or industry concerned in the district where the work is carried on, by collective agreement, arbitration award or national laws or regulations.

In 1949 when public contracts were being largely entered into in many countries in connection with reconstruction and rehabilitation the adoption of this Convention was highly opportune. The Convention was modelled on the principle of the "fair wages clause" widely applied in the United Kingdom, and its first ratification came from that country.

Incomes Policies and Economic Growth

In more recent years, the ILO has been paying increased attention to the relation of wages to living costs, and indeed to the whole problem of wages and incomes policies and economic growth. Ever since the second world war increases in wages have been accompanied by more or less continuously rising prices. In these circumstances the question has been asked whether the origin of inflation is in rising levels of demand or in wage increases pushing up costs and prices. The answer to this question is clearly important for the determination of policy measures aiming at maintaining economic stability or encouraging economic growth. While most countries seek to avoid both inflation and recession, the views taken on the relative importance of "demand pull" and "cost push" vary in different countries.

In 1963 and 1964 fresh impetus was given to the ILO's efforts to work out a wages and incomes policy in relation to economic development. The Conference, in discussing the Director-General's report on the programme and structure of the ILO, devoted much attention to the ILO's action on problems of incomes policy. In the discussion a considerable measure of agreement emerged that the ILO should have two main objectives. It should strive to work for (a) a distribution of incomes which is socially just, account being taken of the need to achieve high levels of productive employment and an equitable sharing of the responsibilities and rewards of economic growth; and (b) participation of free organisations of workers and employers in taking decisions affecting the distribution of incomes.

In working towards these objectives, the ILO is not concerned merely with wages. The ILO has to examine the problem of fair distribution of all the fruits of production. Consideration of incomes policy thus involves study of a wide range of other matters including taxation, social security, and measures for relating wages and other incomes to national plans or programmes for economic growth.

In all this work a major preoccupation of the ILO must continue to be to hold a proper balance between social progress and economic growth.

A new element in the situation has been created by the urge towards rapid economic development in the newly independent countries. On the one hand research has continued to be undertaken by the ILO on the extent to which real wages can be increased to contribute to improved standards of living without prejudicing long-term economic growth. On the other hand action was taken in preparation for the consideration by the Conference in 1969 of minimum wage-fixing machinery and related problems, with special reference to the developing countries. The steps taken to prepare for that discussion included, in addition to action of the Governing Body, a resolution adopted by the Conference in 1964, conclusions of the African Regional Conference (1964), a meeting of experts (1967) and the Inter-American Advisory Committee (1969). In 1969 the Conference, after the statutory "first discussion", placed the question on the agenda of the 1970 session; a Convention was then adopted (see p. 313).

The Productivity of Labour

Before the war the ILO did nothing constructive in the field of productivity. It is true that in the early 1920's a part of its energies were absorbed in the preparation of the monumental *Enquiry into Production*, but the opposition provoked by that enterprise was so great that throughout the rest of the pre-war period the ILO carefully refrained from touching a question that had proved to be so full of danger.

After the war a complete change occurred. The direction in which the Organisation would work was indeed foreshadowed in certain expressions used in the Declaration of Philadelphia: "poverty anywhere constitutes a danger to prosperity everywhere", "the war against want requires to be carried on with unrelenting vigour", "policies to ensure a just share of the fruits of progress to all". Such phrases as these were not verbiage; they indicated a change in the approach of the ILO. Much of the pre-war work of the ILO had been vulnerable to the criticism that all it aimed at was the redistribution of existing wealth. The new aim of the Organisation was to play its part not only in eliminating poverty and want but in creating wealth and plenty.

In his report to the 1950 session of the Conference, the Director-General included a chapter on this question, with a view to stimulating frank discussion. "From the world point of view the real need in almost every sector is for increased production. I know that measures aimed merely at increasing production may mean little to those who labour throughout the world, and may even in some countries arouse their active and legitimate suspicions unless these measures are closely linked to efforts to ensure the fair distribution of the fruits of their labour. They must also be continuously balanced and harmonised with the ultimate goal of full employment in an expanding economy. However, these considerations, fundamental as they may be, must not blind us to the basic need for increased productivity."[4]

The selection of this question for special consideration by the Conference in 1950 was timely. For a survey of trends in social and economic policy in the various countries in the previous year showed clearly that the main emphasis had not been laid on measures to redistribute income, but rather on measures to increase welfare by stepping up production.

Evidence of this was provided in every major branch of social policy. It was illustrated, in the manpower field, by the clearer realisation of the role of employment services in the implementation of policies aiming at higher levels of production, and by the keener interest taken in vocational guidance and training. It was illustrated, in the field of industrial relations, by the tendency for a new attitude on the part of the workers' organisations towards productivity-raising measures. It was illustrated, in the field of social security, by the tendency to use old-age pensions and other social services as an incentive to higher productivity. It was illustrated, in the

[4] *Report of the Director-General*, Int. Lab. Conf., 1950, p. 2.

field of conditions of work, on the one hand by a reluctance to concede shorter hours of work where this would lead, or was expected to lead, to less production, and on the other hand by an intensified interest in wage incentives and especially in systems of payment by results. It was one of the factors, side by side with humanitarian considerations, leading to progress in the fields of industrial safety and health. It was illustrated by the efforts made to increase productivity in the implementation of housing schemes. Finally, but not least important, it was illustrated by the wide variety of measures taken to increase productivity in agriculture.

The discussion in the Conference revealed a wide measure of agreement among the delegates on the central importance for the ILO of the problem of productivity. The relationship between productivity and full employment was emphasised; it was not enough that every worker should find employment; employment must be as productive as possible. Only if the average man produced more wealth could he enjoy a substantially higher standard of living. But efforts to increase production must be accompanied by measures to ensure fair distribution of the fruits of such efforts, and the claims of workers for security of employment must be reconciled with the drive for higher productivity.

Following upon the general discussion by the Conference, problems of productivity were considered by several Industrial Committees. The Textiles Committee in 1950, the Coal Mines Committee in 1951, the Metal Trades Committee in 1952 and the Chemical Industries Committee in the same year all discussed aspects of productivity in their several industries, and adopted resolutions.

In the meantime the ILO published in 1951 a report on *Methods of Labour Productivity Statistics* which had been submitted to the Seventh International Conference of Labour Statisticians, and undertook further study of the problems involved in the measurement and international comparison of labour productivity.

In the same year it published a report on *Payment by Results* containing the revised working paper submitted to, and the conclusions reached by, a meeting of experts on systems of payment by results convened by the Governing Body in 1951. The experts noted, *inter alia*, that systems of payment by results which are well adapted to the production processes and organisation of the plants concerned can make a substantial contribution to raising productivity, to lower costs of production, and to increased earnings for workers.

In 1952 an important meeting of experts on productivity in manufacturing industries was called by the Governing Body. In their conclusions the experts laid emphasis on the need for labour–management co-operation in all efforts to raise productivity. The experts concluded that the work of the ILO in the field of productivity should have three main objectives: (a) to promote a wider understanding of the meaning of higher productivity and of the results which may be expected from it; (b) to examine and try to promote agreement on the types and sequence of the measures that may need to be taken to ensure that increases in productivity will in fact lead rapidly to improvements in economic and social welfare for the community in general and in particular for those working in the undertakings where productivity is raised; and (c) to provide, in fields within the competence of the ILO, technical assistance and advice on the raising of productivity.

The conclusions of the experts were submitted in full to the 1953 Session of the Conference, and the Director-General in his annual report to the Conference again devoted a special chapter to the problem.

In that report the Director-General pointed out that improved distribution of what was already available and increased production resulting from reduction of unemployment and underemployment were both making enormous contributions to increased welfare. Those sources of improvement in living standards were well understood and widely accepted. But the possibilities of securing increased production by a more effective use of existing resources – that is, by raising productivity – were less well understood and less widely accepted. The Director-General expressed his conviction that higher productivity could offer valuable benefits in the attainment of the Organisation's objectives.

The wide measure of agreement expressed in the Conference provided a firm basis for the further development of the productivity programme of the ILO, particularly in the provision of technical advice and assistance.

Automation and technological change

It followed naturally from the concern of the ILO with productivity that it should devote attention to the labour and social aspects of automation.

In his reports to the 1955, 1956 and 1957 sessions of the Conference the Director-General laid emphasis on the impact of automation and other technological developments on labour and social policy. He urged, in particular, that as technology improved it gave the more advanced industrial countries an increased capacity to help the less advanced countries to accelerate their development. In the discussion at the Conference, in spite of the variety of economic systems represented, one conclusion emerged – there was scope for a common international approach through co-operation in the ILO.

Following up this conclusion of the Conference, the ILO carried out for several years, industry by industry, consideration of automation, mainly through the Industrial Committees. This patient examination added greatly to knowledge of the situations in which special problems arise in the application to industry of automation and technological change.

Returning to the question at the 1963 and subsequent sessions, the Director-General drew special attention to the urgency of measures to deal with the consequences to individuals of automation and technological change[5]. These human problems include displacement and unemployment of individual workers, elimination of traditional occupational skills and initiation of new skills, and transformation of programmes of vocational technical training. Delegates concurred that technological progress presents a complex problem of the adjustment of manpower to changing conditions. Some emphasised the importance of advance planning by governments, comprising analysis of impending technological changes, including automation, and appraisal of their effects on employment in various industries and occupations. Others drew attention to the importance of effective collaboration between management and labour to secure understanding and if possible acceptance of action to be taken in the plants concerned when particular technological changes were envisaged.

From these discussions it resulted that there was general agreement that the ILO should undertake a new and practical programme in this field. That programme embraces various areas of action. In the first place the ILO acts as a general clearing-house of information on the social and economic consequences of automation and technological change and measures to deal with them. This involves not only the collection of data and the prosecution of research but the wide distribution of the results so as to make them practically useful to governments, employers and workers throughout the world.

Operational Activities

While technical co-operation undertaken by the ILO contributes broadly to increasing productivity, many missions have dealt specifically with productivity as such. The results of some of the earlier productivity missions were disappointing. Management attitudes are sometimes resistant to change. Workers fear redundancy. Evidence of the real usefulness of other missions has been provided by requests of the governments concerned, after an initial mission has completed its assignment, for a

---

[5] The 1963 Conference adopted a Recommendation on Termination of Employment at the Initiative of the Employer which is important in connection with redundancy due to automation, though it also has other applications. The underlying principle of this Recommendation is that "termination of employment should not take place unless there is a valid reason for such termination connected with the capacity or conduct of the worker or based on the operational requirements of the undertaking, establishment or service".

continuation and expansion of its work. For example, in India, after a mission had demonstrated increases of up to two hundred per cent in productivity in the engineering and textile industries the government asked the ILO to assist in the establishment of a National Productivity Centre in order that the work started by the experts might be continued and developed on a permanent basis. In Israel, the mission of one of the two experts originally sent out to assist the Israeli Productivity Institute was extended in order to continue that assistance and also to advise the Israeli Institute of Technology. In these Institutes many thousand persons have since been trained in productivity techniques.

Experience has shown that, if ILO technical co-operation in productivity is to be fully effective, it is usually necessary for the assistance to be continued over a period of years. Examples of long-term missions, in different regions of the world, have been those in India, in the United Arab Republic, and in Central America.

In India, after the modest beginning mentioned above, a National Productivity Council was established. The Council includes representatives of the Indian Government, employers' organisations, trade unions and technical and scientific institutes. An ILO productivity expert co-operated with the Council in the formulation of its objectives and the organisation of its work.[6]

In Egypt, the ILO productivity and vocational training mission which began work in 1954 continued to assist the Ministry of Industry in implementing planning for industry. Special advice on organisation and other management questions was also given to individual plants. Possible increases in productivity were worked out and in many cases the new techniques were installed. In addition, courses in productivity improvement methods were attended by top executives in Cairo and Alexandria.

In Central America, ILO co-operation in productivity contributed to the Central American Integration Programme. The ILO mission, after a survey of the factors affecting productivity, gave assistance in the application of productivity improvement techniques in Guatemala, Honduras, Nicaragua and El Salvador. In 1959 this project developed into a combined productivity and vocational training mission.

All these projects, together with other productivity programmes described in Chapter 12, have a common and characteristic aim, to further the application of modern techniques for raising productivity, especially,

---

[6] In one of the earlier ILO projects leading to the establishment of the Indian Productivity Council the results made an immediate impression on public opinion in New Delhi. An ILO productivity specialist had been called in to advise on methods of stepping up repairs on buses in the city's transport workshops. Thanks to new techniques introduced by the ILO expert, the output of repaired vehicles was increased from sixty-four every four weeks to ninety-six.

in view of the lack of capital in developing countries, those which require little new capital investment. For the guidance of ILO productivity missions in such countries the ILO has prepared practical handbooks on methods of raising productivity, to be used in connection with systematic courses of practical training in work study and related techniques. A manual on *Work Study* has proved particularly useful.

In addition, ILO productivity missions have been able to draw on the recommendations of meetings of experts assembled from many parts of the world to work out sound principles for raising productivity. The ILO has published these recommendations under the title *Raising Productivity*.

In contrast to such large-scale, long-term projects, involving training in complicated techniques, one project may be mentioned as an example of a case in which simple methods have been used to effect improvements in simple operations. In Israel an ILO expert was set to work to increase productivity in the orange groves. After studying the methods used, the ILO expert instructed 250 foremen in up-to-date techniques of orange-picking and packing. He introduced tall step-ladders to straddle the low trees so that the workers could pick their way up one side of the tree, then down the other. He showed them how to pile the packing boxes three high, so they could empty their bags more quickly and easily. As a result of these and other changes, productivity increased more than 100 per cent.

However important the technical procedures for raising productivity may be, the underlying purpose is the contribution of higher productivity to improved standards of human well-being. In all its productivity work the ILO has tried to ensure the fullest co-operation of management and workers in carrying out the project; it has done its best to demonstrate that higher productivity is beneficial both to the management and to the workers.

16. LABOUR-MANAGEMENT DEVELOPMENTS

In the Constitution of the ilo the words "labour–management" do not appear. In 1919 the term was not in general use in any country. In the 1920's "industrial relations" began to be used to describe the contacts between organised management and the trade unions, or between individual employers and groups of workers, in collective bargaining and negotiation and also in day-to-day relations in particular plants. After the war "industrial relations" tended to be supplanted by "labour–management relations" in the terminology of the ilo and many of its member States.

This chapter will include a discussion of the ilo's work in labour–management relations and in the connected areas of workers' education and management development. It will also cover its activities in the sphere of labour administration.

Labour–Management Relations

Pre-war approaches

The active concern of the ilo with the promotion of labour–management relations began in 1928. In that year the Conference adopted a resolution requesting the Governing Body to instruct the Office to follow the progress of the spirit of collaboration between employers and employed and to report on the subject from time to time. This resolution was prompted by recent action in the United States, and also in certain European countries and in Australia and New Zealand, to improve "industrial relations", primarily the day-to-day working relationships between management and workers at the place of work.

In implementation of the 1928 resolution the Governing Body adopted a plan of work, the most original feature of which was that members of the Office staff should visit outstandingly successful undertakings having a developed system of labour–management relations. After these visits reports were to be prepared covering the organisation of industrial relations in the undertaking. It was thanks to the financial aid of Industrial Relations Counselors, Inc., of New York, that the ilo was able to embark on these studies.

The reports issued by the ilo covered a wide variety of industrial,

181

commercial, mining and transport undertakings in Belgium, Canada, Czechoslovakia, France, Germany, Great Britain, Italy, Netherlands, the Saar, Sweden and the United States. The undertakings visited included Philips, electricity (Netherlands), Siemens, machinery and electricity (Germany), Sandviken, steel (Sweden), Naumkeag, textiles (USA), Fiat, motors (Italy), coalmines of the Saar, Bata, shoes (Czechoslovakia), London Transport, Canadian National Railways.

These reports proved to be "best-sellers"; this showed that there was a real desire among both employers and workers to know exactly how their day-to-day problems were being handled in individual undertakings in other countries.

In unobtrusive ways during the pre-war period the Organisation made other contributions to labour–management relations practice. Many of the discussions in the Conference constituted a model of what industrial discussions and negotiations should be; these techniques of inter-group discussion and negotiation began in fact to be applied in national practice. Again, membership in the tripartite Organisation gave a stimulus in industrially underdeveloped countries to the growth of effective organisations of employers and workers and to the development of methods of systematic co-operation between them.

Post-war standard-setting

In the post-war period, the work of the ILO on the broad front of industrial relations has been characterised by two approaches.

In the first place, in 1947 the Conference initiated a comprehensive programme aimed at the international regulation of industrial relations through the adoption of Conventions and Recommendations. In Chapter 14 reference has been made to the first two of these standard-setting Conventions, on freedom of association, the right to organise and collective bargaining, adopted in 1948 and 1949.

This work was followed in 1951 by a Recommendation laying down the guiding principles for collective bargaining machinery and a second Recommendation setting standards for voluntary conciliation and arbitration. Both can be implemented either by the parties concerned (employers and workers) or by the public authorities, whichever seems to be the better way in any national situation.

Lastly, in 1952, the Conference adopted a Recommendation on co-operation at the plant level between employers and workers as regards matters not covered by collective bargaining, and also a resolution containing model guiding principles on such co-operation.

The working out and adoption of these standards, in a period of five years, on a group of subjects with which the Conference found it impossible to deal before the war, represent a valuable achievement of the Organisation in the "legislative" field.

As a result of this standard-setting much has been done by and through the ILO to develop the machinery for solving the legislative problems of industrial relations and more generally to lay a basis for more satisfactory relations between employers and workers.

Positive promotion of co-operation

In 1955 the Director-General decided that, as a result of what had been accomplished, the time was ripe to take a wider view of the whole problem of labour–management relations and to seek to develop the work of the Organisation from the standpoint not only of the protection of rights and the prevention of conflict but also of the positive promotion of co-operation. As the special theme of his report to the Conference he therefore selected the question of labour–management relations.

In that report the Director-General emphasised that the relations between labour and management were a vital force in the development of modern industrial society. They had an immediate impact on the critical issues which arise in the transition from one stage of industrialisation to another. If, as many believed, the world was on the threshold of a second industrial revolution produced by modern technology, it was urgent for the Organisation to examine what it could do to promote better labour–management relations. The state of labour–management relations, he pointed out, was an important conditioning factor in attaining the broad goals laid down for the Organisation in recent years: the raising of productivity, the promotion of fuller employment of human resources in the underdeveloped countries, the improvement of working conditions and the guaranteeing to the worker of a higher degree of economic security. In view of the widening recognition that higher productivity was essential for raising standards of material prosperity, there had been a perceptible shift of emphasis in labour–management relations toward what had been called "collective thinking rather than conflicting bargaining".

In the discussion, twenty-two Ministers of Cabinet rank, together with outstanding employers and trade union leaders from many of the seventy-four States represented at the Conference, offered suggestions as to the directions in which the resources of the Organisation might be mobilised. Sir Walter Monckton (now Viscount Monckton), then Minister of Labour and National Service of Great Britain, set forth the five basic elements necessary for the establishment of good human relations, namely (a) payment of fair wages and observance of good conditions, (b) proper and adequate supervision and control, (c) provision of information and perfection of the art of communication, (d) consultation and utilisation of the creative energy of the workpeople, and (e) recognition of the human factor; "man is neither a tool nor a machine, but a complex human personality." James P. Mitchell, Secretary of Labor of the United States, said that in his country the wide area of agreement shown by the making or renewing each year of over 100,000 voluntary collective agreements demonstrated that free employers and free workers had learned to live and work together harmoniously and with mutual respect and understanding.

The Conference, on the basis of proposals jointly made by the government delegates of the five Scandinavian countries, adopted a resolution (a) asking the Director-General, in the light of the observations made by members of the Conference, to consider how the ILO's activities should be modified or supplemented so as to contribute effectively towards promoting labour–management co-operation and better human relations in industry, and (b) asking the Governing Body to draw up a practical programme of ILO action on the basis of the proposals to be submitted by the Director-General, and to consider bringing the matter before a future session of the Conference in some appropriate form.

In pursuance of this resolution and with the assistance of a committee of experts, a programme of action was drawn up, approved by the Governing Body in 1957, and progressively implemented.

In the field of research and information several brochures in a special series of labour–management pamphlets have been issued and widely distributed to employers, employers' organisations, trade unions, government departments and research and educational institutes throughout the world.

A technical meeting on certain aspects of industrial relations inside undertakings was held in 1959 and submitted a report on four questions: the position and responsibilities of the personnel department, the status and duties of workers' representatives, works rules, and dismissal procedures. In their report the experts stressed the value for the promotion of good labour–management relations of the ILO's activities in the field of workers' education and management development. On relations between public authorities and employers' and workers' organisations at the industrial and national level, in 1960 a Recommendation was adopted under which such consultation and co-operation should be provided for or facilitated by voluntary action on the part of employers' and workers' organisations; or by promotional action on the part of public authorities; or by laws or regulations; or by a combination of any of these methods.

In 1967 Recommendations were adopted concerning (a) communications between management and workers within the undertaking, and (b) examination of grievances within the undertaking with a view to their settlement. The provisions in these Recommendations are based on the importance of a climate of mutual understanding and confidence within undertakings "favourable both to the efficiency of the undertaking and to the aspirations of the workers".

Technical co-operation

As a parallel development the ILO has been intensifying its technical co-operation activities in this field.

Experts have been sent to several countries to advise and assist in the formulation of labour–management relations policy and in the drafting of legislation. Among countries receiving assistance have been Afghanistan, Bolivia, Costa Rica, Greece, India, Iran, Paraguay, Peru, the Philippines and Venezuela. Special reference may be made to the assistance furnished to Honduras. In 1954 that country was swept by waves of strikes, and relations between employers and workers were completely disrupted. A conciliation commission recommended that Honduras (which had left the ILO on the eve of the second world war) should rejoin the ILO and request its help in developing a code of labour legislation and practice. The government accordingly applied for readmission and requested the ILO to give the needed assistance. The ILO sent experts who helped not only in drafting new labour legislation, but also in training government officials and labour inspectors in methods of implementation, and in giving guidance to trade union and employers' representatives in the techniques of labour–management relations.

Under the technical co-operation programme, each year a number of fellowships have been granted to management and trade union representatives to enable them to study the techniques and methods in use in industrially advanced countries in the promotion of labour–management co-operation.

From time to time the ILO has arranged joint study tours for employers' and workers' leaders. One of these brought such leaders from Burma, Ceylon, India, Indonesia, Japan and Pakistan to ILO headquarters, the United Kingdom and the Federal Republic of Germany. In these two countries the group was accompanied by an ILO official, and it was able to observe and study practical action in labour–management relations. As a follow-up to this study tour, a team consisting of a management expert and a trade union expert from the Federal Republic of Germany, accompanied by an ILO official, visited Ceylon and Pakistan for exchanges of views with employers and trade union groups and government officials. A team of Turkish employers and workers was brought to study industrial relations in Western European countries.

An activity of a somewhat different kind was the Inter-American Study Conference on Labour–Management Relations, held in 1960 in Montevideo, which afforded opportunity for discussion of a variety of industrial relations problems.

While the ILO has thus been able to render useful assistance in this field, the programme has been much less extensive than in the case of vocational training. Assistance in labour–management co-operation is less identifiably technical in character, and there has consequently been less demand for it. Moreover, assistance in industrial relations is particularly delicate as the problems involve human behaviour, social institutions and even political systems.[1]

Role of Industrial Committees

Among the post-war activities of the ILO in labour–management relations, a prominent place must be assigned to the work of the Industrial Committees. Each Industrial Committee is an integral part of the international machinery of industrial relations, and as a result of attendance at them many a delegate has gained a new insight into the meaning and possibilities of labour–management relations.

In Chapter 6 an account has been given of the setting-up, composition and functions of Industrial Committees, but mention may be made here of three respects in which Industrial Committees have proved to be of special importance from the standpoint of labour–management relations.

In the first place, although each Committee is tripartite, in practice the discussions in the Committees are conducted in the main by the employers' and workers' delegates. This is appropriate, for in each industry the employers and the workers are the parties principally concerned.

In the second place, every Committee has had on its agenda the question of industrial relations in some specific form. In addition to recommending a series of points for the guidance of employers and workers in applying the principles of human relations, the Metal Trades Committee, at its 1952 session, conscious of the broad implications of improved human relations in a wide range of industries closely associated with the metal trades, proposed that the Governing Body should consider bringing the question of human relations before an early session of the International Labour Conference.

In the third place, the meetings of the Committees, apart from any specific conclusions reached, have made an important contribution to the practical development of labour–management relations. Meetings of

---

[1] The ILO very rarely takes action in any national labour–management dispute. An exception occurred in 1957 when the ILO was invited to mediate in a particularly difficult dispute on the most important railway in Peru. The Director-General sent one of his senior officials to Peru, who succeeded after a month's negotiations in securing a lasting settlement.

Industrial Committees have facilitated personal contacts between delegates of different groups and various countries, have encouraged the exchange of information on questions not on the agenda of the Committees, and have exerted an influence on the minds and actions of the delegates in the direction of improved collaboration. In reaching agreement on the resolutions to be adopted by the Committees there has generally been a large measure of accommodation on all sides. Quite apart from the actual results achieved the discussions themselves have been of value to many delegates as an exercise in management–worker negotiation.

In this respect, the work of the Industrial Committees has been closely akin to the operational activities of the ILO. This "operational" aspect has also been in evidence in the meetings of Committees held in various countries where it has been possible for delegates to visit plants in the countries concerned and to see for themselves how their industry is carried on in those countries, in respect both of technical organisation and of labour–management relations.

Future prospects

The Director-General has more than once emphasised that the ILO's work in this field is "promotional". For its success it depends upon education, encouragement, persuasion and example. The promotion of labour–management relations must be a gradual process, suited to the long-term needs to be met. If the ILO has much to give, it has also much to learn. That is why the programme has been, and must continue to be, flexible.

In the early future it is to be expected that more attention will be devoted to certain specific matters indicated in the 1967 Recommendation. One of these is communication within the undertaking. In urging the dissemination and exchange of information, the Recommendation listed meetings for the purpose of exchanging views and information, mass media such as magazines, news-letters and information and induction leaflets, exhibitions, plant visits, radio and television.

What the Recommendation does not sufficiently stress is that communication should be a two-way process. It should not be merely communication by the management to the workers; there should also be communication by the workers to the management. Among the many ways in which this may be done, one of the most important is the provision of opportunity and encouragement to the workers at all levels to communicate to management suggestions and opinions relating to the operations of the undertaking as well as to individual or group grievances.

Another question in worker–management relations to which the ILO will give attention is that of workers' representation within the undertaking. In 1970 the Conference conducted a first discussion on the protection of, and facilities to be afforded to, workers' representatives within the undertaking.

On certain aspects of that matter some preliminary discussion took place in 1967 at an ILO technical meeting. That meeting agreed that under any type of industrial relations there was a need for representatives of workers' interests at the level of the plant, provided it reached a certain minimum size, and that the effective functioning of such representatives was in the interest not only of the workers but of the management as well. The meeting also agreed that these workers' representatives were bound often to find themselves in conflict with management by reason of the nature of their duties; this made it necessary that they should have protection against discriminatory measures, together with facilities to carry out their responsibilities. On the thorny question of how the workers should be represented, the discussion at the meeting was inconclusive – should representation be exclusively trade union in character, or based on election by all the workers, unionised or not? No agreement appeared possible at that time.

While many other similarly refractory problems will have to continue to be debated, the progress already made seems to suggest that the future will see, in countries of differing economic systems and stages of development, a gradual approach towards fuller comprehension both by management and by workers of the importance of working out flexible measures within the plant providing for mutual communication, negotiation and participation.

Speeches at the Conference in the discussion of the Director-General's Report, the discussion by Industrial Committees of human relations in industry, various passages in studies published by the Office – all these indicate that the world is now approaching a point in its social evolution, if it has not already reached it, where, in order to be a good worker a man needs not only decent working and living conditions and a measure of economic security but also something else which may be called either job-satisfaction or a sense of the dignity of labour. To be really satisfying work must have a social purpose as well as an economic reward. Is there not some hope that the dissatisfactions and frustrations from which the industrial world suffers may be overcome if workers and employers can feel that their labour has a social content and value, that in their work they are effectively participating in a common constructive effort?

Workers' Education

It was only after the war that the ILO became actively conscious of needs and opportunities for service in connection with workers' education. In this field its work is closely allied to its promotional activities in labour–

management relations. It was in 1956–57 that the workers' education programme was launched and the first steps taken to implement it. A meeting of experts reviewed the work already done by the ILO, and formulated recommendations for carrying out the programme. Its aim is to help equip the workers with the knowledge and understanding they need not only to discharge their functional and civic responsibilities but also to contribute fully to balanced economic growth and social development.

In many countries, especially the economically underdeveloped, the trade unions are young and inexperienced. They need help to educate the leaders and the rank and file in sound methods of union activity and in the process of collective negotiation.

In this work the ILO has been careful not to undertake tasks that are properly those of the unions themselves. The programme consists essentially of education in questions falling within the framework of the ILO's normal activities, such as labour law and administration, collective negotiation, social security and co-operative organisation.

As a beginning, the ILO issued a necessary technical tool – a manual on workers' education methods and techniques, sufficiently flexible to be adapted to meet the varying needs in different countries and regions. This was followed by a series of workers' education manuals on co-operation, social security, freedom of association, industrial accident prevention, industrial hygiene and other matters falling within the field of action of the ILO. Each of these handbooks was issued in English, French, German, Spanish, Arabic, Japanese, Hindi and Urdu. Some of them have been translated at the expense of the organisation concerned into other languages, such as Burmese, Chinese, Greek and Sindhi.

Other basic documentary work includes elementary reading matter on economic and social subjects for newly literate workers, and a collection of 300 films and film-strips in six languages for loan to workers' education bodies. These are being utilised throughout the world.

One of the ILO's most useful forms of educational activity consists in convening or participating in international and regional seminars on workers' education. Thus, in 1958 the ILO organised an international seminar in Geneva with participants from twenty-one countries in all parts of the world, in 1959 a regional seminar for Asian workers' education organisers and instructors, in 1960 a seminar for Latin America and the Caribbean, and in 1961 two similar seminars, one for Arab States and one for Africa.

The topics discussed in these seminars vary. The question of trade union participation in development planning formed the theme of three seminars held respectively in Santiago (Chile) in 1966 for union leaders in eighteen Latin American countries, in Dakar also in 1966 for a group of union leaders from a number of African countries, and in Delhi in 1968 for participants from eight Asian countries. A seminar on trade union research and documentation services met in Geneva in 1967, attended by twenty-four trade union research workers and experts on workers' education from all over the world. Another seminar held in Geneva in 1967 on the use of radio and television for workers' education was the first international meeting specially to discuss this topic. In cases in which the seminars are convened by the ILO, the participants' travelling and subsistence expenses are defrayed by the ILO. But the ILO also participates in many courses or symposia convened by international trade union organisations, national trade union bodies or educational institutions; it sends experts, supplies teaching equipment and allocates fellowships to trainees.

The ILO has sent advisory missions to about forty countries, in addition to twenty more in Africa for which it organised an experimental leadership training scheme. The ILO has a staff of regional experts, who more particularly in Africa train local leaders and give advice to any trade union organisation seeking it.

It will be seen that the ILO's work in this field has assumed many shapes. But the aim is uniform. All the activities are directed to assist workers' organisations which are being called upon more and more to undertake responsible participation in social and economic institutions at both national and international levels.

Management Development

As a result of the recent rapid technological changes in industry, and the increased momentum of industrialisation in developing countries, management, like labour, has been faced with new problems and wider responsibilities. This has given an impetus to the study of new management techniques and methods.

In many developing countries lack of skill and experience in management has naturally proved an obstacle to industrial efficiency and success. The need has therefore been felt for assistance in educating management in modern principles of industrial organisation and administration, including the development of human relationships in industry.

Recognising the opportunities for service by the ILO presented by this situation, the Conference adopted in 1958 a resolution on management development submitted by the government delegation of India. This resolution emphasised the importance of spreading a knowledge of economically and socially sound principles and techniques of management; and proposed that the ILO give a high priority in its work to activities which would contribute to meeting the need for management development and training, more particularly in the industrially less advanced countries.

In pursuance of this resolution the ILO has been carrying out a programme providing for two main branches of action.

This programme covers the technical planning, execution and control of management development activities, involving training for managerial posts in all economic sectors except public administration. It includes the execution and technical supervision of projects relating to small-scale industries and handicrafts. It also includes research on management techniques and the organisation of production and on the adaptation of these techniques to the needs and conditions of developing countries.

All the research activities within this programme are designed either to support or to promote technical co-operation projects and in this sense the whole programme is operational, whether carried out in Geneva or in the field. By 1970 centres devoted wholly or mainly to management development and training will have been set up, generally with ILO co-operation, in most of the countries sufficiently industrialised to support them.

Technical co-operation in 1969 included a total of thirty projects under the UNDP Special Fund for management development and management aspects of employment development, in addition to UNDP/TA, regular budget and trust fund projects.

On the research side of the programme, the ILO has issued some thirty practical instructional manuals on different aspects of management, and also a series of textbooks. In 1969 a revised edition of *Introduction to Work Study* was issued. First published in 1957, this book sold approximately 130,000 copies in the original edition. Other publications in 1968 and 1969 were *Creating a Market, Introduction to Quality Management, Business Diagnosis* and *Management in the Small Enterprise*.

Of the new work items the most important is the development of electronic data processing centres for management. The spread of the use of computers for processing management information as a means of planning and control is extremely rapid and soon many developing countries will need common service centres where individual enterprises can not only buy time on computers but also be advised on the development of systems for data processing to meet their specific needs. Such centres would be attached to existing management development and productivity institutes and would represent a further phase in the evolution of institutes which the ILO has helped to establish.

Labour Administration

Before the establishment of the ILO very few countries had a Ministry of Labour. In most countries in which there was some form of labour

administration, the services concerned were attached, as subsidiary departments, to Ministries such as the Ministry of the Interior (Home Office)
and the Ministry of Commerce (Board of Trade). Now, Ministries of
Labour exist in most countries, and they have found it necessary to set up
administrative departments to implement the various sectors of social
policy. As new nations have come into being and the world has become
increasingly industrialised, new problems of labour administration have
arisen and new needs have been generated.

Since the war the ILO has devoted much attention to helping to solve
these new problems and to assisting new countries to organise appropriate
services of labour administration.

At the 1953 session of the Conference these needs were considered in
detail in the discussion of the organisation and working of national labour
departments, and the ILO's operational programme has included much
technical co-operation with governments in the development of their
labour administration services.

On this front a practical basis was provided for technical co-operation
by the standards set in Conference decisions, such as the Labour Inspection
Convention and Recommendation, 1947, the Convention concerning
Statistics of Wages and Hours of Work, 1938, and the Employment Service
Convention and Recommendation, 1948.

Technical co-operation has been furnished on two main groups of
questions.

In the first place advisory missions have been sent to individual countries
to assist in the setting-up or reorganisation of their labour administration
in general or specific technical labour services. For example, missions to
Burma, Cambodia, Libya, Morocco, Thailand and Venezuela have advised
on labour administration in general; while missions to Iran, Iraq and the
Philippines have helped with the development of national labour inspection
services. In some cases the results of the missions have been disappointing
owing to the inability of the governments to appoint inspectors or other
officials or to give them adequate powers. Other missions have given
assistance in developing labour statistical services; such services are
essential for the formulation and application of policy in employment,
wages, hours and other fields.

The other main area in which technical co-operation has been given is
the training of labour administration staff, particularly labour inspectors,
employment service officers and junior officials. A regional labour administration institute set up in 1955 in Istanbul under the joint auspices
of the ILO and the Turkish Government, trained over five hundred labour
officials from sixteen countries of the Near and Middle East in five years.
A similar institute set up in 1956 in Mexico City in collaboration with the

Mexican Government trained seventy Mexican officials in two years. Both these institutes have, in accordance with the original plans, been handed over to the governments concerned, which are continuing to operate them. Assistance in the training of labour administration staff has also been given by the ILO through participation in regional or national seminars in Africa and elsewhere

In addition to these forms of technical co-operation, many ILO activities contribute to the development of labour and industrial institutions other than the central government departments. Thus, productivity missions help to set up national productivity centres. Vocational training missions help to establish or reorganise technical schools and colleges. Social security missions help to found or reform social security institutions. Co-operative missions help to organise co-operative societies and guide their activities in rural and community development.

In all these ways the ILO is helping countries to provide administrative machinery adequate to the increasing complexity of the new industrial world. Good labour administration is not only a means of enforcing minimum standards; it can be a positive force in surmounting many of the problems of growth in an expanding economy.

Economic and Social Policy

Although it may not be easy, at first sight, to discern the relationship to economic and social policy of some of the diverse questions discussed in this chapter, a little reflection will help to indicate their place in a balanced programme.

The first purpose of labour–management development is to solve the problem of conflict between trade unions and employers' organisations. The elimination of the class-war is a basic feature of the economic and social policy of modern democracies. But even where outmoded conceptions of class-war have been abandoned, relations between management and labour may assume the form of a conflict between an economic standpoint on the one hand and a social standpoint on the other. The tension and friction in the community resulting from such conflict may be reduced both by the adoption of legislative or other measures for the settlement or, better still, the prevention of disputes, and by the promotion of a better understanding of the social and economic problems involved.

Within this framework the ILO has made a major contribution. In the first place, the Conventions on freedom of association, the right to organise and collective bargaining, and the Recommendations on voluntary conciliation and arbitration, and on co-operation between employers and trade unions have set international standards on these basic matters. In the second place, through the parallel programmes of workers' education and management development, much is being done to implement the standards by creating a new sense of social and economic responsibility in trade unions and employers' organisations and thus promoting labour–management relationships beneficial to the community as a whole.

Finally, the ILO International Institute for Labour Studies is doing much to encourage an impartial appreciation among trade unionists, managerial staffs and public servants of the problems confronting them in their day-to-day work, and thus to contribute to balanced economic and social progress.

17. SOCIAL SECURITY

IN no other sphere has the record of the ILO showed such consistent and conspicuous success. The reasons for this are not difficult to identify.

In the first place, in this field the ILO started from scratch. In 1919 no country in the world had a comprehensive system of social insurance. The term "social insurance" was not in general use, and the term "social security" had not been invented. Only two important industrial countries, Germany and Great Britain, had protected the workers against sickness, invalidity and old age. Elsewhere social insurance, if it existed, covered only one risk or one section of the wage earners. The ILO could therefore be a pioneer.

In the second place, the world was ready for a lead. Partly because of, and partly in spite of, the conditions produced by the economic depression which followed the first world war there was a growing recognition of the responsibility of the State for protecting the worker against occupational and social risks. The State should make arrangements by law for covering these risks by insurance and the individual should in his own interest and that of society be compelled to insure. This was the social philosophy which began to gain ground, and every type of economic system gradually began to prepare itself to adopt the method of insurance for providing security for the wage earner.

But while the problem and its solution were both essentially simple, implementation involved extremely difficult administrative, financial, actuarial, medical and other questions. States felt that while the application of social insurance in a particular field in their own countries had necessarily to take account of special needs and conditions they could learn much by meeting with other States and exchanging experience. This was the ILO's opportunity, and it was seized.

The third reason for the success of the ILO in this field was that it was able at an early stage to adopt a comprehensive programme. That programme owed little if anything to the Constitution. In the Constitution there is no organic conception of social insurance; the term itself is never used. As early as 1925 the Conference, on the basis of proposals submitted by the Office, approved a comprehensive programme of action and study.[1]

---

[1] Throughout the pre-war period the ILO's work on social insurance was directed by Adrien Tixier, an ILO official who after the war became Minister of Labour and subsequently Minister of the Interior in de Gaulle's first government.

As the years wore on, that programme was amended, amplified and extended but it was never thrown off course by external pressures, and it governed the whole subsequent development of the social insurance work of the ILO.

The Pre-War Conventions and Recommendations

In implementation of this programme of action the Conference adopted at its sessions in 1925, 1927, 1933, and 1934 a series of Conventions and Recommendations covering the whole area of social insurance.

In 1925 two Conventions and three Recommendations concerning compensation for industrial accidents were approved. The first Convention was of fundamental importance. It provides that the basic principle of occupational risk set forth in legislation on workmen's compensation and accident insurance should cover all workers, employees and apprentices employed by an enterprise, undertaking, or establishment, whether public or private, irrespective of its nature, its size or the degree of risk involved. Provisions are included specifying the nature of the compensation to be made.

The Convention is supplemented by two Recommendations, one dealing with the minimum scale of compensation, the other with jurisdiction in disputes.

The second Convention adopted in 1925, followed by a Recommendation for its application, binds every member which ratifies the Convention to grant to the nationals of any other member which shall have ratified, who suffer personal injury due to industrial accidents happening in its territory, the same terms in respect of workmen's compensation as it grants to its own nationals, without any condition as to residence.

In addition, the 1925 Conference adopted a Convention and Recommendation on compensation for occupational diseases, which are pendants to the instruments on industrial accidents. Members undertake to consider as occupational diseases those diseases and poisonings produced by the substances set forth in a Schedule appended to the Convention when such diseases or poisonings affect workers engaged in the trades or industries placed opposite in the Schedule, and result from occupation in an undertaking covered by the national legislation.[2]

In 1927 the Conference adopted two parallel Conventions on sickness insurance, one for workers in industry and commerce and the other for those in agriculture. These Conventions bind the States which ratify to

---

[2] The Convention was revised in 1934; the list of diseases and toxic substances in the Schedule was augmented. In later years suggestions were made to add still further diseases to the list, and in 1964 a new Schedule was approved.

institute compulsory sickness insurance for wage-earners. The insured persons and their employers should share in providing the financial resources of the sickness insurance system. In addition a Recommendation lays down the general principles which had been found in practice most effective for the reasonable and equitable application of sickness insurance.

In 1933 the Conference adopted a group of six Conventions supplemented by a Recommendation, on old age, invalidity and survivors' insurance, for "industry etc." and for agriculture respectively. The scope of all the "industry etc." conventions is very wide; they apply to "manual and non-manual workers, including apprentices, employed in industrial or commercial undertakings or in the liberal professions, and to outworkers and domestic servants". In each case the insured persons and their employers shall contribute to the insurance scheme. A Recommendation contains a number of general principles shown by experience to be best calculated to promote a just, effective and appropriate organisation of these branches of insurance.

Finally, in 1934, the Conference adopted the Unemployment Provision Convention and Recommendation. The Convention provides for the setting up of either a compulsory insurance scheme or a voluntary insurance scheme or a combination of both or any of these alternatives combined with a complementary assistance scheme. The supplementary Recommendation indicates a number of general principles shown in practice to be best calculated to promote a satisfactory organisation of unemployment insurance and assistance.

With the adoption of the 1934 Convention and Recommendation, the Conference had completed the legislative programme laid down in 1925; it had covered, in as great detail as was possible at that time, the whole field of social insurance.

The social insurance Conventions and Recommendations soon began to influence national legislation and practice. Ratifications began to come in quickly.

The annual surveys made by the ILO of the progress of national legislation present an impressive picture. In the 1920's the extension of social insurance over the countries of Europe was broad and uninterrupted, in the 1930's it spread overseas and in the 1940's the Latin-American countries in particular were widely influenced. The 1950's and 1960's saw the implementation of schemes in some Asian and African States.

The 1944 Recommendations

When the Philadelphia Conference was being planned, the time appeared opportune to place social insurance again on the agenda. Since 1933–34, when the Conference had last dealt with social insurance, much had happened. The standards set up by the early Conventions and Recommendations had in some respects been rendered out of date by subsequent progress, much of it inspired by these very Conventions and Recommendations; the Office had gained much experience from the advisory missions undertaken at the request of governments to advise on the detailed application in their national legislation of the international principles. Furthermore, there was evidence that the world was ready for a fresh international formulation of the guiding principles of social security in the spirit of the fifth Article of the Atlantic Charter which contemplated "the fullest collaboration between all nations in the economic field with the object of securing for all, improved labour standards, economic advancement and social security".

In the Declaration of Philadelphia, the Conference recognised the need for meeting the aspirations of the world in this field by committing the Organisation to "the extension of social security to provide a basic income to all in need of such protection, and comprehensive medical care".

As a first step towards the implementation of this mandate, the Conference adopted the Income Security Recommendation and the Medical Care Recommendation. In addition the Conference adopted a Recommendation concerning income security and medical care for persons discharged from the armed forces and assimilated services and from war employment.

Significant as the 1944 Recommendations were, none was intended to have a permanent value. While the third Recommendation was of a purely temporary character, the other two were only intended to provide guidance, as is, indeed, stated in the Preamble to the Income Security Recommendation, "pending the unification and amplification" of the provisions of the pre-war Conventions and Recommendations.

The Post-War Conventions: Comprehensive Legislation

This process of "unification and amplification" was undertaken by the Conference in 1951-52, and in the latter year it adopted a comprehensive Convention on minimum standards of social security. This covers the whole field of social security which is subdivided into nine types of contingency. It recognises coverage by compulsory and voluntary social insurance, schemes providing benefit as a public service, and social assistance.

A member ratifying the Convention undertakes to comply with (a) certain general provisions, (b) the standards laid down in at least three of the nine parts dealing with each of the nine contingencies – medical care, sickness benefit, unemployment benefit, old-age benefit, employment injury benefit, family benefit, maternity benefit, invalidity benefit, and survivors' benefit (including at least one of the parts dealing with unemployment, old age, employment injury, invalidity and survivors' benefits), and (c) certain common provisions relevant to the parts covered by the ratification. A member whose economy and medical facilities are insufficiently developed may avail itself of temporary exceptions provided for in the Convention.

For each of the nine branches of social security the Convention defines the contingency or contingencies covered, and specifies the range of persons protected, the nature of benefit, the qualifying period that may be required and the permitted limitations of the duration of benefit. Members ratifying the Convention undertake to guarantee the same rights to national and non-national residents. Nevertheless, they may prescribe special rules for non-nationals and nationals born outside their territory in respect of benefits paid out of public funds.

This Convention, which crowned the legislative work of the Organisation in the field of social security, is an admirable example of the combination in an international instrument of the formulation of positive standards combined with flexibility in their application.

But the Conference, in adopting the Convention, was far from achieving unanimity. The vote was 123 for, 32 against, and 22 abstentions. Opposition came principally from the employers, who considered that the coverage of the Convention was too wide. They insisted on the desirability of encouraging social security through voluntary insurance and voluntary non-governmental arrangements. They maintained that, by allowing the individual countries to choose which branches of social security should be covered by their ratification, the text contradicted the principle that a Convention should impose equivalent obligations upon each ratifying member.

Opposition to Social Security

Throughout the whole of the social security work of the ILO, opposition and even hostility has been forcefully expressed. The opposition has been directed chiefly against (a) the compulsory principle and (b) the comprehensive principle. In view of the magnitude of the issues involved the opposition encountered has never been a matter of surprise.

Before the advent of social insurance, in many States voluntary or non-official organisations existed offering the services provided compulsorily under systems of social insurance. Some of these organisations were commercial or profit making, such as insurance companies or medical associations, others were profit sharing, such as mutual or friendly societies, others were non-profit making, such as charitable bodies. Most of them were doing good work in their limited fields, and they naturally resented the imposition of the compulsory principle and the increasing intervention of the State. The hostility manifested nationally by these bodies had international repercussions in the discussions in the Conference.

Opposition was also widely manifested to the comprehensive principle. The various interests referred to above might be divided in their opposition to certain aspects of compulsion, but all were united in their hostility to the systematic extension of the principle of collective social security to cover all contingencies. In this they saw what was to them the menacing shadow of the "Welfare State".

Although these powerful forces of opposition have not been able to prevent progress, they have sometimes been able to retard it. The ILO has necessarily had to take account of the social, economic, financial and political evolution of its members and to avoid getting out of step with the rhythm of progress conditioned by that evolution.

It was considerations such as these that led the Conference in 1952, when it adopted the Convention on minimum standards, to decide not to go any further for the moment. The Conference did, in fact, also have on its agenda the question of objectives and advanced standards of social security on which the Office had submitted a detailed report. But the Conference felt that it would be premature to consider adopting a Convention on advanced standards before allowing time for effect to be given to the Convention on minimum standards, and it contented itself with adopting a resolution inviting the Governing Body to re-examine the question of objectives and advanced standards of social security and to choose an appropriate time for placing it on the agenda of the Conference.

Revision of Earlier Standards

The standard-setting work of the ILO is never completed. As time goes on the earlier standards become out of date and need revision. Thus in 1959 the ILO Committee of Social Security Experts recommended that the ILO undertake the establishment of new standards of social security for migrant and non-national workers and also the revision of the pre-war Conventions. As a first step in this process the 1962 Conference adopted a Convention on equality of treatment in respect of social security for migrant and foreign workers.

In 1964 a comprehensive Convention and Recommendation on benefits in case of industrial accidents and occupational diseases was adopted, under which national legislation would protect virtually all employed persons in the case of employment injury. In accordance with the overriding preoccupation of the ILO with the promotion of balanced progress, the Convention provides that countries whose economic and medical facilities are insufficiently developed may avail themselves of temporary exceptions in implementing its provisions.

Three years later the Conference adopted a Convention concerning invalidity, old age and survivors' benefits, together with a supplementary Recommendation. The Convention constitutes a revision of the six Conventions adopted in 1933. As regards qualifying conditions and the benefits to be provided, it follows closely the Social Security (Minimum Standards) Convention, 1952. Its obligations may be accepted separately in respect of the three sorts of benefit, and the Convention may be accepted subject to certain specified exclusions. A degree of flexibility is thus provided.

Flexibility also characterises a Convention, supplemented by a Recommendation, concerning medical care and sickness benefits, adopted in 1969.

The Cost of Social Security

Another of the grounds on which opposition to social security has been formulated is its cost. The cost expressed in pounds, shillings and pence or in dollars and cents is undoubtedly high. But is it too high? In other words, when a country invests in social security is it getting its money's worth?

The study of this problem is difficult, because it involves questions that are not only social, economic and financial but political as well. Social security is advocated and opposed not only because it affords protection for the worker and his family in certain contingencies, but because it constitutes one of the means of effecting a redistribution of national income. This is recognised whether social security is provided in a country with a Communist economy such as the Soviet Union or in a country of free enterprise such as the United States. Even if the political aspects are left out of account, the problem remains more than difficult. How can a balance-sheet of social security be drawn up, calculating on the debit side all the factors which must be included in financing it, and on the credit side all the benefits which flow from it in increased health, strength, peace of mind and well-being?

The steps taken by the ILO to calculate the cost of social security are of some historical interest.

In 1926 the British Government requested the ILO to undertake an extensive enquiry into the cost of social services in a number of countries, which would cover the different forms of social insurance and assistance services, excluding war pensions and education.

It was understood that the proposed enquiry had a double purpose, on the one hand to calculate the social charges imposed upon the national economy and on the other to measure the social protection afforded by each country to its insured population and to those to whom social assistance was provided.

In view of the importance and complexity of the task the Office consulted a panel of members of the Correspondence Committee on Social Insurance. The Committee pointed out in its report that the cost of social insurance and assistance services formed merely one factor in the cost of production: it was extremely difficult if not impossible to arrive at any scientific and exact determination of the real incidence of the financial burdens involved; social expenditure was in reality productive because of the economic and financial benefits it procured for the community as a whole (e.g. social stability, improvement of the health and earning capacity of the workers) but any attempt to assess the economic value of social legislation would meet with insuperable difficulties.

The results of the enquiry relating to 1930–31 were published in 1933 under the title *International Survey of Social Charges*. A second survey, relating to 1933, was published in two volumes in 1935–36. Both these surveys contained very detailed national monographs, comprising, on a uniform plan, detailed descriptions and financial and other statistics of social insurance and social services in a large number of countries, but neither survey included any attempt at an international comparison of the charges involved.

The question was not again raised in its entirety until after the war. The post-war expansion of social security led to an increase in the volume of the financial operations of social security schemes, with the result that their repercussions on economic life also increased. In 1949 the Seventh International Conference of Labour Statisticians in a resolution, which was supported by the Committee of Social Security Experts, requested the Governing Body to invite members to supply the Office with detailed information with regard to the cost to employers, employees and governments of social security schemes in order to enable the ILO to continue and expand its studies in that field.

In 1952–53 the Office prepared and published in the *International Labour Review* two comparative studies on the cost of social security, and in 1955 it published detailed statistical tables both in the statistical supplement of the *International Labour Review* and in the report on the *Financing of Social Security* submitted to the first European Regional Conference.

Since the ILO initiated its enquiries into the cost of social security several countries have begun to publish consolidated statements of the cost of their schemes, in most cases according to the principles adopted for the

ILO enquiries. This development has, in turn, facilitated the preparation of subsequent ILO studies, the most recent of which was published in 1967.

Administrative Practice

Although before the war the ILO devoted attention to the practical administration of social insurance schemes, it was only after 1952 when the legislative work of the Conference was completed, at least for a time, that the Office was able to concentrate a major part of its activities on administrative aspects.

As the Director-General observed in connection with the adoption of the 1952 Convention, the problem in a great many countries "is not so much one of determining standards as of meeting the practical difficulties that arise in their day-to-day application. It is for this purpose that the ILO is being called upon in increasing measure to render practical and direct assistance in evolving administrative techniques, in simplifying procedures and rendering them more easily comprehensible, and in ensuring that schemes have an adequate actuarial basis."

In pursuance of this programme of work, social security administrative questions have been considered by regional Conferences, and research has been carried out to try to clarify the special problems of each region. Technical co-operation missions have been sent to many countries in all parts of the world.

Finally, close co-operation has been maintained with the International Social Security Association in issuing reports and organising meetings on specific problems of social security administration.

With a view to providing a practical manual of assistance in social security procedures the Office issued in 1955 a report entitled *Administrative Practice of Social Insurance*. More recently handbooks have been prepared and published by the ILO intended to give guidance in setting up schemes of social insurance in countries where none exist.

Operational Activities

Social insurance was the first field in which the ILO was called upon before the war to give technical advice and assistance to governments. There were two reasons for this.

In the first place social insurance involves highly technical questions, on which certain States wishing to set up schemes possessed little knowledge and no experience, and other States, even with wide experience, realised that they had still much to learn. In the second place, the Social Insurance Branch of the Office soon acquired an international reputation as a body of experts possessing not only theoretical knowledge and practical experience but also ability to apply that knowledge and experience to the special needs and circumstances of particular countries.

The participation of the ILO in the Expanded Technical Assistance Programme enabled it to give a wide extension to its social security operational activities. In the developing countries the need for some sort of social security was beginning to be felt. The process of industrialisation in these countries was bringing in its train a series of far-reaching social changes. Workers were wrenched from their traditional environment, where by custom they had enjoyed a certain amount of social protection through the family and the community. The loss of their former protection made them feel insecure, especially in the earlier stages of the transition from the traditional system to a more developed industrial economy. It therefore became necessary, on both economic and social grounds, to protect these workers and their families from emergencies beyond their control. Most of the requests from governments for technical co-operation in this field fell into one or other of two categories.

The first involved the planning of a social security system, which may be comprehensive, applicable to certain sectors of the population or certain groups of workers, or limited to certain risks. As a first step (e.g. in the case of projects in Burma, Indonesia, Iraq and Pakistan) an attempt was made to draw up a plan of social security covering both immediate needs and long-term activities. After the general plan had been prepared work could begin on detailed projects for its practical implementation. In Burma as a result of the ILO project 80,000 Burmese workers and their families are entitled to maternity, injury, unemployment and death benefits.

The second category of requests for technical co-operation concerned the extension of an existing system of social security by widening its geographical scope or by increasing the number of persons or risks covered. Requests of this kind came from Bolivia, the Dominican Republic, Guatemala, Paraguay and Venezuela.

Technical co-operation in such cases included the analysis and revision of existing legislation and preparation of appropriate amendments. It often entailed, in addition, the actuarial revision of the financial regime in force and actuarial estimates for the extension of the social security system in either or both of the forms indicated. Furthermore, complicated problems of organisation and administration often had to be solved before the required extension could be effected.

Projects in which the financial problems and reviews of an actuarial type constituted an important part have been undertaken in Bolivia, Cuba, El Salvador, Guatemala, Iran, Libya, Paraguay, Peru, Turkey and Venezuela.

Questions of an administrative nature have been becoming more important in the technical assistance provided by the ILO. This co-operation has been guided by two principles; the administrative burden should be reduced to a reasonable minimum; and the handling of benefits should be so simplified and accelerated that the number of administrative steps and the time elapsing between the submission of a request and the award of the corresponding benefit are cut down as much as possible.

Although the needs in individual countries vary, the administrative, technical and financial problems of social security are often somewhat similar in countries in the same geographical area. In order to provide opportunity for discussion of these problems the ILO has organised a series of regional seminars, attended by officials of social security institutions in the region together with ILO experts.

It is not only in the developing countries that the technical advice and assistance of the ILO has been sought. Three examples of this may be given. In co-operation with the Central Commission for Rhine Navigation the ILO succeeded in drafting and submitting to special Conferences a Convention co-ordinating the application of national social security schemes to boatmen navigating the Rhine, so that the boatman will always be covered by the system of social protection, wherever he may be at the time.

The second example is the technical co-operation of the ILO with the Council of Europe in developing draft texts on social security to serve as a basis for multilateral Conventions to improve the protection of workers migrating between the eighteen countries belonging to the Council.

Thirdly, under a working arrangement with the European Economic Community and the European Coal and Steel Community a European system of social security for migrant workers has been prepared. The six countries of EEC are parties to an agreement governing the social security coverage of migrant workers, which facilitates the free movement of labour among the countries of the Community. It covers all wage earners of the countries in question, and applies to all existing or future legislation in the matter and to all branches of social security – sickness, maternity, invalidity, old age, death, employment injuries, unemployment, and family allowances. Constant co-ordination is needed in drafting the relevant legislation and in its application and extension. Hence those responsible for social security in the six member States regularly meet in a special committee; the ILO is represented at its sessions and offers technical advice. Several million workers and their dependants benefit from this international co-operation.

One of the secrets of the success of the ILO in its operational activities on social security has been its constant insistence on the need to restrict the scope of social security legislation within the limits of what is practicable at the time in the country concerned in the light of its administrative organisation, medical services, financial resources and other elements. Especially where long-term benefits are involved, the ILO has therefore always advised starting on a modest basis and gradually extending the scope of the legislation when administrative, financial and other conditions warrant such extension. In this way the ultimate objectives of a comprehensive social security programme can be attained more surely than by the hasty promulgation of wide but ill-considered schemes.

The need to proceed gradually has been borne in upon the ILO by the whole history of social security. Gradual development has been characteristic not only of the procedures and techniques of social security but also of its aims and purposes. At the beginning there was no comprehensive aim, but merely an unco-ordinated series of limited objectives, namely protection against specified risks. Gradually, not as a result of any one dramatic change, but as a consequence of a process of evolution, sometimes slower, sometimes faster, social security has developed a comprehensive threefold aim, to prevent contingencies arising wherever possible, to provide protection against the consequences of a contingency or a situation in which standards of living are seriously threatened, and to share the cost of comprehensive protection in an equitable and rational manner.

"Economically Possible" and "Socially Desirable"

In few areas of its work has it been more difficult for the ILO to hold the balance equally between the socially desirable and the economically possible.

With respect to the "economically possible", employers have shown opposition on the ground that the contributions to be paid for financing the schemes raise the cost of employing labour and hence the cost of their products. Governments have been anxious to avoid increasing unduly the burdens to be imposed on the taxpayers. Hostility has also been manifested by powerful groups who feared that their interests were threatened.

With respect to the "socially desirable", workers have insisted on the obvious social value of sickness, invalidity and old-age benefits and the other advantages provided by social security. Governments, conscious of the contribution of social security to the welfare of the community, have generally supported the workers, while advocating caution not to embark on schemes beyond the financial means of the countries concerned.

Faced by such conflicts of attitude the ILO has always endeavoured to arrive at a fair balance. In the case of the Conventions and Recommendations adopted by the Conference this balance has been attained by the process of discussion and negotiation between the various groups. Governments, employers and workers have made an effort to adjust their views to reach agreement on solutions internationally practicable at a given time.

In providing technical advice to individual countries, the ILO has sought to devise balanced systems suited to the special conditions of each country, account being taken of both social desirability and economic possibility. What forms of social security are most needed in the country concerned? How can such needs be met in the general context of the country's economic and social development? How much social security can it really afford? Answers to such questions make it possible to determine the nature of the social security scheme representing a fair balance between what the country needs socially and what it can afford economically. The best proof of the wisdom of this balanced approach is that countries have usually been able to operate successfully such systems, whereas other countries setting up schemes based on theoretical studies have been forced after a few years either to remodel them or to abandon them completely.

Some developing countries, eager to provide social security, at least for certain sectors of their people, have adopted schemes based on foreign models, ill-adapted to local needs and conditions. It has sometimes been possible for the ILO, through technical co-operation, to secure the rehabilitation of such schemes on a more realistic basis. In other cases, however, the failure of the initial schemes has led to frustration and disinclination to attempt to reform them. The difficulty of establishing viable social security schemes in developing countries arises not only from the problem of financing them, but also from the lack of the elementary factors essential for the functioning of social security, such as qualified medical, nursing and auxiliary staff; administrative, clerical and accountancy personnel; hospitals, training establishments and other health and welfare amenities. These practical deficiencies sometimes do not deter developing countries from regarding social security as a target symbolising the struggle for emancipation from want. The ILO recognises its responsibility to assist these countries, and it has continued, through technical co-operation, to simplify, consolidate and otherwise improve existing schemes.

In such ways the social security work of the ILO has proved an outstanding contribution to balanced economic and social progress. Through its operation the distribution of national income in accordance with the free play of economic forces has been moderated by diverting a proportion of that income into socially beneficial channels for the welfare of the less well-provided sectors of the community. In the modern world a sound system of social security is not only an indispensable factor of social progress; it also constitutes an important element in economic stability and even in economic expansion.

18. OCCUPATIONAL HEALTH, SAFETY, AND WELFARE

THE Preamble to the Constitution mentions among the essential tasks of the ILO "the protection of the worker against sickness, disease and injury arising out of his employment".

The Declaration of Philadelphia amplifies this by listing among the aims to be achieved "adequate protection of the life and health of workers in all occupations".

This is an immense field, which is constantly changing with the development of working conditions and production methods. Very few industries are unhealthy in themselves. There are, however, numerous industries in which under certain conditions, dealing with certain products, working in premises heated, lighted or ventilated in a certain way, the worker finds himself exposed to avoidable dangers to his health. A danger which menaced the workers' health and safety may be removed by a change in technique, while some other danger may arise. All these dangers are not equally urgent or equally easy to guard against; in such a vast field progress must be made by gradual stages.

Programme of Work

Although the ILO began work on this front at the first session of the Conference, its activities pursued a somewhat haphazard course. It took up particular questions, some of them of relatively minor importance, in response to individual demands, without reference to any overall scheme. While good work was done on specific items, no organic plan was followed, and it was not until after the war that a comprehensive programme was adopted.

In 1950 the Governing Body set up an *ad hoc* Committee to enquire into the programme of work of the ILO in the sphere of industrial health and safety and to define the particular aspects of the protection of the health of workers in dangerous or unhealthy occupations towards which proposed international regulations should be directed.

The Committee laid particular stress on two essential principles; the programme must be practical and must apply directly to the needs of governments, employers and workers; occupational health and safety are indivisible and should therefore be treated as aspects of the same problem.

208

The Committee supplemented these general directives by a number of recommendations on specific points in the programme. In 1951 the Governing Body approved the recommendations, and the comprehensive programme thus laid down has since determined the course of the activities of the ILO.

If this programme had been agreed upon at the beginning of the work of the ILO, its contribution to the solution of problems of industrial health, safety and welfare would naturally have been much more systematic. Nevertheless, although the earlier work of the ILO in this field consisted, for the most part, of a series of disjointed and unconnected acts, nearly every isolated initiative achieved a measure of success.

Occupational Health

White phosphorus, white lead and anthrax

These early isolated measures included the adoption by the Conference in 1919 of a Recommendation urging adherence to the 1906 Berne Convention prohibiting the use of white phosphorus in match manufacture, in 1921 of a Convention prohibiting the use of white lead in interior painting, and in the same year of a Recommendation for the disinfection of wool with anthrax spores.

Silicosis and pneumoconiosis

Silicosis, which is a disease of the respiratory organs caused by siliceous dust, has occupied the attention of the Organisation since 1924.

With the financial assistance of the South African Bureau of Mines, particularly interested in the question because of the ravages of silicosis in that country, a meeting of experts was convened in Johannesburg in 1930. This meeting adopted a series of resolutions which the Office sent to the governments concerned. Further, in accordance with the wishes of the meeting, the ILO undertook research to reach agreement on a uniform terminology and a uniform radiographic technique for discovering silicosis; to ensure the co-ordination of the scientific studies undertaken by various institutions; and to collect additional information as regards the incidence and development of the disease and of rehabilitation schemes.

In 1950 the Governing Body convened, on the invitation and with the financial assistance of the Australian Government, an International Conference on Pneumoconiosis in Sydney. Pneumoconiosis is a wider term than silicosis; it includes diseases of the respiratory tract caused by the inhalation of all kinds of dust, and not only siliceous dust. The Sydney Conference studied the disease from the health, social security and employment points of view, giving consideration to compensation for silicosis and other forms of pneumoconiosis, the notification and prevention of pneumoconiosis and the rehabilitation of those suffering from the disease. Among its conclusions was an agreement on an international classification of radiographs and the ILO followed this up by devising means for making this classification more widely known and used.

The work of the ILO was continued in 1952, when a meeting of experts was held on the prevention and suppression of dust in mining, tunnelling and quarrying. This meeting adopted over a hundred recommendations on practical measures for preventing and suppressing dust in these operations, and it expressed the hope, which has since been realised, that the ILO would act as a centre for the exchange of information and experience on this question. In accordance with recommendations of a meeting of experts on pneumoconiosis the ILO has compiled and issued a set of films illustrating the new classification of radiographs of this disease.

Standard Code of Industrial Hygiene

The ILO recognised at an early date that the work of the Conference left many gaps, and it endeavoured to make a more systematic contribution to the problem of the protection of the health of the workers which would not require action by the Conference. In 1930, with the assistance of the Correspondence Committee on Industrial Hygiene, the Office began drafting a Standard Code of Industrial Hygiene. In 1933 the Code was approved by the Committee and, with the sanction of the Governing Body, it was published. The general rules contained in the Code were not regulations destined to be embodied later in a Convention or Recommendation but a collection of guiding principles intended in particular for use in countries where regulations on workers' health did not exist. They aimed at being comprehensive, covering not only the special health hazards of particular industries, but also the general problems of the protection of the health of workers employed in all occupations.

Protection of workers' health in the places of employment

In 1953, following upon the approval by the Governing Body of the systematic programme of work in the field of industrial health and safety, the Conference adopted a Recommendation containing a comprehensive series of provisions to protect the health of the workers in their places of employment.

The Recommendation is divided into four parts. One of these sets forth a series of technical measures to be taken by the competent authority or by employers to control risks to health at the workplace. The remaining three parts provide that workers in occupations involving special risks to their health should undergo initial or periodical medical examinations; that occupational diseases should be notified to the labour inspectorate and to the authorities responsible for the protection of the health of the workers; and that facilities for first aid and emergency treatment in case of accident, occupational disease, poisoning or indisposition should be provided at the place of employment.

In 1959, the Conference adopted a further Recommendation on the organisation of occupational health services in places of employment. It was agreed that the essential object of occupational health services was preventive; this could be achieved in two ways – by the protection of the worker against occupational hazards, as indicated in the 1953 Recommendation, and by regular medical examinations to assess his fitness for the job. Occupational health services should either be organised by the undertakings themselves or be attached to an outside body.

Hygiene in commerce and offices

The measures described above were supplemented in 1964 by a comprehensive Convention and Recommendation relating to a wide range of principles concerning hygiene in commerce and offices. In view of the great diversity in the establishments and premises covered, the Convention permits gradual implementation to enable different branches of the economy in each country to adjust themselves to the standards laid down. This is still another example of the ILO insistence on the importance of balance between social and economic progress.

Radiation protection

In adopting, in 1960, the Radiation Protection Convention and Recommendation, the Conference broke new ground. In consequence of the ever-increasing and multifarious application of radiations in industry, the adoption of an international instrument by the ILO was agreed to be advisable. The Convention applies to all activities involving exposure of workers to ionising radiations in the course of their work. It specifies the steps to be taken to ensure effective protection of workers. The Recommendation embodies additional detailed provisions.

Supplementing this standard-setting the ILO has published a practical *Manual on Protection against Radiations in Industry* for the use of industrial personnel, and also a *Model Code*.

Workers' health in particular industries

Several of the Industrial Committees have devoted attention to health problems in the industries concerned. Reference may be made in particular to the resolutions adopted by the Committees for the textiles, building, civil engineering and public works, petroleum and chemical industries. In this way, in accordance with the systematic programme of work approved by the Governing Body in 1951, the comprehensive Recommendation adopted by the Conference in 1953 is being supplemented by a series of resolutions relating to the special hazards and the special needs in each of the major industries.

Occupational Safety

When the ILO came into existence two very different doctrines of accident prevention were being advocated by European and American sponsors respectively.

In Europe the principle that workers should be protected against accidents was recognised and applied long before the idea of compulsory accident insurance was accepted. The protection then given consisted of regulations which the public authorities compelled employers to observe. At that time most industrial accidents were attributed to machinery, and it was therefore natural that the public authorities should intervene and supervise the degree of "safety" of the machines, so that suitable protective devices could be made compulsory where required. Thus, the methods of accident prevention which were generally in force were of an administrative and technical character.

In America, on the other hand, accident prevention was mainly a matter for voluntary action, on the basis of the doctrine of "Safety First". When the legislation of several States made the employer legally liable for the payment of compensation for industrial accidents, the employer insured himself, and the possibility of having to pay large sums drew the attention of insurance companies and employers to the problem. The double principle was soon established that an industrial accident is as costly for the worker, who loses the whole or part of his capacity for employment, as for the employer and the insurance companies which have to pay compensation, and that, in the second place, a large proportion of industrial accidents are not due to any fault or lack of protection in the machine which the worker operates, but to the faulty manner in which he carries out his task. This led to the view that those who restricted the work of accident prevention to technical regulations were on the wrong track, and that what was necessary was to inspire in the worker and in the employer the will to avoid accidents, while at the same time giving the workers appropriate training and individual protective equipment.

Very wisely the ILO did not regard these two doctrines as being necessarily in opposition. It recognised that each contained part of the truth and that in practice each had given positive results. Nevertheless, in view of the tenacity with which their respective supporters advocated the two doctrines, it was impossible, for many years, for the ILO to take any action at the Conference in favour of the prevention of accidents. In these circumstances, its early work in the field of industrial safety was limited almost entirely[1] to the collection and distribution of information on practical methods of preventing accidents in industrial undertakings. In particular, in 1925 the Office began to issue the *Industrial Safety Survey*, which included original technical articles, information on new safety legislation, reports on the work of industrial safety associations and safety museums and summaries of labour inspectors' reports dealing with industrial safety. As a result of this informational work, which contributed to creating a general recognition that the two doctrines of accident prevention were not irreconcilable, the Conference was able in 1929 to adopt a series of instruments on industrial safety, one of general scope, the others of limited application.

Prevention of industrial accidents

The general instrument adopted in 1929 was the Recommendation on the prevention of industrial accidents. This Recommendation, which has been called the gospel of the ILO on accident prevention, showed that the Conference fully realised on the one hand the great value of private initiative, that is of the "Safety First" movement, and on the other hand the importance of statutory regulation. The Recommendation invites members to encourage voluntary safety action by all means in their power and to undertake all possible research work concerning industrial accidents, their causes and the accompanying circumstances. At the same time the Recommendation states that any effective system of accident prevention should rest on the basis of statutory requirements ensuring an adequate standard of safety.

In 1929 also the Conference adopted a Recommendation urging members to adopt and apply the principle that it should be prohibited by law to supply or install any machine intended to be driven by mechanical power and to be used within its territory unless it is furnished with the safety appliances required by law for the operation of machines of that type.

The protection afforded by that Recommendation was strengthened in 1963 by the Convention and Recommendation on the Guarding of Machinery. The Convention prohibits the sale, hire, transfer and exhibition of machinery without appropriate guards, and the Recommendation extends the prohibition to the manufacture of such machinery.

[1] The Labour Inspection Recommendation, 1923, and the Workmen's Compensation (Accidents) Convention, 1925, have safety aspects.

Safety provisions for dockers

A Convention adopted in 1929 for the protection against accidents of workers employed in loading or unloading ships is of interest for three reasons.

In the first place it contained a greater amount of technical prescription than any Convention previously adopted. It specifies in minute detail the measures to be taken to protect or render safe approaches over docks, wharves, quays or similar premises, access to and from ships to be loaded or unloaded, access from deck to hold, hatch coverings, hoisting machines and other gear and appliances.

In the second place, it very soon became clear that some of the detailed requirements would have to be amended to enable the Convention to be generally ratified. In 1932 the Convention was revised by the Conference, and in 1935 conclusions designed to constitute common standards for its application were adopted at an intergovernmental meeting.

The third reason why this Convention is of special interest is that it taught the Organisation a lesson. Although the number of ratifications which it ultimately secured was substantial, the history of the Convention showed that the traditional Convention form was not appropriate for the formulation of safety regulations for particular industries or occupations. Extracting wisdom from experience, when the ILO again attempted to adopt a Convention on the prevention of accidents in a particular industry, it adopted a different method.

Safety provisions for the building industry

It was in 1937 that the lesson derived from experience in connection with the Dockers' Convention was applied. In that year the Conference adopted a Convention concerning safety provisions in the building industry. In the preamble to the Convention it is stated that, in view of the desirability of standardising minimum safety provisions without prescribing requirements too rigid for general application, the most appropriate form for the proposed international instrument is that of a Convention accompanied by a Recommendation embodying a model code of safety regulations.

This Convention and Recommendation thus constituted a further experiment in the direction of discovering the best method by which the obligations involved in the ratification of a Convention could be combined with a reasonable degree of discretion in the application of detailed regulations. The experiment did not prove a success. Members have been reluctant to ratify because they feared that ratification of the Convention might somehow involve them in acceptance of the Recommendation; and they did not wish to entangle themselves in international obligations at a time when building techniques were changing.

Model Codes of Safety Regulations

When, after the war, the question arose of adopting safety regulations for industrial establishments and for coal mines, reflection on experience with the Dockers' and Building Industry Conventions led to the conclusion that it would be preferable not to attempt to give these regulations the form of Conventions or Recommendations.

In 1949 the Office published a *Model Code of Safety Regulations for Industrial Establishments for the Guidance of Governments and Industry*, and in the following year a *Model Code of Safety Regulations for Underground Work in Coal Mines for the Guidance of Governments and the Coal Mining Industry*.

These Model Codes differ both in status and in purpose from Conventions or Recommendations. In respect of status, although they do not have the authority derived from approval by the International Labour Conference, everything possible was done to guarantee the technical soundness of the regulations.

In respect to purpose, the Model Codes are not solely or even primarily designed to secure the adoption by governments of minimum standards of legislation. They were placed at the disposal of governments and industries merely for guidance. Governments and industries are free to make such use of the Codes as they see fit in framing or in revising their own safety regulations.

The Office also prepared a Draft Model Code of Safety Regulations for Civil Engineering and sent it to experts for observations. But the Committee on the programme of work mentioned at the beginning of this chapter recommended in 1950 that this draft model code should be replaced by a series of handbooks dealing with particular branches of civil engineering or particular problems relating to civil engineering, to be issued separately as soon as completed.

Inevitably, as a result of technical and other developments, certain provisions of the Codes became, in time, out of date. The ILO has therefore prepared, with the assistance of committees of experts, revisions of certain parts of the Codes. Other codified provisions have been issued in the form of handbooks under the general title of *ILO Codes of Practice*. In addition, "guides" and "manuals" have been published in several languages.

The changes which have taken place in the methods of action of the Organisation on safety regulations have been determined throughout by one dominant consideration to render the work of the ILO more and more practically useful.

Safety in particular industries

The Industrial Committees have shown the same interest in safety questions as in the health problems of the industries concerned. Resolutions on various aspects of safety have been adopted by the Industrial Committees on road transport, iron and steel, metal trades, textiles, building, civil engineering and public works, petroleum and chemical industries. The last-named Committee made a particularly interesting suggestion. Considering that it would be useful to have a limited number of internationally recognised symbols representative of the risks involved in the handling of dangerous substances, the Committee called upon the Office to work towards the adoption, for use in international trade, of five symbols characteristic of the main types of danger associated with the handling of dangerous substances. At a subsequent session the Committee approved the five symbols, and a sixth and seventh have since been added. The symbols are shown in the Reference section.

Weight of Packages

Having a relation both to health and to safety, two Conventions concerning the weight of packages were adopted in 1929 and 1967. The former provides for marking the weight on heavy packages transported by vessels, the latter deals with the maximum permissible weight to be carried by one worker.

International Information Centre

In 1959 the ILO set up an International Occupational Safety and Health Information Centre. As indicated in the chapter on Research and Information (Chapter 11), the services of this Centre have been very widely utilised.

Industrial Welfare and Housing

When the ILO was established the provision of welfare facilities was generally regarded with hostility, suspicion or doubt. Many governments believed that government intervention was inappropriate apart from the legal regulation of specific conditions of employment; many employers considered that the employers' responsibility was sufficiently discharged by conforming to regulations laid down by legislation or provided for by collective agreement; many workers felt that the provision of welfare facilities constituted an interference with the exercise of their personal freedom.

Although the Conference adopted in 1924 a Recommendation concerning the development of facilities for the utilisation of workers' spare time, it was careful to frame the text in such a way as to avoid conflict with strongly held convictions or prejudices. In particular, the Recommendation was confined to welfare facilities outside the undertaking.

War-time changes of attitude

During the war a profound change occurred in many countries in the attitude of workers, employers and governments alike. Workers increasingly recognised that it did not involve a loss of any of their essential freedoms to benefit from certain social services provided either by the employer or by the community or by both. Governments and employers on their side increasingly recognised that it was desirable for them to take action to provide certain amenities and services for the workers. On the international plane this changed attitude was reflected in the Declaration of Philadelphia.

The 1947 resolution

In 1947 the Conference adopted a resolution on welfare facilities for workers which largely determined the subsequent action of the ILO in this field. In that resolution the Conference drew attention to the importance of establishing in undertakings, wherever appropriate in co-operation with representatives of the workers concerned and under properly qualified management, such services, facilities and amenities as adequate canteens, rest and recreation facilities, sanitary and medical facilities, arrangements for travel to and from work, and for the accommodation of workers employed at a distance from their homes, and such other services, amenities and facilities as contribute to improve the conditions under which workers are employed. In addition, the Conference requested the Governing Body: (a) to instruct the Office to expand its studies of the administration and working of such services, facilities and amenities; (b) to consider the desirability of placing the question, or such aspects of it as might be appropriate, on the agenda of an early session of the Conference; and (c) to refer to future Regional Conferences and to the Industrial Committees such aspects of the question as might present special problems in particular regions or industries.

Welfare questions at Regional Conferences and Industrial Committees

In pursuance of the comprehensive programme laid down in the 1947 Resolution, the Governing Body placed aspects of the question of industrial welfare on the agenda of the Asian Regional Conference in 1950, and also on the agenda of sessions of the Industrial Committees on textiles, building, civil engineering and public works, petroleum, iron and steel, coal mines, and inland transport. All these meetings adopted detailed resolutions relating to the aspects of the question of special importance to the industries or region concerned.

Welfare facilities for workers

In 1956 the Conference took a further step in implementing the 1947 resolution by adopting a comprehensive Recommendation on welfare facilities for workers. This relates to provisions in or near the undertakings concerning eating facilities (including canteens, buffets and trolleys, messrooms and mobile canteens), rest facilities (including seats and rest rooms), recreation facilities and transport facilities to and from work.

Workers' housing

Closely connected with welfare is the provision of satisfactory housing accommodation. Under a programme of work agreed between the international organisations, the ILO is recognised as having a major role in certain branches, in particular workers' housing.

In the earlier work of the ILO provisions relating to housing were included in several Conventions and Recommendations and attention was also devoted to housing in ILO publications. Since the war various aspects of workers' housing have been considered at regional conferences and meetings of Industrial Committees and other ILO bodies. In 1961 a comprehensive Recommendation was adopted by the Conference. The Conference recognised the importance of the social and economic problems constituted by workers' housing in all parts of the world, and its close relation to the productivity of the worker. The Recommendation states that "housing policy should be co-ordinated with general social and economic policy, so that workers' housing may be given a degree of priority which takes into account both the need therefor and the requirements of balanced economic development".

Operational Activities

Although relatively few of the operational activities of the ILO have related exclusively to industrial health, safety and welfare, several of the missions sent to various countries to enquire into and make recommendations on labour matters have devoted attention to questions in this field. The report made by Harold Butler on his mission to Egypt in 1932 contains several recommendations on health, safety and welfare, as do the reports issued by the Office in 1949 and 1950 on the missions to Greece and Turkey respectively.

Under the Expanded Programme of Technical Assistance, some of the first projects to be undertaken were in this field. Thus, an expert was sent to Indonesia to advise on the establishment of regulations and standards in connection with the protection of the health and safety of workers, and another to assist in drafting safety legislation relating to the installation and operation of steam plant and electrical equipment. An expert was sent to Burma to advise on social welfare, including occupational health. In a general survey undertaken in Pakistan, particular attention was paid to occupational safety and health. Guatemala received technical assistance on the improvement of safety and health conditions in industry. Special attention was devoted by the Near and Middle East Regional Training Institute at Istanbul to industrial safety and health and a small demonstration centre and industrial museum was set up.

More recently large-scale projects have been initiated in India involving the establishment of research and training centres. Other countries participating in direct technical co-operation on health and safety have included Finland, Israel, Mexico, the Philippines, Sudan, Thailand, Turkey, the United Arab Republic and Venezuela.

In some cases technicians from these countries have been sent to more industrialised countries for training in safety and health procedures. Thus, four days after a methane gas ("fire damp") explosion in a coal mine in Zonguldak, Turkey, killed eight miners and injured fifty more, the ILO sent five of the survivors to France to study safety measures in similar mines. Two and a half months later they were back in the Zonguldak mine, qualified to enforce safety regulations based on an ILO Model Code put into application by a visiting ILO expert.

The ILO has also been giving technical assistance on housing to the Inter-American Housing Centre in Colombia, whose work includes training architects and building technicians from Latin American countries and studying technical aspects of low-cost housing.

In addition to projects relating exclusively or mainly to health, safety and housing, these matters have been included wherever appropriate in technical co-operation missions on vocational training, productivity, labour administration and social security.

In these and other ways the ILO has been steadily endeavouring to make the maximum practical contribution both to the health, safety and well-being of the individual workers, and to the overall efficiency and productivity of industry.

In this important sector the ILO has thus been of real assistance not only to social progress, by protecting the worker against sickness and accident, but also to economic advancement, by protecting the community against the loss of millions of man-days.

19. WOMEN, CHILDREN AND YOUNG PERSONS

ON behalf of women, children and young persons, the record of the ILO is one of sustained, if unspectacular, usefulness. In contrast to its activities in some other areas its work on this group of problems has followed a continuous and consistent line. The line has been continuous; policy, programme and procedure in the pre-war and post-war periods have shown no substantial change. It has been consistent; less than in any other field it has been affected by political and economic vicissitudes.

This does not mean that in its work for women, children and young persons the ILO has pursued a course remote from the realities of the industrial world. This branch of its work has provided an example of the interaction and mutual influence of international and national progress. For example, international standards set by the Conference in 1919 influenced national progress and that national progress enabled the Conference in 1937 to raise the international norms which in turn again influenced national action. So the spiral of social progress continued to mount.

The Protection of Children and Young Persons

When the ILO came into being legislation on the employment of children and young persons was already well established in many countries. In some, indeed, it had been the earliest labour legislation. There was no doubt that children and young persons should be protected internationally. The only questions were which aspects should be assigned priority and what limits should be fixed in the international standards.[1]

Age for admission to employment

Logically, the first matter to be regulated was the minimum age for admission to employment. In the Minimum Age (Industry) Convention the Washington Conference fixed the minimum age at 14, in the case of industrial undertakings other than those in which only members of the same family are employed.

When the Convention was adopted some doubt was felt whether the

---

[1] The present chapter relates to all industries and occupations except the mercantile marine and agriculture. For those two sectors see Chapters 21 and 22.

age of 14 was high enough. Obviously physical development is not complete at the age of 14, and equally obviously schooling could with advantage be continued beyond that age. But the ILO had to recognise that at that time only in very few countries or parts of countries was school attendance compulsory beyond the age of 14. If compulsory school attendance does not last until the age when the child is permitted to enter employment there is a gap during which children are "at a loose end", neither in school nor in employment, clearly an extremely undesirable situation. In many countries there was a movement in favour of raising the school-leaving age to 15 or even 16, and when this movement had gained sufficient momentum and the school-leaving age had actually been raised in a certain number of countries the Conference was able in 1937 to raise to 15 the minimum age for admission to employment.[2]

Another respect in which the Washington Convention had been felt to be unsatisfactory was the limitation of its scope to industrial undertakings. This excluded many occupations in which children are widely employed, such as shops and offices, hotels, cafes and places of entertainment. In 1932 the Conference filled this gap with the Minimum Age (Non-Industrial Employment) Convention (together with a supporting Recommendation) which fixes the minimum age at 14 provided that children over 12 may, outside the hours fixed for school attendance, be employed on light work. Five years later, in 1937, this Convention was revised by the session of the Conference which revised the Minimum Age (Industry) Convention. Under the revised Convention the minimum age is fixed at 15, while the minimum age for employment on light work is fixed in some cases at 13 and in others at 14.

Night work

When the Washington Conference met, the principle was already generally recognised that night work was prejudicial to the health of young persons. The Conference therefore had no hesitation in adopting a Convention prohibiting the employment of young persons under 18 during the night in industrial undertakings.[3] There are, however, two important exceptions: (a) the Convention does not apply to undertakings in which members of the same family are employed; and (b) young persons over 16 may be employed during the night in certain continuous process industries specified in the Convention.

[2] Two years previously, in 1935, the Conference had adopted the Unemployment (Young Persons) Recommendation, in which it had urged that the minimum age for leaving school and being admitted to employment should be fixed at not less than fifteen years.
[3] It was only in 1946 that it was found possible to extend night work regulation to non-industrial occupations.

After the adoption of this Convention it was nearly thirty years before the interaction of international and national progress justified, in the revised Convention of 1948, the removal or limitation of these exceptions.

Medical examination

In 1946 the Conference adopted two Conventions and one Recommendation on the medical examination of young persons, in industrial undertakings and in non-industrial occupations respectively.

Employment of young persons underground

In 1965 a series of instruments concerning young persons employed underground in mines and quarries carried a stage further the protection embodied in a 1953 Recommendation. A Convention stipulates a minimum age of at least 16, and a Recommendation urges a minimum of 18 as an objective to be aimed at. A Convention provides for an initial medical examination, with periodic re-examinations until 21. Finally, a Recommendation covers safety and health, hygiene and feeding facilities, weekly rest, holidays with pay, training facilities and availability of sports.

Employment and training for development

In 1969 the Conference, undertaking a first discussion on "Special Youth Employment and Training Schemes for Development Purposes", adopted conclusions with a view to the adoption of a Recommendation in 1970. The seriousness of the problem of unemployed and untrained youth in developing countries, described by one government speaker as "frightening", was fully recognised by the Conference. It was agreed that the Recommendation "should cover special schemes designed to enable young persons to take part in activities directed to the economic and social development of their country and to acquire education, skills and experience facilitating their subsequent economic activity on a lasting basis and promoting their participation in society".

These schemes are called "special" because they differ both from normal training schemes and from adult education programmes. The conclusions provide guidelines on the nature of the schemes, the selection of young persons to participate in them, and the conditions of service in the schemes. Participation in the schemes should be voluntary; provided that where existing international standards dealing with forced labour and employment policy are not contravened, exceptional methods of recruitment, involving obligatory enrolment, may be permitted. In the discussion, some delegates, while reluctant to contemplate the use of compulsion, recognised that the situation in many developing countries was so grave that some measure of obligation could not be avoided; several speakers emphasised that the schemes should aim at balanced economic and social objectives.

Other action on behalf of young persons

In addition to adopting Conventions and Recommendations designed specially to afford protection to children and young persons, the Conference has constantly borne in mind, in adopting instruments regulating conditions of adult workers, the need to make provision for the special circumstances of young workers. These special provisions for juveniles are so numerous that only a few illustrative examples can be given.

In the manpower field the Public Works (National Planning) Recommendation, 1937, urges that consideration should be given to including works to give employment to special classes of workers, such as young workers; and the Employment Service Convention, 1948, provides that special arrangements for juveniles shall be initiated and developed within the framework of the employment and vocational guidance services.

The Conventions on holidays with pay, forced labour and penal sanctions all afford a higher standard of protection to young persons.

Finally, several of the social security and occupational health instruments provide, in one way or another, more favourable conditions for young persons.

Young persons in particular regions and industries

The special claims of young persons have not been overlooked by Regional Conferences and Industrial Committees. Resolutions relating in whole or in part to the protection of children and young workers have been adopted by several of the American, Asian and African Regional Conferences, from the earliest session in 1936 down to the most recent.

This chapter is entitled "Women, Children and Young Persons" because there are many points of contact between the protection of children and young persons and problems of women's employment. Child protection begins in the maternity protection of the working mother, continues in the provision made for factory crèches and nurseries where working mothers may leave their babies, is connected with the regulation of night work for women, and moves on through family welfare and social security for families.

Employment of Women

While the protection of children and young persons reposes on universally accepted humanitarian principles, the protection of women has been the arena of acute controversy. In the early years, certain women's organisations, more vocal than representative, the most active of which was the Open Door International, protested against special protection for women workers on the ground that it accentuated the unfavourable position of women on the labour market.

In contrast to this extreme position, most of the women's organisations, particularly those including working women, recognised the need for some special protection for women on the occasion of child-birth and also in connection with employment on certain processes or in certain industries in which the products used or manufactured or the trying conditions of work might cause physiological injury to the reproductive organs.

It was in accordance with this second point of view, and in the teeth of violent opposition from the opponents of special protective legislation for women, that the ILO carried out its programme. That programme provided in the first place for maternity protection and for protection in connection with employment involving special dangers.

On more than one occasion, e.g. 1937 and 1939, the Conference, in special resolutions, emphasised that while it was of the greatest importance that women workers should be protected by legislative safeguards against physically harmful conditions of employment, it was even more important that women should be protected against economic exploitation by ensuring to women equal rights with men in industrial and public life. In any event, the special protective measures for women adopted by the Conference represent only a small fraction of the total legislative effort from which women benefit equally with men. The great majority of the Conventions and Recommendations adopted by the Conference apply equally to women and to men without distinction of sex.

In each of the three fields of special protection – maternity, night work and health – the first steps were taken by the Washington Conference.

Maternity protection

The Washington Conference adopted a Convention on the employment of women before and after childbirth, the provisions of which were in certain respects more favourable than the legislation in force in the more advanced industrial countries.

In the early years after the adoption of the Convention many suggestions were made that the Convention should be revised in order to bring its provisions down to a level at which immediate ratification would be possible. The Governing Body did not wish, however, to envisage lowering international standards which had once been set by the Conference, and when at last, in 1952, the Convention was revised, it was in the direction of increasing the protection afforded rather than of diminishing it.

The 1952 revision of the Maternity Convention extends the coverage of the Convention to comprise industrial, non-industrial and agricultural undertakings, including women wage-earners living at home. The period of maternity leave is fixed as at least twelve weeks, of which not less than six must be taken after confinement, the remainder being allowed before or after confinement, or partly before and partly after. Finally, the provisions concerning cash and medical benefits and protection against dismissal are rendered more precise. The revised Convention is supplemented by a Recommendation.

Night work

The Washington Conference also adopted a Convention on Night Work for Women, parallel to the Night Work of Young Persons Convention.

In the application of this Convention, which prohibits the night work of women, difficulties were encountered; in order to overcome them, the Convention has been twice revised, in 1934 and 1948. The 1948 revision gave to the term "night" a definition providing reasonable elasticity in national application. Further, it does not apply to (a) women holding responsible positions of a managerial or technical character; and (b) women employed in health and welfare services who are not ordinarily engaged in manual work.

The successive revisions of this Convention, and particularly the 1948 revision, illustrate the increasing desire of the ILO to be practical in its standard-setting work. The standards set must be unequivocal, but conformity to them should be possible without conflict with minor national differences in industrial organisation or custom.

Employment on unhealthy work

It was again the Washington Conference which made a beginning with the special protection of women against risks of unhealthy work. In view of the danger involved to the function of maternity and to the physical development of young persons in employment on certain processes using lead or zinc, the Conference adopted a Recommendation urging the prohibition of the employment of women and young persons in a number of specified processes and the regulation of their employment in other processes.

It was not until 1935 that further action was taken by the Conference to restrict the employment of women on work regarded as unhealthy or dangerous. In that year a Convention was adopted prohibiting the employment of women, with the exception of four specified categories, on underground work in any mine.

Other action on behalf of women

In addition to the Conventions and Recommendations relating exclusively to women or exclusively to women and young persons, the Conference has, in certain Conventions and Recommendations of general applicability, made special provision for women. Examples are the Conventions concerning White Lead (1921), Inspection of Emigrants (1926), and Minimum Wage Fixing Machinery (1928).

The interests of women are also safeguarded by certain instruments which emphasise the principle of equality of treatment in cases in which such equality of treatment had frequently been denied. By far the most important of these is the Equal Remuneration Convention, 1951, described in Chapter 14. The adoption of that Convention crowned the efforts of a generation of women to see the principle affirmed in the Constitution effectively embodied in a Convention.

In other instruments of less importance the principle of equality was also expressly enunciated. Thus, the Vocational Training Recommendation, 1939, urges that women should have equal rights of admission to all technical and vocational schools, and should have equal rights to obtain the same certificates and diplomas on completion of the same studies. The Employment (Transition from War to Peace) Recommendation, 1944, urges that the redistribution of women workers in the economy should be organised on the principle of complete equality of opportunity for men and women on the basis of their individual merit, skill and experience.

Participation of women in the administration of social legislation

In a number of cases provision is made for the participation of women in the administration of social legislation.

Thus, the Minimum Wage-Fixing Machinery Recommendation, 1928, urges that wherever a considerable number of women are employed, provision should be made for the inclusion of women among the workers' representatives and the independent persons on wage-fixing bodies. The Invalidity, Old Age and Survivors' Insurance Recommendation, 1933, suggests that national laws and regulations should provide that insured women are adequately represented on the administrative bodies of invalidity, old age and widows' and orphans' insurance. The Unemployment (Young Persons) Recommendation, 1935, recommends that the central supervisory councils to supervise the employment centre system should include a certain number of women.

Most important of all is the provision in the Labour Inspection Recommendation, 1923. "While it is evident that with regard to certain matters and in certain classes of work inspection can be more suitably carried out by men, as in the case of other matters and other classes of work inspection can be more suitably carried out by women, the women inspectors should in general have the same powers and duties and exercise the same authority as the men inspectors, subject to their having had the necessary training and experience, and should have equal opportunity of promotion to the higher ranks."

Employment of women in particular regions and industries

At Regional Conferences questions relating to the employment of women have occupied a prominent place. At the first Regional Conference in Santiago de Chile in 1936 resolutions were adopted which constituted a genuine contribution to the protection of women employed under the special conditions ruling in many Latin-American countries. At the Asian Regional Conferences and at the Near and Middle East Regional Meeting useful resolutions were also adopted relating to the special circumstances of those areas.

The Industrial Committees have devoted less attention to women's work. This was to be expected, for with the exception of the textile industry the industries for which Industrial Committees have been established do not employ a large proportion of women workers.

Employment of women with family responsibilities

In 1965 a comprehensive Recommendation was adopted on the employment of women with family responsibilities, which notes that in many countries women are working outside their homes in increasing numbers. The Recommendation calls upon public authorities to encourage services to enable women to fulfil their responsibilities at home and at work harmoniously, and to promote research into, and general understanding of, the problems involved. Provisions are included on child-care; on the entry and re-entry of women into employment; and on the need for balance between, on the one hand, equality of opportunity for both sexes in the world of work, and, on the other, help for working women in combining the tasks of worker, mother and home-maker.

General trends of policy

The general trend of the work of the ILO on behalf of women workers has gradually shifted from special protective measures involving the prohibition of the employment of women or the authorisation of their employment only under special conditions, towards measures designed to make more effective use of the services of women in the labour force and the promotion of equality of opportunity and treatment for women and men as regards vocational preparation, employment and wages.

This more positive approach is illustrated in the expression of policy contained in a resolution adopted by the Conference in 1947. That resolution concludes by "considering the desirability of eliminating the inequitable treatment of women workers with full understanding of the specific problems which arise from actual but changing social, economic and industrial conditions in the various parts of the world", and recommending that "the Governing Body should instruct the Office to continue the detailed study of the employment of women and its effect on the labour market and to undertake the study of the employment of mothers of families, industrial home work, the status of domestic workers and the steps to be taken to protect women workers, bearing in mind their role as mothers and home-makers".

In accordance with the general policy of the ILO, meetings of experts have been held from time to time to consider problems relating to special categories of women workers, e.g. domestic workers in 1951 and nurses in 1958.

In addition, meetings of consultants have been convened from time to time to consider new trends and emphases in employment techniques and opportunities.

The 1959 meeting found that employment opportunities had greatly increased almost everywhere and pointed out the importance of the full utilisation of women workers as a factor in the efficient employment of human resources. Looking at the future programme of the ILO on behalf of women workers, the consultants expressed the view that the vocational preparation of girls and women should be given the highest priority, that further attention should be paid to the conditions of women in agriculture, that continued stress should be placed on the question of equal remuneration for work of equal value, and that further study should be given to the problems of the employment of married women, and to the impact of technological developments on women's employment opportunities.

At the 1965 meeting special attention was devoted to intensifying the activities of the ILO for promoting economic and social progress of women in developing countries.

Effective Results

Measured in terms of ratifications, the work of the ILO on behalf of women, children and young persons ranks as a solid achievement. Ratifications of the Washington Conventions came in quickly. Thus, by 1931, the Night Work (Women) Convention had received 19 ratifications, the Night Work (Young Persons) 21, and the Minimum Age 19. By 1 January 1970 the ratifications of these three Conventions had increased to 56, 51 and 60.

On the other hand, the Conventions adopted since Washington, including the revised Conventions, have been less well ratified. This is due, in the main, to the higher standards embodied in these Conventions or the enlargement of their scope. None of these Conventions was still-born; all have come into force, and their provisions constitute goals for future attainment by States which have not yet been able to ratify them.

In addition to its impact on national legislation the ILO has also exerted an appreciable influence on behalf of women, children and young persons through its participation in the work of other intergovernmental organisations. Before the war the ILO was represented on Committees of Experts set up by the League of Nations, first the Committee on Child Welfare and the Committee on the Traffic in Women and Children, and later the Committee on Social Questions. With these Committees which worked under the inspiring guidance of Dame Rachel Crowdy the ILO collaborated actively, and it was able to exercise a real influence on the solution of problems which were outside the area of its own competence.

Since the war the ILO has taken an even more prominent part in the work of Committees established by the United Nations. With the Commission on the Status of Women its relations have been particularly close. It has prepared papers for the Commission, at its request, on such questions as part-time employment of women, equal remuneration for men and women workers for work of equal value, and vocational guidance and vocational and technical education of women.

In regard to the protection of children, the ILO has collaborated with the United Nations and with other specialised agencies in a co-ordinated long-range programme. This work originated in the activities of the United Nations Children's Emergency Fund (UNICEF), now called the United Nations Children's Fund.

Throughout the whole of its history the ILO has maintained relations with the international voluntary women's and child welfare organisations some of which have been, and continue to be, influential in their particular fields. The purpose of this relations work has always been double; firstly to gain and maintain the support of these organisations and their national branches for the policies and activities of the ILO, and secondly, to make the influence of the ILO felt in the action of these voluntary organisations.

Operational Activities

In the operational activities of the ILO a greater amount of attention has been devoted to women, children and young persons than would appear from a glance at the titles of the various technical co-operation and advisory missions.

In the less developed countries, as, indeed, in all countries, problems arising in connection with women, children and young persons often form part of wider questions relating to all employed persons. In these circumstances the requests made to the ILO for technical co-operation or advice have rarely related exclusively to women, children or young persons. But in the course of general missions, the recommendations of the ILO have often related, to a very large extent, to conditions of work of women, children and young persons. Thus, in 1932 Harold Butler's recommendations after his advisory mission to Egypt largely concerned women, children and young persons, and the legislation adopted by the Egyptian Government included measures for the regulation of their employment. Similarly, when, after the war, ILO missions were sent to Greece and Turkey, their recommendations called particular attention to measures for the protection of women, children and young persons.

When the Expanded Programme of Technical Assistance came into being, it was clear that the technique developed by the ILO in its earlier advisory missions should continue to be followed; in other words, problems relating to the employment of women, children and young persons should be considered as special aspects of conditions of work in general. Accordingly, the ILO has given technical co-operation on the employment of women, children and young workers within the framework of more general projects concerning the drafting of labour legislation and the establishment of services for the administration of labour law. Such projects have been carried out in such widely different countries as Burma, El Salvador, Pakistan, the Philippines and Thailand.

In the protection of young workers and particularly in the restriction of child labour, the ILO has realised the need for the application of social measures other than labour laws, such as compulsory primary schooling and social welfare services. The ILO has co-operated closely with the United Nations and with other specialised agencies having primary responsibility in these fields.

Similar co-operation with other intergovernmental agencies has taken place in the training of women and young persons in handicrafts and village industries, with a view to increasing their efficiency and productivity. In developing countries employment of women and young persons is largely concentrated in agriculture, handicrafts and village industries. These projects, which cover the training of men as well as women, have mostly been undertaken in co-operation with UNESCO. For example, ILO experts working in the UNESCO Latin-American Fundamental Education Centre in Mexico have trained nationals of several Latin-American countries who will in turn train craftsmen when they return to their own countries. The experts have also helped to set up village centres teaching woodworking, weaving, embroidery, cloth-dyeing and pottery-making. In Ceylon, an ILO expert working in the UNESCO Fundamental Education Centre has assisted in the establishment of twenty-five village centres where training is given in textile production, coconut fibre crafts, rope-making, basket-making, brick-making, pottery and carpentry. In Afghanistan, Libya and Malaya ILO experts have assisted governments in establishing and carrying out plans for the organisation and promotion of handicrafts in the light of their economic needs and possibilities.

By such missions as these the essentially practical and positive character of the work of the ILO is illustrated. While the programme of the ILO has inevitably included prohibition and restriction, for abuses and mal-practices must be abolished and risks must be limited, its dominant aim has increasingly been to enable women and young persons, working under reasonable conditions and with technical training, to make the maximum contribution to their own well-being and the economic progress of the communities in which they live.

20. NON-METROPOLITAN TERRITORIES

WHEN the ILO was founded in 1919, a large proportion of the world's surface consisted of colonies, protectorates and possessions not fully self-governing. The peoples of these "non-metropolitan" territories were dependent for their social and economic rights as well as their political rights on the colonial Powers.

In the ILO's Constitution these dependent peoples were not forgotten.[1] Under Article 35 of the original Constitution, members undertook to apply Conventions which they ratified to their colonies, protectorates and possessions, (a) except where owing to the local conditions the Convention is inapplicable, or (b) subject to such modifications as may be necessary to adapt the Convention to local conditions.

This provision represented a compromise between two attitudes in the Commission on International Labour Legislation of the Paris Peace Conference. On the one hand it was clear that conditions of labour of the type which the ILO was to attempt to improve were to be found at least as frequently in colonial or other non-self-governing territories as in the great majority of sovereign States. On the other hand, it would have been impossible to expect the States responsible for administering dependent territories to agree, by the ratification of a Convention, automatically to apply it not only in the home country but in all the colonial territories, with their wide range of economic development. The compromise formula placed a real but realistic obligation upon ratifying States. They do have an obligation in respect of the application of the Convention in non-metropolitan territories, but on the other hand they have discretion to decide whether the local conditions are such as to permit application of

---

[1] The terminology used by the ILO in this field has not been uniform. This is because of the changes that have occurred in the social philosophy relating to these territories. The original Constitution spoke of "colonies, protectorates and possessions which are not self-governing"; the Forced Labour Convention, 1930, referred to "territories placed under (a member's) sovereignty, jurisdiction, protection, suzerainty, tutelage or authority"; the Social Policy in Dependent Territories Recommendation, 1944, used "dependent territories"; a Committee of the 1946 Conference preferred "non-self-governing territories" (which also figures in the Charter of the United Nations). The term "non-metropolitan territories" was first employed in the Constitution as amended in 1946, and since then it has been uniformly used in all Conventions, in the title of the Committee of Experts on Social Policy in Non-Metropolitan Territories, and in all the publications of the Office. (The title given to the original Committee of Experts, set up in 1926, was Committee of Experts on Native Labour).

the provisions, and if so, to what extent and subject to what modifications.

When the Constitution was revised in 1946 Article 35 was amended to take account on the one hand of political evolution in regard to the status of such territories since 1919 and on the other of the institution of the Trusteeship system of the United Nations.

Application of Conventions to Non-Metropolitan Territories

In order to emphasise the importance of the constitutional obligation, the first session of the Conference included in each of the Conventions which it adopted a "colonial" article, in the following terms:

"Each Member of the International Labour Organisation which ratifies this Convention engages to apply it to its colonies, protectorates and possessions which are not fully self-governing, except (a) where owing to the local conditions its provisions are inapplicable; or (b) subject to such modifications as may be necessary to adapt its provisions to local conditions. Each Member shall notify to the International Labour Office the action taken in respect of each of its colonies, protectorates and possessions which are not fully self-governing."

Articles in the same sense were also included in some of the Conventions adopted by other sessions of the Conference, but it later came to be agreed that it was unnecessary to include in individual Conventions an obligation unequivocally imposed by the Constitution.

With a view to facilitating the practical discharge of this obligation the forms for annual report sent by the Office to members which had ratified Conventions included a series of detailed questions relating to the application of the Conventions in non-self-governing territories, and special importance was attached by the Committee of Experts on the Application of Conventions to the replies of governments on these points.

Some of the governments with colonial responsibilities, particularly the United Kingdom, took very seriously their obligations under these provisions. They gave careful consideration, after consultation with the Governors of each of the various territories, to the application of all or some of the provisions of Conventions, with or without modifications, in each of their dependent territories. As a result, substantial improvements were effected in some dependent territories, particularly in the Caribbean area.

It soon became clear, however, that something more should be done. After all, the Conventions and Recommendations were primarily designed to cover conditions of labour in countries with developed or relatively developed forms of economic and industrial organisation. While some of their provisions could be usefully modified to meet conditions in undeveloped or underdeveloped areas, there were certain specific problems in those areas which cried out for direct and immediate treatment.

The stimulus to take action in this new field came not from within the ILO itself, but from its relationship with the League of Nations. When in 1920 the League Council set up a Permanent Mandates Commission it invited the Office to appoint an expert on labour questions. The Office appointed H. A. Grimshaw, and it soon became apparent that consideration of labour conditions in mandated territories involved study also of conditions in other types of dependent territories.

The ILO was also represented on the temporary Commission on Slavery, the appointment of which by the League in 1924 resulted in the adoption of the Slavery Convention in 1926. In adopting this Convention the Assembly of the League called attention to the work undertaken by the ILO to examine the best means of preventing forced or compulsory labour from developing into conditions analogous to slavery.

Forced Labour

After careful preparation, involving consultation of the Committee on Native Labour on three occasions, the Conference adopted in 1930 a Convention and two Recommendations on forced labour.

In its action to deal with forced labour, the ILO had to overcome strenuous opposition. It was argued that, as the non-colonial Powers far outnumbered the colonial Powers in the ILO, it was the non-colonial Powers who would in effect dictate to the countries directly concerned how they should administer their dependent territories. But this argument was not supported by the facts. At each stage the colonial Powers were able to exercise a preponderant influence on the decisions taken. On the final vote on the Convention five of the eight colonial Powers represented at the Conference declared in favour of it, the remaining three abstaining.

It was also argued that a policy of prohibition or restriction of forced labour, involving limitation of the rights of the colonial Powers, could only result in hindering the work of economic and social development in the colonies. But the ILO had never lost sight of the necessity for a constructive policy. Its attention had first been turned to forced labour because this system has been shown to be an obsolete, uneconomic and anti-social method of employment, which should be abolished before any economic and social system could be established on modern lines.

Under the Convention, each member undertakes to suppress the use of forced or compulsory labour in all its forms within the shortest possible time. With a view to this complete suppression, recourse to forced or compulsory labour could be had, during a five-year transitional period, for public purposes only and as an exceptional measure, subject to conditions and guarantees provided in the Convention.

In addition, the Conference adopted a Recommendation enumerating principles and rules designed to render the application of the Convention more effective, and also a Recommendation stating the principles that appear best fitted to guide the policy of members in endeavouring to avoid any indirect compulsion to labour which would lay too heavy a burden upon the populations of the territories concerned.

It should be noted that, although the Forced Labour Convention and the supplementary Recommendations are applicable to metropolitan territories, their provisions were mainly designed for non-metropolitan territories.

In 1936 and again in 1939 the Conference adopted a series of instruments for the protection of indigenous workers, reference to which is made in the chapter on Agriculture and Rural Development. Like the Forced Labour Convention, these instruments, though generally applicable, were mainly intended for the protection of the peoples of non-metropolitan territories.

The Pre-War Balance Sheet

The Forced Labour Convention was ratified widely, 105 by 1 January 1970; on the other hand the Conventions on indigenous workers secured very few ratifications, although the principal colonial Power, the United Kingdom, rapidly ratified them.

A survey of the activities of the ILO in the pre-war years leads to the conclusion that in a somewhat limited field distinctly useful work was done. At the time the approach of the ILO to these problems was sometimes stigmatised as negative on the ground that it was essentially limited to the prohibition of socially and individually injurious practices and the elimination of abuses and hardships. It would be truer to call it preparatory. In addition to the Conventions and Recommendations that the Conference adopted on specific questions, the discussions in that international forum on conditions of employment of the backward peoples were doing much to awaken the social conscience of the world. The pre-war work of the ILO was a necessary preliminary stage towards the new orientation given by the Philadelphia Conference.

The New Orientation

The Declaration of Philadelphia has been given many titles; perhaps its best name is the "Charter of the Dependent Peoples". Consideration for the dependent peoples runs through the Charter like a recurring theme in a symphony. "All human beings, irrespective of race, creed or sex, have the right to pursue both their material well-being and their spiritual development in conditions of freedom and dignity, of economic security and equal opportunity"; "poverty anywhere constitutes a danger to prosperity everywhere"; "measures to promote the economic and social advancement of the less developed regions of the world" – phrases such as these recur in every movement of the Declaration, and the theme culminates in the resounding concluding paragraph: "The Conference affirms that the principles set forth in this Declaration are fully applicable to all peoples everywhere and that, while the manner of their application must be determined with due regard to the stage of social and economic development reached by each people, their progressive application to peoples who are still dependent, as well as to those who have already achieved self-government, is a matter of concern to the whole civilised world."

Standards of Social and Economic Policy

The Conference started immediately to carry out this new and comprehensive mandate. Its dominant aim was no longer the correction of abuses and the prevention of hardships; its primary concern was to secure progressive improvement in a wide range of standards of life and work of the teeming peoples of the dependent areas of the world. As a first step in the implementation of this objective, the Conference adopted in 1944 the Social Policy in Dependent Territories Recommendation and in the following year the Social Policy in Dependent Territories (Supplementary Provisions) Recommendation. These provisions were given the form of international obligations in an important series of Conventions adopted in 1947.

The basic 1947 Convention is the Social Policy (Non-Metropolitan Territories) Convention. This boldly declares: "The improvement of standards of living shall be regarded as the principal objective in the planning of economic development." It lays down broad principles concerning the predominance of the interests of the peoples of non-metropolitan territories in the planning of policies; the provision of financial and technical assistance to further their economic development; the promotion of improved social standards in such fields as public health, housing, nutrition, education, conditions of employment; and the association of the peoples of non-metropolitan territories in the framing and execution of policy. It is to be an aim of policy to abolish all discrimination among workers on grounds of race, colour, sex, belief, tribal association or trade union affiliation.

On the adoption of this Convention, the general consensus of the Conference was expressed by the United Kingdom delegate, who described the Convention as an instrument which would improve the lives and increase the happiness of vast millions of peoples in non-metropolitan territories.

The 1947 Conference also adopted three supporting Conventions. One relates to the right of association, conclusion of collective agreements, settlement of labour disputes and similar matters, another to the establishment of labour inspection services. The third provides for the application to non-metropolitan territories of thirteen general Conventions, reproduced in a schedule, the provisions of which appeared most likely to be applicable to the conditions ruling in such territories. The importance of this Convention resides in the new procedure it introduced, under which any Convention listed in the schedule can be applied in part or with modifications to non-metropolitan territories even though the Convention has not been ratified by the metropolitan country.

In subsequent years many non-metropolitan territories attained independence. In order to take account of this, the Conference adopted in 1962 the Social Policy (Basic Aims and Standards) Convention. Its main purpose is to enable the 1947 basic Convention to be ratified by States now independent which it previously covered as non-metropolitan territories.

Effective Results

In no other field has the ILO's work had such a direct impact on the lives of so many people. While that estimate is not susceptible of mathematical proof, it is supported by a number of corroborative facts.

In the first place, in this area, the Conference has always attached quite special importance to the effective enforcement of the rules and regulations which it has formulated. In 1930, when it adopted the Forced Labour Convention, it also passed a Recommendation designed to render more effective the application of the Convention; in 1939, when it adopted two Conventions for the protection of indigenous workers, it added a Recommendation urging the setting-up of labour inspection services; and in 1947, when it adopted a series of instruments on social policy in non-metropolitan territories, it included a Convention making the establishment of labour inspection services an obligation. In only one other field has the Conference shown such continuing concern with the practical application of the standards it has laid down.

In the second place, ratification of any one of these Conventions has peculiarly wide and varied effects. Such ratifications are accompanied by declarations listing in four categories the territories administered under the authority of the ratifying member, namely (a) those to which the provisions of the Convention shall apply without modification, (b) those to which the provisions shall apply subject to modification, (c) those to which the Convention is inapplicable, and (d) those in respect to which the decision as to the application of the Convention is reserved. In the case of the United Kingdom, the various declarations classified under these various heads over forty separate territories, some small, others with many millions of inhabitants; the great majority of the territories were placed in the first category, i.e. the provisions of the Conventions apply to them without modification.

Further, under the provisions of Article 35 of the revised Constitution, members ratifying any Convention undertake to communicate to the Office a declaration stating the extent to which the provisions of the Convention will be applied to the non-metropolitan territories for whose international relations they are responsible.

As a result of these various measures of application and the reports supplied by governments, a mass of detailed information has become available on the extent to which conditions of life and labour in these countries have been progressively improved. Thanks to the stimulus provided by the home governments, the personal interest displayed by many of the colonial Governors, the collaboration of the local legislatures, employers and trade unions, and not least to the patience and ingenuity of the local administrators, changes have been progressively made to bring more protection, more security and higher living standards to individual workers and their families.

In addition to its direct action for the welfare of these peoples, the ILO has been able to exercise some influence in the councils of the various international organisations. Before the war in the Permanent Mandates Commission of the League of Nations, since the war in the Trusteeship Council of the United Nations and through its collaboration with such specialised agencies as FAO, WHO and UNESCO, which are doing much, each in its special sphere, to create the practical conditions of social and economic advance, the ILO "has served as the stimulant as well as the guardian of the welfare of dependent peoples".

In one increasingly important area of the world the results of the work of the ILO have been particularly significant. At the outset of an address to the Dakar session (1955) of the Committee on Social Policy in Non-Metropolitan Territories, C. Wilfred Jenks, using words uttered by David Livingstone nearly 100 years before, "invited attention to Africa". After referring to the economic, political and strategic importance of Africa, he pointed out that throughout the whole of non-metropolitan Africa south of the Sahara, with the exception of the Portuguese territories, a substantial group of International Labour Conventions were already in force.

When non-metropolitan territories attain independence, one of their first acts is usually to apply for admission to the ILO. In so doing, they assume the obligations to be bound by the Conventions previously contracted on their behalf by the Power responsible for their international relations. In this way the influence of these international measures continues to be effective.

Evidence of the usefulness of the work of the ILO on behalf of the peoples of non-metropolitan territories was afforded in 1960 at the first African Regional Conference in Lagos, Nigeria. The majority of the States represented at that Conference had recently attained independence. They had previously benefited, as non-metropolitan territories, from the work of the ILO. All were eager to show their appreciation of its work, and all expressed themselves anxious, as independent States, to co-operate in its programmes for integrated social and economic betterment in Africa.

21. WORK AT SEA

LONG before Ulysses sailed forth on the "wine-dark river of Ocean" work at sea had its special characteristics, which have been accentuated with the passing of the centuries. Of all trades, the mercantile marine is the most international. Its sphere of activity is the high seas, on which ships of all flags ply equally. In no other industry is international commercial competition so severe. On the ships of most countries, the crews are drawn from many nationalities. Shipowners and seafarers alike have always been proud of their special position in the world's economy, and have always been jealous to maintain their special prerogatives.

It was, therefore, not surprising that when the Peace Treaties were being drafted in 1919 the Commission on International Labour Legislation was requested by the seamen's associations to set up a special body, side by side with the projected International Labour Organisation, to deal with maritime questions. That request was rejected; but the Commission decided to recommend that "the very special questions concerning the minimum conditions to be accorded to seamen might be dealt with at a special meeting of the International Labour Conference devoted exclusively to the affairs of seamen".

In pursuance of this recommendation the second session of the Conference, meeting appropriately in the great seaport of Genoa, was concerned with maritime questions, and it thereafter became customary for all such questions to be considered at special maritime sessions. Further, an arrangement was made, to which both the shipowners and the seafarers have always attached the greatest importance, that the Governing Body, before placing a maritime question on the agenda of the Conference, would consult the Joint Maritime Commission, composed of representatives of the shipowners' and seafarers' organisations. In this way, within the framework of the ILO the special circumstances and needs of the mercantile marine have been recognised and largely satisfied.

In addition to the second session (1920), the ninth (1926), thirteenth (1929), twenty-first (1936), twenty-second (1936), twenty-eighth (1946) and forty-first (1958) were maritime sessions. Exceptionally, maritime questions were also considered at two ordinary sessions, the third (1921) and the thirty-second (1949). As a result of the work of these sessions twenty-seven Conventions and fifteen Recommendations have been adopted, a larger number of legislative decisions than in any other field of activity of the Organisation.

The International Seafarers' Code

Among the questions placed on the agenda of the first maritime session was "consideration of the possibility of drawing up an international seamen's code". The Conference adopted a Recommendation, in order that the task of establishing an international seamen's code might be facilitated, that each member should undertake the embodiment in a seamen's code of all its laws and regulations relating to seamen.

More important than this Recommendation, a resolution urged that the preparation of an international seafarers' code should be undertaken gradually by the adoption of Conventions and Recommendations dealing with particular subjects.

Historically, it was of great importance for the ILO to have its attention focused, at the very outset of its work, on the desirability of gradually building up a comprehensive international code. From the start the ILO was able to plan with the objective of such a code always in view. In the actual work of moving towards this objective the ILO experienced many disappointments, and when advances were made, they were often apparently haphazard. In a very special degree, the progress of the ILO in the maritime sphere has been conditioned by the economic and political circumstances of the particular time.

It would be a relatively simple matter for an international lawyer to codify, in logical and systematic order, international legal prescriptions regulating the work of the seafarer. That would, however, be a purely theoretical exercise. The practical work of the ILO has involved making progress gradually, when and where it could, as a resultant of masses of conflicting pressures, national and occupational, humanitarian and commercial, political, economic and financial.

In the following account of the principal provisions of the International Seafarers' Code an attempt has been made to present the legislative action of the Conference in a systematic rather than in a chronological form, but at the same time, under each main head, to arrange the matter with a view to bringing out, as clearly as possible, the historical relationship of the parts to the whole.

Conditions for Admission to Employment

Minimum age for admission to employment

In 1920 the Conference, applying to seamen the Convention adopted in the previous year fixing fourteen as the minimum age for admission to industrial employment, adopted a Convention providing that children under the age of fourteen shall not be employed or work on vessels, other than vessels upon which only members of the same family are employed.

In 1936, taking account of the progress realised in the sixteen years since the adoption of the 1920 Convention, the Conference revised that Convention by raising the minimum age to fifteen. In the case of trimmers and stokers, the Conference in 1921 fixed the minimum age at eighteen.

Medical examination

In 1921 the Conference adopted a Convention providing that the employment of any person under eighteen on any vessel, other than vessels upon which only members of the same family are employed, shall be conditional on the production of a medical certificate attesting fitness for such work.

Twenty-five years later, in 1946, the Conference extended the requirement of medical inspection to apply to all seafarers, without regard to age.

Entry to, and Training for, Employment

Entry to employment

In 1920 the Conference adopted the Placing of Seamen Convention, under which each member agrees that a system of public employment offices for finding employment for seamen without charge shall be organised and maintained. This Convention put an end to the exploitation of seamen by unscrupulous commercial employment agencies which sometimes charged exorbitant fees for finding them a ship. An important feature of the Convention is that it expressly provides that freedom of choice of ship shall be assured to seamen and freedom of choice of crew shall be assured to shipowners.

In 1958 the Conference adopted the Seafarers' Engagement (Foreign Vessels) Recommendation. Under this each member should discourage seafarers from joining vessels registered in a foreign country where conditions are not equivalent to those accepted by *bona fide* organisations of shipowners and seafarers of maritime countries.

Articles of agreement

In 1926, the Conference adopted a Convention on seamen's articles of agreement, which laid down rules and standards of value for countries which were, at that time, projecting legislation on seamen's conditions of work.

Vocational training

It was not until 1946 that the Conference dealt with vocational training for seafarers. The reason why action was delayed was partly that it was only just before and during the second world war that much progress was made nationally in vocational training for seamen and partly that it was only in 1939, at the last pre-war Conference, that action had been taken by the Conference to lay down standards for vocational training for persons other than seafarers. The Vocational Training (Seafarers) Recommendation specifies principles and rules for training for sea service. The Recommendation deals not only with pre-sea training but also with refresher courses, and it applies not only to those who intend to serve as ratings but also to those training to become officers.

Certificates of qualification

Closely allied to vocational training is the question of the technical qualifications which the various categories of officers and men of the mercantile marine should possess. The question of the professional capacity of mercantile marine officers was discussed but adjourned at the 1926 session. Following the collision later in that year between the French liner *Lotus* and the Turkish collier *Boz-Kourt*, the International Association of Mercantile Marine Officers asked the ILO to take it up anew. In 1936 the Conference adopted a Convention laying down minimum standards of professional capacity for persons performing the duties of master or skipper, navigating officer in charge of a watch, chief engineer or engineer officer in charge of a watch.

In 1946 the Conference added two further Conventions on minimum qualifications. One requires proper certification of all ships' cooks so as to ensure that they have adequate training and are capable of preparing well-cooked and well-balanced meals. The other deals with the certificates of qualification of able seamen.

Social Security

Unemployment, indemnity and insurance

In 1920 the Conference adopted a Convention requiring the shipowner, in case of loss or foundering of any vessel, to pay to every seaman employed on it an indemnity against resulting unemployment, not exceeding two months' wages. At the same session a Recommendation of more general scope urges members to establish for seamen an effective system of insurance against unemployment arising either out of shipwreck or any other cause.

Repatriation

A special risk to which the seafarer's calling exposes him is the risk of being abandoned in a foreign port. This risk was covered in 1926 by the Repatriation of Seamen Convention which, besides guaranteeing that a seaman shall not be abandoned in a foreign port, lays down definite regulations as regards his repatriation. States were urged by a Recommendation to extend the repatriation provisions to masters and apprentices.

Provision for sickness, injury or death

In 1936 two further steps were taken by the Conference in building up a social security system for seafarers.

One of the 1936 Conventions, which concerns the liability of the shipowner in case of sickness, injury or death of seamen, provides that the shipowner shall be liable: (a) to defray the expenses of medical care and maintenance until the sick or injured person has been cured, or until the sickness or incapacity has been declared of a permanent character; (b) where the sickness or injury results in incapacity for work, to pay full wages as long as he remains on board, and, it he has dependants, to pay wages in whole or in part from the time when he has landed until he has been cured or the sickness or incapacity has been declared of a permanent character; (c) to defray repatriation expenses; or (d) to defray burial expenses.

The other 1936 Convention is more general in scope. It provides for compulsory sickness insurance, and lays down standards in respect to right to benefit, benefits payable and other matters.

Comprehensive social security

Finally, in 1946, the Conference by adopting two Conventions and two Recommendations completed in its main outlines a social security code for seafarers. The Convention concerning social security for seafarers is based on the principle that seafarers and their dependants shall be entitled to benefits not less favourable in respect of conditions of award, extent and duration than those to which industrial workers are entitled. That Convention was supplemented by a special measure relating to seafarers, which provides for compulsory contributory pensions schemes under which seafarers would become entitled to retirement pensions at the age of fifty-five or sixty.

Finally, two Recommendations call for reciprocal agreements in regard to social security benefits and for the provision of medical care to seamen's dependants.

From this account of the work of the Conference on social security for seafarers it will be seen that, little by little, and from modest beginnings, each maritime session in 1920, 1926, 1936 and 1946 made a progressive and substantial contribution to the international social security code by which seafarers are now protected.

Hours of Work and Related Questions

In marked contrast to the smooth development of the social security work of the ILO its activities in respect of hours of work and related questions have encountered all the vicissitudes of the seafarer's life – near shipwreck, adverse winds and currents, becalming, sheltering in a friendly port.

Hours of work

In 1920, after a stormy debate and an exciting vote, the Conference failed to adopt a Convention. After this setback many attempts were made, both at meetings of the Joint Maritime Commission and at sessions of the Conference, to find a solution for the problem.

It was not until 1936 that the Conference succeeded in adopting, by a *tour de force*, a detailed Convention on hours of work and manning. It might perhaps have been better if that Convention had shared the fate of the Genoa draft, for it never came into force. Nevertheless, the international discussions in 1936 were largely instrumental in leading to the adoption of the three-watch system in place of the two-watch system.

At long last, in 1946, came the moment when real progress could be made. Governments were anxious to give practical recognition to the magnificent war-time record of the merchant navies. Shipowners shared the governments' appreciation of the war-time work of the seamen, while cautiously weighing the future economic prospects of the industry. The general atmosphere in those early summer days in Seattle, where after an interval of a quarter of a century a maritime Conference was again meeting in a great seaport, could hardly have been more favourable.

The Conference adopted a Convention determining standards of wages, hours of work and manning, which revised and superseded the 1936 Convention. The Convention fixes in terms of sterling and United States dollars the minimum basic pay of an able seaman, fixes maximum hours of work – a basic eight-hour day for distant-trade ships, with special provisions for near-trade ships, and prescribes joint machinery for fixing the manning scale with a view to ensuring the safety of life at sea and preventing excessive strain upon the crew.

After revision on minor points in 1949, this Convention underwent a comprehensive revision in 1958. The purpose of the revision was to remove difficulties in the ratification and application of the previous instruments and to take account of progress in the intervening years.

Holidays with pay

In 1936 the Conference adopted a Convention providing that, after one year of continuous service in one undertaking, masters, officers and wireless operators should be entitled to not less than twelve working days, and other members of the crew to not less than nine working days, annual holiday with pay.

In 1946 this Convention was revised by the Paid Vacations (Seafarers) Convention, which fixes substantially improved standards. In terminology the Convention provided evidence of the growth in the importance of the United States mercantile marine since the adoption of the original Convention ten years earlier and in content it was symptomatic of the general raising of seafarers' conditions of employment. The 1946 Convention provides that after twelve months of continuous service, masters, officers and radio officers or operators shall be entitled to not less than eighteen working days for each year of service, and other members of the crew to not less than twelve working days for each year of service.

Welfare of Seafarers

While it would have been more logical for the ILO, in building up an international Seafarers' Code, to have dealt with welfare on board ship before welfare in ports, circumstances made it necessary to attack the two problems in the reverse order. When the Conference first approached seamen's welfare it would have been quite impossible, in view of the economic situation of the industry at the time, to reach agreement on welfare on board ship. Under these conditions, the Conference dealt first with the easier, if less important, question, seamen's welfare in ports.

Welfare in ports

In 1936 the Conference adopted a Recommendation which urges the creation in every important port of an official or officially recognised body, comprising representatives of shipowners, seamen, national and local authorities and the chief associations concerned, with a view to the promotion of seamen's welfare in that port. In addition to measures designed to protect the safety, health and savings of seamen, the Recommendation provides for arrangements to set up, at least in the larger ports, seamen's hostels, clubs, recreation rooms and other amenities.

Welfare on board ship

By 1946 economic conditions in the shipping industry were sufficiently favourable and the public conscience was sufficiently awakened to render it possible for the Conference to adopt two Conventions and one Recommendation on the most important aspects of welfare on board ship, namely crew accommodation and food and catering. These instruments set international standards of a level undreamt of before the war.

Medical care

For the benefit of sick or injured seafarers on board ship two Recommendations adopted in 1958 provide for the carrying of medical chests on all vessels, and for the provision of free medical advice by radio to ships at sea.

Identity documents

Also in 1958 a Convention provided for the issue to seafarers of seafarers' identity documents.

"Flags of Convenience"

In recent years the organisations of shipowners and seafarers have been increasingly concerned at the tendency of certain shipowners in the traditional maritime countries to register their ships in countries such as Panama, Honduras and Liberia because of the advantages offered by such "flags of convenience" in respect of taxation and freedom from regulation. The aspect of this matter of special interest to the ILO was the safety and welfare of the seafarers serving on such ships.

Accordingly in 1958 the Conference adopted the Social Conditions and Safety (Seafarers) Recommendation which provides that the country of registration should accept the full obligations implied by registration and exercise effective jurisdiction and control for the safety and welfare of seafarers; to that effect, the country concerned should, in particular, adopt regulations to ensure that all ships on its register observe internationally accepted safety standards, and satisfy itself that the conditions under which the seafarers serve are in accordance with the standards generally accepted by the traditional maritime countries.

Atomic Powered Vessels

In the shipping industry, as in other industries, new problems are constantly arising, and the ILO must keep abreast of them. It has therefore undertaken a study of the problems created by the application of atomic power to shipping, in particular in connection with the protection of the crew. An article in the *International Labour Review*[1] has described the operating and training procedures evolved to protect crews and others from the risks peculiar to atomic powered vessels.

[1] *International Labour Review*, Vol. LXXX, No. 3, September 1959, pp. 236–249.

Effective Application of the Code

The maritime sessions have always shown themselves particularly anxious to ensure that effective measures should be taken to enforce the provisions of Conventions, and in 1926 a Recommendation was adopted on general principles for the inspection of the conditions of work of seamen.

The Conventions adopted in 1920, 1921 and 1926 have been widely ratified. By 1931 the Placing of Seamen Convention had been ratified by 17 States, Unemployment Indemnity (Shipwreck) by 16, Minimum Age (Sea) by 22, Minimum Age (Trimmers and Stokers) by 23, Medical Examination by 23, Seamen's Articles of Agreement by 11, and Repatriation of Seamen by 10. By 1 January 1970 the number of ratifications of these seven Conventions had grown to 28, 39, 43, 58, 56, 41 and 25.

These figures compare favourably with those of any other group of Conventions, particularly when it is borne in mind that maritime Conventions are normally only ratified by maritime States.

On the other hand the 1936 Conventions have been poorly ratified; some of them contain such detailed provisions that ratifications have been prevented because States have been unable to bring their national regulations into conformity with the Convention on some quite minor point. The process of bringing the Seattle (1946) Conventions into full operation has proved slow, because, with one exception, before any of them comes into force it has to be ratified by a certain number of leading maritime countries possessing a specified minimum total of tonnage.

Even where Conventions have not been ratified evidence has been forthcoming that they have had some practical effect. Further, some of the Recommendations, for example the Seamen's Welfare in Ports Recommendation, 1936, and the Vocational Training Recommendation, 1946, have been widely translated into action in leading maritime countries.

In recent years, as countries which did not previously possess distant-trade shipping have begun to operate a mercantile marine they have found the maritime Conventions of great practical value as a basis for drawing up the social legislation required for their seafarers. In addition, the standards laid down in the Conventions have had an influence on collective agreements in the mercantile marine of several countries.

Future Action

A maritime session of the Conference is to be convened in 1970. That session will re-examine certain maritime Conventions previously adopted by the Conference and will review the need for other instruments in the light of conclusions reached by a preparatory maritime conference in

1969, which considered among other questions the social effects of technological development and modernisation on board ship.

Conditions of Work of Fishermen

Criticism has sometimes been levelled at the ILO on the ground that it neglected fishermen for so long. But the fishing industry is clearly in much less need of international regulation than the mercantile marine. That is the reason why the ILO did not take effective action for nearly forty years in this sector. (The 1920 Recommendation is valueless.)

In 1959 the Conference adopted three Conventions. The minimum age Convention provides that, subject to certain exceptions, children under fifteen years shall not be employed or work on fishing vessels, and young persons under eighteen shall not be employed or work on coal-burning fishing vessels as trimmers or stokers. In accordance with another Convention no person shall be engaged for employment in any capacity on a fishing vessel unless he produces a medical certificate attesting his fitness for the work for which he is to be employed. A third Convention provides, in effect, that fishermen shall be covered by contracts and employment records similar to those used in the merchant marine.

In 1966 the Conference adopted a further series of measures of importance to the fishing industry. These include Conventions concerning fishermen's certificates of competency and crew accommodation on board fishing vessels, and a Recommendation concerning the vocational training of fishermen.

Regional Action

Much of the ILO's recent work has been inspired by the desire to be of direct technical service to particular governments or groups of governments and to the shipowners and seafarers concerned.

An example is the work done by a subcommittee of the Joint Maritime Commission to cope with the effect on seamen's conditions of competition in the short-sea trades in North and North-West Europe. The subcommittee concentrated on practical problems, such as hours of work, in an effort to co-ordinate national and bilateral practices on the basis of standards affording reasonable conditions to the seamen.

Seamen's conditions in Asia have been given special attention in an effort to eliminate certain practices, especially in the recruitment of seamen, and to bring about better conditions for Asian seafarers generally. The Joint Maritime Commission in 1951 suggested that the best approach would be to make a first-hand survey of conditions in order to see whether a conference on the subject could have real practical results. This was done by the Office, which had already, in 1950, made a direct survey of seamen's conditions in India and Pakistan. After this preliminary work, an Asian Maritime Conference was held in Ceylon in 1953 which, in five resolutions, made a series of practical suggestions relating in particular to methods of recruitment and engagement of Asian seafarers and welfare facilities for Asian seafarers in Asian ports.

In Latin America, following a mission undertaken by an ILO official, a draft Maritime Code for five republics of Central America was prepared in co-operation with other organisations.

The preceding pages show that the results attained have not been secured easily. In no other field has the ILO encountered so many temporary set-backs, in no other field has so much patience and perseverance been necessary, but in few other fields have the effective achievements been more rewarding.

Undoubtedly the main reason for the success of the ILO has lain in the confidence which both the shipowners and the seafarers of the world have never ceased to repose in it. The seafarers have been appreciative of the substantial improvement in their conditions of employment and social security. The shipowners have been appreciative of the resulting co-operation and loyalty of the seafarers and the relative absence of strikes.

22. AGRICULTURE AND RURAL DEVELOPMENT

In the early years of the ILO, while it was not overlooked that the greater part of the world's population lived and worked in rural areas, and that the number of workers on the land far outnumbered those in all other occupations, the ILO devoted relatively little attention to agricultural conditions.

In quite recent years, mainly as a result of the accession to ILO membership of many countries with a predominantly rural economy, a transformation has occurred in the policies and programmes of the ILO. A comprehensive rural development programme has already been planned in association with the World Employment Programme. In the part of this book entitled "The Future" it is suggested that rural development may well become a major field of activity for the ILO in the next half-century.

Although the ILO began work on agriculture only a year later than on conditions at sea, it was not until after the war that it succeeded in constructing the framework of an International Agricultural Workers' Code. Why did the field of agriculture prove so barren, and why in the early years was the work of the Organisation so unproductive?

Reflection suggests several closely connected explanations. In the first place, in most countries, even in primarily agricultural countries, agricultural labour legislation was almost non-existent in 1920. It is impossible for the ILO to adopt useful Conventions on matters on which there does not already exist in some countries at least the beginnings of basic national legislation.

In the second place, not only was agricultural legislation lacking, but even reliable information on conditions of work in agriculture. When the Office was preparing the agricultural reports for the 1921 session of the Conference, it was hampered by the absence of the official or other information normally available for other industries.

Another reason for the lack of progress is to be found in the slowness of agricultural workers to form trade unions. The relative absence in agriculture both of workers' organisation and of national legislation is not an accidental phenomenon but is due to the nature of agricultural exploitation. In most countries agriculture, unlike manufacturing industry, is carried on in small units. Land is divided up into thousands of small undertakings, most of which are family undertakings with little capital and

251

still less reserves, held on widely different forms of tenure. Where workers are employed on the farms, there is often but little difference in status or in economic position between the farmer and the agricultural labourer. Both suffer from periods of underemployment and both have to face periods of prolonged toil, the alternation of which in many countries can be foreseen and planned only very partially, as it is dependent on irregular seasons and the vagaries of the weather.

Early Conference Action

When, in 1921, a session of the Conference was held which included a substantial number of delegates and advisers with knowledge and responsibilities in the field of agriculture, the proceedings of the Conference were marked by confusion and inconsistency.[1]

Agricultural questions appeared on the agenda of the 1921 session in deference to a wish expressed at the Washington Conference, and the general approach was the adaptation to agricultural labour of various decisions of that Conference. In regard to the regulation of hours of work the Conference realistically deleted the item from its agenda.

The Conference dealt with the remaining agricultural questions in three different ways, without any very clear underlying basis of policy. On one group it adapted and modified the Washington decisions in the endeavour to render them applicable to agricultural conditions; on a second group it confined itself to recommending in general terms extension to agricultural workers of measures relating to other persons; and on a third group it adopted instruments which frankly took account of the fact that regulation of labour conditions in agriculture differs fundamentally from other fields of labour regulation.

Adaptation of Washington decisions

The Conference adopted one Convention and three Recommendations adapting to agriculture four Washington Conventions relating to the

---

[1] The Conference met under the shadow of doubt whether the ILO was constitutionally competent to consider agricultural matters. Although the Conference by a large majority maintained the view that it was competent, the French Government requested that the Permanent Court of International Justice be asked for an advisory opinion. The Court gave as its opinion that the competence of the Organisation does extend to international regulation of the conditions of labour of persons employed in agriculture. In reply to a supplementary question the Court gave as its opinion that the Organisation is not obliged to exclude from its consideration the effect upon production of measures which it may seek to promote for the benefit of workers. The importance for the future of the ILO of these Court findings cannot be overestimated. Not only did they determine once and for all the competence of the ILO in agriculture, but they were accepted as justifying a wide interpretation of the scope of its Constitution.

protection of women and children. The Convention fixes the minimum age at fourteen, but its terms are much less rigid than those of the Washington Convention. Thus, employment under fourteen is prohibited only outside the hours fixed for school attendance, and provided such employment does not prejudice school attendance. Further, employment on light agricultural work is permitted, provided it does not reduce the total annual period of school attendance to less than eight months.

The three Recommendations apply to agriculture the provisions of three Washington Conventions, namely those on maternity protection, night work of women and night work of young persons. In each case the less stringent form of the Recommendation was adopted.

Simple extension of protection

Two Conventions and two Recommendations provide for the extension to agricultural workers of measures relating to workmen's compensation, social insurance, right of association and vocational education.

Specific agricultural provisions

The remaining two decisions of the 1921 Conference are the only ones which reveal a real appreciation and understanding of the specific needs and problems of agriculture. In framing its Recommendation on unemployment the Conference clearly realised that in agriculture the essential problem is underemployment and seasonal absence of employment rather than unemployment in any of the forms usually known in industry, and it agreed on an instrument which wisely concentrates on a comprehensive statement of measures of a permanent character rather than on proposals of a merely remedial type. The Recommendation urges members to consider measures for preventing or providing against unemployment amongst agricultural workers suitable to the economic and agricultural conditions of its country, and to examine particularly from this point of view the advisability of encouraging improved technical methods by which unworked or partially worked land might be brought under cultivation, of encouraging the adoption of improved systems of cultivation and the more intensive use of the land, of providing facilities for land settlement, of affording transport facilities for the movement of unemployed agricultural workers, of developing supplementary forms of employment through seasonal industries and of encouraging co-operative action by the provision of credits.

Finally, the Conference adopted a Recommendation on living-in conditions.

Other Pre-War Action

After 1921, only two pre-war sessions (1927 and 1933) adopted agricultural instruments. These were all social insurance Conventions, parallel to the Conventions relating to other workers adopted at the same sessions.

When the Conference adopted these Conventions for agricultural workers, it was contemplated that governments would be more reluctant to ratify them than the Conventions providing coverage for industrial and other workers. That forecast was borne out by events, although ratification of the agricultural Conventions did not lag so far behind as had been expected.

No survey of the pre-war activities of the ILO in the agricultural field could lead to any other conclusion than that agriculture had been both misunderstood and neglected by it. Misunderstood, because the ILO had, though without any consistent plan, attempted to apply to agriculture solutions which had been found appropriate in other fields of labour regulation; neglected, because the ILO in its preoccupation with the urgent problems of the more vocal industrial and commercial workers had left on one side the claims of the Cinderella of international labour legislation.

Post-War Progress

After the war a number of circumstances combined to enable the ILO to do something to redress the balance in favour of the agricultural worker.

In the first place, the Permanent Agricultural Committee, at its sessions in 1947 and 1949, made a substantial contribution to the formulation of a comprehensive programme of work for the ILO.

In the second place, all the Regional Conferences in the years immediately after the war devoted attention to agricultural problems. In most of the States attending these Conferences the vast majority of the population is engaged in agriculture, and improvement of their standard of living is basic to the problem of the economic development of the countries concerned. The Asian Regional Conference at New Delhi in 1947, the Near and Middle East regional meeting at Istanbul in the same year, and the American Regional Conference at Montevideo in 1949 all adopted resolutions on a wide range of agricultural problems. An important feature of all these resolutions was that they did not base the solutions for agricultural problems on experience in other branches of production; they took their stand on the conditions of the agricultural economy of the countries of the region and realistically endeavoured to work out practical proposals to meet the special needs that had been identified. Furthermore, these regional resolutions did not limit themselves to agricultural labour conditions in the narrow sense; they dealt also with such problems as land tenure, agricultural credit, and agricultural productivity.

The other circumstance which favoured, after the war, a practical comprehensive approach by the ILO to agricultural problems was the collaboration which it instituted with the Food and Agriculture Organization. In pursuance of the formal agreement entered into with that organisation in 1947, practical working arrangements were made between the ILO and FAO, which not only prevented duplication and overlapping, but also provided stimulus and encouragement to both.

Taking account of all these elements in the situation, in 1950 the Conference adopted a resolution requesting the Governing Body to consider including successively on the agenda of future sessions agricultural questions which, after examination by its appropriate advisory bodies and particularly by the Permanent Agricultural Committee, and in consultation with other specialised agencies of the United Nations, were considered ripe for international action. As examples of such questions the Conference mentioned social security, vocational training, hours of work, manpower and employment, safety and hygiene. In addition the Conference drew special attention to the special problems of agriculture in underdeveloped countries.

Gradual implementation of the programme

In implementation of this comprehensive programme, action immediately began to be taken.

In 1951 the Conference adopted a Convention and Recommendation on minimum wage fixing machinery, and in the following year a Convention and Recommendation on holidays with pay. In the same year the comprehensive Convention on Minimum Standards of Social Security defined the persons protected in such a way that those engaged in agriculture are not excluded under the terms of the Convention. Whether they are covered in any particular country which ratifies the Convention depends on which of a number of alternative formulae on coverage is selected by the government concerned.

In 1956 the Conference adopted a Recommendation on the organisation of vocational training in an effective, rational, systematic and co-ordinated programme.

For consideration by the Asian Advisory Committee, the Office undertook a study on living and working conditions of tenants, share-croppers and other categories of agricultural workers in Asia. A similar study was also prepared relating to Latin-American countries. In 1968 the Conference gave international effect to discussion at those regional meetings by adopting a Recommendation on improvement of conditions of life and work of tenants, share-croppers and similar categories of agricultural workers. This was the first international instrument specifically covering non-wage-earning agricultural workers. The Recommendation lays down guidelines to be followed by governments, indicates the methods to be used, and outlines the facilities to be made available to the workers concerned.

In 1969 a Convention and Recommendation on labour inspection in agriculture embodied the principle of the active association of employers' and workers' organisations in labour inspection.

Agrarian Reform

In 1951 the ILO began to deal actively with a question the importance of which it had previously emphasised in several of its publications – agrarian reform. The opportunity for action was presented by the consideration then being given to problems of land reform in connection with economic development by the United Nations Economic and Social Council and General Assembly. The Governing Body placed on record the willingness of the ILO to co-operate with the United Nations and with other specialised agencies in taking action on the question.

The ILO also took a large share in drafting two reports on *Progress and Land Reform*, prepared jointly with the United Nations and FAO, in response to a request made by the Economic and Social Council. These reports, based on replies of governments to a questionnaire sent out jointly by the three agencies, were submitted to the Economic and Social Council in 1954 and 1956.

Plantation Labour

Another new field of action for the ILO was plantation labour. Plantation labour is agricultural labour, but of a special kind. As plantations, which are particularly important in the economies of the tropical and semi-tropical countries of Asia and Latin America, are usually large units, conditions in plantations differ substantially from conditions in most forms of agriculture and involve labour problems akin in some respects to those in industry. It was in 1947 that the attention of the ILO was drawn to the urgency of these questions by the Asian Regional Conference. The Governing Body immediately set up a Committee on Work on Plantations, similar in structure and functions to the Industrial Committees.

Appropriately, in view of the continents and countries specially concerned, the first two meetings of the Committee were held in Indonesia and Cuba, in 1950 and 1953. At those first meetings the Committee carried out a workmanlike survey of basic matters common to plantation labour as a whole. It made recommendations relating to recruitment and engagement of labour, regulation of working hours, fixing of minimum wages, and social services, including medical care, housing and sanitation. It paid special attention to productivity; on the one hand it recommended that additional payments should be made to workers in connection with the achievement of higher output, and on the other it stressed the importance of good working and living conditions in securing a high general level of productivity. Approaching wider problems, the Committee recommended that steps should be taken by the ILO, in collaboration with the United Nations and the other specialised agencies, to promote national and international action for safeguarding the income and employment of plantation workers, who are at the mercy of the violent fluctuations in world market prices of the primary commodities which they produce.

In 1958 the Conference considered the conditions of employment of plantation workers with a view to codifying provisions of existing Conventions and Recommendations into an instrument applicable to plantations. The Convention adopted provides for ratification by parts, some obligatory, others optional. Each member ratifying must comply with the parts relating to wages, the right to organise and collective bargaining, and labour inspection, together with at least two of the other parts. A supplementary Recommendation includes vocational training, hours of work and overtime, welfare facilities and prevention of accidents.

Operational Activities in Agriculture

Although in most of the economically underdeveloped areas of the world agriculture is by far the most important occupation, the number of requests for technical co-operation made to the ILO has so far remained small. For this there are two reasons. In the first place, governments desiring to receive technical assistance have undoubtedly given priority to projects concerned with the technological aspects of agriculture designed to increase food production, and have therefore applied to FAO, the competent agency on such matters. In the second place, governments were aware of the disappointing record of the ILO in the agricultural field in the pre-war years and were not convinced of the value of the assistance it could give. Happily, the new practical approach of the ILO to agricultural questions since the war, and in particular the contribution it has been making to such problems as the productivity of labour and rural development, are also becoming known. The number of requests for technical co-operation has therefore been increasing, and some significant work has been accomplished.

On the one hand, projects undertaken in manpower assessment and vocational training often have a direct bearing on rural development.

On the other hand, some projects have dealt more directly with the problems of agricultural workers, including hired labour, tenants and share-croppers. For instance, ILO experts have carried out surveys of labour and social problems in agriculture in Burma and Pakistan with a view to assisting the governments to take remedial action. Advice has also been given to governments in El Salvador and Guatemala on drafting agricultural labour legislation and establishing enforcement machinery.

The most important work, however, has consisted in providing assistance for indigenous rural peoples.

Assistance for Indigenous Peoples

The work of the Organisation on behalf of rural workers was extended in the 1950's in a special direction.[2] Following upon suggestions made at American Regional Conferences in 1946 and 1949, the ILO set up a Committee of Experts on Indigenous Labour which met at La Paz in 1951.

The Committee approached the various questions submitted to it, not as problems peculiar to particular racial groups, but rather as problems affecting sectors of the population which for historical reasons have not as yet been fully integrated into the social and economic life of the communities surrounding them. Among the factors which continued to prevent such integration the Committee considered that the economic inferiority of the indigenous groups and their deficient education play an important part. The Committee recommended the development of vocational training, the improvement and extension of social security schemes, the protection of indigenous homecrafts, the organisation and control of the recruitment of indigenous workers, the improvement of the measures designed to protect the health and safety of workers in industry and mining, and the dissemination among indigenous populations of

[2] Before the war the ILO had initiated action to protect indigenous workers in a limited sector. In 1936 the Conference adopted a Convention under which each member undertakes to regulate the recruiting of indigenous workers. The two main aims of the Convention are to avoid pressure being brought to bear upon the indigenous populations to offer their labour, and to ensure that the political, ethnical and social organisation of the populations concerned and their power of adjustment to changed economic conditions will not be endangered by the demand for labour. A supplementary Recommendation urges members to take steps to hasten the progressive elimination of the recruiting of labour and the development of the spontaneous offer of labour. In 1939 the Conference continued its work for the protection of indigenous workers by adopting a series of closely connected Conventions and Recommendations relating to contracts of employment and penal sanctions for breach of contract. These measures were strengthened by further Conventions adopted in 1947 and 1955.

information concerning their constitutional rights and labour and welfare laws. Finally, the Committee recommended the setting up of a joint field working party to carry out studies which require co-ordinated field work.

The Governing Body concurred in these proposals, and in 1952 a joint field working party was set up, whose work led to the most ambitious and adventurous undertaking under the Expanded Technical Assistance Programme.

The so-called Andean Indian Programme was designed to help the governments of Bolivia, Ecuador, Peru and Colombia to integrate in-digenous peoples into their respective national communities. It is a vast undertaking. On the high plateaux between 11,000 and 16,000 feet in altitude among the snow-capped peaks of the Andes live seven million Andean Indians. Conquered successively by the Incas and the Spaniards, impoverished and backward, these people need assistance of many kinds to raise their standard of living and enable them to contribute to the economic and cultural life of their countries.

Under the leadership of the ILO, this scheme has been operating since 1954 with the collaboration of many United Nations agencies. WHO has provided doctors and nurses, FAO agricultural and animal breeding specialists, UNESCO teachers and anthropologists, UN social welfare assist-ants, and the ILO vocational training instructors and handicrafts and co-operative experts.

The governments of the countries receiving this assistance have con-tributed money, men and materials. The Indians themselves have provided voluntary labour and surrendered land for the setting-up of training centres and experimental farms. In each country pilot action bases were estab-lished. These demonstration centres provided examples of what the Indians, by a process of self-help and with assistance furnished by their own governments, would be able to do for themselves.

At first it was not easy to secure the confidence and participation of the Indians. Neglected for centuries, they not unnaturally suspected the motives of the foreign experts. Gradually that spirit of doubt and suspicion began to disappear. From among the local communities "social promoters" were appointed who could help to explain the proposals of the experts for their own community, whether these related to new methods in tilling the soil, or training in handicrafts, or child care, or sanitation, or cottage-building, or the formation of a co-operative society.

From 1960 onwards the undertaking has been supplemented and extended both by national arrangements under the control of the govern-ments, in which Argentina and Chile have joined, and by long-term projects financed by the United Nations Special Fund.

Throughout the years the ILO continued to act as co-ordinating agency and major participant in the programme. In accordance with the Indigenous and Tribal Populations Convention, its purpose continued to be the integration of the indigenous peoples of the Andean region into the social, economic and cultural life of their respective countries, and the improvement of their living and working conditions. After many difficulties and disappointments in the early stages, this programme has been successful in inspiring the Indians with the will to raise the standard of living of their communities within the national economy of their countries.

In preparation for the gradual handing over of the undertaking to the countries concerned, executive responsibility in the various countries began to be transferred to the national authorities in 1966, the international experts playing an advisory role. This process of transfer has continued, and since 1970 the scheme has operated under the form of a long-term regional project, financed by the UN Special Fund, in which Bolivia, Ecuador and Peru will participate.

This was the first concerted international undertaking on behalf of the many millions of the world's indigenous and other tribal populations with a view to enabling them to share in the benefits of balanced social and economic progress. By qualified observers it has been regarded as an example worth following elsewhere; the ILO panel of consultants on indigenous and tribal populations considered that the experience gained under the Andean Indian Programme could be made to benefit countries in other parts of the world.

As a result in part of the attention focused by the Andean Programme on the living and working conditions of indigenous populations, the Conference adopted in 1957 the Indigenous and Tribal Populations Convention and Recommendation. These lay down principles and standards for the protection of these peoples and their progressive integration into the life of their respective countries.

In the following years action was taken to implement these provisions. In accordance with proposals made by an ILO meeting on indigenous and tribal populations in 1962, an ILO committee on nomadism and sedentarisation formulated in 1964 a programme of research and operations to secure improvement of the living and working conditions of nomadic peoples, particularly in Africa and the Middle East. In pursuance of the 1964 programme, policies and methods relating to sedentarisation of nomadic populations in the Central Asian USSR republics were examined in a study tour and seminar in 1966, with participation from sixteen countries concerned with such problems. In Africa in 1968 a meeting of experts appointed by the governments of seven countries (Chad, Ethiopia, Mali, Mauritania, Niger, Somalia and Sudan) considered problems of nomadism in their region and the appropriate action for the ILO to take, in conjunction with other agencies. Action on the results of that meeting is being taken by the ILO through technical co-operation.

The Co-operative Movement

Although by no means confined to rural areas, the co-operative movement has played a particularly important role in rural development. Throughout the years the ILO has issued a periodical bulletin *Co-operative Information*, an *International Directory of Co-operative Organisations*, of which the 12th edition was in preparation in 1970, and various specialised publications.

In its work on co-operation the ILO is advised by an international panel of thirty consultants from all parts of the world who give the benefit of their knowledge and experience either by correspondence or in meetings.

A large part of its activities on this front consists in providing technical assistance to agricultural and other rural co-operatives. Many of the ILO projects have been devoted to promoting sound organisational and administrative processes in existing co-operative societies. Others have aimed at helping to provide the legislative and institutional framework necessary before co-operatives could be set up. In co-operative organisation one of the main problems is to ensure that sufficient numbers of persons are being trained in the necessary techniques of leadership and management, so that efficient operation and control may be obtained. To meet this need many of the ILO's activities have been of an educational character.

Most of the countries which have received direct technical assistance are in Africa, Asia, the Caribbean and Latin America. Sound co-operative development is a slow process, and experience has shown that the most fruitful ILO work has been undertaken on long-term projects, such as those in Burma and Haiti.

In addition to giving assistance to individual countries, the ILO (sometimes in co-operation with FAO) has organised every year since 1953 co-operative training courses in the form of regional or inter-regional seminars; these combine lectures, group discussions and study tours; the participants are co-operative leaders and high-level officials of government co-operative departments.

To meet the demand for manuals suitable for use in co-operative training courses and elsewhere the ILO has published several handbooks. These include *Introduction to Co-operative Practice*, first published in 1952 and since translated into many languages, which is in use in study groups in many countries. The workers' education manual *Co-operation* is in great demand for co-operative training purposes. A manual on co-operative administration and management is designed as a guide for persons engaged in the day-to-day working of co-operative undertakings in developing countries.

In 1966 the Conference took the important step of adopting a Recommendation concerning the role of co-operatives in the economic and social development of developing countries. Applying to all categories of co-operative societies, the Recommendation covers in detail the policy objectives of co-operatives, methods of implementing those objectives (including legislation, education and training, financial and administrative aid, and supervision and responsibility for implementation), and international collaboration.

Handicrafts and Small-scale Industries

In developing countries handicrafts and small-scale industries are of great importance. If they are wisely promoted, they can do much to raise living standards in rural areas and to facilitate the transition to industrialisation. In this sector the ILO's technical co-operation missions have included training in selected crafts, initiating practical measures to promote new techniques and industries, and providing appropriate institutional conditions for their development. Care is taken to ensure that ILO projects fit in with national development schemes and encourage economically sound occupations.

A volume on *Services for Small-Scale Industry* published by the ILO in 1961 includes practical information on training, research and financial and other facilities contributing to raising productivity.

The main aim of all the ILO's work in this field is to promote the leadership and organisation required in the transition of backward rural areas into communities enjoying economic growth and social progress.

Raising of Incomes and Living Conditions in Rural Communities

In 1960 the Conference undertook a comprehensive discussion of the future action of the Organisation directed towards raising incomes and living conditions in rural communities, with particular reference to countries in process of development. The Conference unanimously recommended that a special long-term programme of research and operational activities should be established by the ILO. The new programme was supported not only by representatives of developing countries with large rural populations but also by those of highly industrial countries.

As subjects for research, the recommendations included employment promotion in rural areas, capital building projects (irrigation, drainage, school and road building, etc.), co-operatives or analogous organisations for production, supply and marketing, conditions of life and work of various categories of workers in agriculture, forestry and small-scale industries.

As regards operational activities, the Conference considered it best to concentrate on a few key subjects, such as survey of manpower resources as a basis for rural development planning, vocational guidance and training, modernisation of rural industries and improvement of their productivity, extension of social security to rural populations.

The continuing implementation of this broad programme, on which about $800,000 has been spent on operational activities, should enable the ILO to carry still further its socio-economic contribution to rural development.

From its early tentative endeavours to secure an improvement in the conditions of life and work of agricultural workers the ILO has travelled far. Its experience has shown that action in the agricultural field requires for its success a comprehensive series of interrelated economic and social measures.

Rural development is a many-sided process. Agrarian reform, to be successful, means more than land redistribution. Adjustments in land tenure need to be accompanied by measures for overhauling the rural organisational structure with a view to enhancing agricultural productivity. Agricultural training is of the highest importance. Better facilities for credit and marketing are required through government action or through co-operatives. Fuller employment in rural areas can result from industrial decentralisation through the encouragement of small-scale industries and otherwise.

Such measures, primarily of an economic order, have valuable social objectives. The achievement of a larger volume of agricultural production should make it possible to feed a growing population on a better level. The more rational use of land, combined with education and training, should facilitate on the one hand the attainment of a higher standard of living for those who remain in the rural community and on the other the orderly movement of surplus rural workers to full employment in industrial areas.

To these closely interconnected questions the ILO has already devoted attention, particularly at its American and Asian Regional Conferences and through its technical co-operation activities. In the future the success of each new venture will depend on the extent to which it is consciously planned and undertaken as a contribution to the social and economic betterment of the rural community.

PART III

THE FUTURE; CONCLUSION

23. THE FUTURE

REFLECTION on past history rarely provides dependable guidance for forecasting the future. While the truth of this generalisation will be confirmed by almost any period of political history, or economic history, or labour and industrial history, the degree of its applicability depends on the length of the period for which the forecast is to be made. If the estimate is to cover a period of a few years only, a careful study of trends in the recent past may provide some evidence to facilitate a judgment of the extent to which such tendencies will continue to develop on similar lines in the future.

On the other hand, if the forecast is intended to identify the shape of things to come over a much longer time, any possible guidance afforded by the past may become so blurred by the emergence of totally unforeseen and unforeseeable events or developments as to become completely unreliable.

In the light of these considerations, perhaps the most rewarding way to peer into the future of the ILO will be to divide the estimate into two parts, one dealing with the near future – the next decade, and the other extending to the more remote future – the next half-century.

The Next Decade

This attempt to sketch the future of the ILO during the next ten years is limited to consideration of its major comprehensive programme, to the exclusion of its structure and functions. Structure and function have a greater degree of permanence than programmes, which may well vary from year to year. While some adjustments in structure and function may perhaps be expected in the next decade, it will be appropriate to consider reference to them in connection with possible changes in the longer term which will be dealt with in the next part.

In examining the probable evolution of the ILO's major programme in the next decade, it will be useful to bear in mind an essential world condition which must be satisfied if the ILO's contributions are to be effective. That condition is that the "rich" countries should accept in word and deed the proposition that they have a responsibility to assist the "poor" countries. The corollary to that condition is that the "poor" countries should equally genuinely accept the proposition that they should channel that assistance into national projects designed to secure balanced economic and social development.

If the lessons learned in the 1960's from the partial failure of the United Nations First Development Decade are put to good use, it is fair to expect that the Second Development Decade which has now been declared by the United Nations, to which both "rich" and "poor" countries subscribe, will see these conditions more fully satisfied than before. Nevertheless, "Unless we pay far more attention than we have hitherto to the human factor," U Thant said in addressing the International Labour Conference, "the Second Development Decade may fail."[1] Within the United Nations family it is the ILO that has the special responsibility for the human factor.

In the coming decade, the United Nations Development Programme, embracing the Technical Assistance and Special Fund components, will continue to finance on a comprehensive scale the technical co-operation provided by the specialised agencies within the United Nations system. It is to be expected, also, that various bilateral schemes of assistance will continue to operate, and that some may even be augmented. The World Bank and the other international financial bodies will continue to grant massive loans for productive purposes on favourable terms to developing countries.

The World Employment Programme

In the coming years, the "World Employment Programme", launched in 1969, is intended to spearhead a major part of the ILO's activities.

The World Employment Programme is a broadly conceived long-term programme to stimulate and organise international and national action in revalorising human resources in an expanding world economy. It aims at the highest possible level of economically and socially sound employment and at increasing the value of that employment through proper training and through proper working conditions.

While this programme is intended to cover the whole world, industrialised countries as well as developing countries, its implementation may be expected to have its main impact in the developing countries in which large and growing sections of the population are bypassed by the process of development, knowing neither the efforts demanded by it nor the promises that it holds. The programme seeks to provide these peoples with opportunities for contributing to the development of their countries, and to improve their ability to do so.

Some indications of the size of the problem are provided by ILO statistical projections. These show that in 1970 the world's population may be about 3,600 million and the labour force some 1,510 million. During the present

[1] *Prov. Rec.*, Int. Lab. Conf., 53rd session, Geneva, 1969, p. 287.

decade the labour force has been increasing by about 20 million persons per year, and during the next decade it is expected to grow by about 28 million a year. Thus, during the period 1970 to 1980 over 280 million people will be added to the world's labour force. Of these, 226 million will be in the less developed regions, and 56 million in the more developed regions. Another significant figure is the number of persons in the world's labour force under the age of twenty-five. In the same decade the increase in the world's labour force under the age of twenty-five will amount to approximately 68 million, nearly all of whom will be in the less developed regions of the world.

The need for this World Programme did not arise from any sudden emergency; the decision to launch it in 1969 was the culmination of the recognition of needs which found expression throughout the previous two years in various organs of the ILO. The increasing concern of member States about problems of unemployment, underemployment and man-power planning has been reflected in recent meetings of ILO regional advisory committees and regional conferences. These included proposals and plans adopted at the Regional Conference of American States in 1966 (the Ottawa Plan of Human Resources Development), at a meeting of the Asian Advisory Committee and at the Asian Regional Conference in 1968 (the Asian Manpower Plan). In 1967 the African Advisory Committee asked the Office to put before the 1969 African Regional Conference a draft "Jobs and Skills Programme" for Africa. At the 1968 session of the International Labour Conference, a formal proposal for the preparation of a world-wide programme was made in a resolution on international co-operation for economic and social development. At previous sessions guidelines for national and international action on employment and training had been laid down by the Vocational Training Recommendation of 1962 and in the Convention and Recommendation concerning Employment Policy of 1964.

While most of the action will be undertaken on a regional basis, the overall programme is intended to remain a true world programme. Some of the questions involved are world-wide in nature, for instance, international migration including the "brain drain", and problems relating to imports from developing countries to industrialising countries. Furthermore, the entire programme will form part of the world's efforts throughout the United Nations family and otherwise to prevent the widening of the gap between the "rich" countries and the "poor".

There are, of course, limits to the ILO's power to create employment. To a very large extent employment is the outcome of the economic policies of the governments concerned. While the ILO intends to take the lead in preparing plans for action in order that the objectives of economic growth and increasing employment can be co-ordinated, it is for the individual countries to give effect to the plans. These plans will contain statements of employment targets – of projected increases in the level of employment – and of the volume and type of training needed to permit such increases, within the limits of what the appropriate and practicable economic and social policy measures could achieve. Targets of this kind are a matter of very careful manpower assessment in which the ILO is equipped to play a leading role. It will not be enough, however, for governments to receive carefully prepared plans, assessments and targets. They will need to be satisfied that more employment, however great its social value, will also contribute to foster economic growth.

In attempting to assess the prospects of success for the World Employment Programme it is necessary to emphasise that many matters of decisive importance to employment are the responsibility not of the ILO but of other international agencies, for example, international action regarding investment, trade, agricultural production and general education. It is therefore imperative for success that these agencies should be associated as closely as possible with the programme.

The Director-General has, indeed, stated that he has had consultations with the executive heads of these international agencies, and also that the necessary co-operation has been established with the United Nations in the preparation of the Second Development Decade.

As planned by the ILO, the programme is to be carried out in two phases. Phase I will concentrate on preparing assessments on a regional basis on what needs to be done, and in planning necessary action to provide jobs and training. The regional teams will consist of specialists comprising economists, manpower planners, labour statisticians, educational and training planners, industrial and rural development specialists, labour market specialists or others in such fields of specialisation as the needs may dictate. While the specific tasks of the teams will depend on the priorities in each region, their basic functions will include assistance to countries in formulating national employment and manpower policies, on the basis of a thorough analysis of the situation and prospects, in evaluating progress, and in training national personnel in various aspects of manpower planning and policy. Close relations will be established between the teams and experts responsible for technical co-operation projects in the manpower and employment field in individual countries. The ILO realises that it is only through action taken by the countries themselves that the programme can be implemented, and the essential aim must be to help them in this task.

In Phase II, the programme is to provide international help in the implementation of the plans of action – technical assistance by the ILO, and technical and economic assistance by such other international organisations and administrations for bilateral aid as are willing to participate in the programme. Finally, the programme is to include procedures for periodic review and evaluation of progress made.

By the end of 1971, the ILO expects (perhaps too optimistically) that the regional teams will have prepared a diagnosis of the present and past manpower situation in the countries of their respective regions (in particular employment, unemployment and underemployment by sectors, supply and demand of trained personnel, influence on employment and skill levels of past development policies, identification of other factors affecting the situation and trends), and have examined arrangements existing in the various countries for human resources planning and for implementing employment and training programmes, and identified areas where international assistance could help to render such arrangements more effective.

As the ILO conceives it, the World Employment Programme will also include a series of research projects in manpower planning, employment policy and training organisation.

The ILO recognises that the various regional programmes will not develop on the same rhythm and that Phase I of the World Programme will be completed sooner in some regions than in others. It therefore seems unlikely that much progress can be made in Phase II (implementation) until after the end of 1971. Indeed, all experience suggests that the progressive international, regional and national implementation of the various measures comprised in the programme will extend over the whole of the Second Development Decade.

The Next Half-Century

Any attempt to look into the future of the ILO in the next half-century must necessarily proceed on the assumption that the ILO will continue to exist. The future may hold many hazards – world war, conflict between the "third world" and the rest provoking schism and disruption, ideological exacerbation resulting in the withdrawal of groups of States, incompatibility and impatience, leading to frustration or boycotting by groups of employers or workers. The ILO has known all these dangers, either in fact or in menace, and it has survived. The assumption is that, come what may, it will survive.

Universality

Without sacrificing its ideal of universality, the ILO may well experience a sharp fall in the number of its members. That would result not from withdrawal of existing members but from their amalgamation into larger unitary or federal States. In the last twenty years the world has seen a proliferation of new independent States, accompanied by separatist manifestations of a desire for independence by areas forming part of existing States. At some stage in the future the present mystique of "independence" may well give place to a general reversal of policy and recognition by small States of the importance of ensuring an economically viable existence by some form of merger into larger units. However unpopular the notion of federation may be at present, the hard facts of life may well lead to a change in that attitude.

Within the international organisations, the present increase in the number of very small States ("Mini-States") is creating problems. While it is not a new problem, attention has recently been drawn to it by the admission to membership of the United Nations of Gambia and the Maldives. The United States has proposed that consideration should be given to the creation of a category of associate membership for very small States.

Neither of the two States mentioned has applied for admission to the ILO, and it would be unwise for the ILO to encourage them to apply, as there has been evidence that some very small States admitted to the ILO experience difficulty in observing the obligations of membership. Many such very small States have previously been territories with colonial or trusteeship status. It might be possible for arrangements to be made with such States to continue to respect the obligations in respect of Conventions undertaken for them by the State with which they had previously been associated. Some such arrangements for continuing relations, which could be flexible, might be preferable to the creation of a new category of associate members.

Tripartism

The tripartite structure of the ILO is the unique feature which distinguishes it from all other organisations in the United Nations system. What is its future? It is only too easy to stress the underlying community of interest between the three sides – workers, employers and governments. In hard reality, it is the divergence of interest that creates the problems that the ILO has to attempt to solve internationally.

Whether emphasis is laid on divergence or community of interest, unless the economic world is to fall into complete anarchy, the processes of orderly production will inevitably continue to involve interaction of three factors. There is first the factor of providing employment, whether that factor is an individual or a corporation in a free-enterprise economy, or a nationalised "Board" or "Authority" in a partially socialised economy, or a functional organism in a completely socialised economy. There is, secondly, the factor of receiving or taking employment,[2] whether that factor is an unskilled worker, a skilled worker, a technician or a salaried employee. Finally, there is the factor of government, representative of the civic interests of the population as a whole in the protection of basic human rights and the maintenance of order and security, without which the productive interaction of the other two factors would be ineffective.

Rigorous economic analysis can hardly fail to confirm the soundness of the three-sided structure on which the ILO is based. But tripartism depends not only on economics but also on politics. During the last fifteen years, while strains in the employers' side of the ILO triangle have caused some distortion in the pattern of tripartism, recent developments, fully discussed in the chapters on the Conference and Governing Body, have definitely strengthened the employers' side and therefore the equilibrium of the whole structure. If the slow approach towards approximation of policy and practice in management between West and East should continue to be accompanied by mutual comprehension of aims and purposes, the menace to tripartism would be removed. That, in turn, would result in eliminating the conflict between the two principles of tripartism and universality which has been a matter of such serious concern to the ILO both in its thinking and its action.

On the basis of universality and tripartism, the ILO's two fundamental principles, what developments may be expected in structure, functions and programmes?

The International Labour Conference

If the present experiment of adopting the budget on a biennial basis should prove a success, that would strengthen the argument in favour of holding the Conference only every second year. The standard-setting procedure of the Conference would not necessarily be prejudiced, as some double-discussion arrangement could still be provided for; the first discussion could take place at a preparatory technical meeting (similar to the preparatory technical maritime conference) or possibly at an industrial committee or some *ad hoc* tripartite meeting. It would be inadvisable to arrange for the first discussion to take place at a regional conference, as that might precipitate conflict between the regional and the supreme international body.

In view of prospective developments in multi-radiovisual communication, the question might indeed be asked whether it would be necessary to bring delegates to Geneva at all; they could participate in the Conference

---

[2] The relationship between the two factors stands out clearly in German – *arbeitgeber* (work-giver), *arbeitnehmer* (work-taker).

from their own capitals or even from their own homes. But however such new forms of collective communication may develop, it seems unlikely that they could ever provide for such necessary adjuncts to discussion as private meetings and confidential man-to-man consultations which do so much to secure agreement on controversial issues. In any case, so long as the spirit of man inhabits a physical body, the need will be felt for physical presence and congregation in a deliberative assembly.

The Governing Body

The principal change that may possibly be made in the structure of the Governing Body is the abolition of the right of the ten States of chief industrial importance to permanent seats. While the continuous presence in the Governing Body of representatives of States of chief industrial importance has exercised a valuable stabilising influence, the world will no doubt be increasingly reluctant to recognise any form of prerogative or privilege, however generally beneficial it may be.

The International Labour Office

The Office will of course undergo reorganisation from time to time, to take account on the one hand of changing world needs and demands and changing programmes of action to meet them, and on the other of advances in the techniques of office management. Nevertheless, it will continue to be a secretariat, an executive agency, and an operational centre.

Standard-setting

In recent years the view has sometimes been expressed that the need for the adoption of new standards will soon cease. But the world does not stand still, and changing economic and social conditions will demand not only the revision of existing Conventions and Recommendations but also the adoption of new ones. Both an instrument and a buttress of social policy, legislation, supplemented by, or associated with, other forms of regulation, will still be necessary to guarantee the objectives of economic and social progress and to reinforce its infrastructure.

Research and information

Research and information will continue to be necessary. No doubt research and the compilation of information will be facilitated by the increasing use of computerised and data-processing methods, while the dissemination of information will utilise, in addition to the traditional methods, telecommunication and the mass media. But the end-products will be the same.

Operational activities

While the ILO will continue to exercise an operational function, the forms of operation will necessarily be adjusted to respond to the needs of a rapidly changing world. If successive United Nations Development Decades, supported by ILO Employment Programmes and bilateral agreements, should attain their objective of narrowing, if not eliminating, the gap between the "rich" and the "poor" countries, technical co-operation would undergo definite changes. For example, large financial contributions to central funds for providing technical assistance would no longer be required. That would not necessarily mean that ILO co-operation in providing technical advice and training would cease. On the contrary, to whatever extent "developing" countries should become "developed", certain branches of industrial, agricultural or other activity, in an era of continuing technological and electronic advance, would need technical advice and assistance from an international organisation in which confidence was reposed. Such assistance, including organisation of pilot projects and demonstration centres, would be financed on an expenses basis by trust funds deposited by the country making the request.

Programmes

If in its first quarter-century the concern of the ILO was mainly with industrialised countries and in its second quarter-century mainly with developing countries, in the next half-century it may be expected to chart a more balanced course, working equally for developed and developing countries until the distinction between them gradually disappears.

Another basic change may also be foreseen. In the past half-century the ILO has been mainly concerned with the protection of the worker – protection against unduly long hours of work at unduly low wages, protection against contingencies of unemployment, sickness, accidents and old age, protection of freedom of association. In the future, while that work of *protection* will still be necessary in certain fields, the main emphasis of the ILO programmes will increasingly be placed on the positive *promotion* of human rights and the enjoyment of the fruits of balanced economic and social progress.

In future, in determining on which tasks its resources should be concentrated, the ILO should doubtless give priority to those which make a constructive contribution to increasing productivity, stimulating national prosperity and raising individual living standards. Major importance should be assigned to organisation of optimum manpower utilisation, creation of wider employment opportunities, and training in the new skills required by modern technology. Closely allied to this primary pole of activity, and indeed necessary for its success, will come the re-planning and re-tooling of the ILO's programme for the improvement of labour–management relations, trade union organisation and management development. In the complex task of associating free organisations of workers and free organisations of employers with free governments in working for the common good new methods and new procedures will have to be devised and implemented.

In this spirit, ILO programmes to which special attention may be devoted will include rural development designed to ensure that rural workers participate fully in the process of development and that they benefit from such progress. This implies (a) that they have opportunities of engaging in remunerative and productive employment; (b) that they receive necessary training to this end; and (c) that they enjoy working and living conditions compatible with human rights and with opportunities for improvement.

Another problem that will become more and more important will be work and leisure in the industrialised community. The increase of workers' leisure – by day, by week and by year – will affect many industries, and in turn will be affected by them – the tourist industry (already developing rapidly) with its influence on hotels and restaurants, the transport industry for travelling to and from work and on holiday, and, most important of all, the building industry for workers' housing. All these will present new problems for the ILO, particularly in employment, industrial relations and safety.

From among the vast array of problems that the ILO will be called upon to attack, these two have been singled out, because in each case, if a real impact is to be made, it must be the result of carefully planned campaigns undertaken together by the United Nations organisations working in concert.

24. CONCLUSION

REFLECTION on the long road travelled by the ILO during the fifty years of its existence would indeed be sterile if it did not suggest certain conclusions.

The first of these is the rapidity of the changes in the economic and social world in which the ILO has been at work. At the beginning of the period it was customary to say that the world was entering upon "the industrial era", the order in which commodities are produced by labour specialised and organised to operate machinery on a large scale. Now, the world has entered "the technological era", and the "era of automation", the widespread application of technology and electronics to industrial production and distribution.

Almost without realising it, the world has plunged into a second industrial revolution. Machines work almost automatically in the performance of even the most delicate industrial operations, controlled by other machines which operate more rapidly and efficiently than human overseers. The world has learned to apply power on a scale vast indeed but destined to be dwarfed by generation resulting from atomic and nuclear research, and in the further future by the incalculable potentialities of the exploitation of space.

These epoch-making transformations are not, of course, taking place with equal rapidity or equal completeness in all parts of the world. But in most developing countries the ideal of industrialisation is being cherished with almost religious fervour. A Philippine delegate at a Conference was applauded as he cried, "When I see smoke belching from the factory chimneys, I behold a vision of incense arising before the face of the Lord." It is in this spirit that many of the developing countries of Asia and Latin America have been pursuing, with the technical and financial assistance of economically developed countries, a policy of active industrialisation. Africa is now following. The technological advances which shape the new industrial order have been surging from one country to another with a speed that would never have been thought possible when the ILO first came into existence.

Alongside these technical developments the ILO has witnessed significant changes in the control and management of production and distribution. The State has progressively begun to play a more prominent role. In an important group of countries the State has assumed the ownership of

277

almost the whole range of industry and commerce. In other countries it has nationalised important sectors of production, transportation and public utilities. In almost all countries it has widened the area of its intervention in industrial and social relations, and promoted community and individual welfare through social security and other measures.

Within the State, the organisations of workers and employers have emerged as major influences in the developing industrial society. Increasingly conscious of its social responsibilities, the trade union movement has achieved immense power in many countries. Side by side with the trade unions, working sometimes in harmony with them, sometimes in opposition to them, employers' associations have attained a position of far-reaching importance in the operation of new forms of ownership, control and management of industry and commerce.

In no country have these various developments followed a smoothly continuous course. In all countries they have been affected by political and economic convulsions, by wars and rumours of war, by booms and slumps, by depressions and recoveries. Living and working in a world of continuous movement, the ILO has constantly had to adjust its techniques and procedures to the changes in the political and economic climate. Nevertheless the ILO has at no time abandoned the fundamental principles of its social philosophy.

Although the ILO has never been a doctrinaire body (for every doctrine is necessarily false in some respect; no doctrine can ever be completely true to reality), the ILO does have a social philosophy.

The two interrelated ideas on which its social philosophy is based are social justice and universal peace, both of which are manifestations of the principle of synthesis. In social justice the fundamental conception is that of a synthesis of opposing claims. Social justice does not mean simply the absence of conflict. That would be a negative approach. It is something positive, and implies the ultimate conciliation of differences in freedom and harmony. Similarly, universal peace does not mean simply the absence of war, merely "peaceful coexistence"; it involves the overcoming of national enmities, the attainment of international co-operation.

Inspired by such a social philosophy, the ILO has aimed at a constant new creation of social justice, incarnating social progress in an expanding economy in a world at peace.

Between philosophic aspirations and practical realisations a yawning gulf frequently exists. The day-to-day action of the ILO takes place in a workaday world where success or failure is judged on a rough and ready basis, and criticism is often vigorously expressed. In any assessment of the impact of the ILO such criticisms call for examination.

The criticism is sometimes made that the ILO has grown unduly accustomed to compromise in solving its problems. There are, of course, different kinds of compromise. Compromise may be simply a kind of market-place give-and-take bargain, or it may be consensus reached after careful presentation of arguments, laborious efforts to avoid misunderstandings, accommodation of divergent views, and reasoned modifications and adjustments in original positions. It would be idle to suppose that compromise in the first sense never occurs in the ILO, but in the second sense compromise is essential to its working. All its problems are controversial. These controversial problems have to be solved not by governments alone, nor by employers alone, nor by workers alone, but by all three groups, of different nationalities and ideologies. Almost all the decisions of the Conference and the Governing Body can be reached only through negotiation and discussion – in the last resort, compromise, or more correctly, consensus.

Arising out of the criticism that the ILO relies too much on compromise is the further criticism that it is constitutionally too weak, it has no teeth; should its machinery not be strengthened to enable it to put more pressure on governments? When the Constitution of the ILO was being drafted in Paris in 1919, some members of the Commission strongly urged that the Conventions adopted by the Conference should have immediate status and effect of national labour legislation in all member States. If that proposal had been adopted the ILO would inevitably have foundered. The world was not ready then for such a supranational power; it is not ready for it now. National sovereignty is a very tender plant; it has to be handled very carefully.

Weakness of the ILO can also be asserted in respect to finance. Under its regular budget it has no resources other than those contributed by States members. Undoubtedly financial problems exist, but in recent years the members have shown themselves increasingly willing to provide the funds necessary for its work. For example, at the 1969 Conference the budget for the biennium 1970/71 was adopted by 342 votes in favour, 2 against (the two government delegates of China), and 4 abstentions.

A criticism of a different kind is sometimes heard – that the ILO is too aggressive in extending its action into fields with which other intergovernmental organisations are concerned. The ILO is certainly not backward in advocating its claims in what are called "grey areas" on the frontier zones of the adjoining territories occupied by other agencies. But the resulting negotiations, in particular with FAO and UNESCO, have been conducted within the framework of the basic Agreements with the organisations concerned.

Other criticisms, relating to specific questions, have been discussed in the chapters concerned with those problems.

One last criticism of a general character perhaps deserves a word of examination. The ILO, it is sometimes said, is complacent and self-satisfied. What does the historical record show? In the pre-war and war-time years the trials and anxieties of the ILO provided no occasion for complacency. After the war it was in no complacent spirit that the ILO, by amending its Constitution, remodelled itself to meet new conditions, and so made possible the operational action, advocated by David A. Morse on his election as Director-General, which has grown into the technical co-operation programme in the developing countries. Since 1963, Conference, Governing Body and Office have been continuously engaged in self-criticism and self-examination with a view to adjusting structure and programmes to keep them attuned to the needs and problems of a changing world. Indeed, instead of complacency, it is often the ILO's spirit of adventure, experiment and innovation that comes in for criticism.

The survey of the ILO's action in this book has shown on the one hand the historical continuity of its basic policies throughout the whole period of its existence and on the other the significant differences between the pre-war and the post-war approach. These differences have been due in the first place to the fresh orientation given by the Declaration of Philadelphia, the importance of which was perhaps but imperfectly realised by many who voted for it in 1944.

By the Declaration of Philadelphia the original mandate given to the ILO was formulated in more constructive and comprehensive terms. For example, the original aim of preventing unemployment was restated in terms of full employment, not as an end in itself but as contributing towards higher living standards. The earlier concept of protecting workers against the hazards of sickness, accidents and old age was replaced by a wider ideal of social security to provide a basic income, comprehensive medical care and effective protection for the life and health of all persons. The problem of working conditions was no longer defined by enumerating a number of separate issues but was placed in a broad context of wage, hour and other policies, designed to ensure a fair share to all of the fruits of economic and social progress.

As a result of technological changes, the wider use of electronic devices and other recent applications of science to industry, a greatly increased need has arisen for vocational and technical education and training. As a result of the impact on working conditions of the use of atomic and nuclear energy, the need has developed for special measures of protection against radiations and other effects. As a result of agricultural mechanisation, new problems of redeployment in rural communities have had to be solved. As a result of the emergence of a keener social conscience, the demand has grown for effective measures for safeguarding freedom of association, abolishing forced labour and eliminating discrimination in employment. As a result of higher levels of education and rising standards of living, opportunities have increased for new methods of labour–management co-operation and management development.

Most important of all, the attainment of independence by many new nations, coupled with the institution of new international financial and economic arrangements to help them, have created new demands on the ILO to assist in promoting the progress of developing countries towards greater productivity and higher living standards.

In addressing itself to these duties, the ILO is continuing to apply the principles of balance which are fundamental to its operations. It has endeavoured to view each new task in a balanced socio-economic context, and to demonstrate that social progress and economic growth are inconsistent only when there is failure to promote proper balance between them.

In the coming years, while measures for economic advancement must continue to bulk largely in all socio-economic programmes, it is possible and indeed desirable that social policy should become more and more closely identified with the furtherance of respect for human rights. Throughout the world there are signs of growing frustration in the race for financial rewards; there are signs of increasing awareness that material prosperity is worthwhile only to the extent that it enhances human personality and human dignity. In view of this, the ILO may well intensify its efforts to promote those human rights which are fundamental to its objective of balanced social and economic progress.

While the value of the ILO's mission to work for peace through social justice has been recognised in the award of the Nobel Peace Prize, it is only too obvious that social justice has not yet been realised, and that while another world war has been averted the menace still persists. Must the conclusion follow that the ILO has so far been a failure? If the "Big Three" at the Peace Conference in 1919, who gave their blessing to the ILO at its birth, could have met in Elysium on its 50th anniversary to ask themselves whether their hopes for it had been justified, Clemenceau the realist might have said "Yes", Woodrow Wilson the idealist certainly "No", while Lloyd George, that master of compromise, might have said: "Failure or success, the ILO has never stopped trying."

PART IV
REFERENCE

The Constitution of the International Labour Organisation

Preamble

Whereas universal and lasting peace can be established only if it is based upon social justice;

And whereas conditions of labour exist involving such injustice, hardship and privation to large numbers of people as to produce unrest so great that the peace and harmony of the world are imperilled; and an improvement of those conditions is urgently required: as, for example, by the regulation of the hours of work, including the establishment of a maximum working day and week, the regulation of the labour supply, the prevention of unemployment, the provision of an adequate living wage, the protection of the worker against sickness, disease and injury arising out of his employment, the protection of children, young persons and women, provision for old age and injury, protection of the interests of workers when employed in countries other than their own, recognition of the principle of equal remuneration for work of equal value, recognition of the principle of freedom of association, the organisation of vocational and technical education and other measures;

Whereas also the failure of any nation to adopt humane conditions of labour is an obstacle in the way of other nations which desire to improve the conditions in their own countries;

The High Contracting Parties, moved by sentiments of justice and humanity as well as by the desire to secure the permanent peace of the world, and with a view to attaining the objectives set forth in this Preamble, agree to the following Constitution of the International Labour Organisation:

Chapter I – Organisation

Article 1 *Establishment*

1. A Permanent organisation is hereby established for the promotion of the objects set forth in the Preamble to this Constitution and in the Declaration concerning the aims and purposes of the International Labour Organisation adopted at Philadelphia on 10 May 1944 the text of which is annexed to this Constitution.

2. The Members of the International Labour Organisation shall be the *Membership* States which were Members of the Organisation on 1 November 1945, and such other States as may become Members in pursuance of the provisions of paragraphs 3 and 4 of this article.

3. Any original Member of the United Nations and any State admitted to membership of the United Nations by a decision of the General Assembly in accordance with the provisions of the Charter may become a Member of the International Labour Organisation by communicating to the Director-General of the International Labour Office its formal acceptance of the obligations of the Constitution of the International Labour Organisation.

4. The General Conference of the International Labour Organisation may also admit Members to the Organisation by a vote concurred in by two-thirds of the delegates attending the session, including two-thirds of the Government delegates present and voting. Such admission shall take effect on the communication to the Director-General of the International Labour Office by the government of the new Member of its formal acceptance of the obligations of the Constitution of the Organisation.

Withdrawal 5. No Member of the International Labour Organisation may withdraw from the Organisation without giving notice of its intention so to do to the Director-General of the International Labour Office. Such notice shall take effect two years after the date of its reception by the Director-General, subject to the Member having at that time fulfilled all financial obligations arising out of its membership. When a Member has ratified any international labour Convention, such withdrawal shall not affect the continued validity for the period provided for in the Convention of all obligations arising thereunder or relating thereto.

Readmission 6. In the event of any State having ceased to be a Member of the Organisation, its readmission to membership shall be governed by the provisions of paragraph 3 or paragraph 4 of this article as the case may be.

Organs ## Article 2

The permanent organisation shall consist of –

(a) a General Conference of representatives of the Members;

(b) a Governing Body composed as described in article 7; and

(c) an International Labour Office controlled by the Governing Body.

Conference ## Article 3

Meetings and delegates 1. The meetings of the General Conference of representatives of the Members shall be held from time to time as occasion may require, and at least once in every year. It shall be composed of four representatives of each of the Members, of whom two shall be Government delegates and the two others shall be delegates representing respectively the employers and the workpeople of each of the Members.

2. Each delegate may be accompanied by advisers, who shall not exceed *Advisers*
two in number for each item on the agenda of the meeting. When questions
specially affecting women are to be considered by the Conference, one at
least of the advisers should be a woman.

3. Each Member which is responsible for the international relations of *Advisers from*
non-metropolitan territories may appoint as additional advisers to each of *non-metropoli-*
its delegates – *tan territories*

(a) persons nominated by it as representatives of any such territory in
    regard to matters within the self-governing powers of that territory;
    and

(b) persons nominated by it to advise its delegates in regard to matters
    concerning non-self-governing territories.

4. In the case of a territory under the joint authority of two or more
Members, persons may be nominated to advise the delegates of such
Members.

5. The Members undertake to nominate non-Government delegates *Nomination of*
and advisers chosen in agreement with the industrial organisations, if such *non-govern-*
organisations exist, which are most representative of employers or work- *mental repre-*
people, as the case may be, in their respective countries. *sentatives*

6. Advisers shall not speak except on a request made by the delegate *Status of ad-*
whom they accompany and by the special authorisation of the President of *visers*
the Conference, and may not vote.

7. A delegate may by notice in writing addressed to the President
appoint one of his advisers to act as his deputy, and the adviser, while so
acting, shall be allowed to speak and vote.

8. The names of the delegates and their advisers will be communicated *Credentials*
to the International Labour Office by the government of each of the
Members.

9. The credentials of delegates and their advisers shall be subject to
scrutiny by the Conference, which may, by two-thirds of the votes cast by
the delegates present, refuse to admit any delegate or adviser whom it
deems not to have been nominated in accordance with this article.

Article 4   *Voting rights*

1. Every delegate shall be entitled to vote individually on all matters
which are taken into consideration by the Conference.

2. If one of the Members fails to nominate one of the non-Government
delegates whom it is entitled to nominate, the other non-Government
delegate shall be allowed to sit and speak at the Conference, but not to
vote.

3. If in accordance with article 3 the Conference refuses admission to a delegate of one of the Members, the provisions of the present article shall apply as if that delegate had not been nominated.

Place of meetings of the Conference

Article 5

The meetings of the Conference shall, subject to any decisions which may have been taken by the Conference itself at a previous meeting, be held at such place as may be decided by the Governing Body.

Seat of the International Labour Office

Article 6

Any change in the seat of the International Labour Office shall be decided by the Conference by a two-thirds majority of the votes cast by the delegates present.

Governing Body

Composition

Article 7

1. The Governing Body shall consist of forty-eight persons –

Twenty-four representing governments,
Twelve representing the employers, and
Twelve representing the workers.

Government representatives

2. Of the twenty-four persons representing governments, ten shall be appointed by the Members of chief industrial importance, and fourteen shall be appointed by the Members selected for that purpose by the Government delegates to the Conference, excluding the delegates of the ten Members mentioned above.

States of chief industrial importance

3. The Governing Body shall as occasion requires determine which are the Members of the Organisation of chief industrial importance and shall make rules to ensure that all questions relating to the selection of the Members of chief industrial importance are considered by an impartial committee before being decided by the Governing Body. Any appeal made by a Member from the declaration of the Governing Body as to which are the Members of chief industrial importance shall be decided by the Conference, but an appeal to the Conference shall not suspend the application of the declaration until such time as the Conference decides the appeal.

Employers' and Workers' representatives

4. The persons representing the employers and the persons representing the workers shall be elected respectively by the Employers' delegates and the Workers' delegates to the Conference.

Term of office

5. The period of office of the Governing Body shall be three years. If for any reason the Governing Body elections do not take place on the expiry of this period, the Governing Body shall remain in office until such elections are held.

6. The method of filling vacancies and of appointing substitutes and other similar questions may be decided by the Governing Body subject to the approval of the Conference.

Vacancies, substitutes, etc.

7. The Governing Body shall, from time to time, elect from its number a chairman and two vice-chairmen, of whom one shall be a person representing a government, one a person representing the employers, and one a person representing the workers.

Officers

8. The Governing Body shall regulate its own procedure and shall fix its own times of meeting. A special meeting shall be held if a written request to that effect is made by at least sixteen of the representatives on the Governing Body.

Procedure

Article 8

Director-General

1. There shall be a Director-General of the International Labour Office, who shall be appointed by the Governing Body, and, subject to the instructions of the Governing Body, shall be responsible for the efficient conduct of the International Labour Office and for such other duties as may be assigned to him.

2. The Director-General or his deputy shall attend all meetings of the Governing Body.

Article 9

Staff

1. The staff of the International Labour Office shall be appointed by the Director-General under regulations approved by the Governing Body.

Appointment

2. So far as is possible with due regard to the efficiency of the work of the Office, the Director-General shall select persons of different nationalities.

3. A certain number of these persons shall be women.

4. The responsibilities of the Director-General and the staff shall be exclusively international in character. In the performance of their duties, the Director-General and the staff shall not seek or receive instructions from any government or from any other authority external to the Organisation. They shall refrain from any action which might reflect on their position as international officials responsible only to the Organisation.

International character of responsibilities

5. Each Member of the Organisation undertakes to respect the exclusively international character of the responsibilities of the Director-General and the staff and not to seek to influence them in the discharge of their responsibilities.

Article 10

1. The functions of the International Labour Office shall include the collection and distribution of information on all subjects relating to the international adjustment of conditions of industrial life and labour, and particularly the examination of subjects which it is proposed to bring before the Conference with a view to the conclusion of international Conventions, and the conduct of such special investigations as may be ordered by the Conference or by the Governing Body.

2. Subject to such directions as the Governing Body may give, the Office shall –

(a) prepare the documents on the various items of the agenda for the meetings of the Conference;

(b) accord to governments at their request all appropriate assistance within its power in connection with the framing of laws and regulations on the basis of the decisions of the Conference and the improvement of administrative practices and systems of inspection;

(c) carry out the duties required of it by the provisions of this Constitution in connection with the effective observance of Conventions;

(d) edit and issue, in such languages as the Governing Body may think desirable, publications dealing with problems of industry and employment of international interest.

3. Generally, it shall have such other powers and duties as may be assigned to it by the Conference or by the Governing Body.

*Relations with
governments*

Article 11

The government departments of any of the Members which deal with questions of industry and employment may communicate directly with the Director-General through the representative of their government on the Governing Body of the International Labour Office or, failing any such representative, through such other qualified official as the government may nominate for the purpose.

*Relations with
international
organisations*

Article 12

1. The International Labour Organisation shall co-operate within the terms of this Constitution with any general international organisation entrusted with the co-ordination of the activities of public international organisations having specialised responsibilities and with public international organisations having specialised responsibilities in related fields.

2. The International Labour Organisation may make appropriate arrangements for the representatives of public international organisations to participate without vote in its deliberations.

3. The International Labour Organisation may make suitable arrangements for such consultation as it may think desirable with recognised non-governmental international organisations, including international organisations of employers, workers, agriculturists and co-operators.

Article 13

Financial and budgetary arrangements

1. The International Labour Organisation may make such financial and budgetary arrangements with the United Nations as may appear appropriate.

2. Pending the conclusion of such arrangements or if at any time no such arrangements are in force –

(a) each of the Members will pay the travelling and subsistence expenses of its delegates and their advisers and of its representatives attending the meetings of the Conference or the Governing Body, as the case may be;

(b) all other expenses of the International Labour Office and of the meetings of the Conference or Governing Body shall be paid by the Director-General of the International Labour Office out of the general funds of the International Labour Organisation;

(c) the arrangements for the approval, allocation and collection of the budget of the International Labour Organisation shall be determined by the Conference by a two-thirds majority of the votes cast by the delegates present, and shall provide for the approval of the budget and of the arrangements for the allocation of expenses among the Members of the Organisation by a committee of Government representatives.

3. The expenses of the International Labour Organisation shall be borne by the Members in accordance with the arrangements in force in virtue of paragraph 1 or paragraph 2 (c) of this article.

4. A Member of the Organisation which is in arrears in the payment of its financial contribution to the Organisation shall have no vote in the Conference, in the Governing Body, in any committee, or in the elections of members of the Governing Body, if the amount of its arrears equals or exceeds the amount of the contributions due from it for the preceding two full years: Provided that the Conference may by a two-thirds majority of the votes cast by the delegates present permit such a Member to vote if it is satisfied that the failure to pay is due to conditions beyond the control of the Member.

Arrears in payment of contributions

5. The Director-General of the International Labour Office shall be responsible to the Governing Body for the proper expenditure of the funds of the International Labour Organisation.

Financial responsibility of Director-General

Chapter II – Procedure

Article 14

Agenda for Conference

1. The agenda for all meetings of the Conference will be settled by the Governing Body, which shall consider any suggestion as to the agenda that may be made by the government of any of the Members or by any representative organisation recognised for the purpose of article 3, or by any public international organisation.

Preparation for Conference

2. The Governing Body shall make rules to ensure thorough technical preparation and adequate consultation of the Members primarily concerned, by means of a preparatory conference or otherwise, prior to the adoption of a Convention or Recommendation by the Conference.

Transmission of agenda and reports for Conference

Article 15

1. The Director-General shall act as the Secretary-General of the Conference, and shall transmit the agenda so as to reach the Members four months before the meeting of the Conference, and, through them, the non-Government delegates when appointed.

2. The reports on each item of the agenda shall be despatched so as to reach the Members in time to permit adequate consideration before the meeting of the Conference. The Governing Body shall make rules for the application of this provision.

Objections to agenda

Article 16

1. Any of the governments of the Members may formally object to the inclusion of any item or items in the agenda. The grounds for such objection shall be set forth in a statement addressed to the Director-General who shall circulate it to all the Members of the Organisation.

2. Items to which such objection has been made shall not, however, be excluded from the agenda, if at the Conference a majority of two-thirds of the votes cast by the delegates present is in favour of considering them.

Inclusion of new items by Conference

3. If the Conference decides (otherwise than under the preceding paragraph) by two-thirds of the votes cast by the delegates present that any subject shall be considered by the Conference, that subject shall be included in the agenda for the following meeting.

Officers of Conference, procedure and committees

Article 17

1. The Conference shall elect a president and three vice-presidents. One of the vice-presidents shall be a Government delegate, one an Employers' delegate and one a Workers' delegate. The Conference shall regulate its own procedure and may appoint committees to consider and report on any matter.

2. Except as otherwise expressly provided in this Constitution or by the *Voting* terms of any Convention or other instrument conferring powers on the Conference or of the financial and budgetary arrangements adopted in virtue of article 13, all matters shall be decided by a simple majority of the votes cast by the delegates present.

3. The voting is void unless the total number of votes cast is equal to *Quorum* half the number of the delegates attending the Conference.

Article 18

Technical experts

The Conference may add to any committees which it appoints technical experts without power to vote.

Article 19

Conventions and Recommendations

1. When the Conference has decided on the adoption of proposals with regard to an item on the agenda, it will rest with the Conference to determine whether these proposals should take the form: (a) of an international Convention, or (b) of a Recommendation to meet circumstances where the subject, or aspect of it, dealt with is not considered suitable or appropriate at that time for a Convention.

Decisions of the Conference

2. In either case a majority of two-thirds of the votes cast by the *Vote required* delegates present shall be necessary on the final vote for the adoption of the Convention or Recommendation, as the case may be, by the Conference.

3. In framing any Convention or Recommendation of general applica- *Modifications* tion the Conference shall have due regard to those countries in which *for special local* climatic conditions, the imperfect development of industrial organisation, *conditions* or other special circumstances make the industrial conditions substantially different and shall suggest the modifications, if any, which it considers may be required to meet the case of such countries.

4. Two copies of the Convention or Recommendation shall be authenti- *Authentic texts* cated by the signatures of the President of the Conference and of the Director-General. Of these copies one shall be deposited in the archives of the International Labour Office and the other with the Secretary-General of the United Nations. The Director-General will communicate a certified copy of the Convention or Recommendation to each of the Members.

5. In the case of a Convention –

Obligations of Members in respect of Conventions

(a) the Convention will be communicated to all Members for ratification;

(b) each of the Members undertakes that it will, within the period of one year at most from the closing of the session of the Conference, or if it is impossible owing to exceptional circumstances to do so within the period of one year, then at the earliest practicable moment and in no case later than 18 months from the closing of the session of the Conference, bring the Convention before the authority or authorities within whose competence the matter lies, for the enactment of legislation or other action;

(c) Members shall inform the Director-General of the International Labour Office of the measures taken in accordance with this article to bring the Convention before the said competent authority or authorities, with particulars of the authority or authorities regarded as competent, and of the action taken by them;

(d) if the Member obtains the consent of the authority or authorities within whose competence the matter lies, it will communicate the formal ratification of the Convention to the Director-General and will take such action as may be necessary to make effective the provisions of such Convention;

(e) if the Member does not obtain the consent of the authority or authorities within whose competence the matter lies, no further obligation shall rest upon the Member except that it shall report to the Director-General of the International Labour Office, at appropriate intervals as requested by the Governing Body, the position of its law and practice in regard to the matters dealt with in the Convention, showing the extent to which effect has been given, or is proposed to be given, to any of the provisions of the Convention by legislation, administrative action, collective agreement or otherwise and stating the difficulties which prevent or delay the ratification of such Convention.

Obligations of Members in respect of Recommendations

6. In the case of a Recommendation –

(a) the Recommendation will be communicated to all Members for their consideration with a view to effect being given to it by national legislation or otherwise;

(b) each of the Members undertakes that it will, within a period or one year at most from the closing of the session of the Conference, or if it is impossible owing to exceptional circumstances to do so within the period of one year, then at the earliest practicable moment and in no case later than 18 months after the closing of the Conference, bring the Recommendation before the authority or authorities within whose competence the matter lies for the enactment of legislation or other action;

(c) the Members shall inform the Director-General of the International Labour Office of the measures taken in accordance with this article to bring the Recommendation before the said competent authority or authorities with particulars of the authority or authorities regarded as competent, and of the action taken by them;

(d) apart from bringing the Recommendation before the said competent authority or authorities, no further obligation shall rest upon the

Members, except that they shall report to the Director-General of the International Labour Office, at appropriate intervals as requested by the Governing Body, the position of the law and practice in their country in regard to the matters dealt with in the Recommendation, showing the extent to which effect has been given, or is proposed to be given, to the provisions of the Recommendation and such modifications of these provisions as it has been found or may be found necessary to make in adopting or applying them.

7. In the case of a federal State, the following provisions shall apply: *Obligations of federal States*

(a) in respect of Conventions and Recommendations which the federal government regards as appropriate under its constitutional system for federal action, the obligations of the federal State shall be the same as those of Members which are not federal States;

(b) in respect of Conventions and Recommendations which the federal government regards as appropriate under its constitutional system, in whole or in part, for action by the constituent states, provinces, or cantons rather than for federal action, the federal government shall –

   (i) make, in accordance with its Constitution and the Constitutions of the states, provinces or cantons concerned, effective arrangements for the reference of such Conventions and Recommendations not later than 18 months from the closing of the session of the Conference to the appropriate federal, state, provincial or cantonal authorities for the enactment of legislation or other action;

   (ii) arrange, subject to the concurrence of the state, provincial or cantonal governments concerned, for periodical consultations between the federal and the state, provincial or cantonal authorities with a view to promoting within the federal State co-ordinated action to give effect to the provisions of such Conventions and Recommendations;

   (iii) inform the Director-General of the International Labour Office of the measures taken in accordance with this article to bring such Conventions and Recommendations before the appropriate federal, state, provincial or cantonal authorities with particulars of the authorities regarded as appropriate and of the action taken by them;

   (iv) in respect of each such Convention which it has not ratified, report to the Director-General of the International Labour Office, at appropriate intervals as requested by the Governing Body, the position of the law and practice of the federation and its constituent states, provinces or cantons in regard to the Convention, showing the extent to which effect has been given, or is proposed to be given, to any of the provisions of the Convention by legislation, administrative action, collective agreement, or otherwise;

(v) in respect of each such Recommendation, report to the Director-General of the International Labour Office, at appropriate intervals as requested by the Governing Body, the position of the law and practice of the federation and its constituent states, provinces or cantons in regard to the Recommendation, showing the extent to which effect has been given, or is proposed to be given, to the provisions of the Recommendation and such modifications of these provisions as have been found or may be found necessary in adopting or applying them.

Effect of Conventions and Recommendations on more favourable existing provisions

8. In no case shall the adoption of any Convention or Recommendation by the Conference, or the ratification of any Convention by any Member, be deemed to affect any law, award, custom or agreement which ensures more favourable conditions to the workers concerned than those provided for in the Convention or Recommendation.

Registration with the United Nations

Article 20

Any Convention so ratified shall be communicated by the Director-General of the International Labour Office to the Secretary-General of the United Nations for registration in accordance with the provisions of article 102 of the Charter of the United Nations but shall only be binding upon the Members which ratify it.

Conventions not adopted by the Conference

Article 21

1. If any Convention coming before the Conference for final consideration fails to secure the support of two-thirds of the votes cast by the delegates present, it shall nevertheless be within the right of any of the Members of the Organisation to agree to such Convention among themselves.

2. Any Convention so agreed to shall be communicated by the governments concerned to the Director-General of the International Labour Office and to the Secretary-General of the United Nations for registration in accordance with the provisions of article 102 of the Charter of the United Nations.

Annual reports on ratified Conventions

Article 22

Each of the Members agrees to make an annual report to the International Labour Office on the measures which it has taken to give effect to the provisions of Conventions to which it is a party. These reports shall be made in such form and shall contain such particulars as the Governing Body may request.

Article 23

1. The Director-General shall lay before the next meeting of the Conference a summary of the information and reports communicated to him by Members in pursuance of articles 19 and 22.

2. Each Member shall communicate to the representative organisations recognised for the purpose of article 3 copies of the information and reports communicated to the Director-General in pursuance of articles 19 and 22.

Article 24

In the event of any representation being made to the International Labour Office by an industrial association of employers or of workers that any of the Members has failed to secure in any respect the effective observance within its jurisdiction of any Convention to which it is a party, the Governing Body may communicate this representation to the government against which it is made, and may invite that government to make such statement on the subject as it may think fit.

Article 25

If no statement is received within a reasonable time from the government in question, or if the statement when received is not deemed to be satisfactory by the Governing Body, the latter shall have the right to publish the representation and the statement, if any, made in reply to it.

Article 26

1. Any of the Members shall have the right to file a complaint with the International Labour Office if it is not satisfied that any other Member is securing the effective observance of any Convention which both have ratified in accordance with the foregoing articles.

2. The Governing Body may, if it thinks fit, before referring such a complaint to a Commission of Inquiry, as hereinafter provided for, communicate with the government in question in the manner described in article 24.

3. If the Governing Body does not think it necessary to communicate the complaint to the government in question, or if, when it has made such communication, no statement in reply has been received within a reasonable time which the Governing Body considers to be satisfactory, the Governing Body may appoint a Commission of Inquiry to consider the complaint and to report thereon.

4. The Governing Body may adopt the same procedure either of its own motion or on receipt of a complaint from a delegate to the Conference.

5. When any matter arising out of article 25 or 26 is being considered by the Governing Body, the government in question shall, if not already represented thereon, be entitled to send a representative to take part in the proceedings of the Governing Body while the matter is under consideration. Adequate notice of the date on which the matter will be considered shall be given to the government in question.

Co-operation with Commission of Inquiry

Article 27

The Members agree that, in the event of the reference of a complaint to a Commission of Inquiry under article 26, they will each, whether directly concerned in the complaint or not, place at the disposal of the Commission all the information in their possession which bears upon the subject-matter of the complaint.

Report of Commission of Inquiry

Article 28

When the Commission of Inquiry has fully considered the complaint, it shall prepare a report embodying its findings on all questions of fact relevant to determining the issue between the parties and containing such recommendations as it may think proper as to the steps which should be taken to meet the complaint and the time within which they should be taken.

Action on report of Commission of Inquiry

Article 29

1. The Director-General of the International Labour Office shall communicate the report of the Commission of Inquiry to the Governing Body and to each of the governments concerned in the complaint, and shall cause it to be published.

2. Each of these governments shall within three months inform the Director-General of the International Labour Office whether or not it accepts the recommendations contained in the report of the Commission; and if not, whether it proposes to refer the complaint to the International Court of Justice.

Failure to submit Conventions or Recommendations to competent authorities

Article 30

In the event of any Member failing to take the action required by paragraphs 5 (b), 6 (b) or 7 (b) (i) of article 19 with regard to a Convention or Recommendation, any other Member shall be entitled to refer the matter to the Governing Body. In the event of the Governing Body finding that there has been such a failure, it shall report the matter to the Conference.

Article 31

The decision of the International Court of Justice in regard to a complaint or matter which has been referred to it in pursuance of article 29 shall be final.

Decisions of International Court of Justice

Article 32

The International Court of Justice may affirm, vary or reverse any of the findings or recommendations of the Commission of Inquiry, if any.

Article 33

In the event of any Member failing to carry out within the time specified the recommendations, if any, contained in the report of the Commission of Inquiry, or in the decision of the International Court of Justice, as the case may be, the Governing Body may recommend to the Conference such action as it may deem wise and expedient to secure compliance therewith.

Failure to carry out recommendations of Commission of Inquiry or ICJ

Article 34

The defaulting government may at any time inform the Governing Body that it has taken the steps necessary to comply with the recommendations of the Commission of Inquiry or with those in the decision of the International Court of Justice, as the case may be, and may request it to constitute a Commission of Inquiry to verify its contention. In this case the provisions of articles 27, 28, 29, 31 and 32 shall apply, and if the report of the Commission of Inquiry or the decision of the International Court of Justice is in favour of the defaulting government, the Governing Body shall forthwith recommend the discontinuance of any action taken in pursuance of article 33.

Compliance with recommendations of Commission of Inquiry or ICJ

Chapter III – General

Article 35

1. The Members undertake that Conventions which they have ratified in accordance with the provisions of this Constitution shall be applied to the non-metropolitan territories for whose international relations they are responsible, including any trust territories for which they are the administering authority, except where the subject-matter of the Convention is within the self-governing powers of the territory or the Convention is inapplicable owing to the local conditions or subject to such modifications as may be necessary to adapt the Convention to local conditions.

Application of Conventions to non-metropolitan territories

2. Each Member which ratifies a Convention shall as soon as possible after ratification communicate to the Director-General of the International

Labour Office a declaration stating in respect of the territories other than those referred to in paragraphs 4 and 5 below the extent to which it undertakes that the provisions of the Convention shall be applied and giving such particulars as may be prescribed by the Convention.

3. Each Member which has communicated a declaration in virtue of the preceding paragraph may from time to time, in accordance with the terms of the Convention, communicate a further declaration modifying the terms of any former declaration and stating the present position in respect of such territories.

4. Where the subject-matter of the Convention is within the self-governing powers of any non-metropolitan territory the Member responsible for the international relations of that territory shall bring the Convention to the notice of the government of the territory as soon as possible with a view to the enactment of legislation or other action by such government. Thereafter the Member, in agreement with the government of the territory, may communicate to the Director-General of the International Labour Office a declaration accepting the obligations of the Convention on behalf of such territory.

5. A declaration accepting the obligations of any Convention may be communicated to the Director-General of the International Labour Office –

(a) by two or more Members of the Organisation in respect of any territory which is under their joint authority; or

(b) by any international authority responsible for the administration of any territory, in virtue of the Charter of the United Nations or otherwise, in respect of any such territory.

6. Acceptance of the obligations of a Convention in virtue of paragraph 4 or paragraph 5 shall involve the acceptance on behalf of the territory concerned of the obligations stipulated by the terms of the Convention and the obligations under the Constitution of the Organisation which apply to ratified Conventions. A declaration of acceptance may specify such modification of the provisions of the Conventions as may be necessary to adapt the Convention to local conditions.

7. Each Member or international authority which has communicated a declaration in virtue of paragraph 4 or paragraph 5 of this article may from time to time, in accordance with the terms of the Convention, communicate a further declaration modifying the terms of any former declaration or terminating the acceptance of the obligations of the Convention on behalf of the territory concerned.

8. If the obligations of a Convention are not accepted on behalf of a territory to which paragraph 4 or paragraph 5 of this article relates, the Member or Members or international authority concerned shall report to

the Director-General of the International Labour Office the position of the law and practice of that territory in regard to the matters dealt with in the Convention and the report shall show the extent to which effect has been given, or is proposed to be given, to any of the provisions of the Convention by legislation, administrative action, collective agreement or otherwise and shall state the difficulties which prevent or delay the acceptance of such Convention.

Article 36

Amendments to Constitution

Amendments to this Constitution which are adopted by the Conference by a majority of two-thirds of the votes cast by the delegates present shall take effect when ratified or accepted by two-thirds of the Members of the Organisation including five of the ten Members which are represented on the Governing Body as Members of chief industrial importance in accordance with the provisions of paragraph 3 of article 7 of this Constitution.

Article 37

Interpretation of Constitution and Conventions

1. Any question or dispute relating to the interpretation of this Constitution or of any subsequent Convention concluded by the Members in pursuance of the provisions of this Constitution shall be referred for decision to the International Court of Justice.

2. Notwithstanding the provisions of paragraph 1 of this article the Governing Body may make and submit to the Conference for approval rules providing for the appointment of a tribunal for the expeditious determination of any dispute or question relating to the interpretation of a Convention which may be referred thereto by the Governing Body or in accordance with the terms of the Convention. Any applicable judgment or advisory opinion of the International Court of Justice shall be binding upon any tribunal established in virtue of this paragraph. Any award made by such a tribunal shall be circulated to the Members of the Organisation and any observations which they may make thereon shall be brought before the Conference.

Article 38

Regional Conferences

1. The International Labour Organisation may convene such regional conferences and establish such regional agencies as may be desirable to promote the aims and purposes of the Organisation.

2. The powers, functions and procedure of regional conferences shall be governed by rules drawn up by the Governing Body and submitted to the General Conference for confirmation.

Chapter IV – Miscellaneous Provisions

Legal status
of Organisation

Article 39

The International Labour Organisation shall possess full juridical personality and in particular the capacity –

(a) to contract;

(b) to acquire and dispose of immovable and movable property;

(c) to institute legal proceedings.

Privileges and
immunities

Article 40

1. The International Labour Organisation shall enjoy in the territory of each of its Members such privileges and immunities as are necessary for the fulfilment of its purposes.

2. Delegates to the Conference, members of the Governing Body and the Director-General and officials of the Office shall likewise enjoy such privileges and immunities as are necessary for the independent exercise of their functions in connection with the Organisation.

3. Such privileges and immunities shall be defined in a separate agreement to be prepared by the Organisation with a view to its acceptance by the States Members.

ANNEX

Declaration concerning the Aims and Purposes of the International Labour Organisation

The General Conference of the International Labour Organisation, meeting in its Twenty-sixth Session in Philadelphia, hereby adopts, this tenth day of May in the year nineteen hundred and forty-four, the present Declaration of the aims and purposes of the International Labour Organisation and of the principles which should inspire the policy of its Members.

I

The Conference reaffirms the fundamental principles on which the Organisation is based and, in particular, that –

(a) labour is not a commodity;

(b) freedom of expression and of association are essential to sustained progress;

(c) poverty anywhere constitutes a danger to prosperity everywhere;

(d) the war against want requires to be carried on with unrelenting vigour within each nation, and by continuous and concerted international effort in which the representatives of workers and employers, enjoying equal status with those of governments, join with them in free discussion and democratic decision with a view to the promotion of the common welfare.

II

Believing that experience has fully demonstrated the truth of the statement in the Constitution of the International Labour Organisation that lasting peace can be established only if it is based on social justice, the Conference affirms that –

(a) all human beings, irrespective of race, creed or sex, have the right to pursue both their material well-being and their spiritual development in conditions of freedom and dignity, of economic security and equal opportunity;

(b) the attainment of the conditions in which this shall be possible must constitute the central aim of national and international policy;

(c) all national and international policies and measures, in particular those of an economic and financial character, should be judged in this light and accepted only in so far as they may be held to promote and not to hinder the achievement of this fundamental objective;

(d) it is a responsibility of the International Labour Organisation to examine and consider all international economic and financial policies and measures in the light of this fundamental objective;

(e) in discharging the tasks entrusted to it the International Labour Organisation, having considered all relevant economic and financial factors, may include in its decisions and recommendations any provisions which it considers appropriate.

III

The Conference recognises the solemn obligation of the International Labour Organisation to further among the nations of the world programmes which will achieve:

(a) full employment and the raising of standards of living;

(b) the employment of workers in the occupations in which they can have the satisfaction of giving the fullest measure of their skill and attainments and make their greatest contribution to the common well-being;

(c) the provision, as a means to the attainment of this end and under adequate guarantees for all concerned, of facilities for training and the transfer of labour, including migration for employment and settlement;

(d) policies in regard to wages and earnings, hours and other conditions of work calculated to ensure a just share of the fruits of progress to all, and a minimum living wage to all employed and in need of such protection;

(e) the effective recognition of the right of collective bargaining, the co-operation of management and labour in the continuous improvement of productive efficiency, and the collaboration of workers and employers in the preparation and application of social and economic measures;

(f) the extension of social security measures to provide a basic income to all in need of such protection and comprehensive medical care;

(g) adequate protection for the life and health of workers in all occupations;

(h) provision for child welfare and maternity protection;

(i) the provision of adequate nutrition, housing and facilities for recreation and culture;

(j) the assurance of equality of educational and vocational opportunity.

IV

Confident that the fuller and broader utilisation of the world's productive resources necessary for the achievement of the objectives set forth in this Declaration can be secured by effective international and national action, including measures to expand production and consumption, to avoid severe economic fluctuations, to promote the economic and social advancement of the less developed regions of the world, to assure greater stability in world prices of primary products, and to promote a high and steady volume of international trade, the Conference pledges the full co-operation of the International Labour Organisation with such international bodies as may be entrusted with a share of the responsibility for this great task and for the promotion of the health, education and well-being of all peoples.

V

The Conference affirms that the principles set forth in this Declaration are fully applicable to all peoples everywhere and that, while the manner of their application must be determined with due regard to the stage of social and economic development reached by each people, their progressive application to peoples who are still dependent, as well as to those who have already achieved self-government, is a matter of concern to the whole civilised world.

Chronology

Antecedents

1818	Robert Owen's memorial to the Congress of Aix-la-Chapelle
1838–59	Daniel Legrand's memoranda to governments
1881	Swiss Federal Council's proposals for international negotiations on factory legislation
1890	The Berlin International Conference
1900	Formation of the International Association for Labour Legislation
1906	Adoption of two Conventions by Berne diplomatic Conference
1913	Adoption of two drafts of Conventions by Berne technical Conference
1916	Inter-Allied Trade Union Conference

International Labour Organisation

1919 (Jan.)	Appointment by the Peace Conference of the Commission on International Labour Legislation
1919 (April)	Adoption by the Peace Conference of the Constitution of the ILO
1919 (Oct.)	First Session of the International Labour Conference
1919 (Nov.)	First Session of the Governing Body
1920 (Jan.)	Election of Albert Thomas as Director
1920 (June)	First maritime session of the Conference
1920 (July)	Seat of the ILO established at Geneva
1922	Advisory opinions of the Permanent Court of International Justice confirming constitutional competence of the ILO
1926	Opening of the ILO building in Geneva
1926	Advisory opinion of the PCIJ on the regulation of the work of employers
1927	Beginning of the System of Mutual Supervision
1930	First advisory missions (Greece and Romania)
1930 onwards	"The Great Depression"
1932	Death of Albert Thomas
1932	Election of Harold Butler as Director
1932	Advisory opinion of the PCIJ on Night Work of Women
1934	Admission of the United States

305

1934	Admission of the USSR
1935	Withdrawal of Germany
1936	First American Regional Conference (Santiago)
1938	Resignation of Harold Butler
1939	Election of John G. Winant as Director
1939	Withdrawal of Italy
1940	Withdrawal of Japan
1940	Cessation of membership of USSR
1940	Establishment of the Working Centre of the ILO in Montreal
1941	Resignation of John G. Winant
1941	Edward Phelan Acting Director
1941	New York Conference of the ILO
1944	Philadelphia session of the International Labour Conference
1945	Setting up of Industrial Committees
1945	Adoption of the Charter of the United Nations
1945	Readmission of Italy
1945–46	Amendments of the Constitution
1946	Dissolution of the League of Nations
1946	Appointment (retroactive to 1941) of Edward Phelan as Director-General
1946	Agreement with the United Nations
1947	First Asian Regional Conference (Delhi)
1947	First Agreement with a specialised agency (FAO)
1948	Retirement of Edward Phelan
1948	Election of David A. Morse as Director-General
1948	Return of Montreal staff to Geneva completed
1948	Inauguration of Policy of Operational Activities
1948	Manpower Programme
1950	Special Migration Programme
1950	Expanded Programme of Technical Assistance
1950	Adoption in collaboration with the United Nations of Machinery for the Protection of Freedom of Association
1951	Establishment of the Freedom of Association Committee of the Governing Body
1951	Readmission of Germany (Federal Republic)
1951	Readmission of Japan
1951	Failure of the Naples Migration Conference

1954	Readmission of USSR
1955	First European Regional Conference (Geneva)
1959	UN Special Fund for Economic Development
1960	First African Regional Conference (Lagos)
1962	Setting up of International Institute of Labour Studies
1964	Adoption of Declaration and Programme on Apartheid
1964	Adoption of Instruments of Amendment to the Constitution concerning suspension or expulsion of members
1964	Notice of withdrawal of South Africa
1965	Setting up of International Centre for Advanced Vocational and Technical Training
1966	UN Development Programme
1967	Administrative Decentralisation and Regionalisation
1968	"Human Rights Year"
1969	50th anniversary of the ILO
1969	Launching of World Employment Programme
1969	Award to ILO of Nobel Peace Prize
1970	Resignation of David A. Morse
1970	Election of C. Wilfred Jenks as Director-General

Member States of ILO
with Membership Dates
and Number of Conventions ratified
(as at 1 January 1970)

STATES	NUMBER OF RATIFICATIONS	STATES	NUMBER OF RATIFICATIONS
Afghanistan (1934)	10	Ecuador (1934)	31
Algeria (1962)	48	El Salvador (1919–1939 and since 1948)	4
Argentina (1919)	57		
Australia (1919)	28	Ethiopia (1923)	8
Austria (1919–1938 and since 1947)	37	Finland (1920)	47
		France (1919)	80
Barbados (1967)	25	Gabon (1960)	27
Belgium (1919)	70	Germany (Fed. Rep.) (1919–1935 [Germany] and since 1951)	40
Bolivia (1919)	9		
Brazil (1919)	51		
Bulgaria (1920)	77	Ghana (1957)	36
Burma (1948)	21	Greece (1919)	36
Burundi (1963)	17	Guatemala (1919–1938 and since 1945)	37
Byelorussia (1954)	26		
Cambodia (1969)	4	Guinea (1959)	39
Cameroon (1960)	10	Guyana (1966)	25
Eastern Cameroon	6	Haiti (1919)	21
Western Cameroon	8	Honduras (1919–1938 and since 1955)	16
Canada (1919)	24		
Central African Rep. (1960)	35	Hungary (1922)	39
Ceylon (1948)	20	Iceland (1945)	12
Chad (1960)	19	India (1919)	30
Chile (1919)	37	Indonesia (1950)	7
China (1919)	35	Iran (1919)	6
Colombia (1919)	41	Iraq (1932)	33
Congo (Brazzaville) (1960)	13	Ireland (1923)	46
Congo (Kinshasa) (1960)	27	Israel (1949)	35
Costa Rica (1920–1927 and since 1944)	25	Italy (1919–1939 and since 1945)	67
Cuba (1919)	65	Ivory Coast (1960)	25
Cyprus (1960)	28	Jamaica (1962)	20
Czechoslovakia (1919)	44	Japan (1919–1940 and since 1951)	26
Dahomey (1960)	17		
Denmark (1919)	35	Jordan (1956)	14
Dominican Rep. (1924)	24	Kenya (1964)	27

STATES	NUMBER OF RATIFICATIONS	STATES	NUMBER OF RATIFICATIONS
Kuwait (1961)	13	Singapore (1965)	21
Laos (1964)	4	Somalia (1960)	4
Lebanon (1948)	7	*former Trust Territory*	6
Lesotho (1966)	11	*of Somaliland*	
Liberia (1919)	14	*former British Somaliland*	4
Libya (1952)	11	Southern Yemen (1969)	13
Luxembourg (1920)	50	Spain (1919–1941 and	55
Madagascar (1960)	26	since 1956)	
Malawi (1965)	18	Sudan (1956)	5
Malaysia (1957)	8	Sweden (1919)	48
States of Malaya	5	Switzerland (1919)	31
State of Sabah	5	Syrian Arab Rep. (1947–	38
State of Sarawak	9	1958 [Syria] and since	
Mali (1960)	21	1961)	
Malta (1965)	27	Tanzania (1962)	18
Mauritania (1961)	36	*Tanganyika*	6
Mauritius (1969)	31	*Zanzibar*	4
Mexico (1931)	51	Thailand (1919)	11
Mongolia (1968)	6	Togo (1960)	12
Morocco (1956)	30	Trinidad and Tobago	10
Nepal (1966)	0	(1963)	
Netherlands (1919)	66	Tunisia (1956)	38
New Zealand (1919)	45	Turkey (1932)	21
Nicaragua (1919–1938	35	Uganda (1963)	20
and since 1957)		Ukraine (1954)	27
Niger (1961)	23	USSR (1934–1940 and	40
Nigeria (1960)	24	since 1954)	
Norway (1919)	64	United Arab Rep. (1936–	34
Pakistan (1947)	30	1958 [Egypt] and	
Panama (1919)	15	since 1958)	
Paraguay (1919–1937	33	United Kingdom (1919)	65
and since 1956)		United States (1934)	7
Peru (1919)	59	Upper Volta (1960)	23
Philippines (1948)	18	Uruguay (1919)	58
Poland (1919)	59	Venezuela (1919–1957	24
Portugal (1919)	29	and since 1958)	
Romania (1919–1942	23	Viet-Nam (1950)	15
and since 1956)		Yemen (1965)	2
Rwanda (1962)	15	Yugoslavia (1919–1949	53
Senegal (1960)	33	and since 1951)	
Sierra Leone (1961)	32	Zambia (1964)	19

Total of ratifications* 3,567

* The total includes ratifications of Albania (1920-67) (17) and South Africa (1919-66) (12) which have withdrawn from the ILO.

Conventions adopted by the International Labour Conference
(as at 1 July 1970)

The number of ratifications registered in each case is shown in brackets.

* Convention which has not yet received the required number of ratifications for entry into force.

† Convention revised by a subsequent Convention.

‡ Convention no longer open to ratification as a result of the entry into force of a revising Convention.

1. Hours of Work (Industry), 1919 (32)
2. Unemployment, 1919 (46)
3. Maternity Protection, 1919 (26)†
4. Night Work (Women), 1919 (56)†
5. Minimum Age (Industry), 1919 (60)†
6. Night Work of Young Persons (Industry), 1919 (51)†
7. Minimum Age (Sea), 1920 (43)†
8. Unemployment Indemnity (Shipwreck), 1920 (39)
9. Placing of Seamen, 1920 (28)
10. Minimum Age (Agriculture), 1921 (39)
11. Right of Association (Agriculture), 1921 (87)
12. Workmen's Compensation (Agriculture), 1921 (53)†
13. White Lead (Painting), 1921 (48)
14. Weekly Rest (Industry), 1921 (77)
15. Minimum Age (Trimmers and Stokers), 1921 (58)
16. Medical Examination of Young Persons (Sea), 1921 (55)
17. Workmen's Compensation (Accidents), 1925 (52)†
18. Workmen's Compensation (Occupational Diseases), 1925 (52)†
19. Equality of Treatment (Accident Compensation), 1925 (85)
20. Night Work (Bakeries), 1925 (14)
21. Inspection of Emigrants, 1926 (29)
22. Seamen's Articles of Agreement, 1926 (41)
23. Repatriation of Seamen, 1926 (25)
24. Sickness Insurance (Industry), 1927 (22)

310

25. Sickness Insurance (Agriculture), 1927 (17)
26. Minimum Wage-Fixing Machinery, 1928 (77)
27. Marking of Weight (Packages Transported by Vessels), 1929 (45)
28. Protection against Accidents (Dockers), 1929 (4)‡
29. Forced Labour, 1930 (105)
30. Hours of Work (Commerce and Offices), 1930 (23)
31. Hours of Work (Coal Mines), 1931 (2)*†
32. Protection against Accidents (Dockers) (Revised), 1932 (31)
33. Minimum Age (Non-Industrial Employment), 1932 (23)‡
34. Fee-Charging Employment Agencies, 1933 (10)‡
35. Old-Age Insurance (Industry, etc.), 1933 (11)†
36. Old-Age Insurance (Agriculture), 1933 (10)†
37. Invalidity Insurance (Industry, etc.), 1933 (9)†
38. Invalidity Insurance (Agriculture), 1933 (8)†
39. Survivors' Insurance (Industry, etc.), 1933 (7)†
40. Survivors' Insurance (Agriculture), 1933 (6)†
41. Night Work (Women) (Revised), 1934 (36)‡
42. Workmen's Compensation (Occupational Diseases) (Revised), 1934 (45)†
43. Sheet-Glass Works, 1934 (9)
44. Unemployment Provision, 1934 (13)
45. Underground Work (Women), 1935 (74)
46. Hours of Work (Coal Mines) (Revised), 1935 (2)*
47. Forty-Hour Week, 1935 (4)
48. Maintenance of Migrants' Pension Rights, 1935 (8)
49. Reduction of Hours of Work (Glass-Bottle Works), 1935 (7)
50. Recruiting of Indigenous Workers, 1936 (26)
51. Reduction of Hours of Work (Public Works), 1936 (0)*
52. Holidays with Pay, 1936 (45)†
53. Officers' Competency Certificates, 1936 (21)
54. Holidays with Pay (Sea), 1936 (6)*‡
55. Shipowners' Liability (Sick and Injured Seamen), 1936 (10)
56. Sickness Insurance (Sea), 1936 (9)
57. Hours of Work and Manning (Sea), 1936 (5)*†
58. Minimum Age (Sea) (Revised), 1936 (42)
59. Minimum Age (Industry) (Revised), 1937 (25)
60. Minimum Age (Non-Industrial Employment) (Revised), 1937 (10)

61. Reduction of Hours of Work (Textiles), 1937 (0)*
62. Safety Provisions (Building), 1937 (23)
63. Statistics of Wages and Hours of Work, 1938 (30)
64. Contracts of Employment (Indigenous Workers), 1939 (23)
65. Penal Sanctions (Indigenous Workers), 1939 (26)
66. Migration for Employment, 1939 (0)*‡
67. Hours of Work and Rest Periods (Road Transport), 1939 (4)
68. Food and Catering (Ships' Crews), 1946 (14)
69. Certification of Ships' Cooks, 1946 (17)
70. Social Security (Seafarers), 1946 (6)*
71. Seafarers' Pensions, 1946 (8)
72. Paid Vacations (Seafarers), 1946 (5)*‡
73. Medical Examination (Seafarers), 1946 (19)
74. Certification of Able Seamen, 1946 (16)
75. Accommodation of Crews, 1946 (5)*‡
76. Wages, Hours of Work and Manning (Sea), 1946 (1)*†
77. Medical Examination of Young Persons (Industry), 1946 (21)
78. Medical Examination of Young Persons (Non-Industrial Occupations), 1946 (21)
79. Night Work of Young Persons (Non-Industrial Occupations), 1946 (15)
80. Final Articles Revision, 1946 (50)
81. Labour Inspection, 1947 (72)
82. Social Policy (Non-Metropolitan Territories), 1947 (4)
83. Labour Standards (Non-Metropolitan Territories), 1947 (1)*
84. Right of Association (Non-Metropolitan Territories), 1947 (4)
85. Labour Inspectorates (Non-Metropolitan Territories), 1947 (4)
86. Contracts of Employment (Indigenous Workers), 1947 (16)
87. Freedom of Association and Protection of the Right to Organise, 1948 (77)
88. Employment Service, 1948 (51)
89. Night Work (Women) (Revised), 1948 (48)
90. Night Work of Young Persons (Industry) (Revised), 1948 (32)
91. Paid Vacations (Seafarers) (Revised), 1949 (15)
92. Accommodation of Crews (Revised), 1949 (18)
93. Wages, Hours of Work and Manning (Sea) (Revised), 1949 (5)*†
94. Labour Clauses (Public Contracts), 1949 (43)
95. Protection of Wages, 1949 (64)
96. Fee-Charging Employment Agencies (Revised), 1949 (28)

97. Migration for Employment (Revised), 1949 (30)

98. Right to Organise and Collective Bargaining, 1949 (90)

99. Minimum Wage-Fixing Machinery (Agriculture), 1951 (34)

100. Equal Remuneration, 1951 (69)

101. Holidays with Pay (Agriculture), 1952 (35)

102. Social Security (Minimum Standards), 1952 (20)

103. Maternity Protection (Revised), 1952 (13)

104. Abolition of Penal Sanctions (Indigenous Workers), 1955 (22)

105. Abolition of Forced Labour, 1957 (88)

106. Weekly Rest (Commerce and Offices), 1957 (30)

107. Indigenous and Tribal Populations, 1957 (23)

108. Seafarers' Identity Documents, 1958 (20)

109. Wages, Hours of Work and Manning (Sea) (Revised), 1958 (7)*

110. Plantations, 1958 (8)

111. Discrimination (Employment and Occupation), 1958 (71)

112. Minimum Age (Fishermen), 1959 (24)

113. Medical Examination (Fishermen), 1959 (15)

114. Fishermen's Articles of Agreement, 1959 (15)

115. Radiation Protection, 1960 (23)

116. Final Articles Revision, 1961 (59)

117. Social Policy (Basic Aims and Standards), 1962 (19)

118. Equality of Treatment (Social Security), 1962 (21)

119. Guarding of Machinery, 1963 (23)

120. Hygiene (Commerce and Offices), 1964 (24)

121. Employment Injury Benefits, 1964 (8)

122. Employment Policy, 1964 (29)

123. Minimum Age (Underground Work), 1965 (21)

124. Medical Examination of Young Persons (Underground Work), 1965 (18)

125. Fishermen's Competency Certificates, 1966 (4)

126. Accommodation of Crews (Fishermen), 1966 (5)

127. Maximum Weight, 1967 (4)

128. Invalidity, Old-Age and Survivors' Benefits, 1967 (5)

129. Labour Inspection in Agriculture, 1969 (0)*

130. Medical Care and Sickness Benefits, 1969 (0)*

131. Minimum wage-fixing, with special reference to developing countries, 1970 (0)*

132. Annual holidays with pay (Revised), 1970 (0)*

List of Ratifications
(as at 1 January 1970)

An asterisk denotes conditional ratification registered.
Figure in italics denotes denunciation following or followed by
ratification of a revising Convention.
Figure in bold denotes other denunciation.

STATE	TOTAL	CONVENTIONS RATIFIED
Afghanistan	10	4, 13, 14, 41, 45, 95, 100, 105, 106, 111.
Albania	17	**4**, 5, 6, 10, 11, 16, 21, 29, 52, 58, 59, 77, 78, 87, 98, 100, 112.
Algeria	48	3, 6, 10, 11, 13, 14, 17–19, 24, 29, 32, 42, 44, 56, 58, 62, 63, 68–71, *72*, 73, 74, 77, 78, 80, 81, 87–89, 91, 92, 94–101, 105, 111, 119, 120, 122, 127.
Argentina	57	1–23, 26, 27, 29–36, 41, 42, 45, 50, 52, 53, 58, 68, 71, 73, 77–81, 87, 88, 90, 95, 98, 100, 105, 107, 111.
Australia	28	7–12, 15, 16, 18, 19, 21, 22, 26, 27, 29, 42, 45, 57, 63, 76, 80, 85, 88, 93, 99, 105, 116, 122.
Austria	37	1*, 2, 4–6, 10–13, 17–19, 21, 24, 25, 27, 29, 30*, 33, 42, 45, 63, 80, 81, 87, 89, 94, 95, 98–103, 105, 116, 128.
Barbados	25	5, 7, 11, 12, 17, 19, 22, 26, 29, 42, 50, 63, 65, 74, 81, 86, 87, 94, 95, 97, 98, 101, 105, 108, 115.
Belgium	70	1, 2, *4*, 5–19, 21–23, 26, 27, 29, 32, 33, *41*, 42, 43, 45, 50, 53, *54*, 55–58, 62, 64, 68, 69, 73, 74, 80–82, 84, 85, 87–89, 91, 92, 94, 96–102, 105, 107, 112–115, 122, 125, 126.
Bolivia	9	5, 14, 19, 26, 42, 87, 96, 107, 116.
Brazil	51	*3*, *4*, 5–7, 11, 12, 14, 16, 19, 21, 22, 26, 29, *41*, 42, 45, 52, 53, 58, 80, 81, 88, 89, 91–101, 103–111, 113, 115–118, 120, 122.

314

STATE	TOTAL	CONVENTIONS RATIFIED
Bulgaria	77	1, **2**, 3, **4**, *5*, 6–27, 29, 30, 32, 34–40, 42–45, 49, 52–60, 62, 68, 69, 71–73, 75, 77–81, 87, **88**, 94, 95, 98, 100, 106, 111–113, 116, 120, 123, 124.
Burma	21	1, 2, **4**, 6, 11, 14–19, 21, 22, 26, 27, 29, **41**, 42, 52, 63, 87.
Burundi	17	4, 11, 12, 14, 17–19, 26, 27, 29, 42, 50, 62, 64, 89, 94, 105.
Byelorussia	26	10, 11, 14–16, 29, 45, 47, 52, 58–60, 77–79, 87, 90, 95, 98, 100, 103, 106, 111, 115, 120, 122.
Cambodia	4	4, 6, 13, 29.
Cameroon	10	11, 19, 26, 29, 45, 87, 94, 95, 98, 116.
Eastern Cameroon	6	4–6, 13, 14, 33.
Western Cameroon	8	15, 16, 50, 64, 65, 81, 97, 105.
Canada	24	1, 7, 8, 14–16, 22, 26, 27, 32, 45, 58, 63, 68, 69, 73, 74, 80, 88, 105, 108, 111, 116, 122.
Central African Republic	35	2–6, 10, 11, 13, 14, 17–19, 26, 29, 33, 41, 52, 62, 67, 81, 87, 88, 94, 95, 98–101, 104, 105, 111, 116–119.
Ceylon	20	*4*, 5, *6*, 7, 8, 11, 15, 16, 18, 29, *41*, 45, 58, 63, 80, 81, 89, 90, 96, 99.
Chad	19	4–6, 11, 13, 14, 26, 29, 33, 41, 52, 81, 87, 95, 98, 100, 105, 111, 116.
Chile	37	1–20, 22, 24–27, 29, 30, 32, 34–38, 45, 63, 80, 122.
China	35	7, 11, 14–16, 19, 22, 23, 26, 27, 42, 45, 53, 58, 59, 73, 80, 81, 91, 95, 98, 100, 104, 105, 107, 111–114, 116–119. 123 124.
Colombia	41	1–5, 7–9, 11–26, 29, 30, 52, 62, 80, 81, 88 95, 99–101, 104–107, 111, 116.
Congo (Brazzaville)	13	4–6, 11, 13, 14, 26, 29, 33, 41, 87, 95, 119.
Congo (Kinshasa)	27	4, 11, 12, 14, 17–19, 26, 27, 29, *42*, 50, 62, 64, 81, 88, 89, 94, 95, 98, 100, 116–121.

STATE	TOTAL	CONVENTIONS RATIFIED
Costa Rica	25	11, 29, 45, 81, 87–90, 92, 94, 96, 98–100, 105–107, 111–114, 117, 120, 122.
Cuba	65	1, 3–23, 26, 27, 29, 30, 32, *33*, 42, 45, 46, 52, 58–60, 63, 67, *72*, 77–81, 87–101, 103–107, 110, 111.
Cyprus	28	2, 11, 15, 16, 19, 29, 44, 45, 81, 87–90, 94, 95, 97, 98, 105, 106, 111, 114, 116, 119, 121–124, 128.
Czechoslovakia	44	1, *4*, 5, 10–14, 17–19, 21, 24–27, 29, 34–40, 42–45, **48,** 49, 52, 63, 80, 87–90, 98–100, 111, 115, 116, 123.
Dahomey	17	4–6, 11, 13, 14, 18, 26, 29, 33, 41, 87, 95, 98, 100, 105, 111.
Denmark	35	2, 5–9, 11, 12, 14–16, 18, 19, 21, 27*,29, 42, 52, 53, 58, 63, 80, 81, 87, 92, 94, 98, 100, 102, 105, 106, 111, 112, 116, 118.
Dominican Republic	24	1, 5, 7, 10, 19, 26, 29, 45, 52, 79–81, 87–90, 98, 100, 104–107, 111, 119.
Ecuador	31	2, 11, 24, 26, 29, 35, 37, 39, 45, 86, 87, 95, 98, 100, 101, 103–107, 110–113, 116, 117, 119, 120, 123, 124, 127.
El Salvador	4	12, 104, 105, 107.
Ethiopia	8	2, 11, 80, 87, 88, 98, 111, 116.
Finland	47	2, 7–9, 11–22, 27, 29, 30, 32, *34*, *42*, 45, 52, 53, 62, 63, *72*, 73, *75*, 80, 81, 87, 91, 92, 94, 96, 98, 100, 105, 116, 118–122, 124.
France	80	1*, 2, 3, *4*, 5, 6, 8–19, 21*, 22–24, 26, 27, 29, 32, 33, 35–38, *41*, 42–45, 49, 52, 53, *54*, 55, 56, 58, 62, 63, 68–71, *72*, 73, 74, *75*, 77, 78, 80–82, 84, 85, 87–89, 91, 92, 94–101, 105, 108, 109, 112–114, 116.
Gabon	27	3–6, 10–14, 19, 26, 29, 33, 41, 45, 52, 87, 95, 96, 98–101, 105, 111, 123, 124.
German Federal Republic	40	2, 3, 7–12, 15–19, 22–27, 29, 42, 45, 56, 62, 63, 81, 87, 88, 96–102, 105, 111, 112, 114, 116.

STATE	TOTAL	CONVENTIONS RATIFIED
Ghana	36	8, 11, 15, 16, 19, 22, 23, 26, 29, 45, 50, 58, 59, 64, 65, 69, 74, 81, 87–90, 92, 94, 98, 100, 105–108, 111, 115–117, 119–120.
Greece	36	1–3, *4*, 5–9, 11, 13–17, 19, 27, 29, *41*, 42, 45, 52, 55, 58, 69, 80, 81, 87–90, 95, 98, 102, 105, 108.
Guatemala	37	19, 26, 30, 45, 58, 63, 65, 77–81, 86–90, 94–101, 105, 106, 108–114, 116, 118, 119.
Guinea	39	3, *4*, 5, *6*, 10, 11, 13, 14, 16–18, 26, 29, 33, *41*, 45, 52, 62, 81, 87, 89, 90, 94, 95, 98–100, 105, 111–115, 117–122.
Guyana	25	2, 5, 7, 10–12, 15, 19, 26, 29, 42, 45, 50, 64, 65, 81, 86, 87, 94, 95, 97, 98, 105, 108, 115.
Haiti	21	1, 5, 12, 14, 17, 19, 24, 25, 29, 30, 42, 45, 77, 78, 81, 90, 98, 100, 104–107.
Honduras	16	14, 29, 32, 42, 45, 62, 78, 87, 95, 98, 100, 105, 106, 108, 111, 116.
Hungary	39	2, 3, *4*, 6, 7, 10, 12–19, 21, 24, 26, 27, 29, 41, 42, 45, 48, 52, 62, 77, 78, 87, 95, 98–101, 103, 111, 115, 122–124.
Iceland	12	2, 11, 15, 29, 58, 87, 91, 98, 100, 102, 105, 111.
India	30	1, **2,** 4–6, 11, 14–16, 18, 19, 21, 22, 26, 27, 29, 32, *41*, 42, 45, 80, 81, 88–90, 100, 107, 111, 116, 118.
Indonesia	7	19, 27, 29, 45, 98, 100, 120.
Iran	6	29, 104–106, 108, 111.
Iraq	33	1, 8, 13–19, 22, 26, 27, 29, 30, 41, 42, 52, 58, 59, 77, 78, 80, 81, 88, 89, 95, 98, 100, 105, 106, 111, 115, 116.
Ireland	46	2, *4*, 5–8, 10–12, 14–16, *18*, 19–23, 26–29, *41*, 42–45, 49, 63, 68, 69, 74, 80, 81, 87–89, 92, 98, 102, 105, 108, 116, 118, 121, 122.

STATE	TOTAL	CONVENTIONS RATIFIED
Israel	35	1, 5, 9, 10, 14, 19, 20, 29, 30, 48, 52, 53, 77–79, 81, 87, 88, 90, 91, 94–98, 100–102, 105, 106, 111, 112, 116–118.
Italy	67	1*, 2–4, 6–16, 18, 19, 22, 23, 26, 27, 29, 32, 35–40, 42, 44, 45, 48, 52, 53, 55, 58–60, 68, 69, 71, 73, 77–81, 87–90, 94–98, 100–102, 105, 106, 108, 111, 114, 117, 118.
Ivory Coast	25	3–6, 11, 13, 14, 18, 19, 26, 29, 33, 41, 45, 52, 87, 95, 96, 98–100, 105, 110, 111, 116.
Jamaica	20	7, 8, 11, 15, 16, 19, 26, 29, 50, 58, 64, 65, 81, 86, 87, 94, 97, 98, 105, 117.
Japan	26	2, 5, 7–10, 15, 16, 18, 19, 21, 22, 27, 29, 42, 45, 50, 58, 73, 80, 81, 87, 88, 96, 98, 100.
Jordan	14	29, 81, 98, 100, 105, 111, 116–120, 122–124.
Kenya	27	2, 5, 11, 12, 14, 15, 17, 19, 26, 29, 32, 45, 50, 58, 59, 63–65, 81, 86, 88, 89, 94, 97, 98, 105, 123.
Kuwait	13	1, 29, 30, 52, 81, 87, 89, 105, 106, 111, 116, 117, 119.
Laos	4	4, 6, 13, 29.
Lebanon	7	14, 26, 45, 52, 81, 89, 90.
Lesotho	11	5, 11, 14, 19, 26, 29, 45, 64, 65, 87, 98.
Liberia	14	29, 53, 55, 58, 65, 87, 98, 104, 105, 110–114.
Libya	11	29, 52, 88, 89, 95, 96, 98, 100, 104, 105, 111.
Luxembourg	50	1–30, 42, 45, 59, 60, 77–88, 87–90, 96, 98, 100, 102, 103, 105, 116.
Madagascar	26	4–6, 11–14, 19, 96, 29, 33, 41, 52, 87, 95, 100, 101, 111, 116–120, 122–124.
Malawi	18	11, 12, 19, 26, 45, 50, 64, 65, 81, 86, 89, 97–100, 104, 107, 111.

STATE	TOTAL	CONVENTIONS RATIFIED
Malaysia	8	29, 50, 64, 65, 81, 95, 98, 105.
States of Malaya	5	11, 12, 17, 19, 45.
State of Sabah	5	15, 16, 86, 94, 97.
State of Sarawak	9	7, 11, 12, 14–16, 19, 86, 94.
Mali	21	4–6, 11, 13, 14, 17–19, 26, 29, 33, 41, 52, 81, 87, 95, 98, 100, 105, 111.
Malta	27	2, 5, 7, 8, 10–12, 15, 16, 19, 22, 26, 29, 32, 35, 36, 42, 81, 87–89, 95, 98, 99, 105, 108, 111.
Mauritania	36	3, *4*, 5, 6, 11, 13–15, 17–19, 22, 23, 26, 29, 33, *41*, 52, 53, 58, 62, 81, 87, 89–91, 94–96, 101, 102, 111, 112, 114, 116, 118.
Mauritius	31	2, 5, 7, 8, 11, 12, 14–17, 19, 26, 29, 32, 42, 50, 58, 59, 63–65, 74, 81, 86, 94, 95, 97–99, 105, 108.
Mexico	51	*6*, 7, 8, 9, 11–14, 16, 17, 19, 21–23, 26, 27, 29, 30, 32, 34, 42, 43, 45, 46, 49, 52–55, 58, 62, 63, 80, 87, 90, 95, 99, 100, 102, 105–112, 116, 120, 123, 124.
Mongolia	6	59, 87, 98, 100, 103, 111.
Morocco	30	2, 4, 11–15, 17–19, 22, 26, 27, 29, 41, 42, 45, 52, 55, 65, 80, 81, 94, 98, 99, 101, 104, 105, 111, 116.
Nepal	0	
Netherlands	66	2, *4*, 5, *6*, 7, 8–17, *18*, 19, 21–27, 29, 32, 33, *41*, *42*, 44, 45, 48, 58, 62, 63, 68–71, 73, 74, 80, 81, 87–92, 94–97, 99, 101, 102, 105, 112, 115, 116, 118, 121–124, 128.
New Zealand	45	1, 2, 9–12, 14–17, 21, 22, 26, 29, 30, 32, *41*, 42, 44, 45, 47, 49, 50, 52, 53, 58, 59, **60,** 63–65, 74, 80–82, 84, 88, 89, 97, 99, 101, 104, 105, 116, 122.
Nicaragua	35	1–19, **20,** 21–30, 87, 98, 100, 105, 111.
Niger	23	4–6, 11, 13, 14, 18, 26, 29, 33, 41, 65, 87, 95, 98, 100, 102, 104, 105, 111, 116, 117, 119.

STATE	TOTAL	CONVENTIONS RATIFIED
Nigeria	24	8, 11, 15, 16, 19, 26, 29, 32, 45, 50, 58, 59, 64, 65, 81, 87, 88, 94, 95, 97, 98, 104, 105, 116.
Norway	64	2, 5, 7–15, 18, 19, 21, 22, 24–27, 29, 30, 32, *34*, 42–44, 49, 50, 53, 56, 58, 59, 63, 68, 69, 71, 73, *75*, 80, 81, 87, 88, 90–92, 95–98, 100–102, 105, 109*, 111, 112, 115, 116, 118–120, 122, 126, 128.
Pakistan	30	1, 4, 6, 11, 14–16, 18, 19, 21, 22, 27, 29, 32, *41*, 45, 59, 80, 81, 87, 89, 90, 96, 98, 105–107, 111, 116, 118.
Paraguay	33	1, 11, 14, 26, 29, 30, 52, 59, 60, 77–79, 81, 87, 89, 90, 95, 98–101, 105–107, 111, 115–117, 119, 120, 122–124.
Peru	59	1, 4, 8–12, 14, 19, 20, 22–27, 29, 32, 35–41, 44, 45, 52, 53, 55, 56, 58, 59, 62, 67–71, 73, 77–81, 87, 88, 90, 98–102, 105, 107, 112–114, 122.
Philippines	18	17, 23, 53, 59, 77, 87–90, 93–95, 98–100, 105, 110, 111.
Poland	59	2, 5–19, 22–25, 27, 29, 35–40, 42, 45, 48, 62, 68–70, 73, 74, 77–80, 87, 90–92, 95, 96, 98, 100, 101, 105, 111, 112, 115, 116, 120, 122–124.
Portugal	29	1, 4, 6, 7, 12, 14, 17–19, 26, 27, 29, 45, 68, 69, 73, 74, 81, 89, 91, 92, 98, 100, 104–108, 111.
Romania	23	1–3, *4*, 5–11, 13–16, 24, 27, 29, 87, 89, 98, 100, 116.
Rwanda	15	4, 11, 12, 14, 17–19, 26, 42, 50, 62, 64, 89, 94, 105.
Senegal	33	4–6, 10–14, 18, 19, 26, 29, 33, *41*, 52, 81, 87, 89, 95, 96, 98–102, 105, 111, 116, 117, 120–122, 125.
Sierra Leone	32	5, 7, 8, 15–17, 19, 22, 26, 29, 32, 45, 50, 58, 59, 64, 65, 81, 86–88, 94, 95, 98–101, 105, 111, 119, 125, 126.

STATE	TOTAL	CONVENTIONS RATIFIED
Singapore	21	5, 7, 8, 11, 12, 15, 16, 19, 22, 29, 32, 45, 50, 64, 65, 81, 86, 88, 94, 98, 105.
Somalia	4	29, 65, 105, 111.
former Trust Territory of Somaliland	6	16, 17, 19, 22, 23, 45.
former British Somaliland	4	50, 64, 94, 95.
South Africa	12	2, *4*, 19, 26, 27*, *41*, 42, 45, 63, 80, 89, 116.
Southern Yemen (Aden)	13	15, 16, 19, 29, 58, 59, 64, 65, 86, 94, 95, 98, 105.
Spain	55	1–20, 22–27, *28*, 29–34, 42, 45, 48, 62, 80, 81, 88, 89, 95, 97, 100, 103, 105, 111–116, 123, 126, 127.
Sudan	5	2, 19, 26, 29, 98.
Sweden	48	2, 7–16, *17*, *18*, 19–21, 27, 29, 32, *34*, *42*, **45,** 57*, 58, 63, 73, *75*, 80, 81, 87, 88, 92, 96, 98, 100–102, 105, 109*, 111, 115, 116, 118–122, 128.
Switzerland	31	2, *4*, 5, 6, 8, 11, 14–16, 18, 19, 23, 26, 27, 29, *41*, 44, 45, 58, 62, 63, 80, 81, 88, 89, 105, 111, 115, 116, 120, 123.
Syria	38	1, 2, 11, 14, 17–19, 26, 29, 30, 45, 52, 53, 63, 80, 81, 87–89, 94–96, 98–101, 104–107, 111, 115–120, 125.
Tanzania	18	11, 12, 15–17, 19, 26, 29, 50, 59, 63–65, 86, 94, 95, 98, 105.
Tanganyika	6	32, 45, 81, 88, 101, 108.
Zanzibar	4	5, 7, 58, 97.
Thailand	11	14, 19, 29, 80, 88, 104, 105, 116, 122, 123, 127.
Togo	12	4–6, 11, 13, 14, 26, 29, 33, 41, 87, 95.
Trinidad & Tobago	10	15, 16, 19, 29, 50, 65, 87, 97, 98, 105.
Tunisia	38	4, 6, 11–14, 17–19, 26, 29, 45, 52, 62, 65, 81, 87–90, 95, 98–100, 104–108, 111–114, 116, 118, 122–124.

STATE	TOTAL	CONVENTIONS RATIFIED
Turkey	21	2, 11, 14, 15, *34*, 42, 45, 58, 80, 81, 88, 94–96, 98, 100, 105, 111, 115, 116, 119.
Uganda	20	5, 11, 12, 17, 19, 26, 29, 45, 50, 64, 65, 81, 86, 94, 95, 98, 105, 122–124.
Ukraine	27	10, 11, 14–16, 29, 45, 47, 52, 58–60, 77–79, 87, 90, 95, 98, 100, 103, 106, 111, 112, 115, 120, 122.
USSR	40	10, 11, 14–16, 23, 27, 29, 32, 45, 47, 52, 58–60, 69, 73, 77–79, 87, 90, 92, 95, 98, 100, 103, 106, 108, 111–113, 115, 116, 119, 120, 122–124, 126.
UAR	34	1, 2, 11, 14, 17–19, 26, 29, 30, *41*, 45, 52, 53, 63, 74, 80, 81, 87–89, 94–96, 98, 100, 101, 104–107, 111, 115, 116.
UK	65	2, **4**, 5, **6**, 7, 8, 10–12, 15–17, *18*, 19, 21*, 22, 24–26, 29, 32, 35–40, **41, 42, 43,** 44, 45, 50, 56, 63–65, 68–70, 74, 80–88, 92, 94, 95, 97–99, 101, 102, 105, 108, 115, 116, 120, 122, 124.
USA	7	53–55, 57, 58, 74, 80.
Upper Volta	23	3–6, 11, 13, 14, 17–19, 26, 29, 33, 41, 52, 87, 95, 97, 98, 100, 101, 111, 116.
Uruguay	58	1, 2, *3–7*, 8–17, *18*, 19–27, 30, 32, *33*, 42, 43, 45, 52, 54, 58–60, 62, 63, 67, 73, 77–80, 87, 89, 90, 93–95, 97–99, 101, 103, 105.
Venezuela	24	1–3, *4*, 5–7, 11, 13, 14, 19, 21, 22, 26, 27, 29, 41, 45, 80, 81, 88, 98, 105, 116.
Viet-Nam	15	*4*, 5, 6, 13, 14, 26, 27, 29, 45, 52, 80, 81, 89, 98, 111.
Yemen	2	104, 111.
Yugoslavia	53	2, 3, *4*, 5, *6*, 7–9, 11–19, 22–25, 27, 29, 45, 48, 52, 53, 56, 58, 69, 73, 74, 80, 81, 87–92, 97, 98, 100–103, 106, 109, 111–114, 116.
Zambia	19	5, 11, 12, 17–19, 26, 29, 45, 50, 64, 65, 86, 89, 97, 105, 117, 123, 124.

Recommendations adopted by the International Labour Conference

1. Unemployment, 1919
2. Reciprocity of Treatment, 1919
3. Anthrax Prevention, 1919
4. Lead Poisoning (Women and Children), 1919
5. Labour Inspection (Health Services), 1919
6. White Phosphorus, 1919
7. Hours of Work (Fishing), 1920
8. Hours of Work (Inland Navigation), 1920
9. National Seamen's Codes, 1920
10. Unemployment Insurance (Seamen), 1920
11. Unemployment (Agriculture), 1921
12. Maternity Protection (Agriculture), 1921
13. Night Work of Women (Agriculture), 1921
14. Night Work of Children and Young Persons (Agriculture), 1921
15. Vocational Education (Agriculture), 1921
16. Living-in Conditions (Agriculture), 1921
17. Social Insurance (Agriculture), 1921
18. Weekly Rest (Commerce), 1921
19. Migration Statistics, 1922
20. Labour Inspection, 1923
21. Utilisation of Spare Time, 1924
22. Workmen's Compensation (Minimum Scale), 1925
23. Workmen's Compensation (Jurisdiction), 1925
24. Workmen's Compensation (Occupational Diseases), 1925
25. Equality of Treatment (Accident Compensation), 1925
26. Migration (Protection of Females at Sea), 1926
27. Repatriation (Ship Masters and Apprentices), 1926
28. Labour Inspection (Seamen), 1926
29. Sickness Insurance, 1927
30. Minimum Wage-Fixing Machinery, 1928

31. Prevention of Industrial Accidents, 1929
32. Power-driven Machinery, 1929
33. Protection against Accidents (Dockers) Reciprocity, 1929
34. Protection against Accidents (Dockers) Consultation of Organisations, 1929
35. Forced Labour (Indirect Compulsion), 1930
36. Forced Labour (Regulation), 1930
37. Hours of Work (Hotels, etc.), 1930
38. Hours of Work (Theatres, etc.), 1930
39. Hours of Work (Hospitals, etc.), 1930
40. Protection against Accidents (Dockers) Reciprocity, 1932
41. Minimum Age (Non-Industrial Employment), 1932
42. Employment Agencies, 1933
43. Invalidity, Old-Age and Survivors' Insurance, 1934
44. Unemployment Provision, 1934
45. Unemployment (Young Persons), 1935
46. Elimination of Recruiting, 1936
47. Holidays with Pay, 1936
48. Seamen's Welfare in Ports, 1936
49. Hours of Work and Manning (Sea), 1936
50. Public Works (International Co-operation), 1937
51. Public Works (National Planning), 1937
52. Minimum Age (Family Undertakings), 1937
53. Safety Provisions (Building), 1937
54. Inspection (Building), 1937
55. Co-operation in Accident Prevention (Building), 1937
56. Vocational Education (Building), 1937
57. Vocational Training, 1939
58. Contracts of Employment (Indigenous Workers), 1939
59. Labour Inspectorates (Indigenous Workers), 1939
60. Apprenticeship, 1939
61. Migration for Employment, 1939
62. Migration for Employment (Co-operation between States), 1939
63. Control Books (Road Transport), 1939
64. Night Work (Road Transport), 1939
65. Methods of Regulating Hours (Road Transport), 1939
66. Rest Periods (Private Chauffeurs), 1939

67. Income Security, 1944

68. Social Security (Armed Forces), 1944

69. Medical Care, 1944

70. Social Policy in Dependent Territories, 1944

71. Employment (Transition from War to Peace), 1944

72. Employment Service, 1944

73. Public Works (National Planning), 1944

74. Social Policy in Dependent Territories (Supplementary Provisions), 1945

75. Seafarers' Social Security (Agreements), 1946

76. Seafarers' (Medical Care for Dependants), 1946

77. Vocational Training (Seafarers), 1946

78. Bedding, Mess Utensils and Miscellaneous Provisions (Ships' Crews), 1946

79. Medical Examination of Young Persons, 1946

80. Night Work of Young Persons (Non-Industrial Occupations), 1946

81. Labour Inspection, 1947

82. Labour Inspection (Mining and Transport), 1947

83. Employment Service, 1948

84. Labour Clauses (Public Contracts), 1949

85. Protection of Wages, 1949

86. Migration for Employment (Revised), 1949

87. Vocational Guidance, 1949

88. Vocational Training (Adults), 1950

89. Minimum Wage-Fixing Machinery (Agriculture), 1951

90. Equal Remuneration, 1951

91. Collective Agreements, 1951

92. Voluntary Conciliation and Arbitration, 1951

93. Holidays with Pay (Agriculture), 1952

94. Co-operation at the Level of the Undertaking, 1952

95. Maternity Protection, 1952

96. Minimum Age (Coal Mines), 1953

97. Protection of Workers' Health, 1953

98. Holidays with Pay, 1954

99. Vocational Rehabilitation (Disabled), 1955

100. Protection of Migrant Workers (Underdeveloped Countries), 1955

101. Vocational Training (Agriculture), 1956

102. Welfare Facilities, 1956

103. Weekly Rest (Commerce and Offices), 1957
104. Indigenous and Tribal Populations, 1957
105. Ships' Medicine Chests, 1958
106. Medical Advice at Sea, 1958
107. Seafarers' Engagement (Foreign Vessels), 1958
108. Social Conditions and Safety (Seafarers), 1958
109. Wages, Hours of Work and Manning (Sea), 1958
110. Plantations, 1958
111. Discrimination (Employment and Occupation), 1958
112. Occupational Health Services, 1959
113. Consultation (Industrial and National Levels), 1960
114. Radiation Protection, 1960
115. Workers' Housing, 1961
116. Reduction of Hours of Work, 1962
117. Vocational Training, 1962
118. Guarding of Machinery, 1963
119. Termination of Employment, 1963
120. Hygiene (Commerce and Offices), 1964
121. Employment Injury Benefits, 1964
122. Employment Policy, 1964
123. Employment (Women with Family Responsibilities), 1965
124. Minimum Age (Underground Work), 1965
125. Conditions of Employment of Young Persons (Underground Work), 1965
126. Vocational Training (Fishermen), 1966
127. Co-operatives (Developing Countries), 1966
128. Maximum Weight, 1967
129. Communications within the Undertaking, 1967
130. Examination of Grievances, 1967
131. Invalidity, Old-Age and Survivors' Benefits, 1967
132. Tenants and Share-croppers, 1968
133. Labour Inspection in Agriculture, 1969
134. Medical Care and Sickness Benefits, 1969
135. Minimum wage-fixing, machinery, with special reference to developing countries, 1970
136. Special youth employment and training schemes for development purposes, 1970

External Offices

Algeria: Bureau de l'OIT, 19 avenue Claude-Debussy, BP 226, Algiers ("Interlab Alger"; Tel. 60 37 31, 60 29 70, 60 29 71 and 60 29 72).

Argentina: Oficina de la OIT, avenida Córdoba 333, 3.er piso, Buenos Aires ("Interlab Buenos Aires"; Tel. 32-0016).

Belgium: Correspondant du BIT (M. J. Fafchamps), 51–53, rue Belliard, 1040 Brussels ("Interlab Bruxelles"; Tel. 13 40 90).

Brazil: Bureau Internacional do Trabalho, Escritório no Brasil, rua da Glória 190, apt. 201, Caixa Postal 607-ZC-00, Rio de Janeiro, Estado da Guanabara ("Interlab Rio de Janeiro"; Tel. 242-0455 and 222-9034).

Bulgaria: Correspondant du BIT (M. Alexandre Mintcheff), boulevard Evlogui Guéorguiev 136, Sofia-C ("Interlab Sofia"; Tel. 66 20 56).

Cameroon: Bureau de l'OIT, Immeuble de l'OAMPI, 2me étage, BP 13, Yaoundé ("Interlab Yaoundé"; Tel. 47-14).

Canada: ILO Branch Office, 3rd Floor, Room 307, 178 Queen Street, Ottawa 4, Ontario ("Interlab Ottawa"; Tel. 233-1114 and 233-1115).

Chile: Oficina de Enlace de la OIT con CEPAL, Concepción 351, Casilla 2353, Santiago de Chile ("Interlab Santiago de Chile"; Tel. 25 24 89. Telex 3520123).

China: ILO Correspondent (Mr Fu-Sen Hu), 84-3, Roosevelt Road, Section 4, PO Box 4200, Taipei, Taiwan (Formosa) ("Interlab Taipei"; Tel. 365174).

Congo (Kinshasa): ILO Country Representative in the Congo, Kinshasa, PO Box 7248 ("Interlab Kinshasa").

Costa Rica: Oficina de la OIT, avenida Central y 6.ª Calle, edificio Raventos 7.° piso, Apartado postal 10170, San José ("Interlab San José"; Tel. 22 95 33 and 22 97 11).

Czechoslovakia: Correspondant du BIT (M. Jirí Fischer), UTEIN, Konviktská 5, Prague 1 ("Interlab Praha"; Tel. 239 241).

Ethiopia: ILO Regional Office for Africa, Africa Avenue, PO Box 2788, Addis Ababa ("Interlab Addis Ababa"; Tel. 47320, 47321 and 47322).

France: Bureau de correspondance du BIT, 205 boulevard Saint-Germain, F-75 Paris 7e ("Interlab Paris 044"; Tel. 548-92-02).

Germany (Federal Republic): Internationales Arbeitsamt, Zweigamt Bonn, Hohenzollernstrasse 21, D-53 Bonn-Bad Godesberg ("Interlab Bonn"; Tel. Bad Godesberg 62322 and 64322).

Hungary: Correspondant du BIT (M. J. Benyi), Bem rakpart 47, Budapest II ("Interlab Budapest"; Tel. 350-100).

India: ILO Branch Office, Mandi House, New Delhi 1 ("Interlab New Delhi"; Tel. 44481 and 47567).

Italy: Ufficio internazionale del Lavoro, Ufficio di Corrispondenza, Villa Aldobrandini, via Panisperna 28, I-00184 Rome ("Interlab Roma"; Tel. 684334 and 672197).

Japan: ILO Branch Office, Zenkoku-Choson-Kaikan, 11-35 Nagatachô 1-Chome, Chiyoda-Ku, Tokyo 100 ("Interlab Tokyo"; Tel. Kasumigaseki (581) 3551 and 3552).

Lebanon: Bureau de l'OIT, BP 4656, Beirut ("Interlab Beyrouth"; Tel. 27 30 78 and 27 30 79).

Luxembourg: See under Belgium.

Mexico: Oficina de la OIT, Edificio B, 10.° piso, avenida Juárez 42, Apartado Postal 8636, Mexico 1, DF ("Interlab Mexico DF"; Tel. 12 26 78 and 13 55 48).

Nigeria: ILO Area Office, 11 Okotie-Eboh Street, PO Box 2331, Lagos ("Interlab Lagos"; Tel. 25072 and 26514).

Pakistan: ILO Correspondent, Room No. 8, Block No. 17, Pakistan Secretariat Hutments, Near Chief Court, Karachi ("Interlab Karachi"; Tel. 52889).

Peru: Oficina Regional de la OIT para las Américas, Mariscal Miller 2621, San Isidro, Apartado Postal 3638, Lima ("Interlab Lima"; Tel. 404800 and 404850).

Poland: Correspondant du BIT (M. Zdzislaw Wierzbicki), Ul. Szopena 1, Warsaw 61 ("Interlab Warszawa"; Tel. 28 80 30).

Senegal: Bureau de l'OIT, 22 rue Thiers, BP 414, Dakar ("Interlab Dakar"; Tel. 23 23 0 and 23 23 1).

Tanzania: ILO Area Office, Independence Avenue at corner of Mkwepu Street, PO Box 9212, Dar-es-Salaam ("Interlab Dar-es-Salaam"; Tel. 21674).

Thailand: ILO Regional Office for Asia, 302 Silom Road, Bangkok Insurance Building, PO Box 1759, Bangkok ("Interlab Bangkok"; Tel. 35924, 35925 and 35926).

Trinidad and Tobago: ILO Area Office, 19 Keate Street, PO Box 1201, Port-of-Spain ("Interlab Port-of-Spain"; Tel. 37574 and 37611).

Turkey: Bureau de l'OIT, Gümüssuyu caddesi 96, Ayazpasa, Istanbul ("Interlab Istanbul"; Tel. 49 69 20).

Union of Soviet Socialist Republics: Bureau de correspondance du BIT, Petrovka 15, Apt. 23, Moscow K 9 ("Interlab Moscow"; Tel. K 5-90-54).

United Arab Republic: ILO Area Office, 9 Sh. Willcocks, Zamalek, Cairo ("Interlab Cairo"; Tel. 819961 and 819889).

United Kingdom: ILO Branch Office, Sackville House, 40 Piccadilly, London W1V 9PA ("Interlab London W1"; Tel. 01 734 6521).

United Nations: ILO Liaison Office with the United Nations, 345 East 46th Street, New York, N.Y. 10017 ("Interlabor New York"; Tel. Oxford 7-0150).

United States: ILO Branch Office, 666 Eleventh Street, NW, Washington DC 20001 ("Interlab Washington DC"; Tel. (202) 638 5656).

Uruguay: Inter-American Research and Documentation Centre on Vocational Training, Calle Colonia 993, 7.° piso, Casilla de Correo 1761, Montevideo ("Cinterfor Montevideo"; Tel. 8 48 13).

Yugoslavia: Correspondant du BIT (M. Ratko Pešić), Fruškogorski put 23, Novi Sad (Vojvodine) ("Interlab Novi Sad"; Tel. 52 713).

Zambia: ILO Area Office, PO Box 2181, Design House Ltd., Third Floor, Dar-es-Salaam Place, Cairo Road, Lusaka ("Interlab Lusaka"; Tel. 75474, 75475 and 75476).

Summary of Staff Resources by Major Programme (Posts and Man-Years) for 1969 and 1970/71

MAJOR PROGRAMME	POSTS*				ADDITIONAL MAN-YEARS/MONTHS				TOTAL MAN-YEARS/MONTHS			
	1969		1970–71		1969		1970–71		1969		1970–71	
	Professional	General Service	Professional	General Service	Professional	General Service	Professional	General Service	Professional	General Service	Professional	General Service
General Management	22/0	21/0	46/0	40/0	0/4	—	0/8	2/0	22/4	21/0	46/8	42/0
Central Research and Planning	64/0	55/0	138/0	108/0	11/1	13/2	18/10	27/4	75/1	68/2	156/10	135/4
Conditions of Work and Life	64/0	18/0	128/0	36/0	11/2	9/0	26/8	21/6	75/2	27/0	154/8	57/6
Human Resources	71/0	23/0	144/0	46/0	24/5	23/0	48/11	52/5	95/5	46/0	192/11	98/5
Social Institutions Development	49/0	15/0	104/0	28/0	18/1	6/6	35/1	13/10	67/1	21/6	139/1	41/10
International Labour Standards	30/0	11/0	62/0	22/0	1/3	—	6/2	—	31/3	11/0	68/2	22/0
Management of Field Programmes	125/0	128/0	262/0	260/0	5/0	112/0	2/2	261/10	130/0	240/0	264/2	521/10
Relations and Conference Services	79/0	178/0	146/0	370/0	1/0	37/2	1/6	89/4	80/0	215/2	147/6	459/4
Publications and Public Information	90/0	35/0	182/0	70/0	7/1	3/4	17/6	8/0	97/1	38/4	199/6	78/0
Legal Services	5/0	3/0	10/0	6/0	—	0/1	1/0	0/2	5/0	3/1	11/0	6/2
Personnel and Administrative Services	39/0	127/0	78/0	254/0	1/3	30/0	6/6	73/2	40/3	157/0	84/6	327/2
Financial and General Services	39/0	70/0	82/0	138/0	8/3	15/2	20/6	31/4	47/3	85/2	102/6	169/4
Totals	677/0†	684/0‡	1,382/0†‡	1,378/0‡	88/11	249/5	185/6	580/11	765/11	933/5	1,567/6	1,958/11

* Each post represents one man-year in 1969 and two man-years in 1970–71.
† Excludes four reserve posts for officials seconded to other organisations.
‡ Excludes six posts of removal men and thirteen posts of full-time cleaners.

Senior Officials of the International Labour Office
(as at 1 June 1970)

		Date of appointment to present post
C. Wilfred Jenks (British)	Director-General	1 June 70
Abbas M. Ammar (UAR)	Deputy Director-General	22 Nov. 64
Francis Blanchard (French)	Deputy Director-General	1 March 68
Edward J. Riches (New Zealand)	Assistant Director-General/ Treasurer and Financial Comptroller	3 Jan. 61
Bertil Bolin (Swedish)	Assistant Director-General	25 Nov. 68
Albert Tévoédjré (Dahomey)	Assistant Director-General	1 Jan. 69
Xavier Caballero-Tamayo (Bolivian)	Assistant Director-General	1 Aug. 69
Yujiro Ohno (Japanese)	Assistant Director-General	11 May 70
Francis Wolf (French)	Legal Adviser on level of Assistant Director-General	1 June 70
Robert W. Cox (Canadian)	Director of the International Institute for Labour Studies	1 May 65
Philippe L. Blamont (French)	Director of the International Centre for Advanced Technical and Vocational Training, Turin	1 Nov. 66
Aamir Ali (Indian)	Chief, Relations and Conference Dept.	1 March 66
Patrick M. Denby (British)	Chief, Finance and General Services Dept.	1 Jan. 70
Tien-kai Djang (Chinese)	Special Assistant to the Director-General	1 April 62
Alexandre Flores-Zorrilla (Chilean)	Seconded to UNDP	1 Oct. 67
Warren W. Furth (USA)	Chief, Personnel and Administrative Services Dept.	1 Jan. 70

Date of appointment to present post

Jean de Givry (French)	Chief, Social Institutions Dept.	1 April 68
S. K. Jain (Indian)	Regional Co-ordinator for Asia	1 June 66
René Livchen (USA)	Chief, Conditions of Work and Life Dept.	1 Nov. 67
Meshak Ndisi (Kenya)	Regional Co-ordinator for Africa	1 July 69
Horst W. Quednau (German)	Chief, Human Resources Dept.	1 Nov. 69
Anwar A. Shaheed (Pakistani)	Director of the Liaison Office with the UN, New York	1 May 67
C. G. S. von Stedingk (Swedish)	Chief, Field Dept.	1 Nov. 69
Vladimir N. Timofeev (USSR)	Chief, Editorial and Public Information Dept.	27 Aug. 66
Nicolas Valticos (Greek)	Chief, International Labour Standards Dept.	1 Jan. 66
Vladimir Velebit (Yugoslav)	Chief, Research and Planning Dept.	1 Jan. 68
	(12 months' special leave without pay)	16 Feb. 70
George L.-P. Weaver (USA)	Special Assistant to the Director-General, Washington	1 Sept. 69
C. R. Wynne-Roberts (British)	Director of ILO Activities, Middle East and Europe	1 Nov. 69
Hubertus Zoeteweij (Netherlands)	Chief, Research and Planning Dept.	16 Feb. 70

Biographical Notes

Abbas M. Ammar, b. 1907; ed. Cairo Univ., Manchester Univ., Cambridge Univ.; lecturer and assistant professor Cairo Univ. 1942–48; UN Trusteeship Department 1948–50 and 1950–52; Director UNESCO Arab States Fundamental Education Centre 1952; Minister of Social Affairs, UAR 1952–54; Minister of Education 1954; Assistant Director-General ILO 1954–64, Deputy Director-General 1964–.

Gullmar Bergenstrom, b. 1909; ed. Uppsala Univ.; judiciary service at Court of Justice 1934–37; Secretary-General Swedish Employers' Confederation 1937, Assistant Director 1941, Vice-Director 1944, Director 1949–; member Permanent Commission of Employers' Federations in the Nordic Countries 1950–, Chairman of its International Affairs Council 1957–; Vice-President Executive Committee of the International Organisation of Employers 1952–62, President 1963–; Swedish employers' delegate International Labour Conference 1950–; Vice-Chairman Selection Committee 1952–; member of the Governing Body of ILO 1950–, Vice-Chairman 1969–.

Francis Blanchard, b. 1916; ed. Ecole des Sciences Politiques, Paris; attaché French Résidence-Générale, Tunisia; civil administration, Ministry of the Interior, France; Ministry of Foreign Affairs, detached to International Refugee Organization, Geneva 1947–51; Chief of Division, ILO 1951–56, Assistant Director-General 1956–65, Deputy Director-General 1965–.

Bertil Bolin, b. 1923; ed. Uppsala Univ.; Legal Adviser, Swedish Confederation of Trade Unions 1954–62, Director for International Affairs 1962–68; member Swedish delegation UN General Assembly 1961; Chairman General Assembly Committee on Industrial Development 1965; member Swedish delegations UNCTAD and UNIDO; Swedish workers' delegate International Labour Conference 1962–68; member ILO Governing Body 1965–68; Assistant Director-General ILO 1968–.

Sir Harold B. Butler, 1883–1951; ed. Balliol, Fellow All Souls, Oxford; entered British Civil Service 1907; Ministry of Labour 1917–19; Assistant General Secretary International Labour Commission, Peace Conference 1919; Deputy Director ILO 1920–32, Director 1932–38; Warden Nuffield College, Oxford 1939–43; Commissioner for Civil Defence 1939–41; Minister at British Embassy, Washington 1942–46.

Xavier Caballero-Tamayo, b. 1918; ed. San Andrés Univ., La Paz; Secretary-General, Chief of Personnel, Assistant Inspector-General, Central Bank of Bolivia 1939–48; joined ILO 1948; Deputy Director Field Office for Near and Middle East 1957–63, Director 1963–66; Acting Regional Co-ordinator for the Americas 1966, Regional Co-ordinator 1967–69; Assistant Director-General 1969–.

Robert W. Cox, b. 1926; ed. McGill Univ., Montreal; joined ILO 1947; executive assistant to the Director-General 1957–61; Chief of Research Division 1961–63; professor Graduate Institute of International Studies, Geneva 1963–65; Chief of Research and Planning Department 1965; Director International Institute of Labour Studies, Geneva 1965–.

Héctor Gros Espiell, b. 1926; ed. Montevideo Univ.; Professor of Constitutional Law, Montevideo Univ.; Editor *Tribuna* 1960–63; Under-Secretary for Foreign Affairs 1963–64; Ambassador representing Uruguay at inter-American and international conferences since 1965; Permanent Representative of Uruguay to the European Office of UN and other intergovernmental organisations since 1967; member of the ILO Governing Body 1969–, Chairman 1969–70.

C. Wilfred Jenks, b. 1909; ed. Gonville and Caius College, Cambridge, Graduate Institute of International Studies, Geneva; Legal Section of ILO 1931–40, Legal Adviser 1940–48, Assistant Director-General 1948–64, Deputy Director-General 1964–67, Principal Deputy Director-General 1967–70; Director-General 1970–; member ILO delegations to UN Conference on International Organisations, San Francisco 1945, UN General Assembly, and ECOSOC and other international conferences and committees; member Institute of International Law, International Academy of Comparative Law.

George Alexander Johnston, b. 1888; ed. Glasgow Univ., Berlin Univ.; lecturer St Andrews Univ. 1912–14, Glasgow Univ. 1914–16; military service Macedonia, War Office, GHQ Palestine and Cairo 1916–19; Ministry of Labour 1919–20; ILO 1920–40; visiting Professor of Social Legislation, Columbia Univ. 1931–32; Assistant Secretary, Ministry of Labour and National Service 1941–45; member UK delegation, International Labour Conference 1944; Assistant Director ILO 1945, Assistant Director-General 1946–48, Treasurer and Financial Comptroller 1948–53, Secretary-General, Training Institute, Istanbul 1954; member UN Economic Mission to Viet-Nam 1955–56; Director ILO London Office 1956–57.

Hafiz Abdul Majid, b. 1907; ed. Punjab Univ., Christ Church, Oxford; Indian Civil Service 1931–47; Pakistan Civil Service, Chief Secretary to Punjab Government 1947–57; Secretary to Pakistan Government, Ministry of Labour 1957; Ministry of Finance 1958–62; Pakistan government member of ILO Governing Body 1958; Special Assistant to Director-General 1962–64; Assistant Director-General 1964–69.

Jean Möri, 1902–70; after primary studies became printer, typesetting machine operator, proofreader, journalist and trade union secretary; Editor of *Gutenberg* 1935–40; Secretary of Swiss Federation of Typographers 1939–46; Secretary of Swiss Federation of Trade Unions and Editor of *Swiss Trade Union Review* 1946–70; Swiss workers' delegate, International Labour Conference 1947–70, Vice-President 1956–69, President 1969; member of the Governing Body 1947–70, Vice-Chairman 1960–70.

David A. Morse, b. 1907; ed. Somerville High School, N.J., Rutgers Univ., Harvard Law School; law, private practice and government posts 1932–38; lecturer on Labour Relations, Labour Law and Administrative Law, various colleges and law schools 1938–47; us Forces in North Africa and Europe 1943–45; General Counsel National Labor Relations Board, Washington 1945–46; Assistant Secretary of Labor 1946–47; Under-Secretary of Labor 1947–48; Acting Secretary of Labor, June–August 1948; us government member of ILO Governing Body and government delegate to International Labour Conferences; Director-General ILO 1948–70; Pierce Lecturer, Cornell Univ. 1968; Board of Directors, Graduate Institute of International Studies, Geneva; Chairman of the Board, International Institute of Labour Studies, Geneva.

Yujiro Ohno, b. 1920; ed. Tokyo Univ.; Office of the Japanese Central Labour Relations Commission 1949–53; studied on an ILO fellowship in the Federal Republic of Germany 1953–54; chief of the Labour Policy Section, Japanese Ministry of Labour 1955–61; Director-General, Workmen's Accident Compensation Department 1961–63; Director-General, Office of the Public Corporation and National Enterprise Labour Relations Commission 1963–67; Director-General Industrial Safety and Health Bureau 1967–68; Special Assistant to the Minister of Labour to advise on labour policy issues 1968–70; personal representative of the Director-General of ILO at ILO Asian Headquarters in Bangkok 1969–70; Assistant Director-General ILO 1970–.

Alexandre Parodi, b. 1901; ed. Paris Univ., faculties of law and letters; entered Council of State 1926; delegate-general in occupied France of General de Gaulle's provisional government 1944; Minister of Labour and Social Security 1944–45; Ambassador of Provisional Government to Rome; Permanent Representative of France, UN Security Council 1946–49; Secretary-General, Ministry of Foreign Affairs 1949–55; Ambassador and Permanent Representative to NATO 1955–57; Ambassador to Morocco 1957–60; Vice-President Council of State 1960–; President International Labour Conference 1945, delegate 1961–, French government member Governing Body 1945 and 1961–, Chairman 1962–63.

Edward J. Phelan, 1888–1968; ed. Liverpool Univ.; Ministry of Labour; member UK mission to Russia 1917; secretariat International Labour Commission 1919; secretariat ILO Organising Committee 1919; Chief of Division ILO 1920, Assistant Director 1932, Deputy Director 1939, Acting Director 1941, Director-General 1946 (retroactive to 1941).

Edward John Riches, b. 1905; ed. New Zealand Univ.; joined ILO 1927; Rockefeller fellow Michigan Univ. 1930–31; Assistant Economic Adviser ILO 1941, Acting Chief, Economic and Statistical Section 1941–46, Economic Adviser 1946–60, Treasurer and Financial Comptroller (Assistant Director-General) 1961–.

Naval Hormusji Tata, b. 1904; ed. Bombay Univ.; industrialist, Chairman Tata Group of Textile Mills, Tata Group of Hydro-electric Cos., Deputy

Chairman Tata Industries, Tata Sons, Vice-Chairman Tata Oil Mills; President Employers' Federation of India; President National Institute of Labour Management; Indian employers' delegate International Labour Conference 1949–, member Governing Body 1949–.

Albert Tévoédjré, b. 1929; ed. Toulouse Univ., Fribourg Univ., Graduate Institute of International Studies, Geneva; teaching posts in Dahomey and France; teaching and research appointments at Harvard and Georgetown Univs.; Secretary of State for Information, Dahomey 1960–61; Secretary-General Union Africaine et Malgache 1961–63 and chief delegate of the Union to UN General Assembly 1961–62; joined ILO 1965, Regional Co-ordinator for Africa 1967, Assistant Director-General 1969–.

Albert Thomas, 1878–1932; ed. Ecole Normale Supérieure, Paris; teacher, journalist and author; Deputy, Chambre des Députés 1910; Mayor of Champigny 1912; Under-Secretary of State for Artillery and Munitions 1915, Minister of Munitions 1916; Ambassador to Russia 1917; Director ILO 1920–32.

John G. Winant, 1889–1947; ed. Princeton Univ.; American Expeditionary Force 1917–19; Governor New Hampshire 1925–27, 31–33, 33–35; Chairman Social Security Board 1935–37; Assistant Director ILO 1935 and 1937, Director 1939–41; United States Ambassador to UK 1941–46; United States representative, UN Economic and Social Council 1947.

Francis Wolf, b. 1923; ed. Strasbourg Univ., Geneva Univ., Montreal Univ.; Mobile Group of Alsace (First French Army) 1944; attached to Military Mission German Affairs, later French Group, Inter-allied Control Commission, Berlin 1945; ILO Legal Division 1945–56, Chief 1956–63, Legal Adviser 1963– (promoted to level of Assistant Director-General 1970); lecturer Academy of International Law, The Hague, 1967.

Statement of Contributions due from Member States for 1970/71

(In US dollars)

STATE	% 1970	NET CONTRIBUTION 1970*	% 1971	NET CONTRIBUTION 1971*
Afghanistan . . .	0·09	26,852	0·08	23,868
Algeria . . .	0·12	35,803	0·12	35,803
Argentina . . .	1·35	402,779	1·28	381,895
Australia . . .	1·83	545,990	1·83	545,990
Austria . . .	0·40	119,342	0·42	125,310
Barbados . . .	0·09	29,852	0·08	23,868
Belgium . . .	1·35	402,779	1·35	402,780
Bolivia . . .	0·09	26,852	0·08	23,868
Brazil . . .	1·29	384,878	1·23	366,977
Bulgaria . . .	0·19	56,687	0·19	56,688
Burma . . .	0·09	26,852	0·09	26,852
Burundi . . .	0·09	26,852	0·08	23,868
Byelorussia . .	0·45	134,260	0·45	134,260
Cambodia . . .	0·09	26,852	0·08	23,868
Cameroon . . .	0·09	26,852	0·08	23,868
Canada . . .	3·36	1,002,473	3·36	1,002,473
Central African Republic .	0·09	26,852	0·08	23,868
Ceylon . . .	0·09	26,852	0·09	26,852
Chad . . .	0·09	26,852	0·08	23,868
Chile . . .	0·33	98,457	0·31	92,490
China . . .	2·80	835,394	2·98	889,098
Colombia . . .	0·30	89,506	0·28	83,540
Congo (Brazzaville) . .	0·09	26,852	0·08	23,868
Congo (Kinshasa) . .	0·09	26,852	0·08	23,868
Costa Rica . .	0·09	26,852	0·08	23,868
Cuba . . .	0·28	83,539	0·26	77,573
Cyprus . . .	0·09	26,852	0·08	23,868
Czechoslovakia . .	0·92	274,487	0·92	274,487
Dahomey . . .	0·09	26,852	0·08	23,868
Denmark . . .	0·70	208,848	0·70	208,849
Dominican Republic .	0·09	26,852	0·08	23,868
Ecuador . . .	0·09	26,852	0·08	23,868
El Salvador . . .	0·09	26,852	0·08	23,868
Ethiopia . . .	0·09	26,852	0·08	23,868
Finland . . .	0·35	104,424	0·37	110,392
France . . .	6·07	811,015	6·07	1,811,015
Gabon . . .	0·09	26,852	0·08	23,868
German Federal Republic .	4·90	1,461,939	5·01	1,494,759
Ghana . . .	0·11	32,819	0·10	29,836
Greece . . .	0·21	62,654	0·22	65,639

STATE	% 1970	NET CONTRIBUTION 1970*	% 1971	NET CONTRIBUTION 1971*
Guatemala	0·09	26,852	0·08	23,868
Guinea	0·09	26,852	0·08	23,868
Guyana	0·09	26,852	0·08	23,868
Haiti	0·09	25,852	0·08	23,868
Honduras	0·09	26,852	0·08	23,868
Hungary	0·42	125,309	0·42	125,310
Iceland	0·09	26,852	0·08	23,868
India	2·52	751,854	2·39	713,069
Indonesia	0·43	128,293	0·43	128,293
Iran	0·27	80,556	0·27	80,556
Iraq	0·09	26,852	0·09	26,852
Ireland	0·23	68,622	0·23	68,622
Israel	0·14	41,770	0·15	44,754
Italy	2·35	701,134	2·42	722,020
Ivory Coast . . .	0·09	26,852	0·08	23,868
Jamaica	0·09	26,852	0·08	23,868
Japan	2·64	787,657	2·82	841,361
Jordan	0·09	26,852	0·08	23,868
Kenya	0·09	26,852	0·08	23,868
Kuwait	0·09	26,852	0·09	26,852
Laos	0·09	26,852	0·08	23,868
Lebanon	0·09	26,852	0·08	23,868
Lesotho	0·09	26,852	0·08	23,868
Liberia	0·09	26,852	0·08	23,868
Libya	0·09	26,852	0·08	23,868
Luxembourg . . .	0·09	26,852	0·08	23,868
Madagascar . . .	0·09	26,852	0·08	23,868
Malawi	0·09	26,852	0·08	23,868
Malaysia	0·15	44,753	0·15	44,754
Mali	0·09	26,852	0·08	23,868
Malta	0·09	26,852	0·08	23,868
Mauritania . . .	0·09	26,852	0·08	23,868
Mauritius	0·09	26,852	0·08	23,868
Mexico	0·76	226,750	0·76	226,750
Mongolia	0·09	26,852	0·08	23,868
Morocco	0·14	41,770	0·13	38,787
Nepal	0·09	26,852	0·08	23,868
Netherlands . . .	1·13	337,141	1·13	337,142
New Zealand . . .	0·47	140,227	0·47	140,227
Nicaragua	0·09	26,852	0·08	23,868
Niger	0·09	26,852	0·08	23,868
Nigeria	0·20	59,671	0·19	56,688
Norway	0·51	152,161	0·51	152,161
Pakistan	0·53	158,128	0·50	149,178
Panama	0·09	26,852	0·08	23,868
Paraguay	0·09	26,852	0·08	23,868
Peru	0·13	38,786	0·13	38,787
Philippines . . .	0·37	110,391	0·37	110,392
Poland	1·24	369,960	1·24	369,961
Portugal	0·23	68,622	0·22	65,639

STATE	% 1970	NET CONTRIBUTION 1970*	% 1971	NET CONTRIBUTION 1971*
Romania	0·43	128,293	0·43	128,293
Rwanda	0·09	26,852	0·08	23,868
Senegal	0·09	26,852	0·08	23,868
Sierra Leone . . .	0·09	26,852	0·08	23,868
Singapore	0·09	26,852	0·08	23,868
Somalia	0·09	26,852	0·08	23,868
Southern Yemen . .	0·09	26,852	0·08	23,868
Spain	1·04	310,289	1·04	310,290
Sudan	0·09	26,852	0·08	23,868
Sweden	1·58	471,401	1·58	471,401
Switzerland . . .	1·24	369,960	1·18	352,059
Syria	0·09	26,852	0·08	23,868
Tanzania	0·09	26,852	0·08	23,868
Thailand	0·19	56,687	0·18	53,704
Togo	0·09	26,852	0·08	23,868
Trinidad and Tobago . .	0·09	26,852	0·08	23,868
Tunisia	0·09	26,852	0·08	23,868
Turkey	0·51	152,161	0·49	146,194
Uganda	0·09	26,852	0·08	23,868
Ukraine	1·35	402,779	1·44	429,632
USSR	10·00	2,983,550	10·45	3,117,810
United Arab Republic .	0·30	89,506	0·28	83,540
United Kingdom . .	9·14	2,726,965	9·12	2,720,998
United States . . .	25·00	7,458,875	25·00	7,458,875
Upper Volta . . .	0·09	26,852	0·08	23,868
Uruguay	0·12	35,803	0·12	35,803
Venezuela	0·50	149,177	0·50	149,178
Viet-Nam	0·09	26,852	0·09	26,852
Yemen	0·09	26,852	0·08	23,868
Yugoslavia . . .	0·40	119,342	0·40	119,342
Zambia	0·09	26,852	0·08	23,868
Total . .	100·00	29,835,500	100·00	29,835,500

* In some cases the amounts attributed to States assessed at the same percentage in both years have had to be rounded down in 1970 and rounded up in 1971.

Expenditure Budget for 1970/71 by Major Programme

(In US dollars)

TITLE	1968 EXPENDITURE	1969 BUDGET	1970–71 ESTIMATES
PART I. ORDINARY BUDGET			
Policy-Making Organs:			
International Labour Conference . . .	496,223	514,000	1,339,200
Governing Body	151,777	158,340	362,410
	648,000	672,340	1,701,610
General Management:			
General Management . . .	555,410	748,246	1,655,788
50th Anniversary Celebration . .	40,587	34,500	—
	595,997	782,746	1,655,788
Programmes of Activity:			
Major Advisory Meetings . . .	248,411	493,000	1,064,420
Central Research and Planning . .	1,750,593	1,982,308	4,417,634
Conditions of Work and Life . .	1,955,465	2,043,200	4,506,736
Human Resources	3,076,692	3,432,038	8,232,823
Social Institutions Development .	2,115,654	2,223,652	4,852,260
International Labour Standards . .	588,024	691,096	1,595,829
Management of Field Programmes .	3,448,127	3,862,796	8,688,720
Relations and Conference Services .	2,855,158	3,155,455	7,033,172
Publications and Public Information .	2,171,366	2,411,248	5,332,511
International Institute for Labour Studies .	296,734	325,000	650,000
	18,506,224	20,619,793	46,374,105
Service and Support Activities:			
Legal Services	110,114	117,211	270,954
Personnel and Administrative Services .	2,836,384	2,947,914	6,534,530
	1,433,125	1,725,708	3,873,840

Deduct: Adjustment for Staff Turnover	—	(−284,168)	(−313,493)
	24,861,413	27,220,689	61,361,400
Less: Part of cost of increased salaries and family allowances for General Service category staff in Geneva*	—	—	(−321,400)
Total of Part I	24,861,413	27,220,689	61,040,000
PART II. UNFORESEEN EXPENDITURE			
Unforeseen Expenditure	83,334	130,000	260,000
PART III. WORKING CAPITAL FUND			
Working Capital Fund	690,067	150,000	200,000
Total Gross Expenditure (Parts I–III)	25,634,814	27,500,689	61,500,000
MISCELLANEOUS INCOME			
Deduct: Receipts from UNDP/TA Special Account	844,995	887,950	1,829,000
Total Net Expenditure Budget	24,789,819	26,612,739	59,671,000

* The Governing Body at its 175th (May 1969) Session, in deciding that this amount should not be included in the draft programme and budget, requested the Director-General to try to cover it from savings within the programme and budget for 1970–71 on the understanding that if such savings could not be achieved it would be necessary for the Director-General to submit a proposal for a suppplementary credit to the Governing Body at its November 1971 Session.

Statistical Tables relating to ILO Technical Co-operation Activities

(1969 figures provisional)

Analysis, by Type of Programme and by Field of Activity, of ILO Technical Co-operation Expenditure in 1969

('000 US dollars)*

FIELD OF ACTIVITY	EXPENDITURE			
		UNDP		Special pro-grammes†
	Regular pro-gramme	Tech. Ass.	Spec. Fund	
Overall economic and social development:				
Statistics	105	95	9	10
Economic planning	14	4	—	—
International labour standards . .	10	—	—	—
Labour and social studies . . .	—	31	—	—
Human resources development:				
Manpower planning and organisation .	743	551	533	163
Management development . . .	258	454	6,562	5
Small-scale industries and handicrafts .	107	291	1,171	118
Vocational training	413	1,265	6,638	976
Conditions of work and life:				
Social security	156	250	—	18
Occupational safety and health . .	5	75	249	16
General conditions of work . . .	97	—	86	—
Maritime workers	2	1	27	—
Social institutions development:				
Labour law and labour relations . .	53	84	—	—
Labour administration . . .	209	225	142	56
Workers' education	407	50	—	—
Co-operative, rural and related institu-tions	284	751	526	162
Associate experts	—	—	—	72
Total ILO technical co-operation programmes	2,863	4,127	15,943	1,596

* Administrative costs not included.
† Including trust funds, associate experts and projects on a reimbursable basis.

Analysis of ILO Expenditure under all Technical Co-operation Programmes, by Region, in 1969

REGION*	US $ '000	%
Africa	9,960	40·60
Americas	4,282	17·46
Asia	4,747	19·35
Europe	3,322	13·54
Middle East	1,326	5·41
Inter-regional	892	3·64
Total . .	24,529	100·00

* The regional classification of countries follows the pattern adopted by the United Nations.

Analysis of ILO Expenditure under all Technical Co-operation Programmes, by Type of Assistance, in 1969

TYPE OF ASSISTANCE	US $ '000	%
Experts	17,939	73·13
Fellowships and study grants .	1,275	5·20
Equipment and miscellaneous .	5,315	21·67
Total . .	24,529	100·00

Expenditure on Technical Co-operation Programmes, (1950—1969)*

('000 US dollars)

YEAR	EXPANDED PROGRAMME	SPECIAL FUND	TRUST FUNDS†	REGULAR PROGRAMME	ANNUAL TOTAL
1950–51	341·2	—	—	—	341·2
1952	1,616·4	—	—	—	1,616·4
1953	1,942·0	—	—	—	1,942·0
1954	1,728·2	—	—	—	1,728·2
1955	2,310·1	—	—	—	2,310·1
1956	2,665·3	—	—	116·2	2,781·5
1957	2,759·6	—	42·8	131·0	2,933·4
1958	2,925·1	—	77·2	146·5	3,148·8
1959	2,869·4	—	141·2	140·4	3,151·0
1960	2,744·8	132·0	272·9	334·9	3,484·6
1961	3,120·8	1,304·6	195·8	465·6	5,086·8
1962	4,403·1	3,342·0	299·0	640·5	8,684·6
1963	3,770·3	5,500·2	528·3	1,177·4	10,976·2
1964	5,365·8	5,292·9	525·4	1,331·9	12,516·0
1965	4,516·0	5,908·6	1,029·1	1,620·7	13,074·4
1966	6,213·4	6,663·3	1,248·0	1,979·6	16,104·3
1967	5,654·0	8,393·0	1,660·0	2,171·0	17,878·0
1968	6,429·0	10,642·0	1,393·0	2,339·0	20,803·0
1969	4,127·0	15,943·0	1,596·0	2,863·0	24,529·0
Total	65,501·5	63,121·6	9,008·7	15,457·7	153,089·5

* Administrative costs not included.
† Including costs of associate experts, projects on a reimbursable basis, the special Swedish programme for training women and girls and the United Nations Programme for the Congo (Kinshasa).

Summary of ILO Assistance in the Form of Experts and Fellowships, 1968

(Under all programmes)

CATEGORY	EXPERTS*			FELLOWSHIPS		
	Number of assignments	Man-months	% of total man-months	No.	Man-months	% of total man-months
Overall economic and social development:	*13* *(4)*	*105*	*1·3*	*8*	*38*	*2·0*
Statistics	11 (2)	104	1·3	6	36	2·0
International Labour Standards	2 (2)	1	—	2	2	—
Economic planning	—	—	—	—	—	—
International Institute for Labour Studies	—	—	—	—	—	—
Human resources development:	*853* *(332)*	*6,360*	*79·0*	*336*	*1,419*	*73·0*
Manpower planning and organisation	109 (28)	754	9·4	20	107	5·5
Management development	226 (116)	2,059	25·6	107	501	25·8
Small industries and handicrafts	90 (34)	681	8·4	12	56	2·9
Vocational training	388 (154)	2,866	35·6	197	755	38·8
Conditions of work and life:	*85* *(39)*	*409*	*5·1*	*35*	*153*	*7·8*
Social security	38 (15)	200	2·5	18	76	3·9
Occupational safety and health	22 (11)	116	1·5	16	75	3·9
General conditions of work	25 (13)	93	1·1	1	2	—
Social institutions development:	*171* *(56)*	*1,178*	*14·6*	*67*	*334*	*17·2*
Labour law and labour relations	20 (6)	106	1·3	6	29	1·5
Labour administration	43 (16)	251	3·1	44	229	11·8
Workers' education	15 (6)	79	1·0	8	12	0·6
Co-operative, rural and related institutions development	93 (28)	742	9·2	9	64	3·3
Total	1,122 (431)	8,052	100·0	446	1,944	100·0

* Throughout this table, experts having been on assignment more than once in the same country in the same speciality have been counted for one assignment only. New assignments in 1968 are given in brackets.

345

Danger Symbols

(See Chapter 18)

1. Danger of ignition 2. Oxidising agent 3. Danger of explosion 4. Danger of poisoning 5. Danger of corrosion 6. Symbol for packages or consignments containing large sources of radioactive materials, as defined in the IAEA Regulations for the Safe Transport of Radioactive Materials 7. Symbol for packages or consignments containing radioactive sources of lesser activity than large sources

346

Publications of the International Labour Office

Periodical Publications
(all issued in English, French and Spanish)

International Labour Review. Monthly. Articles on economic and social topics of international interest affecting labour, notes on recent developments, notices of new books received by the ILO.

Official Bulletin. Quarterly. Information on the activities of the International Labour Organisation, and texts adopted by the International Labour Conference, other conferences and meetings, reports of inquiries and other official documents.

Legislative Series. Issued in instalments every two months. A collection of the most important national laws and regulations on labour and social security, translated into English.

Bulletin of Labour Statistics. Quarterly. Current statistics on employment, unemployment, wages, hours of work, consumer prices, etc. Contains also the results of a detailed annual inquiry into wages, hours of work and consumer prices.

Year Book of Labour Statistics. Published at the end of each year. Trilingual. A comprehensive survey of annual data from all parts of the world relating to economically active population, employment and unemployment in different sectors, wages and hours of work, consumer price indices, family living studies, industrial accidents, industrial disputes, etc.

Minutes of the Governing Body. Published three to four times a year.

Documents of the International Labour Conference. (a) Reports prepared for each item on the agenda of the annual Conference; (b) Record of Proceedings, including committee reports and decisions. Parts I and II of the Report of the Director-General to the International Labour Conference are obtainable separately.

ILO Panorama. Issued free of charge six times a year in English, French and Spanish editions. Contains illustrated articles on aspects of the work of the ILO.

ILO Information. Issued free of charge, in a series of bulletins in fifteen languages. Provides news material on ILO activities, suitable for reproduction in newspapers and periodicals, and also as wall-sheets for trade union halls, UN Associations, schools and other groups.

Non-Periodical Publications
Studies and Reports Series: monographs on a wide range of economic and

347

social problems relating to labour conditions and development. Handbooks of occupational safety and health, works of international reference, manuals prepared in relation to international technical co-operation, workers' educational manuals, etc.

Publications in the Series "Studies and Reports" issued 1952–69
(all issued in English, French and Spanish)

Conditions of Work in the Fishing Industry.

Textile Wages: An International Study. Prepared for the Third Session of the Textiles Committee.

An Introduction to Co-operative Practice.

Safety in Coal Mines. Vol. I*; Vol. II.

Minimum Wages in Latin America.*

Indigenous Peoples.

Report of the Ad Hoc Committee on Forced Labour.

Trade Union Rights in Czechoslovakia.

Higher Productivity in Manufacturing Industries.

Vocational Guidance in France.

Administrative Practice of Social Insurance.

Guide for Labour Inspectors.

Unemployment Insurance Schemes.

Problems of Wage Policy in Asian Countries.

Production and Employment in the Metal Trades. The Problem of Regularisation.

International Comparisons of Real Wages.*

Social Aspects of European Economic Co-operation. Report by a Group of Experts.

The Landless Farmer in Latin America.

African Labour Survey.

Trade Union Rights in the USSR.

Trade Union Rights in Hungary.

The Cost of Medical Care.*

Labour Costs in European Industry.

The International Standardisation of Labour Statistics.*

International Migration.

Employment and Conditions of Work of Nurses.*

Job Evaluation.

Co-operative Management and Administration.

The Protection of Trade Union Funds and Property.

Why Labour Leaves the Land.*

Labour Survey of North Africa.

Services for Small-scale Industry.

Employment Objectives in Economic Development. Report of a Meeting of Experts.

Family Living Studies. A Symposium.

Workers' Management in Yugoslavia.

Unemployment and Structural Change.

Housing Co-operatives.

Employment and Economic Growth.

The Quality of Labour and Economic Development in Certain Countries. A Preliminary Study by Walter Galenson and Graham Pyatt.

Plantation Workers.

Prices, Wages and Incomes Policies in Industrialised Market Economies, by H. A. Turner and H. Zoeteweij.

| Human Resources for Industrial Development. | The Organisation of Medical Care under Social Security, by Milton I. Rœmer. |
| Minimum Wage Fixing and Economic Development. | Technical and Social Changes in the World's Ports, by A. A. Evans. |

* English edition out of print.

Handbooks and Manuals: Selected List
(in English, French and Spanish unless otherwise stated)

Collective Bargaining, a workers' education manual. 1960. 157 pp. Also issued in German.

The Cost of Social Security, 1961–1963. 1967. 353 pp. Trilingual (English, French and Spanish). Statistics of the financial operations of social security systems in sixty-one countries, followed by comparative tables.

Creating a Market, an ILO programmed book. 1968. 180 pp. English.

Discrimination in Employment and Occupations: Standards and Policy Statements Adopted under the Auspices of the ILO. 1967. 56 pp.

Employment and Training Problems in New Factories. (in preparation).

The Enterprise and Factors Affecting its Operation. 1965. 193 pp. A course on the "anatomy" of the enterprise, originally designed for participants in the advanced management courses organised by the ILO.

How to Read a Balance Sheet, an ILO programmed book. 1966. 121 pp. Not available in French.

Guide to Safety and Health in Forestry Work. 1968. 223 pp. (illustrated). Detailed practical guidance for employers, supervisors and others on the risks of all types involved in the different forestry operations.

Guide to the Prevention and Suppression of Dust in Mining, Tunnelling and Quarrying. 1965. xviii+421 pp.

International Standard Classification of Occupations, revised edition, 1968. 1969. 355 pp. A completely revised edition of the work originally issued in 1958.

Introduction to Work Study. Revised edition, 1969. 436 pp.+97 illustrations, 14 tables. In English only. A completely revised edition of the original English edition issued in 1957.

Manpower Aspects of Recent Economic Developments in Europe. 1969. 175 pp. Not available in Spanish.

Manual of Industrial Radiation Protection:
Part I: **Convention and Recommendation Concerning the Protection of Workers against Ionising Radiations.** 1963. 24 pp.
Part II: **Model Code of Safety Regulations (Ionising Radiations).** 1959. 54 pp.

Payment by Results. 1951. Tenth impression 1969. 204 pp. 14 charts. An international survey, liberally illustrated by means of charts and statistical tables, of various systems of payment by results and their effects on costs, earnings and output. The extent of their use, their advantages and disadvantages and the necessary preconditions and safeguards are also discussed.

A Tabulation of Case Studies on Technological Change: Economic and Social Problems Reviewed in 160 Case Studies. 1965. 87 pp. Not available in Spanish. Shows what particular aspects have been investigated at plant or industry level by means ot case studies in various countries.

Wages, a workers' education manual. New edition, revised, 1968. 254 pp. An introduction, explaining how wage rates are fixed.

Bibliography

AMERICAN ACADEMY OF POLITICAL AND SOCIAL SCIENCE, *The International Labor Organisation*. Ed. by Alice Cheyney. Philadelphia, 1933.

AYUSAWA, I. F., *History of Labor in Modern Japan*. Honolulu, East-West Center Press, 1966.

BARNES, G. N., *History of the International Labour Office*, with an introduction by Emile Vandervelde. London, Williams, 1926.

BUTLER, H. B., *The Lost Peace, a Personal Impression*. London, Faber and Faber, 1941.

CHISHOLM, A., *Labour's Magna Carta*. London, Green, 1925.

FOLLOWS, J. W., *Antecedents of the International Labour Organization*. Oxford, Clarendon Press, 1951.

GUERREAU, M., *Une nouvelle institution du droit des gens:* L'Organisation permanente du Travail, Paris, 1923.

HAAS, E. B., *Beyond the nation state:* functionalism and international organization. Stanford, Stanford University Press, 1964.

INTERNATIONAL LABOUR OFFICE, *The International Labour Organisation:* the first decade. With a preface by Albert Thomas. London, Allen and Unwin, 1931.

JENKS, C. W., *Human Rights and International Labour Standards*. London, Stevens, 1960.

JENKS, C. W., *The International Protection of Trade Union Freedom*. London, Stevens, 1957.

JENKS, C. W., *The Common Law of Mankind*. London, Stevens, 1958.

JENKS, C. W., *Social Justice in the Law of Nations:* the ILO Impact after Fifty Years. London, Royal Institute of International Affairs and Oxford University Press, 1970.

LANDELIUS, T., *Workers, Employers and Governments*. Stockholm, 1965.

LANDY, E. A., *The Effectiveness of International Supervision:* thirty years of ILO experience. London, Stevens, 1966.

LORWIN, L. L., *The International Labor Movement:* history, policies, outlook. New York, Harper, 1953.

MORSE, D. A., *The Origin and Evolution of the ILO and its Role in the World Community*. Ithaca, New York State School of Industrial and Labor Relations, Cornell University, 1969.

351

PHELAN, E. J., *Yes and Albert Thomas*. London, Cresset Press, 1936.

PILLAI, P. P., *India and the International Labour Organisation*. Patna, Patna University, 1931.

PRICE, J., *The International Labour Movement*. London, Oxford University Press, 1945.

PRICE, J., *ILO: 50 Years On*. London, Fabian Society, 1969.

SCELLE, G., *L'Organisation Internationale du Travail et le B.I.T.* With a preface by Albert Thomas. Paris, Rivière, 1930.

SHOTWELL, J. T., *The Origins of the International Labor Organization*. New York, Columbia University Press, 1934. 2 vols.

STEWART, M., *Britain and the ILO:* the story of fifty years. London, HMSO, 1969.

THOMAS, A., *International Social Policy*. Geneva, ILO, 1948.

TROCLET, L. E., *Législation sociale internationale*. With a preface by Georges Scelle. Brussels, Editions de la Librarie Encyclopédique, 1952.

VALTICOS, N., *Un système de contrôle international: la mise en œuvre des Conventions internationales du Travail*. Leyden, Académie de Droit international, 1968.

WEAVER, G. L.-P., *The International Labor Organization and Human Rights*. Washington, Howard University, School of Law, 1965.

WILSON, F. G., *The International Labor Organization*. New York, Carnegie Endowment for International Peace, Division of Intercourse and Education, 1932.

WILSON, F. G., *Labor in the League System:* a study on the International Labor Organization in relation to international administration. Stanford, Stanford University Press, 1934.

WOLF, F., *L'interdépendance des Conventions internationales du Travail*. Leyden, Académie de Droit international, 1967.

Index